MICHAEL MERANZE

Laboratories of Virtue

Punishment, Revolution, and

Authority in Philadelphia,

1760–1835

Published for the

Institute of Early American History and Culture, Williamsburg, Virginia,

by the University of North Carolina Press,

Chapel Hill and London

The Institute of Early American History and Culture is
sponsored jointly by the College of William and Mary and
the Colonial Williamsburg Foundation

© 1996 The University of North Carolina Press
Manufactured in the United States of America

Library of Congress Cataloging-in-Publication Information

Meranze, Michael.
    Laboratories of virtue : punishment, revolution, and
authority in Philadelphia, 1760–1835 / Michael Meranze.
        p.   cm.
    Includes bibliographical references (p.   ) and index.
    ISBN 0-8078-2277-9 (cloth : alk. paper)
    1. Punishment—Pennsylvania—Philadelphia—History.
2. Prisons—Pennsylvania—Philadelphia—History.
3. Prison reformers—Pennsylvania—Philadelphia—History.
I. Title.
HV9481.P5M47   1996
364.6'09748'11—dc20   95-45117
                                                                    CIP

The paper in this book meets the guidelines for permanence
and durability of the Committee on Production Guidelines for
Book Longevity of the Council on Library Resources.

This volume received indirect support from an unrestricted
book publication grant awarded to the Institute by the L. J.
Skaggs and Mary C. Skaggs Foundation of Oakland, California.

00 99 98 97 96   5 4 3 2 1

For My Mother,
Barbara Meranze

and in Memory of My Father,
Theodore Meranze

ACKNOWLEDGMENTS

Many individuals have helped this work and its author along their way. At Wesleyan University, Peter Dobkin Hall and Donald Meyer introduced me to American history and to the problems of intellectuals and authority that underlies much of my thinking here. At the University of California, Berkeley, James Kettner, Samuel Haber, and Michael Rogin guided the dissertation from which this study grew. They each, in his own way, provided examples of intellectual and personal generosity. I was also fortunate to have the support, financial and intellectual, of the Philadelphia Center for Early American Studies. Richard Beeman, Richard Dunn, and especially Michael Zuckerman made my stay there (and my continuing sojourn in early American history) pleasant and stimulating. The Institute of Early American History and Culture not only provided the time and resources to begin the road from dissertation to book but also a series of challenging friends and colleagues. I would like to thank Edward Ayres, Cynthia Ayres, and Thad Tate for making my stay there far more livable. Fredrika Teute, first friend and then editor, has helped this book and its author greatly; Ronald C. Hoffman, now director of the Institute, has provided unstinting support for this project in its final stages; and Virginia Montijo Chew provided expert editorial assistance in sharpening prose and the argument. Earlier versions of portions of this study have appeared in "The Penitential Ideal in Late Eighteenth-Century Philadelphia," *Pennsylvania Magazine of History and Biography,* CVIII (1984), 419–450, and in my introduction to Benjamin Rush's *Essays: Literary, Moral, and Philosophical,* published by Union College Press.

My colleagues in the history department at the University of California, San Diego, have provided that rarity—a genuine intellectual fellowship. I would especially like to thank Michael Bernstein, Takashi Fujitani, Steven Hahn, Judith Hughes, Rachel Klein, Stephanie McCurry, Eric Van Young, and Robert Westman. Other colleagues across campus—Susan Davis, Page duBois, Valerie Hartouni, Daniel Schiller, and especially George Mariscal and Teresa Odendahl—have provided intellectual and personal companionship.

Several friends have traversed with me the sojourns of this book, and I need to recognize them particularly. Julia Liss has been a true friend to this book's author for longer than seems possible and certainly longer than either of us would like to admit. Cornelia Hughes Dayton has provided unflagging support and suggestions about early American history for more than a decade. Christopher Looby has consistently shared his fascination with things intellectual and written. Paul Rabinow has proved unfailingly generous in support and ideas. Steven Rosswurm disagrees with much, if not most, of the philosophy that underlies this work. That he never failed to argue about it is a sign of intellectual comradeship and caring all too rare.

Numerous others have read and commented on aspects of this work. Karen Halttunen and Allen Steinberg were extremely provocative and thoughtful readers of the manuscript for the Institute of Early American History and Culture. Casey Nelson Blake discussed this work and its implications over many years. I would also like to thank commentators and audiences at the UCLA Center for Seventeenth- and Eighteenth-Century Studies held at the William Andrews Clark Memorial Library, the Philadelphia Center for Early American Studies, the American Studies Association, the Organization of American Historians, and the University of Pennsylvania for their comments and suggestions. G. J. Barker-Benfield, Elizabeth Fischer, Daniel Cohen, Toby L. Ditz, Bryna Goodman, Susan Mackiewicz, Louis P. Masur, Ric Northrup, Jonathan Prude, Julia Stern, Christopher Tomlins, and James Walvin also shared thoughts and suggestions. Gregory Rodriquez provided excellent last-minute research assistance.

The expert aid of staff at several archives and libraries made research far more productive and fulfilling. I would like to thank the staffs at the Historical Society of Pennsylvania, most notably Amy Hardin, Arlene Shaner, and especially Linda Stanley, the reading room crew at the Library Company of Philadelphia (especially Mary Ann Hines), and Ward Childs and the other librarians of the Philadelphia City Archives. I am also indebted to librarians at the Pennsylvania Historical and Museum Commission, the Quaker Collection of the Haverford College Library, the manuscript division of the New York Public Library, and the Special Collections librarians at Van Pelt Library of the University of Pennsylvania.

Financial support has come from a wide range of agencies. I would like to thank the Mabelle Mcleod Lewis Foundation, the Mellon Foundation, the National Endowment for the Humanities, the University of California, Berkeley, and the Academic Senate and Chancellor of the University of California, San Diego.

In dedicating this work to my parents, I seek to acknowledge the love my mother gave and the sacrifices she made as well as the memory of my father's presence. Finally, Helen Elizabeth Deutsch taught me that Propertius was correct. For that, and everything else, I am grateful.

CONTENTS

Newspapers (Philadelphia)

Dem. Press	*Democratic Press*
Ind. Gazetteer	*Independent Gazetteer*
Pa. Eve. Herald	*Pennsylvania Evening Herald*
Pa. Gazette	*Pennsylvania Gazette*
Pa. Journal	*Pennsylvania Journal*
Pa. Mercury	*Pennsylvania Mercury*
Pa. Packet	*Pennsylvania Packet*

Published Collections

Col. Records Samuel Hazard, ed., *Colonial Records of Pennsylvania* (Harrisburg, 1852–1853).

Pa. Archives Samuel Hazard et al., eds., *Pennsylvania Archives* (Harrisburg, 1874–1935).

St. at Large J. T. Mitchell and Henry Flanders, eds., *The Statutes at Large of Pennsylvania from 1682 to 1801* (Harrisburg, 1896–1908).

Manuscript Collections and Depositories

Bd. of Insp., Minutes Inspectors of the Jail and Penitentiary House of the City and County of Philadelphia, Minutes, 1794–1835, Record Group 38, Philadelphia City Archives

MSCMS Standing Committee of the Magdalen Society of Philadelphia, Minutes, Magdalen Society of Philadelphia, Records, Historical Society of Pennsylvania, Philadelphia

PSAMPP Philadelphia Society for Alleviating the Miseries of Public Prisons, Papers, Historical Society of Pennsylvania, Philadelphia

PSAMPP-Society Philadelphia Society for Alleviating the Miseries of Public Prisons, Papers, 1787–1848, Society Collection, Historical Society of Pennsylvania, Philadelphia

HSP Historical Society of Pennsylvania, Philadelphia

PCA Philadelphia City Archives

PHMC Pennsylvania Historical and Museum Commission, Harrisburg, Pennsylvania

Journals

PMHB	*Pennsylvania Magazine of History and Biography*
WMQ	*William and Mary Quarterly*

LABORATORIES OF VIRTUE

On May 22, 1823, Roberts Vaux—Philadelphia gentleman, merchant, and philanthropist—addressed a crowd assembled to mark the laying of the cornerstone of the Eastern State Penitentiary. Vaux praised his state and its legislators for breaking the fetters of penal tradition and abolishing the pillory, the whipping post, and the chain—"those cruel and vindictive penalties which are in use in the European countries"—and substituting "milder correctives" for crime. In the place of public corporal punishments that, he argued, "were not calculated to prevent crime, but to familiarize the mind with cruelty, and consequently to harden the hearts of those who suffered, and those who witnessed such punishments" would stand the penitentiary. There, the community "wisely and compassionately sought to secure and reform the criminal by the most strict solitary confinement."[1] In the brave new world of punishment, Vaux believed, compassion would replace cruelty, and solitude, suffering.

I

Roberts Vaux articulated a widely shared vision, and he spoke for a large number of social and political institutions in Philadelphia. Vaux stood at the center of philanthropic Philadelphia in the early nineteenth century. He was a leading figure in the Historical Society of Pennsylvania, the Pennsylvania Temperance Society, the Pennsylvania Society for the Promotion of Public Economy, and the Pennsylvania Society for Promoting the Abolition of Slavery. He was president of the Board of Controllers of the Philadelphia Public Schools and a driving force behind the creation of Philadelphia's House of Refuge. Indeed, Vaux did as much as any member of his generation to evince the sensibilities of Philadelphia's elite and to shape private intervention and public policy about proper social organization.[2]

Penal reform lay at the heart of Vaux's labors. A member of the Board of Commissioners to Superintend the Construction of the Eastern State Penitentiary and secretary of the Philadelphia Society for Alleviating the Miseries of Public Prisons, Vaux was the most important of the writers who developed, expressed, and defended the Society's vision of punishment. Founded in 1787,

1. Vaux's comments were reproduced in [George Washington Smith], *Description of the Eastern Penitentiary of Pennsylvania* (Philadelphia, 1829), 7.

2. For a complete account of Vaux's efforts at social reform and philanthropy, see Roderick Naylor Ryon, "Roberts Vaux: A Biography of a Reformer" (Ph.D. diss., Pennsylvania State University, 1966).

the Philadelphia Society aimed to prevent illegal and unjust confinement, administer individualized charity to prison inmates, and investigate and propose new "modes of punishment" that would be the "means of restoring our fellow-creatures to virtue and happiness." In the transformation of punishment, the Philadelphia Society believed, both Christian duty and social obligation could be met. Composed primarily of merchants, manufacturers, gentlemen, and professionals (with a smattering of artisans), the Society was the central agitator for penal reform within Pennsylvania and a major participant in late-eighteenth- and early-nineteenth-century transatlantic debates over penal philosophy and practice.[3]

The construction of Eastern State Penitentiary climaxed fifty years of penal transformation. In the aftermath of Independence, elite Philadelphians dramatically overturned the traditional system of punishment. Their efforts proceeded through three distinct moments. First, in 1786, Pennsylvania discontinued the public whipping post, dramatically reduced the number of capital crimes, and experimented with a system of public penal labor in the city streets. Second, in 1790, the state replaced public labor with imprisonment,

3. Philadelphia Society for Alleviating the Miseries of Public Prisons, *Constitution* (Philadelphia, 1787). For some of Vaux's writing, see *Notices of the Original, and Successive Efforts, to Improve the Discipline of the Prison at Philadelphia, and to Reform the Criminal Code of Pennsylvania: With a Few Observations on the Penitentiary System* (Philadelphia, 1826); *Letter on the Penitentiary System of Pennsylvania . . .* (Philadelphia, 1827); *Reply to Two Letters of William Roscoe, Esquire of Liverpool, on the Penitentiary System of Pennsylvania* (Philadelphia, 1827). For examples of the writings of others in a similar mode, see Philadelphia Society for Alleviating the Miseries of Public Prisons, *A Statistical View of the Operations of the Penal Code of Pennsylvania; to Which Is Added, a View of the Present State of the Penitentiary and Prison of the City of Philadelphia* (Philadelphia, 1817); John Sergeant, *Observations and Reflections on the Design and Effects of Punishment . . .* (Philadelphia, 1828); George W. Smith, *A Defence of the System of Solitary Confinement of Prisoners Adopted by the State of Pennsylvania, with Remarks on the Origins, Progress and Extension of This Species of Prison Discipline* (Philadelphia, 1833); Job R. Tyson, *Essay on the Penal Law of Pennsylvania* (Philadelphia, 1827).

Of the 175 individuals who joined the Philadelphia Society for Alleviating the Miseries of Public Prisons in its first year, occupations are available for 145. Of these, 87 were merchants or professionals, 15 were clergymen, and 19 were probably artisans. These numbers are based on lists presented in Negley K. Teeters, *They Were in Prison: A History of the Pennsylvania Prison Society, 1787–1937* (Philadelphia, 1937), 90–93. For the 192 who joined between the summer of 1788 and the end of 1830, merchants and professionals again dominated the lists with 67, 12 were clergy, and 12 were artisans. These latter figures are from Peter Jonitas and Elizabeth Jonitas, "Members of the Prison Society: Biographical Vignettes, 1776–1830, of the Managers of the Philadelphia Society for Assisting Distressed Prisoners and the Members of the PSAMPP 1787–1830," II, Department of Special Collections, Haverford College Library, Philadelphia, Pa., 1982. It is, of course, possible that the ranks of artisans are underrecognized because they would be less likely to appear in the city directories.

and, in 1794, legislators limited capital punishment to first-degree murder. Lastly, at Eastern State, Pennsylvania turned to a system designed to impose solitary confinement on all inmates. Penitential punishments promised an entirely new way of governing society—one based on spiritual engagement, not coercive violence; one that would reclaim rather than expel, that would preserve individual reputation instead of spreading infamy, and that would contain rather than extend the example of criminality.

Each of these penal moments stood in dramatic contrast to pre-Revolutionary punishments. Before the American Revolution, Pennsylvania deployed a system of public punishments modeled on English criminal sanctions. Through corporal and capital penalties, the state seized the body of the condemned and directly inscribed its sanctions on that body. These penalties were not only inflicted in the open; they were openly corporal. The system of public punishments was predicated on display—display of the condemned, display of the penalty, display of violence.

By the 1820s, however, the violent display of authority seemed, to Vaux and his allies, archaic and unwise. Vaux's assured condemnation of "those cruel and vindictive penalties which are in use in the European countries" assumed a number of Enlightenment truisms: that corporal punishments debased spectator, subject, and society alike, that the display of violence only spread violence, that solitude opened the possibility for the reclamation of character, and that the movement toward penitential punishments represented the heightened sensibility and the growing humanity of democratic government. In all, Vaux presumed the moral and political superiority of the new forms of liberal society and government.

Vaux's excitement and confidence were not without cause. Philadelphians transformed more than their penal system in the half-century following the Revolution. From the 1780s through the 1830s, they reorganized their poor-relief system, developed new institutions to control juveniles and prostitutes, constructed a system of free public education, strove to regularize and order the city's streets and parks, and transformed the mechanisms of class relationships and the government of the city's laboring classes.[4] In doing so, they instituted a variety of new techniques for governing social relations.

The late eighteenth and early nineteenth centuries witnessed a dramatic in-

4. For discussions of these developments within Philadelphia, see John K. Alexander, *Render Them Submissive: Responses to Poverty in Philadelphia, 1760–1800* (Amherst, Mass., 1980); Marcia Roberta Carlisle, "Prostitutes and Their Reformers in Nineteenth Century Philadelphia" (Ph.D. diss., Rutgers University, 1982); J. David Lehman, "Explaining Hard Times: Political Economy and the Panic of 1819 in Philadelphia" (Ph.D. diss., University of California, Los Angeles, 1992); O. A. Pendleton, "Poor Relief in Philadelphia, 1790–1840," *PMHB*, LXX (1946), 161–172; Allen Steinberg, *The Transformation of Criminal Justice: Philadelphia, 1800–1880* (Chapel Hill, N.C., 1989).

vention and dissemination of disciplinary techniques and locations through-out the city. Despite a multiplicity of objects, these efforts shared techniques, practices, and effects. Whether the target was poverty, criminality, delin-quency, prostitution, or idleness, reformers and officials believed that social problems could best be contained through the transformation of individual character, that individual character could best be transformed through the careful supervision of individual regimen, and that the supervision of individ-ual regimen could best take place within an environment where time and space were carefully regulated. These laboratories of virtue assembled spaces separate from daily life, arranged according to carefully specified rules and overseen by hierarchical organizations. They sought to inculcate the habits of labor, personal restraint, and submission to the law.

Philadelphians were not alone in these efforts. On both sides of the At-lantic, private reformers and public officials experimented with new tech-niques to contain crime and poverty, to transform the character of delin-quents and offenders, and to increase the capacity of the state to intervene in the everyday life of its citizens. Penitentiaries were only the most fearsome em-bodiment of a widespread strategy to regulate and regularize moral life and create citizens and workers for the new liberal, capitalist societies of the nine-teenth century.

This study examines the controlling assumptions of early liberal America. It traces the replacement of a penal system based on public capital and corpo-ral penalties with one centered on penitence within a system of solitary con-finement—in one place. Philadelphia was a crucial site for the elaboration of Enlightenment ideas in America. It served, along with New York, as the polit-ical capital of the new nation, suffered the social transformations that accom-panied the transition to capitalism in the late eighteenth and early nineteenth centuries, and grew from a small if vibrant seaport to one of the nation's man-ufacturing centers, and its population was at all times diverse in ethnic, racial, religious, and class terms. It was, of course, in cities throughout the northern United States that the contradictions of the emerging bourgeois order ap-peared most clearly and that disciplinary institutions took their greatest hold. All the world was not Philadelphia; the peculiarities of the story that I am about to tell need not be denied. Yet as a central site of the experimentation of liberal discipline, the laboratories of virtue constructed in Philadelphia not only teach us much about the history of early liberalism; they continue to help structure the world in which we live.

II

If the late eighteenth and early nineteenth centuries effectively naturalized the connection between "humanity" and imprisonment, the history and historiography of the later twentieth century have worked to problematize it. The great works of the 1970s—Michael Ignatieff's *Just Measure of Pain,* David Rothman's *Discovery of the Asylum,* and, above all, Michel Foucault's *Discipline and Punish*—returned to the Age of Enlightenment and Revolution to reexamine the historical origins of the humanitarian commitment to incarceration.[5] Each sought to understand the process through which imprisonment, previously a marginal technique in the realm of criminal justice, assumed its seemingly self-evident centrality to the practices of punishment. Each examined how justice in punishment became intertwined with the deprivation of liberty. And each investigated why the perhaps inevitable violence of the social bond became institutionalized in structures of incarceration. Rothman interpreted the prison as the Jacksonian attempt to guard against the effects of increasing social mobility, Ignatieff saw imprisonment as the pure form of an industrial capitalist social order, and Foucault contended that the penitentiary institutionalized a technology of power—one that seemed more humane and rational because of its finer control of time and space and its departure from older political strategies based on the violent seizure of the body.

Foucault, Ignatieff, and Rothman, then, inscribed the emergence of the penitentiary within a wider social strategy. Each as well, by means of his historical construction, sought to show that, whatever the benefits of the decline of corporal and capital punishments—and none denied those—the forms that took their place were not transcendentally rational but were themselves complex institutions of domination.[6] The transformation of punishment, they demonstrated, was more than simply the effect of a growing humanitarianism.

5. Michael Ignatieff, *A Just Measure of Pain: The Penitentiary in the Industrial Revolution, 1750–1850* (New York, 1978); David J. Rothman, *The Discovery of the Asylum: Social Order and Disorder in the New Republic* (Boston, 1971); Michel Foucault, *Discipline and Punish: The Birth of the Prison,* trans. Alan Sheridan (New York, 1977).

6. This work has not gone unchallenged. Social historians have argued that Foucault, Ignatieff, and Rothman overestimated the success of disciplinary institutions—that they conceded them too much power and importance. For different versions of this interpretation, see Peter Linebaugh, *The London Hanged: Crime and Civil Society in the Eighteenth Century* (London, 1991), 3; Michael Ignatieff, "State, Civil Society and Total Institutions: A Critique of Recent Social Histories of Punishment," in Stanley Cohen and Andrew Scull, eds., *Social Control and the State: Historical and Comparative Essays* (Oxford, 1983), 75–105. Legal historians have contended that the notion of a widespread social strategy misconstrues the nature of penal change—that prisons replaced corporal and capital penalties simply because they were more effective means to curtail crime. On this, see John H. Langbein, "Albion's Fatal Flaws," *Past and Present,* no. 98 (1983), 96–120; Adam Jay Hirsch, *The Rise of the Penitentiary: Prisons and Punishment in Early America* (New Haven, Conn., 1992). Lastly, intellectual and cultural historians have maintained that reading penal developments primarily in terms of social control underestimates the transformation of values that accompanied the development of bourgeois society—that questions of culture and

In effect, each of these works argued that the penitentiary spread precisely because it was more than a response to crime. Beyond technical disagreements or immediate policy implications, debates over crime and punishment were overdetermined. The figure of the criminal, the occurrence of crime, and the practices of punishment all condensed issues of authority and insubordination, of selfhood and subjectivity, of philosophy and politics, and of the relationship between the legal order and the contradictions of society at large. As Ignatieff put it: "Force being necessary to the maintenance of any social order, what degree of coercion can the state legitimately exert over those who disobey? Every debate about prison conditions and prison abuses is ultimately about such questions."[7] Without losing sight of the human experiences involved in the practices of crime and punishment (from the victims of crime, through the criminals, to state officials), Foucault, Ignatieff, and Rothman aimed to trace these excessive questions at the heart of the origins of reformative incarceration. Indeed, these works suggested that it was precisely their overdetermined quality that shaped the early structures and strategies of incarceration.

Foucault's work, in particular, provided tools for understanding the multiple implications of the history of punishment. In *Discipline and Punish,* Foucault examined the "birth of the prison" from the perspective of the history of the body. Pondering the seeming spiritualization of punishment, he argued that modern disciplinary practices gave rise to a "non-corporal" double of the "subjected body of the condemned man." This "soul," Foucault insisted, is not "an illusion, or an ideological effect." "On the contrary, it exists, it has a reality, it is produced permanently around, on, within the body by the functioning of a power that is exercised on those punished." Opposed to the Christian soul ("born in sin and subject to punishment"), this penal soul "is born rather out of methods of punishment, supervision and constraint."[8] The growing attention to this penal soul, Foucault implied, helped ground an increasing spiritualization of punishment in which the direct infliction of pain on the body decreased and the body itself, no longer the prime target of the penal apparatus, became a medium to retrain and save convicts' characters.

---

sensibility need to be placed at the center of analysis. For the importance of sensibility, see Pieter Spierenburg, *The Spectacle of Suffering: Executions and the Evolution of Repression: From a Preindustrial Metropolis to the European Experience* (New York, 1984); Louis P. Masur, *Rites of Execution: Capital Punishment and the Transformation of American Culture, 1776–1865* (New York, 1989). V.A.C. Gatrell's magisterial *The Hanging Tree: Execution and the English People, 1770–1868* (New York, 1994) arrived too late for me to incorporate his efforts in this study.

7. Ignatieff, *A Just Measure of Pain,* xii.

8. Foucault, *Discipline and Punish,* 29.

Yet if the penal soul is not an "ideological effect," it is, Foucault suggested, an effect of social practices—particularly the practices that he called "discipline." For Foucault, discipline was a highly specific political technology—a structured set of object and power relations. As he put it, speaking of the early modern plague town:

> The enclosed, segmented space, observed at every point, in which the individuals are inserted in a fixed place, in which the slightest movements are supervised, in which all events are recorded, in which an uninterrupted work of writing links the centre and periphery, in which power is exercised without division, according to a continuous hierarchical figure, in which each individual is constantly located, examined and distributed among the living beings, the sick and the dead—all this constitutes a compact model of the disciplinary mechanism."[9]

Foucault's notion of "discipline," then, does not aim to capture some transhistorical need for "social control" or to redescribe individual "self-discipline" as a form of malevolence. Instead, discipline is a historically specific way of governing groups and individuals that combines the careful division and control of time and space, rigorous surveillance, the accumulation of written records and the production of knowledge about its subjects, and that operates through the systematic retraining of the body.

As a set of practices, discipline provided the ground for the emergence of individuals as both subjects and objects of the penal apparatus. Foucault's emphasis on discipline as a set of practices has led to the assumption (erroneous, I think) that he evacuated all human agency from his histories. There were numberless actors and speakers in *Discipline and Punish*. But they were, in a sense, marginal to Foucault's interpretive objectives. Foucault sought to displace attention from subjective intent to repetitious action, from reformers' beliefs to those social conditions that made such beliefs possible and rational. For Foucault, the humanization of punishment emerged from the spread of disciplinary practices. That historical grounding, however, disappeared from view because of the blinding presence of the penal soul. We have, he suggested, inverted the proper order of things, seeing an effect as an effective cause, our investment in a greater spiritualization of punishment as structuring the dissemination of discipline rather than the other way around. Consequently, *Discipline and Punish* traced a series of historical displacements, from the social practices of discipline, through humanitarian efforts to transform punishment, to their putative target, the soul.

9. Ibid., 197.

But if, as Foucault argued, the penal body was an object for both knowledge and power, it was also a threat and disruption. In late-eighteenth-century Philadelphia, when private reformers and public officials challenged and overturned the inherited system of public punishments and the reformed system of public labor, their criticisms and anxieties focused on the public presence and display of criminals. Proponents of disciplinary institutions argued that individual character was fundamentally unstable, that criminality—spread through example and communication—constituted a veritable social contagion. As they analysed the dynamics of public executions, of whippings and pillorying, or of public labor in the streets, they argued that crowds of onlookers were too drawn to the condemned and the violence inflicted on them. Witnessing public punishments did little, they insisted, to diminish crime. On the contrary, it triggered what I term "mimetic corruption," where the very presence of embodied criminality overwhelmed spectators' virtue and led them to identify with and replicate criminality.

These critics conceived of the public realm as a dangerous theater of miscommunication and misunderstanding. They aimed—literally—to wall off the enticements of criminality, to distance the sources of vice and isolate them within the prison. Having done so, they insisted, they could then subject convicts to a disciplinary regime that would root out habits of crime and idleness and preserve inmates from further corruption. From this perspective, the body was not only subject to various penal technologies; its very presence and materiality had the capacity to disrupt the orderly dissemination of virtue.

Articulated most acutely by Benjamin Rush but shared by a wide range of his contemporaries, this critique suggested that public punishments promoted a series of false or misplaced identifications. These critics insisted that spectators identified with the condemned or with the infliction of suffering on the condemned, rarely with the overall meaning of the ritual. If punishments were to be retained, the connection between the bodies of the condemned and the imagination of the crowd would have to be broken. In a sense, critics of both traditional public punishments and the reformed system of public labor suggested that the problem with public punishments was a too great proximity between the condemned and the crowd. They implied that the body was itself a social character, that its communicative capacity had the power to overturn the script of legal punishment.

This discourse of mimetic corruption was the frame through which subsequent penal problems came to be seen. When onlookers sympathized with convicts, convicts escaped, or inmates protested violently, private reformers and public officials interpreted these developments as signs of a communicative economy in disarray. In attempting to overcome the dangers of mimetic corruption, late-eighteenth- and early-nineteenth-century reformers and officials constructed an ever-expanding network of disciplinary institutions. But their attempts to control communication always returned to the ordering of the body; the contradictions of the penal scene were displaced and deposited onto the body. Penal reformers simultaneously emphasized the communicative element of punishment and turned the question of social communication into an anxiety over corporal presence.

As a result, the transition from public corporal and capital punishments, through public labor and congregate labor, to segregative confinement, while decreasing the apparent violence of the penal scene and expanding the hopes for reformation of convicts, consolidated structures of social distance. Excluding prisoners in order to reclaim them made material the social and psychological separation that already existed between social reformers and their charges. Given the various ways that different classes of spectators viewed the condemned, the turn to the prison effectively imposed on social space (and, consequently, on society as a whole) the distance that reformers already experienced in psychic space.[10] The body as character opened up the space for the emergence of what Foucault termed the penal "soul"; it would also allow punishment to become the site of utopian hopes and social fears.

IV

The twin transformations that restructured the practice of punishment—the increasingly segregated nature of the penal system and the declining impor-

---

10. For three studies that take up the issue of the construction of social distance through the very process of reform, see John Bender, *Imagining the Penitentiary: Fiction and the Architecture of Mind in Eighteenth-Century England* (Chicago, 1987), 231–252; Karen Halttunen, "Humanitarianism and the Pornography of Pain in Anglo-American Culture," *American Historical Review*, C (1995), 303–334; Randall McGowen, "Civilizing Punishment: The End of the Public Execution in England," *Journal of British Studies*, XXXIII (1994), 257–282.

The distanced reclamation of prisoners offers a suggestive vantage point on the claims raised by Thomas L. Haskell on the origins of Anglo-American humanitarian sentiment. Haskell claimed, in his critique of David Brion Davis's treatment of abolition, that the spread of market forces helped create the preconditions for an expansion of moral sensibility; the expansion of market connections and rationality in effect triggered efforts to overcome psychic and social distance on the part of humanitarian reformers. But Haskell's analysis fails to account for the ways in which the very act of reform could not only presuppose but constitute a continuing distance between reformers and their charges. As I argue below in Chapter 4, the spread of notions of humanity not only expanded the realm of possible reformation and reclamation; it also expanded the realm of subordination and exclusion. For Haskell's arguments, see Haskell, "Capitalism and the Origins of the Humanitarian Sensibility," *American Historical Review*, XC (1985), 339–361, 547–566. Has-

tance of penalties aimed openly at the body—implicate the history of what
Jürgen Habermas has called the "bourgeois public sphere." The notion of the
"public sphere" has become central to much critical discussion about the nature of liberal societies, the place of intellectuals in the contemporary world,
and the collapse of a coherent shared culture in the United States as well as the
historical meaning and legacy of the Enlightenment and the Age of Revolution.[11] The attention paid to the public sphere has generated serious reflection
about the basic preconditions of any truly democratic society. Yet these discussions have, it seems to me, placed far too much attention on the spread of
the institutions of the public sphere, as opposed to the social policies produced within it.

As Habermas has shown, the separation of state and society that accompanied the spread of commodity exchange opened the space in which "private
people come together as a public" to debate rationally and criticize social and
political policy. Of particular importance was the emergence of the independent press and the social space of coffeehouses, reading libraries, debating
clubs, and moral societies that made it possible for bourgeois males to communicate and exchange ideas about the nature of society and the course of
contemporary events. In this public sphere, Habermas argues, social standing
was disregarded and discursive victory was made dependent on the force of
the better argument. The debates that took place within the public sphere, he
believes, were crucial to legitimating bourgeois power. Claiming to dissolve
domination in reason, the bourgeoisie conquered state and society, in part,
through the force of its argumentation.[12]

Ultimately, the internal logic of capitalist development rejoined the private

kell's essays, as well as responses by David Brion Davis and John Ashworth, have now been
collected together in Thomas Bender, ed., *The Antislavery Debate: Capitalism and Abolitionism as a Problem in Historical Interpretation* (Berkeley, Calif., 1992).

11. Jürgen Habermas, *The Structural Transformation of the Public Sphere: An Inquiry into
a Category of Bourgeois Society,* trans. Thomas Burger (Cambridge, Mass., 1989). For ex-
amples of historical work inspired by Habermas, see Joan Landes, *Women and the Public
Sphere in the Age of the French Revolution* (Ithaca, N.Y., 1988); Mary P. Ryan, *Women in
Public: Between Banners and Ballots, 1825–1880* (Baltimore, 1990); Michael Warner, *The
Letters of the Republic: Publication and the Public Sphere in Eighteenth-Century America*
(Cambridge, Mass., 1990); and the historical essays in Craig Calhoun, ed., *Habermas and
the Public Sphere* (Cambridge, Mass., 1992). For discussions focused more on the contem-
porary situation, see the Calhoun volume and Bruce Robbins, ed., *The Phantom Public
Sphere* (Minneapolis, Minn., 1993), and the enormous later work of Habermas himself.

12. Habermas, *Structural Transformation of the Public Sphere,* 27, 89–116. It should be
noted that in Habermas, at least, the public sphere designates less a particular space than a
form of interaction that cuts across a variety of institutions and spaces. Consequently, the
common conflation of public sphere with public space misses the essential point about the
public sphere as a disembodied arena of argumentation.

and public realms. Large administrative apparatuses and technologically advanced media effectively colonized the public sphere. Nonetheless, Habermas argued, the public sphere of the late eighteenth and early nineteenth centuries was more than merely an ideological fiction, and, he insisted, a revamped public sphere is a necessary component of any future democratic politics.

Habermas's public-sphere arguments have generated a substantial body of historical and philosophical work. At the same time, they have also been subjected to historical and political criticisms. Feminist critics such as Nancy Fraser and Joan Landes have focused on the utopian nature of Habermas's formulation, highlighting the exclusions (in particular, those along gender lines) that constituted the bourgeois public sphere. Bourgeois universality, they have stressed, concealed bourgeois and patriarchal particularity.[13]

Yet, castigating the public sphere for its exclusions has limited critical power. In its claims to universality, the public sphere contained within itself the grounds for criticizing its own exclusions.[14] Criticisms of the public sphere, I would argue, remain incomplete if they do not engage the content produced in the public sphere—that is, the practical strategies generated by "private people come together as a public." Ignoring the content of the public sphere also means we fail to grasp the significance of its form—that claim to disembodied discourse that remains one of the fundamental ideological fantasies of bourgeois authority.

Nowhere is this clearer than in the history of punishment. What participants in the liberal public sphere generated was a disciplinary strategy that they justified through the fictions of universal and disembodied laws of reason. The disciplinary realm offered an inverted extension of the public sphere. Within disciplinary institutions, the power of the better argument was supplanted by the argument of power, and the reason of the public materialized on the bodies of those without "sufficient" reason. It was not simply that they were excluded from communication with the dominant discourse.[15] Social

13. See Landes, *Women and the Public Sphere;* Nancy Fraser, "What's Critical about Critical Theory: The Case of Habermas and Gender," in Fraser, *Unruly Practices: Power, Discourse, and Gender in Contemporary Social Theory* (Minneapolis, Minn., 1989), 113–143; and Fraser, "Rethinking the Public Sphere: A Contribution to the Critique of Actually Existing Democracy," Mary P. Ryan, "Gender and Public Access: Women's Politics in Nineteenth-Century America," and Geoff Eley, "Nations, Publics, and Political Cultures: Placing Habermas in the Nineteenth Century," all in Calhoun, ed., *Habermas and the Public Sphere,* 109–142, 259–288, 289–339.

14. See Jürgen Habermas, "Further Reflections on the Public Sphere," in Calhoun, ed., *Habermas and the Public Sphere,* 429.

15. In "Michel Foucault: A Young Conservative?" Nancy Fraser questions the applicability of a critique of Habermas based on the practice of discipline. She suggests that Habermas's notion of communicative reason provides the grounds with which to criticize precisely the sorts of hierarchical situations that I discuss here. But even if that is true in the abstract, it

discipline worked to individualize and contain those citizens who remained outside the bourgeois public sphere—and who thereby embodied its limits.

No history, then, of the public sphere can ignore the history of disciplinary institutions and practices. To do so is to conceal and deny the content produced by the public sphere and the content of the form of the public sphere. The institutions of the public sphere not only generated disciplinary strategies; they did so by asserting that they were only concerned with general norms and conditions of debate. It was not merely that other groups were excluded from the public sphere but that such exclusion was predicated on presuming the universality of the norms of the public sphere itself. Those unable or unwilling to participate under those particular rules became objects for disciplinary intervention. The public sphere not only excluded—it helped open up the realm of disciplinary strategies. In saying this, I do not want to imply that the institutions that provided the groundwork of the public sphere (the press, access to information, assembly, speech, and so forth) need to be overcome or denigrated as merely bourgeois. The history of societies that have done away with these institutions as superfluous hardly provide a model to emulate. But it does seem to me that Karl Marx's criticism of the public sphere as possible in its universality only as it abstracts itself from real social antagonism marks the essential limits of a formalist approach to political conflicts.[16]

V

If the emergence of the prison is an important site for the history of the body, and a disturbing complication for the history of the public sphere, its most profound implications are for the history of liberalism. In the half-century following the Revolution, liberalism became the dominant ideology of northern bourgeois society.[17] Although always challenged—by republicanism, ple-

---

does not address the question of how the public sphere functions historically within liberal society. See Fraser, *Unruly Practices,* 43–47.

This notion of a lack of communication would appear to be Habermas's interpretation of the arguments of Michel Foucault: "Foucault considers the formative rules of a hegemonic discourse as mechanisms of exclusion constituting their respective 'other.' In these cases there is no communication between those within and those without. Those who participate in the discourse do not share a common language with the protesting others." Habermas, "Further Reflections on the Public Sphere," in Calhoun, ed., *Habermas and the Public Sphere,* 429.

16. See Karl Marx, "On the Jewish Question," in Marx, *Early Writings,* trans. Rodney Livingstone and Gregor Benton (New York, 1975), 212–241.

17. Joyce Oldham Appleby, *Capitalism and a New Social Order: The Republican Vision of the 1790s* (New York, 1984); Appleby, *Liberalism and Republicanism in American Historiog-*

beian radicalism, and evangelical Protestantism, not to mention the slave South with its own political economy and organicist social vision—liberalism displaced its rivals in shaping the political economy and values of the North.

Liberalism presupposed a particular relationship between individual and society. Conceiving of the individual as a self-possession, a position C. B. Macpherson called "possessive individualism," liberal thinkers presumed that a properly ordered social and political world would place the fewest limits possible on individual action and liberty. Placing their faith in the power of personal choice and reason, they argued that social constraints on the individual held back the progress of humanity. Liberalism presumed a radical distinction between the individual and the social—and liberal thought interpreted this division to the favor of the individual. This faith in individual liberty and reason undergirded many of the major historical accomplishments of the Age of Revolution, including the expansion of civil liberties and attempts to restrain the state's control over speech, assembly, and religion. Liberalism also provided a language of dissent throughout the nineteenth and twentieth centuries. Attempts to dismantle entrenched state and social powers have often occurred under the sign of liberalism.[18]

But the radical distinction between the individual and society could cut another way. Liberalism precluded any consideration of the collective in the individual—if success was individual, so was failure. Most often this problem emerged in the refusal of state support for the poor. Classical political economy, with its critique of older paternalistic state practices, displayed the liberal emphasis on the individualistic nature of success and failure most clearly.

---

raphy (Cambridge, Mass., 1992); Steven Watts, *The Republic Reborn: War and the Making of Liberal America, 1790–1820* (Baltimore, 1987); Gordon S. Wood, *The Radicalism of the American Revolution* (New York, 1992).

As Christopher Tomlins put it: liberalism "spawned a new series of reinforcing routines constitutive of market society with, however, distinctly asymmetrical social relations: social and economic individualism, the protection of property, a filtered democracy, and a hobbled state" (*Law, Labor, and Ideology in the Early American Republic* [New York, 1993], 26). As will be clear throughout this study, I think that Tomlins somewhat overstates the "hobbled" nature of the state because of his focus on labor relations (where the state withdrew in favor of the economic dominant). For a discussion of the intersection between economic laissez-faire and the noneconomic intervention of the state in 19th-century America, see David Montgomery, *Citizen Worker: The Experience of Workers in the United States with Democracy and the Free Market during the Nineteenth Century* (New York, 1993), 52–88.

18. For the notion of "possessive individualism," see C. B. Macpherson, *The Political Theory of Possessive Individualism: Hobbes to Locke* (Oxford, 1962), esp. 3–4. For forceful statements about the necessity of appreciating the long-term transformative and liberating aspects of at least parts of the liberal tradition, see Appleby, *Liberalism and Republicanism in American Historiography;* Wood, *Radicalism of the American Revolution;* and Cornel West, *Keeping Faith: Philosophy and Race in America* (New York, 1993), 195–205.

But the implications of liberal assumptions extended far beyond political economy. The effort to restrain the powers of the state coexisted problematically with the new forms of disciplinary power ushered in with the Age of Revolution.

The simultaneous spread of liberal thinking and disciplinary practices poses a series of analytical problems. Disciplinary institutions—with their concealment, hierarchy, emphasis on submission, and reliance on coercive techniques—would seem contrary to the spread of the liberal values of individualism, self-expression, and expansive opportunities. Yet as Vaux's cornerstone proclamation indicates, the proponents of disciplinary institutions saw few contradictions between their efforts and the spread of liberal values. From their perspective, the new forms of social discipline, especially the penitentiary, were signs of enlightenment and the growth of humanity. The penitentiary represented a new, more humane form of government.

Consequently, I have attempted to tie the spread of discipline more closely to the construction of liberal society than did Foucault, Ignatieff, or Rothman. Liberalism assumed little overt place in *Discipline and Punish* and *A Just Measure of Pain*, whereas the apparent contradiction between liberalism and discipline was the driving force of Rothman's *Discovery of the Asylum*.[19] Rothman interpreted the efflorescence of disciplinary institutions as a Jacksonian attempt to turn back the forces of liberal capitalist change. He argued that such institutions were essentially efforts at social nostalgia that, in the interests of reestablishing eighteenth-century stability, effectively created new bureaucratic forms. While acknowledging the historical coincidence between liberal capitalism and the "discovery of the asylum," Rothman treated them as separate, almost opposed developments.

Yet it is a central contention of this study that discipline was the social equivalent of wage labor; it was an effective underpinning of liberal democracy. Discipline was not contrary to the spread of liberal institutions and values. Instead, it was a central element in it. Just as wage labor freed workers from extra-economic ties and practices only to subject them more directly to the coercions of the market, so discipline restrained the directly violent power of authority only to expand techniques for the more constant oversight and regulation of its subjects.[20] Tracing the transformation of punishment from

19. For Ignatieff's comments on liberalism in *A Just Measure of Pain*, see 211–213. For one neo-Foucaultian effort to link the spread of the prison directly to liberalism, see Thomas L. Dumm, *Democracy and Punishment: Disciplinary Origins of the United States* (Madison, Wis., 1987). Although I share Dumm's interest in connecting discipline to the history of liberalism, I think that he underestimates the tensions between liberal ideals of self-assertion and self-submission and the law and discipline.

20. This connection between wage labor and discipline is the central implication of both Linebaugh's *The London Hanged*, which argues that it was the discipline of the wage rela-

the 1780s through the 1830s, I argue that discipline was a continually renewed effort to shape public communication, individualize social problems, train dutiful citizens, and marginalize social divisions and alternative ways of life.

But, and this is equally crucial, disciplinary institutions proved so compelling because they appeared to make direct physical and corporal coercion unnecessary. Imprisonment emerged as the central practice of punishment, not in a movement away from the body, but rather as a different way of acting on it; the growing emphasis on the reformation of character was inextricably linked to corporeality. Yet proponents of penitentiary punishments believed that what was at stake was not the body, and this denial of the body was linked in an analogous fashion to a wider exercise of bourgeois authority. Whether it is a question of contract over the coercions of the market, love over forced submission, or punishment aimed at the spirit rather than the corporal being, modern bourgeois authority disembodies itself in order to extend its reach.[21]

Advocates of reformative incarceration, while recognizing the irreducible materiality of the penal apparatus, insisted that their target was the convicts' spirit or character. In this way, the body was both part of the penal process and excluded from it; reformers both acknowledged and avoided the continuing corporality of the penal process. This denial was not hypocrisy, however, but its opposite. It was the reformers' commitment to the growing spiritualization of punishment that drove them to disavow the corporality of punishment even as their efforts returned again and again to the body. The dynamic of the process bears a striking resemblance to what Freud called "negation," a concept describing a mechanism through which individuals simultaneously expressed and repudiated wishes or perceptions. According to Freud, what is at stake in such negation or disavowal is the stability of the subject's symbolic world.[22] The denial of corporality helped penal reformers maintain the dis-

---

tion itself that rendered obsolete the older forms of what Linebaugh calls "thanotocracy," i.e., a legal and penal system based on the infliction of public death, as well as Ignatieff's *Just Measure of Pain*, which ties the spread of the penitentiary to struggles over labor discipline and the factory system.

21. On the disembodiment of authority in England—and its connections to the rise of the novel—see Bender, *Imagining the Penitentiary*. For the connections between this disembodiment and the history of architecture, see Robin Evans, *The Fabrication of Virtue: English Prison Architecture, 1750–1840* (New York, 1982).

22. Sigmund Freud suggested in his reflections on "negation," "fetishism," and the "splitting of the ego" that subjects faced with a traumatic disruption to their symbolic world could respond in a way that both avoided knowledge of the trauma and accepted its reality. These mechanisms of "disavowal" achieved their most concrete form in the fetish where, in the psychoanalytic case, the material object enabled the subject to simultaneously acknowledge, deny, and fend off the threat of castration. See Freud, "Negation," in Ernest Jones et al., eds., *Collected Papers*, 5 vols., trans. Joan Riviere et al. (London, 1953), V, 181–185; Freud, "Fetishism," ibid., 198–204; Freud, "Splitting of the Ego in the Defensive

tinction between modern penitential practices and the pre-Revolutionary counterparts of these practices—a distinction, in turn, that signified the difference between the enlightened quality of northern liberal society and the continued corporality of monarchical and slave regimes. What Foucault called the penal soul was, in a sense, the symptom of this negation.

This process of disavowal adds a second twist to the tale of the body in penal reform. If reformers displaced social-communicative issues onto the body, they in turn displaced corporal questions onto the issue of character. Having focused on character, prison officials and private reformers could respond to inmate recalcitrance and resistance by intensifying control over the prisoners' bodies without dissolving the difference between their regime and those that they labeled "cruel." Indeed, from the perspective of the penitential imagination, recalcitrance or insubordination became a sign of the necessity of intensified intervention. Liberal discipline, like liberal society more generally, produced its own specific modes of transgression, transgressions that in turn necessitated new modes of containment.[23] From mimetic corruption through the body to the soul, the spread of discipline transformed the contradictions and limits of liberal values and societies into a source of continually expanding power. But this disciplinary transformation was made possible only by a series of misrecognitions. The denial of corporality enabled the new regime of discipline. And discipline, in turn, sustained and contained the contradictions of liberal thought and society.

Process," ibid., 372–375. See as well the entries for "Disavowal," "Negation," and "Splitting of the Ego," in J. Laplanche and J. B. Pontalis, *The Language of Psycho-analysis,* trans. Donald Nicholson-Smith (New York, 1973), 118–121, 261–263, 427–429.

23. The history of punishment thus stages the fundamental contradictions of early liberalism. While claiming to liberate individual freedom, liberal governments also sought to constrain those freedoms that they deemed inimical to their own organization. The dismantling of the state was, in reality, partial; the disciplinary realm, if anything, expanded. This two-sided development of liberalism, simultaneously liberating and constraining, was justified through discourses of maturity and was accomplished, in part, by severing questions of individual morality and responsibility from social organization. (I would like to thank my colleague Eric Van Young for suggestions on this formulation.) For two recent treatments of this tension at the heart of early liberalism and the ways that human nature and maturity were mobilized to conceal it, see Thomas C. Holt, *The Problem of Freedom: Race, Labor, and Politics in Jamaica and Britain, 1832–1938* (Baltimore, 1992), 4–7, 35–37; Jay Fliegelman, *Declaring Independence: Jefferson, Natural Language, and the Culture of Performance* (Stanford, Calif., 1993), 150–155.

PART ONE

Display

CHAPTER ONE

Public Punishments
in Philadelphia

In eighteenth-century Philadelphia, as elsewhere in the North Atlantic world, the legal system deployed a variety of public punishments to chastise convicted offenders. The whip, the pillory, and the scaffold were all employed, and employed with regularity. Although by the standards of London or Paris the numbers of public punishments may have been low, few months passed without public whippings and few years without executions. All of these penalties dramatically and explicitly merged the symbolic and the corporal, seizing the body to inflict pain or death—and they did so before the eyes of the community.[1]

Pennsylvania's penal practices were modeled on English patterns. In England, the eighteenth century was the heyday of the power of the law; the eighteenth-century English ruling classes depended on the ritual of the law to maintain their authority. English elites combined a legal code of more than two hundred capital offenses with a widespread practice of pardoning that joined terror and mercy in a manner that upheld their claims to justice. In Pennsylvania, the system was less elaborate. Pennsylvania did import the basic rituals and practices of English criminal justice: trial by jury, public punish-

---

1. Between 1682 and 1834, when the state eliminated public executions, Pennsylvania executed at least 257 individuals, 113 in Philadelphia. Of the latter, only 7 occurred after the Revolution. In one particularly intense period of executions, 1780–1785, 32 people were executed in the city (Negley K. Teeters, "Public Executions in Pennsylvania, 1682–1834," *Journal of the Lancaster County Historical Society*, LXIV [1960], 119; Negley K. Teeters, *Scaffold and Chair: A Compilation of Their Use in Pennsylvania, 1682–1962* [Philadelphia, 1963], 79–80). For a discussion of the wider context of criminal punishment in colonial Pennsylvania, see Herbert William Keith Fitzroy, "The Punishment of Crime in Provincial Pennsylvania," *PMHB*, LX (1936), 242–269. And for an analysis of the changing place of corporality in the theory and practice of English executions, see Randall McGowen, "The Body and Punishment in Eighteenth-Century England," *Journal of Modern History*, LIX (1987), 651–679.

ments, and pardon through character references. Still, public punishments, although considerable, were, by English standards, infrequent and the number of capital offenses few. Class formation in colonial Pennsylvania was less well developed, the ownership of property more widespread, and access to the courts greater.[2]

Public punishments were more than just legal rituals. The state had the machinery of terror and death at its disposal, and it was deployed most frequently in the defense of property. Yet, at the same time, the criminal could subvert the official script, and the community could question the justice of the punishment. The public punishment was an inherently unstable social practice, for, if officials could ensure its outcome, they could not control its meaning.

As a result, the government strove to incorporate both the condemned and the community within its ceremony of punishment. Yet that very desire to incorporate indicated the limits of the state's power. The exercise of public punishments depended on the participation, or at least the acquiescence, of the very subjects before whom it was displayed and for whom it was designed. Public punishments staged and restaged the conflicts and insecurities that structured eighteenth-century social relations. They seized the body, but they could not ensure consent.

The ceremony of public punishment enacted in miniature the nature and contradictions of eighteenth-century authority. In eighteenth-century Pennsylvania, social and political authority, although joined, remained unstable. Public punishment depended on both the condemned and their audience for its efficacy; it revealed what E. P. Thompson called the "field of force" of social relations. In eighteenth-century England, Thompson argued, the antagonistic relationship between patricians and plebs structured society. The middling sorts, sometimes allied with the patricians, sometimes with the plebs, were a dependent force—they might change the tone but not the fundamental picture of social relations.[3] In eighteenth-century Pennsylvania, especially Philadelphia, these forces were aligned differently. Most important, the patricians were less dominant and small propertyholders more central to the pub-

2. For a discussion of the implications of 18th-century executions for social and class relations, see Douglas Hay, "Property, Authority, and the Criminal Law," in Hay et al., *Albion's Fatal Tree: Crime and Society in Eighteenth-Century England* (New York, 1975), 17–63. On English criminal procedures, see ibid., 17–63, and John Beattie, *Crime and the Courts in England, 1660–1800* (Princeton, N.J., 1986). On the different context of Pennsylvania's private prosecution system, see Allen Steinberg, "From Private Prosecution to Plea Bargaining: Criminal Prosecution, the District Attorney, and American Legal History" (paper presented to the Philadelphia Center for Early American Studies, Mar. 4, 1983).

3. For the notion of social relations as a "field of force," see E. P. Thompson, *Customs in Common* (London, 1991), 16–96, with the specific notion introduced at 73.

lic realm. The vagaries of a commercial economy rendered wealth and power more insecure. Middling values—perhaps most famously represented by Benjamin Franklin's "Poor Richard"—suffused not only the scene of punishment but society at large. When a public punishment took place, the middling sorts were pivotal to its effectiveness. And their ambiguous status mirrored the ambiguous effects of public punishments.

I

Philadelphia's public punishments possessed a complex historicity. On the level of form, they displayed little change. Throughout the eighteenth and early nineteenth centuries, Philadelphia's executions took place either in one of the city's four public squares or in specially cleared areas. Before a hanging, the condemned walked from the prison through the city streets accompanied by clergy, judges, the sheriff, and guards, in full public display, watched both by crowds along the route and then by thousands at the actual execution. At the site of the execution, the speech of the criminal preceded his or her death. During the eighteenth century, whipping and pillorying normally took place on Wednesdays and Saturdays at the city's market while it was in session. The authorities thus staged punishments to present penal sanctions to the eyes of the public.

Although the rituals of public capital punishment remained relatively constant, their objects, frequency, and context changed dramatically. In the early years of Pennsylvania's colonial history, only murder was punishable by death. But, beginning in 1718, the number of crimes subject to capital sanctions grew steadily. By the late-colonial period, Pennsylvania executed persons for at least eighteen offenses, including arson, murder, rape, treason, burglary, robbery, sodomy, and counterfeiting. In 1786, Pennsylvania removed capital sanctions from robbery, burglary, and sodomy, and, in 1794, from all offenses save first-degree murder.[4]

4. On murder as a capital crime, see *St. at Large,* II, 172. On the general expansion of the death penalty, see William Bradford, *An Enquiry How Far the Punishment of Death Is Necessary in Pennsylvania with Notes and Illustrations . . . to Which Is added, an Account of the Gaol and Penitentiary House of Philadelphia, and of the Interior Management Thereof. By Caleb Lownes, of Philadelphia* (Philadelphia, 1793), 14–20. The actual number of capital crimes depends on how finely one distinguishes within general offense categories (for example, arson could be one offense or several as arson statutes will distinguish different types of buildings that qualify). I have counted conservatively. For the major introduction of the death penalty into Pennsylvania in 1718, see, *St. at Large,* III, 200–205 (for those capital crimes where the condemned could claim benefit of clergy, this right was lost with the second conviction, 208). Additional offenses were made capital throughout the colonial and early Revolutionary period. See ibid., IV, 358 (counterfeiting, uttering, forging), V, 248, 300 (another statute against counterfeiting, uttering, forging), VI, 326, 328 (rioting), VII,

Yet, if the statutory reach of capital punishments steadily declined during the late eighteenth century, the actual practice of public executions followed a different chronology. The Revolutionary period saw the largest exercise of capital sanctions in Philadelphia's eighteenth- and early-nineteenth-century history. Whereas forty-four individuals were hanged in Philadelphia before 1776, sixty-two were executed between 1776 and 1790 alone. Then, following a decade-long drought, Pennsylvania publicly hanged another seven people in the city before the state abolished public executions in 1834.[5]

Throughout most of the eighteenth century, capital punishments took place within a larger penal system geared toward the public display and seizure of the body. Until 1794, manslaughter could be punished with burning in the hand. Before 1786—when the state abolished public whipping—petit larceny, tried summarily before two magistrates, could bring up to fifteen lashes, a first larceny conviction up to twenty-one lashes, a second conviction between twenty-one and forty lashes, and a further conviction from thirty-nine to fifty lashes.[6] Individuals convicted of small property offenses were also fined and forced to make restitution. In some cases, time in the pillory or other non-capital corporal punishments were added. In addition, courts ordered that selected offenders be "carted." This latter punishment most closely approximated the public execution. Here the offender would be strapped to a cart's tail and moved throughout the city's squares in order to be whipped serially. In this way, carting joined a lesser version of the execution procession to the most common corporal punishment. The vast majority of public punishments were for these small property crimes.

A variety of courts oversaw the infliction of public penalties. Capital crimes fell under the jurisdiction of the Supreme Court. The Pennsylvania Supreme Court sat twice a year in Philadelphia, and Supreme Court justices had powers to sit as courts of oyer and terminer when cases demanded immediate attention. The Supreme Court could, and did, impose secondary public punishments as well. Secondary public punishments were also prescribed at the level of the county and the city. Philadelphia had two quarterly courts of record that dealt with criminal cases: the Mayor's Court (renamed the City Court during the Revolution) and the Philadelphia County Court of Quarter Ses-

---

350–351 (specifies penalties for those who committed crimes while blacked and armed), VIII, 183 (expanding the arson statute), X, 110 (non-highway robbery). In many cases, these later laws were clearly intended to close gaps in earlier capital statutes. For the removal of capital sanctions, see ibid., XII, 281, XV, 174–178.

    5. Teeters, *Scaffold and Chair*, 62–67, 79–80.

    6. Bradford, *An Enquiry*, 41–42; *St. at Large*, XV, 176–177. For larceny penalties, see *St. at Large*, III, 211–213. For petit larceny and summary judgment, see ibid., 246–247. On the abolition of whipping, see Chapter 2.

sions of the Peace. The Court of Quarter Sessions was composed of justices of the peace appointed by the governor (except from 1776 to 1790, when they were elected). It possessed jurisdiction over noncapital crimes committed in Philadelphia County. The Mayor's Court was composed of aldermen, the mayor, and the recorder of the city of Philadelphia. In the colonial period, the city was a self-perpetuating corporation with powers of self-government, and the Mayor's Court possessed jurisdiction within the confines of the incorporated city. In the eighteenth century, the Court of Quarter Sessions for the County of Philadelphia met four times a year, in March, June, September, and December. The Mayor's Court met in January, April, July, and November. Throughout the colonial period and the Revolution, these courts routinely ordered that people convicted of small property crimes be whipped. Whipping and pillorying, then, were year-round events in colonial Philadelphia.[7]

By the nineteenth century, however, public capital penalties had become anomalies, not exemplars of the penal system. But no simple spread of humanitarianism or constant progression toward sensibility and discretion marked this change. Instead, the history of capital punishment in Philadelphia witnessed a series of erratic shifts: a steady deployment of capital sanctions during the late-colonial period, a marked upsurge during the Revolutionary era, then a seeming disappearance at the end of the eighteenth century, leading to occasional but repeated hangings during the early nineteenth century. Moreover, there was a complete reversal, within Pennsylvania at least, in the proportion of urban and rural executions from the eighteenth to the nineteenth century. During the former period, 106 individuals were hanged in Philadelphia, compared to 97 in the rest of Pennsylvania. But from 1800 to 1834, only 7 were executed in the city, compared to 47 for the rest of the

---

7. *St. at Large,* III, 302–305. On the Courts of Quarter Sessions, see ibid., 299–300. Theoretically, according to Philadelphia's charter, the city's Mayor's Court had jurisdiction over all crimes within the city limits. See Pa. (Colony) Laws, Statutes, etc., *The Charters and Acts of Assembly of the Province of Pennsylvania* (Philadelphia, 1762), I, 12, and Edwin C. Surrency, "The Evolution of an Urban Judicial System: The Philadelphia Story, 1683–1968," *American Journal of Legal History,* XVIII (1974), 97–99. In practice, the Mayor's Court functioned like the Court of Quarter Sessions.

From December 1780 to December 1785, the Court of Quarter Sessions sat 21 times. During that period, it sentenced 98 individuals to some sort of public punishments (whippings, pillorying, carting). In 23 sittings of the City Court, from April 1779 to July 1785, 186 individuals were sentenced to public punishments. Nor did the courts hesitate to impose corporal public punishments throughout the year. Only two sittings of the Court of Quarter Sessions and no sittings of the City Court failed to impose some form of corporal penalty. By contrast, during the same period, the Court of Quarter Sessions sentenced only 16 people and the City Court just 22 to some form of imprisonment. See the Philadelphia County Court of Quarter Sessions of the Peace, 1780–1785, Philadelphia Court Papers, HSP; Dockets of the Mayor's Court of Philadelphia, Oct. 1779–Apr. 1782, July 1782–July 1785, PCA.

state.[8] It was in the city that the place of public executions changed most dramatically, and, in these developments, the Revolution stands out as a paradoxical turning point in Philadelphia, simultaneously intensifying the use of public penalties and accelerating their demise.

Yet, beyond their numbers and locations, public punishments were complex rituals of bodily pain, degradation, and death. From the most compressed whipping to the most elaborate execution, public punishments visibly inscribed the law's demands on the body of the condemned. They also openly displayed the fact of crime, the presence of violation. In presenting the power of the law to the public, each public punishment encapsulated a drama of transgression and its punishment, of authority and its exercise.

II

February 7, 1823, was "clear and cold" when William Gross, convicted of murdering Keziah Stow, was hanged at Logan Square in northwest Philadelphia. Gross emerged from the Walnut Street Jail shortly before half past ten in the morning wearing "a black hat." "Over his usual clothes was a white cotton garment, which covered his whole body, arms and legs. His arms were pinioned and the rope [was] round his body." Gross was, not surprisingly, "very pale." However, his "step was remarkably firm"—this despite six weeks of confinement with a chain around his ankle. Gross behaved as the authorities wanted: "He did not pause a moment; nor did he then, or at any future time, raise his eye to survey the multitude." At center stage of the theater of punishment, Gross never sought to challenge or subvert the script.[9]

The distance from the prison to the place of execution was approximately a mile and a half, and, despite "occasional obstructions" from the crowd, Gross walked it in under three-quarters of an hour. A sheriff's "officer with a wand," the high constables, the city constables, and "the Captains and Lieutenants of the Watch" headed the procession on horseback. The city and county watchmen carrying their night clubs followed on foot, and then came "chief clerks" on horseback with wands. Then, a "cart in which rode the hangman, disguised in a black mask, an old straw hat and blankets" was followed by Gross and members of the clergy. After the prisoner came the high sheriff and "principal" deputy, the coroner, the hearse, more county constables, the court crier, citizens on foot, a sheriff's officer on horseback, and, lastly, more citizens on horseback. City and county constables on horseback carrying staffs rode

8. Teeters, *Scaffold and Chair,* 33, 79–80. For an argument that stresses the long-term growth of "sensibility" to explain the decline of public penalties, see Pieter Spierenburg, *The Spectacle of Suffering: Executions and the Evolution of Repression: From a Preindustrial Metropolis to the European Experience* (New York, 1984), 183–199.

9. *Dem. Press,* Feb. 8, 1823.

alongside the procession to keep the crowd at a proper distance. No judges took part, nor did the mayor. Yet the procession brought together the keepers of public order and the citizenry. Officials of varying ranks took part, from the high sheriff to common constables; clergymen walked along with the criminal, and citizens of different ranks (on foot and horseback) also participated. The ritual itself proclaimed the integration of state and society.[10]

The execution process was deeply religious. In the days leading up to his hanging, Gross appeared the model penitent. "His feelings were wonderfully subdued and his expression and manner were altogether influenced by his feelings." Philadelphia's newspapers delighted in detailing Gross's growing religious fervor and repentance. Gross declared his peace with his fate and his desire to throw himself on the mercy of God. From the beginning of his imprisonment, clergy visited Gross—counseling him, praying with him, urging his repentance. Their intensity was so great, in fact, that Gross limited the number of his religious visitors to four, complaining that the contradictory advice he received disquieted him. But those who remained continued their endeavors to the very end. On the day of the execution, hymns were sung after the group left the prison and "continued to be sung after the prisoner had arrived on the ground." One witness reported that he heard the prisoner's "voice clear and unbroken, raised to heaven." Clergy surrounded Gross on his way to the scaffold. When he arrived, they joined him in prayer and hymns and all listened as a speaker "addressed the throne of Mercy for some minutes in a strain of fervent piety. . . . A Hymn was then sung."[11]

The religious and the secular joined in the central moments of the ceremony: the prisoner's confession and actual execution. After listening to a brief address, Gross ascended the scaffold. When he reached the top, he paused to talk to the sheriff and his deputy, and then "the Sheriff read, in a loud and distinct manner, the Death Warrant under which he was acting." A call for silence was heard, and Gross began his confessional last statement, detailing his fall into the habits of "sin" and "vice" and providing his last advice to his peers: "*Avoid Bad Company*," he insisted, "it leads to all crimes and plunges in all sin. *Avoid Card Playing.* It has been my ruin. God guard you against these mighty tempters." Despite the seeming banality of the advice, Gross's statement was a moment of great drama and tension. "The anxiety to hear [on the part of the crowd] was so great as somewhat to disturb the serenity of the scene." Gross played out the role of the penitent sinner to the end. He did not denounce the authorities or proclaim his innocence. He refused a drink when it was offered on the scaffold, and, during his last moments, "he exhibited the

10. Ibid. For a general discussion of the relationship between state and society in European public executions, see Spierenburg, *The Spectacle of Suffering,* 200–207.

11. *Dem. Press,* Jan. 30, Feb. 5, 8, 1823; *Saturday Evening Post* (Philadelphia), Feb. 1, 8, 1823; "M. T.," *Poulson's American Daily Advertiser* (Philadelphia), Feb. 10, 1823.

same firmness and resignation which distinguished his deportment through-out the whole of the trying scene." By accepting his sentence and execution with Christian resignation, Gross acknowledged its justice and confirmed the righteousness of the state's actions.

Finally, came the moment of the hanging:

> When the rope was adjusted and every one had left the platform, it was more than a minute before the upright was struck down, yet the criminal did not bend nor sway nor tremble. He kept the same position in which he was left. The upright being taken away, the platform fell, and the culprit dropped about eighteen inches. His neck must have been broken by the sudden shock. No motion of the body was visible, in less than two minutes after the drop fell, except what was given by the wind. In about twenty min-utes the corpse was lowered into a coffin, the coffin was placed in a hearse and the coroner attended to see him buried in the New Potter's Field.

Thus ended the brief public career of William Gross.[12]

Gross stood, during the execution ceremony, poised between this world and the next. But his execution itself also stood perched between two different penal worlds. On the one hand, he was executed only a few months before Roberts Vaux spoke to commemorate the laying of the cornerstone of the Eastern State Penitentiary and only a few miles from the site of that ceremony. On the other, Gross's execution harked back to a long practice of public penalties. William Gross was the last person the state of Pennsylvania publicly executed in Philadelphia. He followed—both literally and figuratively—in the footsteps of numerous predecessors. Before 1823, at least 108 men and 4 women had made their way to the gallows in Philadelphia.[13] For more than one hundred years, the drama of penal death had been played out in the streets of Philadelphia.

III

The celebration of public punishment was designed to spread terror and re-spect for the state's law throughout society. Magistrates orchestrated the prac-tice of public punishment to evoke images of mercy, terror, and repentance. Turning the courtroom and the scaffold into a stage for instructing the com-munity, they aimed to uphold authority and protect property and persons.

12. *Dem. Press,* Feb. 8, 1823. See also *Poulson's,* Feb. 8, 1823; *The Union; United States Gazette and True American* (Philadelphia), Feb. 8, 1823.

13. Teeters, *Scaffold and Chair,* 62–67, 79–80. Given the fragmentary nature of the records, the actual number of those executed may be greater. Two men convicted of federal crimes were hanged in the city after Gross. They were James Porter, convicted of mail rob-bery and executed on July 2, 1830, and James Moran, convicted of piracy and murder and executed on May 19, 1837.

To the eighteenth-century judges who oversaw the law, punishments were rooted in reason and nature. As Thomas McKean, chief justice of the Pennsylvania Supreme Court during the Revolution, informed a grand jury, "Man is a social creature, and formed for a social state." Yet individuals were "not only qualified to *benefit*" their "fellow creatures . . . but likewise to *disquiet* and *injure them*, and is from the variety amd violence of his passions, too often tempted to do so." God, he argued, could not have placed humanity within society if he did not provide the means to preserve order: "Therefore God, in willing the happiness of mankind in society, must necessarily be supposed to will the restraint of such unruly passions as would, if unrestrained, overthrow and destroy all that happiness." [14] The necessity of punishment was written in the nature of humanity.

In effect, penal ideology presupposed a struggle within each person between respect for authority and rebellion. The colony's General Assembly, addressing the governor in 1768, argued, "It is the Dread of exemplary Punishment, steadily and uniformly inflicted on past Delinquents, that alone can deter the Wicked from the Perpetuation of future Offenses." McKean held that "as the passions and perverse humours of men are no otherwise to be restrained but by establishing a coercive power over them," it was necessary that someone "be vested with authority and power to restrain the unruly wills and passions of men, by proper degrees of *terror* and punishment." [15] Pennsylvania's public punishment system presupposed the base nature of most of humanity. Only through fear of pain and death could the passions of the multitudes be controlled.

The terror of the law, its defenders insisted, manifested example and compassion. Edward Shippen in a charge to the grand jury of Philadelphia's Court of Quarter Sessions in October 1785 (on the eve of the first great wave of Pennsylvania's penal reforms) acknowledged that exemplary punishments "are not designed so much to *reform* the offenders . . . as to exhibit *Examples* to others, and by the terrors of the law, to prevent the future Commission of the like Enormities." But, if punishments seemed cruel to the individual subject to them, they freed the rest of society. McKean, recognizing the hesitancy of many to inflict capital penalties, argued that jurors could have "this consolation in the discharge of so disagreeable a duty, that altho' *one* suffereth, *numbers* are protected and relieved; the punishment of a few is the preservation of multitudes." The law's punishments, Edward Shippen insisted in 1762, were

14. Thomas McKean, "Notes on Charges to Grand Juries, 1777–1779," McKean Papers, 1–2, 4, HSP.

15. General Assembly's message to the Governor, Jan. 13, 1768, in *Pa. Archives*, 8th Ser., VII, 6087–6088; McKean, "Notes on Charges to Grand Juries," McKean Papers, 2. See also Edward Shippen, Jr., "Grand Jury Charge," Oct. 24, 1785, Philadelphia Court of Quarter Sessions, Balch-Shippen Papers, II, 88, HSP.

themselves acts of compassion. "We cannot sufficiently admire the Wisdom, Justice, and at the same time, the Lenity of the English Constitution, in providing laws to reach every possible crime, whereby the peace and good order of the Community may be affected." Only the law and its sanctions prevented the dissolution of society.[16]

The judges went further, arguing that Anglo-American law went far to succor the dignity of the condemned. In 1785, Shippen compared Pennsylvania's law to the "severity" of the punishments as they were "exercised in most other Countries of the World." Unlike the rest of the world, "Racks" and "Tortures" were not "permitted to extort Confessions from the unhappy Culprits." If the law seized the body, Shippen suggested in 1762, it was with reluctance and only from necessity. The English legal tradition itself guarded "against every Oppression that the Subject might be liable to under Colour of a legal prosecution." No individual could "be put upon his Tryal, unless a Grand Jury of his Country has first examined the Witnesses . . . after which he is to have an open and Fair Tryal in the Face of the Country . . . where he has every Opportunity of making his Defence that Innocence can Desire."[17] Between its prosecution of every crime and its defenses of the rights of the subject, Shippen implied, the criminal law brought together the claims of justice and mercy within its very design. Despite the apparent severity of punishment, humanity guided the penal law.

McKean also dramatically justified capital punishment while proclaiming the state's reluctance to condemn. It was only after a "sensible and unbiased jury" found guilt, he asserted, that the sentence of death was declared. In his telling, the state was forced to execute, and it did so with the deepest feelings for the condemned. Addressing convicted murderers, McKean turned the sentencing process into a personal travail. "I am very sorry," he informed the

16. Shippen, "Grand Jury Charge," Oct. 24, 1785, Balch-Shippen Papers, II, 88; McKean, "Notes on Charges to Grand Juries," McKean Papers, 3; [Edward Shippen], "Charge to Grand Jury, delivered by Edw at Easton June 1762," Balch-Shippen Papers, II, 85, HSP. I should note that there is a possibility of confusion about this date. Although the document indicates that this charge is from 1762, at that point in time, Edward Shippen IV (who I presume gave the charge) did not hold a position that clearly entitled him to charge juries in capital crimes. Nor did Edward Shippen III. This situation could be the result either of an incorrect date on the document or some irregularity in the court proceedings. Nonetheless, internal evidence in the charge's discussion of law indicates that it is a late colonial charge. It should be noted that McKean and his colleagues are attempting to justify legal punishments in terms of reason and efficacy, not simply in terms of authority or justice. As Foucault has suggested, this utilitarian defense of exemplary punishments may itself indicate growing skepticism of the severity of the law. See Michel Foucault, *Discipline and Punish: The Birth of the Prison*, trans. Alan Sheridan (New York, 1977), 49.

17. Shippen, "Grand Jury Charge," Oct. 24, 1785, Balch-Shippen Papers, II, 88; Shippen, "Charge to Grand Jury, delivered by Edw at Easton June 1762," Balch-Shippen Papers, II, 85.

condemned, "that you have been the occasion of bringing yourselves to unfortunate ends, and that there is this melancholy necessity *on me* to pronounce the sentence of *death* upon you." As McKean presented it, sentencing was an inexorable process, one that allowed for no pleasure, only a recognition of justice served. He cautioned the condemned to hope for no pardon and to prepare themselves for the final judgment before God, to spend what little time was left them repenting their sins and seeking divine mercy. In his discourses, McKean assumed two roles—that of "Christian" and "Judge."[18] In his Christian concern for the soul of the condemned and his judicial concern for the sanctity of the law, a judge, McKean believed, joined justice with mercy in the pronouncement of death.

Yet the claim to mercy was not limited to the next world or concern for the condemned's soul. Despite McKean's assertion of the inexorability of the sentence, pardons did occur in capital cases, and with some frequency. The demands made on the pardoned and the reasons for granting pardons varied. Some were required to leave the colony or the state in exchange for their pardons; others joined the military. A few were required to act as the state's executioner. Women could be reprieved or pardoned owing to pregnancy. Individuals were pardoned because of their youth, because of doubts about their guilt, or because of support from within the community for their character. But the pardon was always a gift by authority either to an individual or to the community. Despite their essentially arbitrary quality (there were no formal rules in Pennsylvania), pardons reaffirmed the state's claim of responsibility to its subjects and the demands of justice and mercy.[19]

18. McKean, "Another [Exordium or Preparatory Discourse to the Pronouncing a Sentence of Death] for Burglary etc.," in "Notes on Charges to Grand Juries," McKean Papers, 60, 62, 69; McKean, "Another [Exordium or Preparatory Discourse to the Pronouncing a Sentence of Death]," ibid., 60; McKean, "Notes on Charges to Grand Juries," McKean Papers, 60–61, 62–63, 66, 69, 70. Greg Dening has recently suggested that the lack of pleasure in inflicting punishment, the distancing of the official act from any personal investment, was a crucial device in upholding the legitimacy of the law. Although his discussion speaks directly to flogging on ships, I think his point that aloofness "directed the gaze from the man in power to the power itself and its necessity" is applicable to the theater of example more generally. See Greg Dening, *Mr. Bligh's Bad Language: Passion, Power and Theatre on the Bounty* (New York, 1992), 116. At the same time, McKean's articulation of reluctant necessity also points to the ambiguities of agency in Revolutionary thought, where many Revolutionaries aimed to displace their own acts of will onto some divine or natural demand. On this latter point, see Jay Fliegelman, *Declaring Independence: Jefferson, Natural Language, and the Culture of Performance* (Stanford, Calif., 1993), 140–164.

19. Teeters has identified 131 reprieves and pardons prior to 1800, excluding cases of treason. See Negley K. Teeters, "Public Executions in Pennsylvania, 1682–1834," *Journal of the Lancaster County Historical Society*, 64 (1960), 153–163. For examples of men pardoned on condition of joining the military, see *Col. Records*, XII, 222; on condition of leaving the colony, IX, 778–779, X, 93–94 (this case involved two slaves to be transported), 172; on

The granting of a pardon involved social and political considerations that extended beyond the legal concerns of the specific case. The entire logic of exemplary punishments demanded a careful consideration of the meaning and effects of specific examples. This calculation emerged most clearly during the Revolution. When Thomas McKean, William Atlee, and John Evans, all Supreme Court judges, recommended a pardon for George Hardy, convicted of treason, they noted that Hardy's behavior toward them had been "decent, respectful, and penitential" and expressed the hope that, if his life was spared, he might reform his ways. But they also stressed their calculation of the effects of his punishment and the context of his pardon. "His death," they suggested, "would afford little benefit by the example," as he was "a man of small note or consideration." Several others, they pointed out, "at least equally criminal with this man," had been acquitted owing to the "extreme lenity and tenderness of the Juries."[20] The judges recognized that exemplary punishments were public spectacles—and that their reception had to be taken into account. If the appearance of justice was violated, the legitimacy of authority was threatened. Punishments were not merely legal sanctions—they were exercises in government.

These calculations intertwined legal, political, and social power. At the heart of the penal system lay the protection of property; this protection was integral both to the criminal codes and to the practices of the courts. Serious crimes against the person were treated severely—but the majority of executions before 1794 were for crimes against property.[21] The large majority of business before the lower criminal courts concerned larceny and assault and

---

women being pardoned or reprieved owing to pregnancy, III, 240. Isaac Bradford was convicted of a robbery in 1737 and sentenced to death, but he was reprieved in exchange for acting as executioner of Henry Wileman and Catherine Smith—a "*very hard choice*," as the newspapers noted. *American Weekly Mercury* (Philadelphia), June 23–30, 1737. For examples of individuals pardoned for their youth, doubts about guilt, or support from the community, see the petition of Cornelius Sweers, Aug. 1 (?) 1778, HSP, and petition of Joseph Taggert, Jan. 28, 1789, HSP. Taggert, in particular, stressed his youth and his good character. Both petitioners had references from community members and the support of the judges who presided over their cases for their requests. On pardons and the state, see Hay, "Property, Authority, and the Criminal Law," in Hay et al., *Albion's Fatal Tree,* 17–63, and, for a dissenting view, John M. Langbein, "Albion's Fatal Flaws," *Past and Present,* no. 98 (1983), 96–120.

20. *Pa. Archives,* 1st Ser., VII, 326–27. On the response of the Supreme Executive Council, see *Col. Records,* XI, 753, 754, 760, 761, 764.

On the broader social calculations and effects of the English pardon process, see Hay, "Property, Authority, and the Criminal Law," in Hay et al., *Albion's Fatal Tree,* 44–49; Beattie, *Crime and the Courts in England,* 439–449, 621–622.

21. Teeters, "Public Executions in Pennsylvania, 1682–1834," *Journal of the Lancaster County Historical Society,* 64 (1960), 119; Teeters, *Scaffold and Chair,* 79–80.

battery. And among the lesser offenses, the protection of property reigned supreme. Although larceny punishments routinely included fines, restitutions, and whippings, for instance, assault and battery usually was punished only with small fines.

The protection of property lay at the ideological heart of the criminal law. Indeed, for Thomas McKean, the defense of property lay at the origin of government itself. "Without *government*," he informed one grand jury, "there can be no such thing as property in any thing beyond our own persons; for nothing but laws can make property, and laws are the effect of government and authority." Without government, he went on, even lives and liberty would be without meaning, each individual could enjoy nothing because of the constant fear of attack. But the connections between protection of property and protection of the law were even closer than in Lockean philosophy. As Edward Shippen argued in 1762, describing high treason ("a crime of the highest Nature that can be committed against Man"), there was "but one kind of it that can be committed in this Country, which is the Counterfeiting the King's Coin." [22] Property, in effect, was the base of individuality and revering the currency the sign of political loyalty.

The defense of property meant the defense of the propertied. And here the connection between property, personal standing, and power made the exercise of criminal punishments even more complex. Take the case of Samson, a slave convicted of arson in 1737. Samson was the slave of James Logan, president of the Governor's Council, and the building Samson burned belonged to Logan. Throughout the Anglo-American world, arson was often a form of class revenge against those with property. Logan and his peers were aware of its implications, and, given Logan's situation, Samson's conviction posed a political quandary. Logan protested that the prosecutor, by basing his entire case on Samson's confession, had failed to convince the jury (and presumably the wider public) of the "wicked Disposition of the Criminal, his Malice, and threatened Resentment against the Owner of the House, and the Person who then lived in it." As a result, the jury had petitioned for mercy toward Samson. This request, Logan complained, meant that he was "laid under some Difficulty." On the one hand, if the Council denied the jury's request, "it may be imagined to proceed from the Injury and Loss he himself has sustained"; on the other, "a Complyance with their Request in suffering so heinous a Crime to pass unpunished" would "be attended with many ill consequences," given that "the insolent Behavior of the Negroes in and about the city, which has of late been so much taken notice of, requires a strict hand to be kept over them." The Council agreed that punishment should not be voided, "yet being

22. McKean, "Notes on Charges to Grand Juries," McKean Papers, 5–6; Shippen, "Charge to Grand Jury, delivered at Edw by Easton June 1762," Balch-Shippen Papers, II, 85.

willing to pay some Regard to the Application" for a pardon, it reprieved
Samson for three months. When that time was passed, it offered to reprieve
Samson for another six months while allowing Logan to sell him out of the
British dominions so that he would never return to Pennsylvania.[23]

Samson's case brought into sharp focus considerations that normally remained implicit. From the vantage of Logan and his colleagues, Samson not
only had committed a "heinous" crime but represented the "insolent Behavior" of the black slaves in the city. Given the recurrent fears in eighteenth-
century Philadelphia of insubordination within the slave community and of
social alliances between black slaves, apprentices, and young men, the Council
was determined to impose severe punishments on slaves. But the Council also
recognized that it could not simply ignore the requests of the community's ju-
rymen, especially given Logan's place in the case. To do so might appear more
concerned with Logan's property than with the sense of the community. It
sought to convey specific, if contradictory, messages to two separate parts of
society—terrible resolve to the city's blacks and merciful responsiveness to
the freeholders who heard the case—while providing for Logan's losses. Protecting property and authority without appearing partial meant devising degrees of terror and punishment that would restrain without revolting.[24]

The jury's action also suggests that public corporal and capital punishments had a complex reception in eighteenth-century Philadelphia. The jurors, after all, did convict Samson. If they questioned the appropriateness of
death in the case, they did not question the law's right to punish crime. They
called for mercy, the temporary suspension of the law's penalties, not for the
overthrow of the law. In this position, they might well have represented the
views of small and middling propertyholders, individuals committed to property and the law but skeptical about the corporal excesses of punishment.
Later in the century, Thomas Paine, writing at the height of Revolutionary upheaval, argued in *The Rights of Man* both for submission to the law and recognition of its potential inhumanity. Declaring his disdain for England's sedi-
tion laws, Paine still averred, "I have always held it an opinion (making it also
my practise) that it is better to obey a bad law, making use at the same time of
every argument to show its errors and procure its repeal, than forcibly to vio-

23. *Col. Records*, IV, 243–244, 259; Gary B. Nash, *Forging Freedom: The Formation of
Philadelphia's Black Community, 1720–1840* (Cambridge, Mass., 1988), 12–13.

24. "Grand Jury Presentment, July 28, 1702," in John W. Wallace, "Ancient Records of
Philadelphia" (Am 3054), HSP; "Grand Jury Presentment, April 4, 1717," ibid.; "Grand Jury
Presentment, 1741," Philadelphia Court Papers, 1732–1744, HSP; Nash, *Forging Freedom*, 14.
Concerns about blacks, it should be noted, led so far as to the use of separate courts to try
black offenders. Samson himself had been tried at such a court. See *Col. Records*, IV, 243.
Councils did not always show such responsiveness to petitioners or concern over owners'
slave property. For the case in 1762 of a slave convicted of burglary whose support did not
save his life, see *Pa. Archives*, 1st Ser., IV, 102–103; *Col. Records*, IX, 5–6.

late it; because the precedent of breaking a bad law might weaken the force, and lead to a discretionary violation of those which are good." Paine, at least implicitly, approved of the criminal law and its protection of property; he never leveled a general criticism of either. But he did express skepticism about the justice of capital punishments. "When, in countries that are called civilized, we see age going to the work-house and youth to the gallows," he contended, "something must be wrong in the system of government. . . . Civil government does not consist in executions; but in making that provision for the instruction of youth, and the support of age, as to exclude, as much as possible, profligacy from the one, and despair from the other." Nor was he without skepticism over the class nature of criminal justice, asking: "Why is it that scarcely any are executed but the poor? The fact is a proof, among other things, of a wretchedness in their condition. Bred up without morals, and cast upon the world without a prospect, they are the exposed sacrifice of vice and legal barbarity." [25] Paine's language is telling on this point. Paine's view that the poor were "bred up without morals" expressed a more widely held middling conviction. As he saw it, the executed poor were doubly victims—of their lives and the laws.

Of course, Paine was not a typical middling man, and *Rights of Man* was from the 1790s. But, paradoxically, that may give more representativeness to his comments. Even at the height of his radicalness, Paine challenged neither the law nor its ties to property, a point that only reinforces his famous, and earlier, assertion of democratic *Common Sense,* that, if in England "the king is law," then in America "the law is king." [26] For Paine at least, the law and its practices powerfully symbolized the possibility (if not always the actuality) of justice.

IV

Paine's remarks, then, may help explain the complexity of popular attitudes toward the law. Although it is impossible to say to what extent Paine's views were shared by the middling and lower sorts in Philadelphia, they suggest that the public had an ambivalent and ambiguous relationship to the public spectacle of justice in eighteenth- and early-nineteenth-century Philadelphia. In England, and London in particular, public executions often precipitated riots and the spread of political dissent. In Pennsylvania, disturbances related to public punishments occurred infrequently. In 1726, a crowd burned down the

25. Thomas Paine, *The Rights of Man,* in Philip S. Foner, ed., *The Life and Major Writings of Thomas Paine* (Secaucus, N.J., 1948), I, 351, 404–405; Hay, "Property, Authority, and the Criminal Law," in Hay et al., *Albion's Fatal Tree,* 37–38.

26. Thomas Paine, *Common Sense,* in Foner, *The Life and Major Writings of Thomas Paine,* 29.

whipping post and the pillory. During the Revolution, issues of class biases in justice intertwined with issues of loyalty to the Revolutionary cause. In 1808, following the executions of John Joyce and Peter Mathias, two blacks convicted of robbery and murder, a black crowd assaulted the hangman. But these instances were exceptional. We have no evidence, at least for Philadelphia, of riots or attempts to free the condemned at the gallows. These actions did occur—but in the rural areas where conflicts over the legitimacy of the law and the courts were greater and more frequent. In Philadelphia, when crowds gathered at the foot of the scaffold or along the procession route, they did not openly challenge the proceedings. Why this was so is unclear, although the relatively widespread possession of property (made manifest in the importance of small-propertyholding artisans) may have generated sympathy for its protection through legal sanctions.[27] Nor is it clear what lesson spectators drew from public punishments. But their behavior allowed eighteenth-century authorities to assume that crowds witnessing the punishment shared the official understanding of its meaning and developed reverence (or at least fear) of the law from the ritual.

Still, as the aftermath of the Joyce and Mathias executions demonstrate, public punishments were volatile events, and their capacity to reach throughout the community was limited. In that instance, it is clear that members of the city's black community suspected that the legal proceedings were racially biased. The city's blacks largely avoided the execution itself, and Richard Allen, minister of the African Methodist Episcopal Church, felt compelled to defend the justice of the proceedings against hostility within his community.[28] The growing segregation of the city's African-American community during

27. William H. Lloyd, *The Early Courts of Pennsylvania* (Boston, 1910), 89; Steven Rosswurm, *Arms, Country, and Class: The Philadelphia Militia and "Lower Sort" during the American Revolution, 1775–1783* (New Brunswick, N.J., 1987), 156–158, 212; *Dem. Press*, Mar. 15, 17, 1808.

Evidence does exist for one planned attempt to free a condemned prisoner. In 1816, Ann Carson plotted to free her lover, Richard Smyth, first from jail and then through a plan to kidnap the governor to force a pardon. She did not carry out either plan. See Negley K. Teeters, *The Cradle of the Penitentiary: The Walnut Street Jail at Philadelphia, 1773–1835* (Philadelphia, 1955), 97–98. Moreover, rumors of escapes at the gallows were considered credible in the 19th century. In 1830, for instance, rumors of a plan to free James Porter from the scaffold nearly caused a riot. *Saturday Bulletin* (Philadelphia), July 3, 1830.

On the importance of petty producers to the city's pre-Revolutionary economy, see Rosswurm, *Arms, Country, and Class*, 13–18; Foner, *Tom Paine and Revolutionary America* (New York, 1976), 19–45. For a general discussion of the economic patterns of the late-18th-century city, see Billy G. Smith, *The "Lower Sort": Philadelphia's Laboring People, 1750–1800* (Ithaca, N.Y., 1990), 63–91.

28. *Dem. Press*, Mar. 15, 17, 1808; "Address to the Public, and People of Colour," in *Confession of John Joyce, alias Davis, Who Was Executed on Monday, the 14th of March, 1808 for the Murder of Mrs. Sarah Cross . . .* (Philadelphia, 1808), 3–6.

the post-Revolutionary period may have opened the space for the city's blacks to express their skepticism of the law, or it may have produced that skepticism itself. But in either case, the ambiguous roots of the black opposition to the Joyce and Mathias executions point to the variable nature of popular support for public executions themselves.

That repetitive yet limited nature of state power was rooted in the material conditions of colonial Philadelphia. Although a dynamic, rapidly growing seaport, throughout much of the eighteenth century Philadelphia remained a relatively small face-to-face community. On the eve of the Revolution, the city contained fewer than twenty-five thousand people. The city's neighborhoods contained individuals from a cross section of the city's classes, and people interacted socially and publicly across class lines. This interaction brought classes together in public life and reinforced class distinctions as the rich publicly displayed their wealth through coaches, dress, and language.[29]

Until the Revolution, the city's economy centered primarily on petty-commodity production within households. Although Philadelphia possessed a growing wage labor sector, bound labor (either apprenticeships, other forms of indentured servitude, or slavery) still predominated, especially among the city's artisans. Artisans worked alongside their apprentices and governed their everyday lives. Patriarchal authority continued to organize the workplace: school, home, and workplace were combined within the master-apprentice relationship. This economic structure helped militate against the development of a class of free wage laborers. Although certain trades were employing more and more workers through the wage system, bound labor in small workplaces was crucial to the city's economy until the eve of the Revolution.[30] This economic structure helped preserve the acceptability of public punishments to the city's elites. It seems likely that the high degree of familiarity across class lines and between employers and employees contributed to the lack of open challenge at public punishments. The freedom of behavior that anonymity brings was not available during these occasions.

Social relations in the city, then, helped shape patterns of display, differentiation, and identification between ranks and classes. The upper and lower classes shared cultural practices of gaming, drinking, and other festivities—practices that set them apart from the middling sorts who would emerge po-

29. Gary B. Nash, *The Urban Crucible: Social Change, Political Consciousness, and the Origins of the American Revolution* (Cambridge, Mass., 1979), 408; Stephen Brobeck, "Revolutionary Change in Colonial Philadelphia: The Brief Life of the Proprietary Gentry," *WMQ,* 3d Ser., XXXIII (1976), 410–434; Rosswurm, *Arms, Country, and Class,* 35–38.

30. Sharon V. Salinger, *"To Serve Well and Faithfully": Labor and Indentured Servants in Pennsylvania, 1682–1800* (New York, 1987), 137–142; Rosswurm, *Arms, Country, and Class,* 14–18; Salinger, "Artisans, Journeymen, and the Transformation of Labor in Late Eighteenth-Century Philadelphia," *WMQ,* 3d Ser., XL (1983), 65.

litically through the Revolution. These practices, of course, did not conceal the actual inequalities that existed (and that were growing in the late-colonial city). The possibility of open social conflict was constant. But the shared living areas and cultural practices helped ensure that these conflicts were sporadic. At the same time, class relations remained personalized and particularistic. The isolation of class from class remained incipient until the nineteenth century.[31] Again, this does not mean that tensions were absent or that those below fully accepted relations of hierarchy. But social and personal relations intertwined in a manner that may have strengthened the appearance of deference.

These social patterns emerged clearly in poor-relief practices. Unlike later institutional forms of poor relief, the colonial system provided relief for the poor in their homes, allowing them to maintain some semblance of normal living patterns in their neighborhoods. The opportunity to receive outrelief, however, depended on a person's receiving a recommendation from one of the city's elites. In this way, the city's leaders not only imposed a distinction between the "deserving" and the "vicious" poor but, by equating deferential behavior with being deserving, were able to give demands for deference an additional material base.[32]

This recommendation system for poor relief paralleled the reference system for pardons. Although recommendations for a pardon came from judges, they were often based on letters or solicitations from friends of the felons. It was important to have reputable people willing to vouch for one's character to the court. Without such recommendations, convicts were less likely to receive mercy, except in cases of real doubt about guilt or of youth. The pardon system, like outrelief, was based on the personal evaluation of character by community leaders. Thus the personalistic nature of class relations extended into the recommendation systems and reinforced the importance of patronage to the city's poor. Both pardons and poor relief reinforced the face-to-face character of social control in the city. And the nature of social relations in the city, in turn, provided the terrain for the practice of public punishments.

The contradictions of public punishment paralleled those in the assumptions about the necessity of terror itself. The ideologists of exemplary punishments argued that individuals were divided internally, making terrible restraint continually necessary. At the same time, the ceremony itself, with its constant danger of reversal, made clear that society itself stood in perpetual deadlock between those who incorporated the lessons of the law and those

31. During the latter half of the century, the city was becoming increasingly segregated along class lines, especially during the 1790s. See, Smith, The "Lower Sort," 164–165.

32. John K. Alexander, Render Them Submissive: Responses to Poverty in Philadelphia, 1760–1800 (Amherst, Mass., 1980), 22, 22–24, 129–133; Rosswurm, Arms, Country, and Class, 24–29.

who remained outside its message. The display of awesome violence lay at the heart of social discipline; public punishments represented the violence of the social bond, and this violence was practiced directly on the body of the condemned. And the repetitive display of public punishments was necessary because the possibility of insubordination seemed ever present.

V

Like the Passion from which it was distantly derived, the execution ritual brought words and flesh together in the symbolism of public death.[33] But it did so in a particular way. Legally, the penalty imposed was death; the state took it upon itself to destroy the life of those who violated certain of its laws. Nothing more was sanctioned, nothing more was required. Technically, the confession was not part of the punishment—the criminal was under no obligation to speak. The confessional statement was incidental to the legal punishment.

Yet the confession of the condemned was central to the event. The speeches of the criminals marked their only moment of freedom. Criminals could, and indeed some did, deny their guilt or challenge the judgment of their sentence. It was this realm of freedom—to speak or not to speak, to question or not to question—that made the confession such a crucial moment in the ritual. When the confession occurred, the criminals acknowledged that the law was just and that they in fact deserved the punishment imposed. The speech of the condemned functioned first of all as a means of reinforcing or denying the legitimacy of punishment and, by extension, the state itself.

Many of the condemned, like William Gross, appeared penitent and remorseful. In 1736, John Whatnell and Michael MacDeirmatt, condemned for burglary, "appeared Penitent, bewailing their Sins, and desirous of Instruction. At the Place of Execution, they seem'd very earnest in their Supplications to Heaven for Mercy, and cautioning the Spectators . . . to take warning by their miserable and shameful End." Of William Cole, executed in 1789 for burglary after escaping from jail, the *Pennsylvania Packet* noted that, "from his sentence to his execution, his behaviour was suitable to his deplorable situation." When Joseph Baker and Joseph Berouse, executed for piracy in 1800, arrived at the "fatal spot," they "kneeled down, and after some time spent in prayer, with much contrition . . . were prepared for the conclusion of the awful scene." Their agitation, the paper noted, "was extreme; and they employed their remaining time in the most earnest supplication to the Almighty for mercy and forgiveness." And Richard Smith, executed in 1816 for murdering his lover's husband, arrived at the execution scene in a cart with the execu-

33. On the connection between the Passion and executions, see Francis Barker, *The Tremulous Private Body: Essays on Subjection* (New York, 1984), 24.

tioner and a minister "with whom he was engaged in deep supplication and prayer."[34] Each seemed to acknowledge his guilt, recognize his sinfulness, and accept the justice of his condemnation. None challenged his fate.

Still, not all of the condemned performed exactly as the authorities wanted. Peter Lacroix, executed with Baker and Berouse for piracy, unlike his compatriots, "discovered to the spectators no external marks of penitence," instead going to his death declaring "his peace with all mankind." James Porter, executed under federal authority in 1830, arrived at the place of execution and "looked upon the immense mass of people without any uncommon concern." Although he joined with the clergy in hymns and prayer, Porter declined making a scaffold confession, and had even, one of the city's papers reported with apparent horror, walked out of prison "with a cheerfulness bordering on hilarity." Nearly one hundred years earlier, Henry Wileman and Catherine Connor each denied the authorities their satisfaction. Neither, the *American Weekly Mercury* reported, "behav'd so concern'd as might have been expected from Persons in their Circumstances." Even Richard Smith subtly threatened the carefully staged ceremony. He went to his death "with great firmness" and "composure," even assisting the hangman with his hood.[35] Smith appeared more dashing adventurer than humble sinner.

Each of these incidents, from Connor's "hardened" behavior at her trial to Smith's "firmness" at his death, threatened the effectiveness of the execution ritual. Each demonstrated that, although the state could take one's life, or seize one's body, it could not control one's will. Each provided a counterpoint to the ceremony, either by manifesting contempt and indifference or by claiming respect above their violations of the law. Smith was no Connor. He did not set out to refuse the authorities their edifying example, and he provided the community with a broadside confession. But just as Connor drew on traditions of insubordinate plebeian womanhood, Smith displayed the demeanor of the seafaring working class. And they, like Wileman, Lacroix,

34. *American Weekly Mercury,* Apr. 29–May 6, 1736; *Pa. Packet,* Aug. 1, 1789; *Claypoole's American Daily Advertiser* (Philadelphia), May 10, 1800; *Poulson's American Daily Advertiser* (Philadelphia), Aug. 12, 1816. For other examples of apparently penitent criminals, see *Pa. Packet,* May 18 (this may have taken place in Chester), Aug. 30, 1787; *Dem. Press,* Mar. 15, 1808 (although, as I discussed above, this case was fraught with racial tensions). For an early example of a penitent confession, see the confession of William Battin, who was executed at Chester, reprinted in *American Weekly Mercury,* Aug. 16–23, 1722.

35. *U.S. Gazette* (Philadelphia), Aug. 10, 1816; *Claypoole's American Daily Advertiser,* May 10, 1800; *Saturday Bulletin,* July 3, 1830; *American Weekly Mercury,* June 30–July 7, 1737. Connor had originally been sentenced to be hanged with Whatnell and MacDeirmatt the previous year but had been reprieved (most likely because she was pregnant). In the interim, she had been committed for another burglary, escaped, and was then caught for the final time. Ibid., Apr. 29–May 6, 1736, May 12–19, 1737; *Col. Records,* IV, 47, 209, 224.

Porter, and others, embodied the specter of a transatlantic plebeian world outside the authorities' effective control.[36]

There was, moreover, the danger of even greater subversion. Edward Hunt is a case in point. Hunt was tried in Pennsylvania for counterfeiting and convicted of high treason. He was hanged in Philadelphia on November 19, 1720. Hunt, like many others, read a final confession before his execution, and, like many others, he assumed the role of Christian martyr. But he did so in a particular fashion, using his statement to condemn both the authorities and those who testified against him.[37]

Hunt began his confession in proper fashion. Acknowledging his failure to live in accord with "the Precepts and Principles of the Church, in which I was bred and educated," he proclaimed his "sincere Repentance and hearty Sorrow" for the course of his life. He then threw himself on the "everflowing Mercy" of "my Savior Jesus Christ . . . who has promised Eternal Life on no other terms to the most Righteous upon Earth." It was a promising beginning.[38]

Hunt also admitted his guilt in the action for which he had been charged. But then the confession moved in new directions. Hunt asked God's forgiveness "since he knows that I did not do it with any Design to cheat or defraud any one . . . being Ignorant of the Breach of any Laws of God or Man, I thought I might cut those impressions as innocently as any other." Hunt claimed to have been led astray by "the Gentlemen" around him who had requested that he make the counterfeit coins and stamps. He challenged the truthfulness of the prosecution's witnesses, denying the testimony of John Butler and implying that the testimony of two other witnesses was unjust. Nonetheless, continuing his self-appointed role as martyr, he forgave those who testified against him.[39]

36. [Richard Smith], *Confession of Lieutenant Richard Smith, Who Is Now under Sentence of Death, for the Murder of Capt. John Carson* (Philadelphia, 1816). For Connor's "hardened" behavior, see *American Weekly Mercury,* May 12–19, 1737. For examples of working-women's insubordination to the law or at the gallows, see Peter Linebaugh, *The London Hanged: Crime and Civil Society in the Eighteenth Century* (London, 1991), 142–150. For discussion of seafaring masculinity, see Marcus Rediker, *Between the Devil and the Deep Blue Sea: Merchant Seamen, Pirates, and the Anglo American Maritime World, 1700–1750* (New York, 1987), 153–253.

In noting this sort of resistance and insubordination, I am not suggesting that we romanticize these individuals. Smith, for instance, murdered his lover's husband while implicitly blaming the lover. But we do need to recognize, in the property cases especially, that property was being redefined in the 18th and 19th centuries and that one of the major tools for enforcing new definitions of absolute property rights was the violence of the law. On this latter point, see Hay et al., *Albion's Fatal Tree;* Linebaugh, *The London Hanged.*

37. *American Weekly Mercury,* Nov. 24, 1720.

38. Ibid.

39. Ibid.

But the injustices did not stop with a few individuals. Without intention, he implied, there could be no true guilt. But in Pennsylvania the "Rights of Englishmen" had been denied him: "I am an *English* Subject, and desired to have the Privilege of the Laws of *England;* but it was not granted in any Point, except in Condemning me." Judicial officials, from the courts up to the governor, were guilty in this regard—they condemned him, he asserted, without fair procedure and denied his request to appeal to the king, and thus, "I could not be tried by the laws of *England* in all Points, as a *Church of England Man* ought to be." He was a martyr, not to the awful necessity of justice, but to the capriciousness of injustice. "Pray God to forgive them all, and everyone that has a hand in taking away my Life any manner of way, and that my Blood be not required at their Hands; *for they know not what they do.*" [40]

Here Hunt completed his process of subversion, transforming himself into an almost Christlike figure. Drawing on both Christian imagery and his own background in the Church of England, Hunt challenged the social and religious character of the (Quaker) authorities and the "gentlemen" who accused him. Taking advantage of the relative novelty of his sentence (he was the first person executed for counterfeiting in the colony), Hunt used the rhetoric of the English legal tradition to suggest that the judicial process was somehow illegitimate. Hunt seized on one of the essential contradictions of the execution scene. The condemned were expected to appear penitent and humble, but it was they, not the officials of the law, who decided whether to display these qualities. Although he could not save his own life, Hunt was able to undermine the effectiveness of the law's actions by wrapping himself in the Christian symbolism of the event. His refusal to acknowledge the justice of his conviction denied the authorities their edifying spectacle.

Contemporaries clearly understood the significance of Hunt's actions. The *American Weekly Mercury,* in publishing his confession, noted, "It is evident, that the following Speech was intended to misrepresent the Administration and Justice of this Government, as well as to infuse both ill Principles and Practices into the Minds of the People." Still, the paper felt compelled to publish the confession: "Yet the Falsehoods, Contradictions and silly Evasions therein contained, will so plainly appear to every impartial and honest Reader, that it has been thought proper to publish this extraordinary Piece here." The *American Weekly Mercury* hoped that by publishing Hunt's last statement with its own commentary it would be able to undo the impact that his actions might have had on his listeners. Otherwise, the terror and education of the execution might be lost.[41] The paper's concern displays the fundamental insecu-

40. Ibid. (emphasis added).
41. Ibid.

rity of those in authority: they could neither control the behavior of the condemned nor be certain how people might interpret the event.

These tensions were not limited to capital punishments proper. If the authorities sought to orchestrate the execution scene in order to spread terror, the pardon ritual combined terror with mercy in a way that heightened the spectacle's emotional effect. Although criminals could be pardoned at any time after their sentence, some underwent the procession from jail to the scaffold before being told of their pardon. Nor would the audience be told in advance; their sympathies and emotions would be played on as if the execution was to occur. In this way, criminals "justly" condemned would undergo the terror of approaching death before being brought back to the world of the living by the governor's mercy.[42]

James Prouse and James Mitchel, having been convicted of burglary, were condemned to be hanged on January 14, 1730. Prouse had not challenged the justice of his conviction but had claimed in open court that Mitchel was innocent. Because of Prouse's youth (he was nineteen) and the possible innocence of Mitchel, the judges had recommended them to the governor's mercy. But the public had little reason to expect clemency. As Benjamin Franklin, writing in the *Pennsylvania Gazette,* noted, "Several Malefactors having been already pardoned, and every Body being sensible, that, considering the great Increase of Vagrants and idle Persons, by the late large Importation of such from several parts of *Europe,* it was become necessary for the common Good to make some Examples, there was but little Reason to hope that either, and less that both of them might escape the Punishment justly due to Crimes of that enormous Nature."[43]

Prouse and Mitchel appeared victims of timing and the social necessities of the authorities. Men like Franklin believed that too many had recently received clemency, and social disorder seemed too great to allow Mitchel and Prouse to escape punishment. Thus, at eleven in the morning, a "numerous Croud of People was gathered near the Prison, to see these unhappy young Men brought forth to suffer." First their irons were removed and their arms bound, then they were "placed in a Cart, together with a Coffin for each of them, and led thro' the Town to the Place of Execution." Arriving at the "fatal Tree," Prouse and Mitchel "were told that it was expected they should make some Confession of their Crimes, and say something by Way of Exhortation to the People." With some difficulty, Prouse was prevailed upon to admit

42. For examples of this practice, see the case of Isaac Bradford, June 23, 1727, in *Col. Records,* IV, 224; *Pennsylvania Journal,* Dec. 10, 1747; "Journal of Samuel Rowland Fisher," *PMHB,* XLI (1917), 167 (this latter pardon took place in 1779); the case of Richard Shirtliffe, June 5, 1786, in *Col. Records,* XV, 31; and the case of James McDonald, *Pa. Packet,* Aug. 30, 1787.

43. *Pa. Gazette,* Jan. 13–20, 1729–1730.

his guilt, although he impeached one of the witnesses against him—one Greyer—alleging that it had been Greyer's idea to commit the burglary. Mitchel, on the other hand, refused to play his role and declared that he was innocent of the charges against him. His confession, however, was crucial to the proceedings: "He was then told, that it did not appear well in him to persist in asserting his Innocence; that he had had a fair Trial, and was found guilty by twelve honest and good Men. He only answer'd, *I am innocent; and it will appear so before God;* and sat down." Frustrated in their efforts, the officials were forced to proceed with the ritual:

> Then they were both bid to stand up, and the Ropes were order'd to be thrown over the Beam; when the Sheriff took a Paper out of his Pocket and began to read. The poor Wretches, whose Souls were at that Time fill'd with the immediate Terrors of approaching Death, having nothing else before their Eyes . . . took but little Notice of what was read; or it seems imagined it to be some previous Matter of Form, as a Warrant for their Execution or the like, 'till they heard the Words PITY and MERCY. . . . Immediately *Mitchel* fell into the most violent Agony; and having only said, *God bless the Governor,* he swooned away in the Cart.

After recovering, Mitchel confessed to being a *"great Sinner,"* although continuing to declare his innocence of theft. Both Prouse and Mitchel, not surprisingly, were "overwhelmed" with joy on their return from the scaffold. Nor was the crowd unaffected. "Concern," Franklin reported, "appeared in every face while these Criminals were leading to Execution, and . . . Joy . . . diffused it self thro' the whole Multitude" after the reprieve.[44]

The pardon scene doubled the ritual of execution. The criminals were taken to the edge of death—accompanied by coffins, paraded through the streets to the scaffold, the rope prepared, their confessions taken—and then, at the last minute, the hand of the state brought them back to life. The psychological terror of the execution scene was combined with a saving forgiveness, the government's need for justice tempered by the "wisdom" of Christian mercy. In the execution, the state displayed its power by killing; here it displayed its strength by sparing the felons. The state, by ignoring its own laws, reaffirmed its own justice.

As with the execution ritual, a confessional conflict lay at the heart of the pardon ceremony. There was no legal necessity for the condemned to confess, yet the officials struggled—if only verbally—with both Prouse and Mitchel to bare their souls, to make public their innermost recognition of the justice of the law and of their sentence. Ultimately, the law could not compel this confession. Prouse undermined his confession by accusing Greyer, and Mitchel

44. Ibid.

refused guilt altogether. But this lack of control only made the agonistic word-play more tense and more desired. Because it could be refused, the con-demned's acknowledgement of the justice of their punishment made the confession an especially powerful legitimation device. With the confession, doubts about state killing could be swept away. If even the condemned recog-nized that the law was just, then who could disagree? With a confession, the condemned fused once more with the community whose laws they had vio-lated. All were one in the acknowledgment of the law. Justice—or in the case of a pardon, justice combined with mercy—was reaffirmed.

But the execution confession, the individual acknowledgment of collective justice, was not an individuating act. Instead, it exemplified the commonali-ties of criminality and the connections between the law-breaking and law-abiding fractions of the community. These confessions were highly formulaic. They were marked by a fairly commonplace set of elements: loss of parents, a lack of (or a poor) religious education, a tendency to transience, some primal fall into vice and viciousness (cardplaying, drinking, a seduction), and then the seemingly irresistible progression to the scaffold.[45]

These statements pointed, not toward some inherent genius for evil (as the Gothic would later have it) or some dangerous class, but rather toward the very banality of the descent to crime. Little distinguished these individuals from any others, or at least any others from the plebeian classes. They were mirrors of everyday life—of the gaming, drinking, violence, and insecurities that marked laboring life. The confession transformed the execution from an event merely providing the terror of example to one that indicated the fine line between the gallows and the games of common culture. Just as the con-fession merged the condemned with collective justice, so it merged them with

45. See *American Weekly Mercury*, Aug. 16–23, 1722 (reprint of the confession of William Battin hanged at Chester); *The Last Words and Dying Confession of the Three Pirates, Who were Executed This Day, (May 9, 1800)* (Philadelphia, 1800); *Confession of John Joyce, alias Davis, Who Was Executed on Monday, the 14th of March, 1808 for the Murder of Mrs. Sarah Cross . . . ; Confession of Peter Mathias, alias Mathews, Who Was Executed on Monday, the 14th of March, 1808 for the Murder of Mrs. Sarah Cross . . .* (Philadelphia, 1808); *Confession of Lieutenant Richard Smith, Who Is Now under Sentence of Death for the murder of Capt. John Carson;* and the discussion of William Gross, below. These confessions were so formulaic, in fact, that they were expertly parodied in [William Cobbett], *The Last Confession and Dy-ing Speech of Peter Porcupine, with an Account of His Dissection* (Philadelphia, 1797). For wider discussions of the genre, see Peter Linebaugh, "The Ordinary of Newgate and His Account," in J. S. Cockburn, ed., *Crime in England, 1550–1800* (London, 1977), 246–269; Daniel A. Cohen, *Pillars of Salt, Monuments of Grace: New England Crime Literature and the Origins of American Popular Culture, 1674–1860* (New York, 1993), 20–26, 117–142; Karen Halttunen, "Early American Murder Narratives: The Birth of Horror," in Richard Wight-man Fox and T. J. Jackson Lears, eds., *The Power of Culture: Critical Essays in American His-tory* (Chicago, 1993), 67–101; Louis P. Masur, *Rites of Execution: Capital Punishment and the Transformation of American Culture, 1776–1865* (New York, 1989), 33–35.

their fellows—who with the slightest false step could follow them on the road to ruin.[46]

The connection with everyday life manifested itself in the very staging of the scaffold spectacle. Eighteenth- and early-nineteenth-century punishments, unlike later Victorian executions, did not take place behind the closed walls of prisons. These punishments occurred in public spaces—spaces that in other times were used for the very activities that, according to the confession, led to the necessity of the gallows.[47] The streets through which the condemned walked or rode were the normal streets of the city—filled as on other days with people out about their business or drawn to the sight of the criminal. An inversion took place as the normal secular spaces of the city were seized for quasi-sacred ceremony. By taking place in public, in the commons as it were, punishments destabilized any simple division between criminal spaces and everyday spaces, just as the confession destabilized any simple distinction between those on the scaffold and those in the crowd.

The very publicness of the punishment, moreover, made the crowd and its understanding crucial to the event. It was, after all, for the "edification" of the populace that the executions were held. Nor does it appear that the curiosity of the people let the authorities down. At William Gross's execution in 1823,

46. Rosswurm, *Arms, Country, and Class,* 21–39; Ric Northrup, "Decomposition and Reconstitution: A Theoretical and Historical Study of Philadelphia Artisans, 1785–1820" (Ph.D. diss., University of North Carolina, 1988), 149–206. For one explicit attempt to demonstrate how little things can lead to the sentence of death, see "The Child Trained Up for the Gallows, by the Late Governor Livingston," in *Freeman's Journal* (Philadelphia), Apr. 20, 1791. Karen Halttunen has argued that criminal narratives in the 19th century were increasingly constructed around Gothic plots and the power of horror. She contends that the new forms of these narratives mark a fundamental break from older notions of criminality, indicating a breakdown of the idea that criminals were similar in nature to the other members of the community. In the 19th century, she argues, criminals were being constituted as moral aliens because of the Enlightenment's inability to rationally explain evil. In this context, murder could only be understood as an inexplicable act, one that assumed horrifying features precisely because it was incomprehensible. See "Early American Murder Narratives," in Fox and Lears, *The Power of Culture,* 86–100. As will be clear from my discussion, however, I would argue that these narratives are transitional, that, as in the story of William Gross, they retain the basic notion that everyone could fall into criminality.

47. On the transition to Victorian "private" executions and its meanings, see Masur, *Rites of Execution,* 93–116. Officials complained repeatedly about the uses of the streets and other public spaces. "Grand Jury Presentment, July 28, 1702," in Wallace, "Ancient Records of Philadelphia" (Am. 3054), HSP (robbing orchards by servants and youth, violations of Sabbath by blacks); "Grand Jury Presentment, 1741," Philadelphia Court Papers, 1732–1744, HSP (violations of the Sabbath by blacks, apprentices, and youth); "Grand Jury Presentment, 1744, in Wallace, "Ancient Records of Philadelphia" (Am. 3054), HSP (tippling houses and disorder in streets); "Grand Jury Presentment, Mayor's Court of Philadelphia, Feb. 14, 1757," Philadelphia Court Papers, 1749–1821, HSP (disorderly people in the marketplace).

crowds lined the entire route from prison to scaffold, and, at the place of execution, "The crowd on the ground seemed to be equal to the whole white male population of Philadelphia." Even in the nineteenth century, the lure of executions cut across class lines as fascination with the condemned's fate overcame the increasingly private nature of bourgeois propriety.[48] Yet the fascination that drew people to the spectacle could also undercut its effectiveness. Breaking the body did not secure the criminal's soul, and the condemned, whether resistant or submissive, could claim the sympathy of the audience. There was no guarantee that the lesson of the scaffold would be learned as it was taught. The state, through a ritual designed to reaffirm the bonds of a public community, risked turning the criminal into a martyr or hero.

The paradoxes of public executions were condensed in the figure of the hangman. Hangmen were, traditionally, objects of popular enmity and contempt. Often felons themselves, in some cases, they were released from jail for assuming the role; in others they were spared execution themselves. In important ways, the condemned had a more exalted station than did the executioner. In the execution of William Gross, Gross was dressed in white, whereas the executioner was disguised in a black mask and wrapped in blankets. The executioner, it would appear, was a felon, brought out of prison for his task and returned there at the conclusion of his duties. At the execution itself, it was the hangman, not Gross, who suffered rebuke and public criticism. When ascending the scaffold, he did so with what the *Democratic Press* deemed "a quickness of step and levity of deportment which was offensive," and the sheriff ordered him down. Shortly thereafter, Gross "advised him [the hangman] to repent and turn from the evil of his ways."[49] Gross achieved the status of Christian sufferer; the hangman remained masked and confined.

Even more than executions, the secondary public punishments were integrated into everyday life. Both the whipping post and the pillory were set up at Third and Market Streets, across from the Old Stone Prison at the head of the

---

48. *Dem. Press,* Feb., 8, 1823; *Saturday Evening Post* (Philadelphia), Feb. 8, 1823. Gross's execution was not unique in this popularity. Other executions also drew crowds into the thousands. See *American Weekly Mercury,* Apr. 29–May 6, 1736; *Claypoole's American Daily Advertiser,* May 10, 1800; *Dem. Press,* Mar. 15, 1808; *Poulson's,* Aug. 12, 1816. For a criticism of public punishment at an earlier execution, that of Richard Smith, see Nicholas B. Wainwright, ed., "The Diary of Samuel Breck, 1814–1822," *PMHB,* CII (1978), 485.

49. *Dem. Press,* Mar. 15, 1808, Feb. 8, 1823; *American Weekly Mercury,* June 23–30, 1737; John F. Watson, *Annals of Philadelphia and Pennsylvania, in the Olden Time; Being a Collection of Memoirs, Anecdotes, and Incidents of the City and Its Inhabitants, and of the Earliest Settlements of the Inland Part of Pennsylvania, from the Days of the Founders . . .* 2 vols. (Philadelphia, 1857), I, 184. This contempt was not peculiar to Pennsylvania. As Pieter Spierenburg has documented, examples of contempt and hostility toward executioners can be found throughout early modern Europe. See Spierenburg, *The Spectacle of Suffering,* 13–42.

city's main marketplace. During both pillorying and whipping, citizens would move from the stalls of commodities to the place of punishment and back again. Those whipped were displayed to the community both before and during their punishment, and those condemned to the pillory were subjected to the crowd's abuse. In 1736, for instance, a woman arrested for picking pockets during market day was "exposed during the Market upon the Balcony of the Court-House with her Face towards the People, that every Body might know her; after which she received a Whipping." The pillory was most often employed in combination with other punishments. The offender's experience of the pillory, even more than other public punishments, depended on the attitude of the crowd. If the crowd sympathized with the offender, the penalty would pass quickly and without too much trauma. On the other hand, if the crowd was hostile, they could actively partake in the punishment of the offender. One shopkeeper, "who, to build up his sinking credit, had made too free with other people's names," was placed in the pillory, where "the populace pelted him with eggs," and then he had his ears cropped.[50] The authorities, it would seem, looked the other way during these "excesses" performed by the crowd—if they did not actually encourage them. The point of the penalty was to expose and humiliate the offender publicly. So long as the crowd did not challenge the penalty or commit new crimes during the punishment, its active participation was welcomed. The ritual incorporated the crowd, thereby implicating it in the practice of the law's justice. And even more than with capital penalties, these rituals could take festive form; when this occurred, the distinctions between penal ceremony and the games and combats of everyday life were even further blurred.

These penalties were not merely symbolic. The authorities might have seen

50. Negley K. Teeters, *The Cradle of the Penitentiary*, 11; *Pa. Gazette*, Oct. 21–28, 1736; J Thomas Scharf and Thompson Westcott, *History of Philadelphia, 1609–1884* (Philadelphia, 1884), II, 857. An example of a case employing the pillory as well as other punishments is David Hovet, convicted of horse theft at the July 1780 session of the Philadelphia City Court, who was sentenced to 39 lashes at the whipping post, to an hour in the pillory, and to having his ears cut off. For another example, see the case of Frederick Conn, convicted of horse theft, who, at the January 1780 session, also received 39 lashes and an hour in the pillory, although he received six months imprisonment and retained his ears. Jan. and July 1780 sessions, Philadelphia County Court of Quarter Sessions of the Peace, Docket, Philadelphia Court Papers, HSP. It is unclear if the entire ear was cut off. It is possible that the ears were cropped instead, both to inflict pain and as a form of branding. See, as well, the cases of John Conrad Latour, John Walter, John Speakert, Christian Peter, Caspar Kirkessol, and Jacob Walter, all convicted of cheating and sentenced to be pilloried and fined. "Minutes of a Court of Oyer and Terminer and General Gaol Delivery," Philadelphia County, Apr. 3, 1786, in Philadelphia Court Papers, IV, 1749–1821, HSP. In England in 1813, an English radical sentenced to the pillory was garlanded by the admiring crowd. See Michael Ignatieff, *A Just Measure of Pain: The Penitentiary in the Industrial Revolution, 1750–1850* (New York, 1978), 21.

a hanging as an edifying display, but, for the condemned, it terminated their lives. A whipping might have provided an opportunity for public scorn, but the number of lashes inflicted during whippings could be great, and they caused serious bodily pain and harm. In 1743, for instance, one man went so far as to slit his own throat at the whipping post rather than undergo his penalty.[51] The intended effect of the punishment was always achieved by the infliction (or the threat of the infliction) of material, bodily harm. The speech of the convict was always preparatory, the punishment always inscribed directly on the body.

Magistrates operated on the body of the condemned to maintain the hierarchical society they governed. This combination of the material and the symbolic gave the ritual its political meaning. In a sense, these punishments demonstrated excess. The treatment of the body of the condemned was, in economic terms at least, unproductive. The condemned was cast out (either temporarily or permanently) from the circuits of social and economic production. The social utility of the practice, then, was entirely representative. Put another way, these rituals were so powerful because they combined the material and the symbolic, the body and speech, in a communal celebration of the law. And they did so without being subordinated to anything but the logic of power.[52]

In sum, then, in traditional public punishments, the speech and the display of the offender served as devices of legitimation and exemplification. As such, the public punishment was a form of what Jürgen Habermas called "representative publicity." In absolutist regimes, he argued, publicity was staged before the people to represent authority as suspended above them; publicity was less a stimulus to debate than a sign of the ubiquity and transcendence of power. This form of publicity would, it seems, mirror the nature of monarchical subjection, in which subjectivity was, not voluntary, but imposed at birth.[53] But as the importance of the confession indicates, the nature of these ceremonies was somewhat more complex. The confession made authority dependent on the actions of the condemned for the stability of its representations. The confession, when it occurred, was a crucial moment in upholding the power and dignity of the law. But it did even more. It also—along with the actual organization of the ceremony itself—served to implicate the community in the fate of the condemned. And it did so by blurring the seemingly clear markers be-

51. Scharf and Westcott, *History of Philadelphia*, II, 857.

52. The most powerful presentation of traditional punishments as manifestations of the excesses of the sovereign is in Foucault's *Discipline and Punish*, 47–57.

53. Jürgen Habermas, *The Structural Transformation of the Public Sphere: An Inquiry into a Category of Bourgeois Society*, trans. Thomas Burger (Cambridge, Mass., 1989), 7–8; James H. Kettner, *The Development of American Citizenship, 1608–1870* (Chapel Hill, N.C., 1978), 18–19.

tween virtue and vice. Rather than demonstrating the impermeability of the social order, the public punishment opened its violence and struggles to the view of the community. "Representative publicity" was more contradictory than it might seem.

Finally, the confession at the scaffold brought into play an additional element of punishment—the possibility of reformation. This is a paradoxical claim. There would, after all, be no reformed life following execution. But, despite this fact, intense efforts were made to persuade the condemned to confess not merely to serve the interests of the state and community but to save their immortal souls. This reformation without reform was preparatory to another judgment—the judgment of the hereafter. That reformation was beyond the powers of the penal system per se can be seen by the lack of attention placed on confession in the lesser punishments, whether the fine, the whipping post, or the pillory. In these cases, where the offenders would rapidly rejoin society, the confession played no role in the penal drama, and there is no evidence that religious or social pressures were placed on them in the days prior to punishment. But the role of confession in capital executions, and the clear evidence that this confession was seen as paving the way to salvation in the next world, already points to a connection between verbalization of sin and the transformation of the self. This confession linked speaking the truth with preparing to live it—even if only in death.[54]

VI

William Gross died in February 1823. The city's newspapers duly reported his actions leading up to and during his execution. His story spread at least as far as Richmond, Virginia.[55] In lesser or greater detail, the papers provided running commentary on Gross's sad situation, describing in great and melodramatic detail his feelings and observations. The public execution might have been a momentary act of state retribution, but it generated a whole set of narratives to explain and justify it.

If the ritual of Gross's execution assumed a traditional shape, its incessant narration was a greater novelty. In the eighteenth century, it was highly uncommon for any extended description of Philadelphia executions to appear in the city's newspapers. Far more typical were mere notices of the event or brief comments. Moreover, whereas all of the nineteenth-century executions generated pamphlets or at least broadsides, few of the eighteenth-century ones

54. That, of course, is an old theme in Christianity. For one treatment of it that I have found helpful for thinking about the relationship of confession, the body, and the transformation of the self, see Michel Foucault, "Truth and Subjectivity," pt. 2, Howison Lecture in Philosophy (paper presented at the University of California, Berkeley, Oct. 21, 1980).
55. *Dem. Press*, Feb. 15, 1823.

did. In other words, Gross (and his nineteenth-century fellows) were both typical and atypical of Philadelphia's condemned. A split had emerged within the very form of the public execution; if the presentation of their death followed long-standing practice, its re-presentation did not. Public executions were no longer so self-evident as to pass without (written) comment. To some extent, the greater coverage may represent simply the growing importance of print to urban culture. But it may also indicate the increasingly anomalous nature of capital punishments, their insecure ideological position, and growing concerns over their effect on the population at large.[56]

Gross himself helped transform his life and death into a tale of melodramatic transgression and decay. He began with his scaffold warning against card playing and "bad" company. Gross authorized a pamphlet (possibly with spurious competitors) detailing his fall into sin and the paths that led to his fateful rendezvous with the hangman. Gross's pamphlet included his autobiographical narrative, a letter to his mother, a warning to youth, a description of his experience in prison, and a copy of the hymn sung at his hanging. Such autobiographies were common on both sides of the Atlantic. By the early nineteenth century, they were part of a wider literature of criminal narrative that explored not only the roots of crime but the social and sexual tensions of the new Republic.[57]

56. This lack of a tradition of extended execution literature stands in contrast to New England where, as Daniel A. Cohen has demonstrated, the literature of crime and punishment took root by the late 17th century. Still, as Cohen indicates, there was a growing complexity to criminal narratives across the 18th and 19th centuries, a development that he links to challenges to authority and the emergence of new forms of print production. Most suggestive in this regard was the aftermath of the Revolution when challenges to the legal system made the system of criminal justice less self-evidently just and consequently required new narrative forms to justify ideologically and epistemologically the legal system. On a smaller level, I think, the increasing production of execution narratives, combined with some of the other literary forms that Cohen discusses (e.g., trial reports), indicates that some of the same ideological uncertainty surrounded executions in Philadelphia. See Cohen, *Pillars of Salt*. For an overview of these developments, see 3–38.

The growing importance and acceptance of discipline—the central theme of Chapters 4 through 8 below—can be seen in the decreasing practice and legitimacy of public spectacles of legal violence.

57. [William Gross], *The Last Words and Dying Confession of William Gross, Who Was Executed on the 7th of February 1823, for the Murder of Kesiah Stow, in the City of Philadelphia* (Philadelphia, 1823). For discussions of this genre, see Linebaugh, "The Ordinary of Newgate and His Account," in Cockburn, ed., *Crime in England*, 246–269; Cohen, *Pillars of Salt*, 20–26, 117–142, 167–194, 199–216; Karen Halttunnen, "Early American Murder Narratives," in Fox and Lears, eds., *The Power of Culture*, 67–101, 94–100; Patricia Cline Cohen, "The Helen Jewett Murder: Violence, Gender, and Sexual Licentiousness in Antebellum America," *Journal of the National Women's Studies Association*, II (1990), 374–389. For an example of a later attempt to circulate an unofficial narrative, see *Saturday Evening Post*, May 28, 1830.

Commentators also viewed Gross's drama as a lesson in propriety and virtue. "M. T.," for example, warned the city's youth to heed Gross's fate. Reflecting on the condemned and his victim, M. T. cautioned Philadelphia's young to recognize that "their sun probably rose as fair as yours." But the "Siren Pleasure drew them aside from the paths of virtue. Heedlessly they wandered, lured by her deceitful melody—till suddenly the demon threw aside her vestment, and engulphed them in ruin and horror inexpressible!" As M. T. saw it, the tale of Keziah Stow and William Gross was one of "female virtue" and the "manly soul." Female virtue, he believed, was "inestimable" to both "individuals and society!" Gross had lost sight of that fact—rendering him outcast in this world and the next. "How hateful then . . . should be he who would profanely dare to tarnish [female virtue]. The wiles of seduction can lurk but in that ignoble bosom—the manly soul discards them—the generous sensibilities shrink from their touch—and piety execrates the garment spotted even by thought!" M. T. aimed to deploy the execution to uphold the proprieties of domesticity. Gross, he believed, was a dying example of the dangers of transgressing sexual and domestic virtues.[58]

As Gross recounted it, instability and wandering marked his early life. Born on New Year's Day 1796, orphaned at age three, he was adopted into the family of John Gross, where he was "treated with all the tenderness that was possible," until apprenticed when nearly nine years old. At this point, the stability of his life was shattered. He remained with his new master, a coppersmith, for only two years, "in consequence of their cruel and inhuman treatment," a treatment he "freely" forgave them for. After spending one more year at home and in school, he proceeded through a series of jobs in and out of Philadelphia, among them tobacco spinning, sheep herding, and butchering. Although he confessed to minor theft while at his parents' house, it was not until he was employed as a butcher, he claimed, that his true descent into vice and crime began. Then, having become "perfectly acquainted with the cursed practice of card playing" (under the tutelage of his master it seems), his fate was sealed. Gross remembered that he became "fond of company" and increasingly spent his time at dance houses and card tables: "In fact, I became so addicted to gambling, dancing, and almost every other vice, that I thought of nothing else, and to support myself, I had to resort to dishonest means to obtain money." Finally, Gross's indenture expired at age twenty, and he returned home.[59]

At first, his return settled Gross. But quickly his old habits revived. Having gained employment as a laborer, Gross began once again to take "frolick[s]"

58. "M. T.," *Poulson's,* Feb. 10, 1823. For other examples of attempts to control the meanings of the Gross affair or to offer insight into his fall from grace, see *Dem. Press,* Jan. 30, 1823; *Saturday Evening Post,* Feb. 1, 8, 1823.

59. [Gross], *The Last Words and Dying Confession of William Gross,* 3–4.

and met Catherine Palmer at a dance house. They married in August of 1818, and, for nearly two years, lived with his adopted parents. But, in the spring of 1820, his old love of dance and gambling began to separate Gross from his wife. Fights ensued, alienation resulted, and Gross, now working as a watchman in a bank, began stealing to support his habits. It was then, he told his posthumous audience, that he met Keziah Stow.[60]

From that point on, Gross's tale was one of transience and melodramatic obsession. Gross reported that he did not notice Stow until she became ill. Becoming devoted to her health, he attended her during her illness and then began to provide for her board. Soon they began living together in the boardinghouse where they had met. Gross, of course, remained married, and his wife did not stand idly by, bringing a complaint for maintenance to a magistrate. After Gross was able to get it dismissed, however, she agreed to a legal separation. In his confession, Gross assumed full responsibility for the failed marriage. Catherine Palmer was the first wronged woman of his tale—but, as the reader knew well, she would not be the last.

As Gross recounted it, the pattern of his life with Stow led inexorably to disaster and destruction. Living together, they began to take in boarders. Then the two began to quarrel over Stow's insistence on going out with her friends. These quarrels became frequent, and they lived together, in Gross's words, "very discontentedly." His desire to keep Stow from her own independent social life led to a quarrel so severe that she prosecuted him for assault and battery—a charge he denied until death. Then, according to Gross, came the final violence. Gross recalled leaving the magistrate to return home. He did not, however, remain long, his mind being "in the most distressed situation immaginable." Tracking Stow to a dance house, he began to drink. Finally, when the dance broke up, the two "went home together, but not in a social manner. I believe their [sic] was no words passed between us on the road." Once there, Gross took the final step:

> After walking about the room a few moments in a distracted state of mind I went up stairs and brought down the *fatal knife*. After I came down I walked once or twice across the room, and walked up to her and asked her whether she still intended to go where she pleased and do as she pleased—she said she did, and wished that I would go about my business, as she did not wish any thing more to do with me; at which I gave her the FATAL BLOW![61]

Keziah Stow lingered for several days before she died. Gross was arrested with the knife almost immediately. He claimed to have been in a stupor

60. Ibid., 4–6.
61. Ibid., 9–10.

through the entire episode "as the witnesses swore to expressions which I should have made use of that I never thought of when I was in my sober senses, nor neither have I the faintest recollection of making use of them that night." [62] He was tried twice for her murder (his first conviction overturned on appeal), and he was convicted both times of first-degree murder.

As with his gallows statement, Gross's autobiography traced a relentless descent from ordinary vice to horrid crime. From the moment that gambling insinuated its way into Gross's life, through the dancing, the violation of marriage vows, the entrance into an alternative world of urban youth, to the jealousies and the struggles over domestic dominance, Gross plunged heedlessly, he implied, into his fate. Overall, the story Gross told was one of domestic propriety desecrated—his path to the gallows a perfect example of the importance of familial oversight and the dangers of youthful (especially sexual) folly.

In these narratives, Keziah Stow appeared only as a victim and backdrop. M. T. showed especial concern for Stow, but that was because she was a woman and therefore "of that interesting class with whom we associate all that is soft, and tender, and endearing." [63] In his telling, she lacked any individuating characteristics, functioning solely as a type. The compilers of Gross's autobiography provided no information about her life. Gross notes her primarily for her effect on him. He is drawn to her by her illness, he is then intoxicated by her, and finally he is enraged by her. Then in a moment that he is unable to recall, he strikes her down. After lingering for several days, she dies.

Yet, if the official versions of Gross's narrative reduced Stow to melodramatic victim, the actual details of their lives suggested another story. After her initial sickness, Stow rather than Gross moved their life along. It was Stow who most frequently changed lodgings (and Gross who followed). It was Stow who determined to take in female boarders. And it was Stow's striving for an independent social life that Gross could not control that precipitated his murderous rage. Stow was no meek victim seeking domesticity. Instead, she actively sought a life in the city, one marked by sociability and enjoyment. And she aimed, as did many other young urban women, at independence. [64] Gross murdered Stow in response, and he endeavored in his narrative to transform her into abject victim. But her actions belied both the religious and the secular morality plays that the execution confession sought to stage.

Gross's narrative, then, was internally contested. Despite attempts to raise

62. Ibid., 10.

63. "M. T.," *Poulson's,* Feb. 10, 1823.

64. [Gross], *The Last Words and Dying Confession of William Gross,* 7–9. For a wider discussion of the strategies of working-class women to control their lives in antebellum cities (lives often ending as Stowe's did), see Christine Stansell, *City of Women: Sex and Class in New York, 1789–1860* (New York, 1986), 3–30, 41–52. As Stansell's work makes clear, Stow's

the story to timeless allegory, the history of William Gross and Keziah Stow was continually drawn back to the particularities of nineteenth-century working-class life. Instead of domesticity transgressed, Gross and Stow lived a life where domesticity was irrelevant. Instead of a simple story of the dangers of gambling and bad company, Gross's violence emerged out of conflicts and struggles over domestic power and authority. The actual lives of Gross and Stow resisted the meanings that Gross and the authorities sought to impose on them. Whereas Gross's autobiography and the commentary surrounding his execution hoped to teach immemorial moral lessons, the actual events leading to his execution exposed the commonness of Gross's experience. And that experience pointed less directly at questions of good and evil than at despair and the violence and conflicts of everyday life.

Of course, these instabilities between the everyday and the timeless did not necessarily undermine the power of Gross's narrative or the moral message it, and the execution itself, sought to convey. Traditionally, after all, the execution ritual highlighted the connections between the mundane and the terror of criminality and death. But, at the same time that Gross affirmed the official meaning of his death, his history marked the dissolution of the social basis of urban public punishments. His repeatedly failed indentures, his movement from one semiskilled job to another, and his cohabitation with Keziah Stow all revealed aspects of the new urban order of the nineteenth-century city. The collapse of older systems of labor discipline and patriarchal authority that accompanied the spread of wage labor in the city opened the space for the elaboration of increasingly separate class cultures. Gross's story epitomized the split society of post-Revolutionary Philadelphia. And, in so doing, it revealed a social order that could no longer be contained within, or sustained by, the rituals of public punishment.[65] William Gross was the last person publicly executed in Philadelphia under Pennsylvania law. That was, perhaps, not a coincidence.

The traditional system of criminal punishments, then, was based upon public spectacle. These punishments aimed to spread either terror of the law or joy at its mercy throughout the population. Operating directly on the body of the

---

entrapment within webs of dependency as well as her efforts to escape them were not unique.

65. On the decline of bound labor in Philadelphia and its implications for class relations, see Salinger, *"To Serve Well and Faithfully,"* 137–152, 165–171. For a reading of the bifurcated nature of antebellum Philadelphia's culture, see Susan G. Davis, *Parades and Power: Street Theatre in Nineteenth-Century Philadelphia* (Philadelphia, 1986). On the connection between the spread of wage discipline and the search for new forms of criminal punishments, see Linebaugh, *The London Hanged,* 329–441.

condemned, the system received its justification from a vision of the depraved character of human nature while revealing the necessity of violence to the social order. Visibility and corporality were the true coin of that penal realm. Public punishments were the most visible sign of a society where power was clearly displayed—and authority openly seized the body.

At the same time, the instabilities of public punishment marked the limits of public authority, demonstrating the dependence of the governors on those they governed. Public punishments required the approval, or at least the acquiescence, of the audience. When the spectators approved the sentence, the execution could operate as the authorities hoped. If the audience doubted the verdict or challenged the justice of the punishment, however, the authorities could inadvertently create bonds between the condemned and the crowd. Public punishments worked, through visible exclusion, to create a society. But if the crowd sympathized with the condemned, then the society created might exclude the stagers, not the subjects, of the execution.

Just as the scaffold defended relations of authority and property, so it drew material support from the structure of the city. In Philadelphia, the prevalence of bound labor fused the power of fathers and employers, the relatively large numbers of artisans and shopkeepers disseminated a Franklinesque commitment to personal property and law, and the discretionary quality of the relief system reinforced relations of personal dependence. Public punishments were the penal currency of this structure of households and paternal authority. The system of public punishments—with its demonstration of the reversibility of penal and common space, of criminality and prosaic life—intensified and embodied the nature of everyday authority. But this system, flourishing in the late-colonial period, would not last long. Although public punishments would not be eliminated until the 1830s, their dismantling began with the Revolution.

CHAPTER TWO

Public Labor

In the autumn of 1786, Pennsylvania's General Assembly established a system of public penal labor. Under public labor, the penal scene broke free of its moorings in semisacred space and spread throughout the city. Those sentenced to public labor would no longer suffer brief, if dramatic, punishments; instead, they would be set to work in the streets. Proponents believed that public labor would turn convicts into constant reminders of the penalties of vice, their visibility would signify the ubiquity of the power to punish. Public labor intensified the display of penality. No longer set off against the everyday, punishment entered mundane life itself.

Public labor marked a new style of punishment. Unlike corporal and capital punishments, public labor (so its proponents claimed) did not act directly on the body; instead, time was at stake. The body aged under public labor; it was not broken. A loss of freedom replaced the painful degradation of the whipping post or the timeless extinction that followed the gallows. At the same time, both labor and reformation moved to the center of punishment. Under the new system, convicts would labor—through labor—to transform their own habits. Time and labor would lead to reformation; the expiation of crime would be linked to the rebirth of character.

Public labor reflected a Revolutionary notion of governance. The new system aimed to make punishment part of a wider, vibrant republican public realm. Public labor's proponents argued that the law could represent universal, rational values in a methodical fashion. Whereas traditional punishments had stressed the singular expression of punitive power, public labor promised an inescapable and generalized scenario of submission—like the law itself, it would spread throughout society. Pennsylvania's authorities continued to employ shame and example but within the context of a greatly reduced reliance on sanguinary penalties; they aimed to curb immorality and control the

spread of vice through fines and lesser terms of public labor. Reason, they believed, finally dominated public policy.

I

During the 1760s and early 1770s, Pennsylvania's polity changed dramatically.
The resistance movement propelled new groups (most significantly artisans)
into political prominence while driving the older political leadership from its
position of dominance. The constitution of 1776 both reflected and reinforced
these transformations. In Pennsylvania, 1776 marked a true internal political
revolution.

Pennsylvania's new Revolutionary leadership thought that government
could embody the general interest of society. A social contract, they believed,
bound communities. Government, Pennsylvania's constitutional convention
declared, "ought to be instituted and supported for the security and protection of the community . . . and to enable the individuals who compose it to
enjoy their natural rights, and the other blessings which the Author of existence has bestowed on man." It was, the convention proclaimed, its "duty" to
form a new government based on "such original principles of government" as
would ensure the "general happiness of the people" and their descendants
"without partiality for, or prejudice against any particular class, sect, or de-
nomination." Government should not institutionalize the interests of the various ranks of society; it should directly represent the interests of the "people"
as a whole.[1]

The convention dramatically broadened the suffrage and, as a result, the
"political nation." All males twenty-one years of age and older who had
resided in the state for more than a year and paid taxes were eligible to vote.
The male children of a "freeholder" were eligible to vote on their twenty-
first birthday even if they were not taxpayers.[2] The constitution still excluded
large numbers of the population (for example, women, servants, and those
not assessed for taxes) and, consequently, maintained the link between sex,
property, and politics. But the new requirements did allow many previously
excluded men (especially mechanics and immigrants) to enter the electoral
process.

Pennsylvania's radical leaders sought to make the "consent of the governed" a reality, not just a rhetorical flourish. The convention established an
annually elected unicameral legislature. It limited Assembly service to four
years in seven—thereby institutionalizing rotation in office. Not only would

1. Francis Thorpe, ed., *The Federal and State Constitutions* (Washington, D.C., 1909), V,
3081–3082.
2. Ibid., 3084.

the Assembly constantly be subject to the judgment of the people—by virtue of annual elections—but rotation would, the convention asserted, prevent members of the Assembly from becoming an interest distinct from the people.[3]

The convention presumed not only that a common good existed but that it could be determined through open discussion. Reason, it believed, would triumph over interest through debate. As the convention saw it, the task of the constitution was to ensure that neither specific interests nor the power of the government foreclosed the open interchange of ideas. The constitution required that all legislative bills be printed in the public papers before they were debated for the last time and forbade any law—except in an emergency—from being passed in the same session in which it was proposed. Theoretically, the public would direct their representatives on specific issues, and the state would guard against "hasty determinations."[4] The public, thereby, would be certain of the appropriateness of the laws, and the legislature would be assured of the consent of the public. Left to its own devices, the public sphere could secure virtuous public policy.

Finally, the convention attempted to preclude the emergence of an aristocratic presence within the government. It established a plural executive of twelve members, each elected for three years. The division of the executive, combined with its relatively frequent elections, would, the convention believed, both "train" greater numbers in the "public business" and preclude the development of "an inconvenient aristocracy."[5] Radical leaders hoped to create a unified political nation that spoke with one voice—the voice of the middling sorts in the city and the yeomen of the countryside, not the "great" of the colonial gentry.

This constitutional vision reconceptualized state and society. Within the framework of monarchical authority, the state was modeled on the family (the court originally being an extended family). Consequently, government remained conceptually intertwined with society. But one of the effects of the Revolutionary period was to separate society from the state—to the advantage of the former.[6] Society became a self-regulating, or potentially self-regulating, unity. Indeed, the state itself now came to be seen as either an effect of evil or the source of social disruptions.

This case was put forward directly in Thomas Paine's *Common Sense* (1776). Paine, writing to encourage Independence from England, did more than attack the claims of Britain to govern its colonies. Instead, he rooted his

3. Ibid.
4. Ibid., 3086.
5. Ibid., 3086–3088.
6. For the larger national story of this theoretical transformation, see Gordon Wood, *The Creation of the American Republic, 1776–1787* (Chapel Hill, N.C., 1969).

challenge in the confines of a theory of social organization. As Paine articulated it, society was a positive phenomenon, government a negative one: "Society is produced by our wants and government by our wickedness; the former promotes our happiness *positively* by uniting our affections, the latter *negatively* by restraining our vices. The one encourages intercourse, the other creates distinctions. The first is a patron, the last a punisher." For Paine, government itself was a "badge of lost innocence," a sign that the original cooperation of humanity that instituted society had failed, "for were the impulses of conscience clear, uniform and irresistibly obeyed, man would need no other law-giver." Such lack of government, he implied, was the case in original society. But—and here Paine typifies the social contract tradition—as the community grew and dispersed, as the benefits of sociality enabled individuals to become more secure, the connectedness of individuals declined. In the end, growing population demanded the expansion of government. If government became necessary, however, it remained undesirable. From that, Paine concluded, the best government was minimal and republican.[7]

Paine, in effect, indicted government while declaring a general amnesty for society itself. Acknowledging the developments of ranks and distinctions, and the possibility of oppression from these ranks, he suggested that these developments were in the natural course of things. Only the division of "KINGS AND SUBJECTS" was incomprehensible. Unlike "male and female," which "are the distinctions of nature," or "good and bad the distinctions of heaven," the distinction of kings and subjects lacked any "truly natural or religious reason" for its existence.[8] Political power, not society, was at fault.

In other words, Paine attempted to delegitimize hereditary political distinctions by comparing them with distinctions of nature and morals—or, at least, comparing them with what Paine purported to be distinctions of nature and morals. Paine, in effect, drew on sexual difference to eternalize moral judgments and rationalize social inequalities. He removed both power and contradiction (or at least unjustified power and collective contradiction) from society. Society, by definition, was the arena of social intercourse and mutual aid. Forces that disrupted this harmony were rooted either in archaic institutions (the monarchy) or in individual failure (vice). Left to its own devices, and with properly reasoning individuals, society would be self-regulating and beneficial to all its members.

7. Thomas Paine, *Common Sense,* in Philip S. Foner, ed., *The Life and Major Writings of Thomas Paine* (Secaucus, N.J., 1948), I, 3–46; quotations on 4, 5.

8. Ibid., 9. For an extended discussion that demonstrates that Paine was both a representative of artisanal notions of male equality and a defender of commercial development with all its economic inequality, see Eric Foner, *Tom Paine and Revolutionary America* (New York, 1976), esp., 71–209.

Paine's vision spoke powerfully to Philadelphia's radicals and artisans. Although merchants and the proprietary elite led the Stamp Act resistance, by the late 1760s conflicts had emerged between the city's upper classes and its radical and middling elements. When the city responded to the Townshend Acts (1767), merchants—as a group—were the most reluctant to enter into a new round of nonimportation and the most eager to end the economic actions when the majority of the Townshend duties were repealed. To the artisanal community and the radical leaders, this reluctance indicated a willingness to sacrifice ideals for interests. At the same time, the Quaker elite continued its withdrawal from colonial politics begun during the Seven Years' War. Leadership passed to individuals identified with the resistance movement.[9]

The displacement of the old political elite was completed in the aftermath of the Coercive Acts (1774). Unlike legislatures in most other colonies, the Pennsylvania Assembly hesitated on the crucial questions of intercolonial cooperation, support for Massachusetts, and, in 1776, the necessity of Independence. In doing so, the Assembly lost its legitimacy with the radicals. The extralegal committees that had directed the economic actions against the British—and who were now dominated by younger, more radical members—led a movement to create a new constitution and to overturn the old legislature. To the authors of the new constitution, it seemed clear that the source of republican virtue did not lie within the old elite.[10]

The political emergence of the artisans within the city heightened this Revolutionary sensibility. Before the Revolution, artisans had deferred to merchants and landed gentry in the matter of politics. But, during the late 1760s and early 1770s, artisans began to break free from their deferential behavior. When the merchants hesitated in response to the Townshend duties by resisting the declaration of nonimportation, or attempted in early 1770 to end the boycott of British goods, or when the Assembly refused to commit to Independence, the artisans pushed resistance forward. By the summer of 1776, practically all of the major radical leaders—James Cannon, Charles Willson Peale, Thomas Paine, Timothy Matlack, Thomas Young, David Rittenhouse—had ties to the artisanal community.[11] No longer could the mechanical part of the community be ignored in politics.

9. For discussions of the transformation of urban politics, see Richard Alan Ryerson, *The Revolution Is Now Begun: The Revolutionary Committees of Philadelphia, 1765–1776* (Philadelphia, 1978), Charles S. Olton, *Artisans for Independence: Philadelphia Mechanics and the American Revolution* (Syracuse, N.Y., 1975), and Foner, *Tom Paine and Revolutionary America,* 56–69.

10. Steven J. Rosswurm, *Arms, Country, and Class: The Philadelphia Militia and "Lower Sort" during the American Revolution, 1775–1783* (New Brunswick, N.J., 1987), 93–108.

11. Ibid., 107–108; Foner, *Tom Paine and Revolutionary America,* 107–138.

In part, the artisans' newfound militancy stemmed from the economic benefits they derived from the various nonimportation agreements. Mechanics had traditionally found it difficult to compete with British goods. The nonimportation agreements eliminated that competition, and the movement for political independence helped strengthen the mechanics' economic position. Unlike the many merchants who found that their economic interests and their patriotic ideals conflicted, the ideals and interests of the manufacturing community meshed. Political and economic independence seemed, to the artisans at least, to go hand in hand.

But the concepts of "independence" and "virtue" had powerful resonances within artisanal culture. "Poor Richard," after all, had long preached the virtue of independence to his middling readers. In his "Way to Wealth" (1758), Franklin had warned against the dangers of debt and dependence: "*The Borrower is a Slave to the Lender, and the Debtor to the Creditor,* disdain the Chain, preserve your Freedom; and maintain your Independency." [12] Artisanal culture linked independence to the goal of a "competency." An eighteenth-century competency indicated the savings or skill to support oneself and one's family and to retire safely in old age. The failure to achieve a competency could, in the end, lead to dependence on poor relief or even the city's workhouse. Personal competence was intertwined with the idea, and reality, of independence. [13]

The middling elements of the Revolutionary city saw threats to their "Independency" all around them. Artisanal culture stood in stark, and often hostile, opposition to the city's upper- and lower-class lifestyles. This hostility to both upper and lower cultures was expressed clearly during 1781 in an article in the *Pennsylvania Packet.* "Wilbraham" argued that the city was divided into three classes. The first consisted of the "commercial projectors: those who make enormous gains of public confidence: speculators, riotous livers, and a kind of loungers." They were "so complaisant to each other as to call themselves THE BETTER SORT OF PEOPLE." The third class was the "thieves, pick-pockets, low-cheats and dirty sots." The only difference between this class and the first sort was, not "principle," but a "want of wealth and public trust." "A fellow who could cheat at cards, a wretch that could betray private confidence, needs only to be entrusted with a few millions of Continental property, to become, instantly, one of the Better Sort of People." The second class, on the other hand, was "a set of honest sober men, who mind their business." This class was generally ignored except when it was "the prey of the first and third

12. L. Jesse Lemisch, ed., *Benjamin Franklin: The Autobiography and Other Writings* (New York, 1961), 195.

13. Ric Northrup, "Decomposition and Reconstitution: A Theoretical and Historical Study of Philadelphia Artisans, 1785–1820" (Ph.D. diss., University of North Carolina, 1988), 121–147.

classes." [14] The cultures of the upper and lower classes enmeshed them in debilitating webs of dependence. Having lost their own virtue, Wilbraham implied, these classes were parasites on the labor of the middling sorts. If their power was not curbed, and their cultures reformed, society would be lost. The values of artisanal culture meshed perfectly with the Revolutionary emphasis on virtue and independence. And these emphases, in turn, resonated not only with the constitution of 1776 but with attempts to restructure the penal system.

II

The constitution's emphasis on virtue and independence extended into its approach to criminal justice. The convention sought to protect individual rights against the abuses of state power, moderate punishments inherited from the colonial codes, and ensure that the government maintained the community's morality. In so doing, the convention carried its vision of a public sphere into the penal realm.

First, the constitution guaranteed a defendant's rights. The constitution's "Declaration of Rights" assured Pennsylvanians a speedy public trial by an "impartial jury of the country," ensured the right to counsel and to confront prosecution witnesses, and protected individuals from being compelled to testify against themselves. It also required the "unanimous consent" of the jury to establish guilt and declared that no one could be deprived of liberty except under the "laws of the land" and by the "judgement of his peers." [15]

The constitution also mandated a reform of the inherited criminal law. The convention rejected the colonial reliance on hangings and whippings, insisting that Pennsylvania's criminal code be based on a correspondence between crimes and their punishments. Section 38 instructed the legislature to reform the penal laws so that punishments be "made in some cases less sanguinary, and in general more proportionate to the crimes." The convention also recommended that labor be a part of punishment. Despite the statutory possibility of imprisonment at labor, colonial sanctions rarely included penal incarceration. The constitution sought to change these practices. In order to "make sanguinary punishments less necessary," section 39 directed that "houses . . . be provided for punishing by hard labour" noncapital offenders, "wherein the criminals shall be imployed for the benefit of the public, or for reparation of injuries done to private persons." [16] Labor would become the linchpin of the new penal system.

14. *Pa. Packet*, Mar. 24, 1781. Also, see Foner, *Tom Paine and Revolutionary America*, 28–45; Rosswurm, *Arms, Class, and Country*, 37–38.

15. Thorpe, ed., *Federal and State Constitutions*, V, 3083.

16. Ibid., 3090.

But the purpose of this new punishment was not merely compensation, nor was the convention concerned only with moderating punishments. The proposed houses of correction were designed not only to "make sanguinary punishments less necessary" but also to "deter more effectually . . . the commission of crimes, by continued visible punishments of long duration." These houses were not to shield their inmates from public scrutiny. "All persons" at "proper times" were to be admitted to watch the "prisoners at their labour."[17] The emphasis on labor and moderation occurred within a philosophy of public punishments. The convention intended that, while inmates compensated their victims and the public with their labor, they would remain, as had colonial subjects of capital and corporal punishments, visible to the community.

Finally, the convention sought to counteract the fragile nature of the people's "virtue." It believed that a republic made old forms of terror unnecessary. But, the convention thought, it also made social order more problematic, since the republic depended on the people's ability both to govern themselves and to guard against the encroachment of the power of the great and of the government.[18] Consequently, nothing could be left to chance in maintaining this virtue. Section 45 instructed that "laws for the encouragement of virtue, and prevention of vice and immorality, shall be made and constantly kept in force, and provision shall be made for their due execution." The constitution protected religious and charitable organizations and provided for the establishment of schools in each county and a university for the state.[19] The convention, then, mandated a moderation of criminal sanctions. But it also insisted that the state curb vice and immorality while spreading education and religious sentiments among the population. The constitutional convention delineated a structure for reforming the criminal law. Pennsylvanians would put that structure into practice during the 1780s.

III

The effort to reform public punishments was widespread. New York experimented with public labor, and in England—because transportation closed down during the American Revolution—criminals sentenced to the hulks on the Thames were condemned to public works. Thomas Jefferson proposed a republican revision of criminal penalties that, although never translated into Virginia's law, would have made the state's sanctions correspond to the crimes they punished. A faith in public punishments was taken up in France, where an entire theory of punishment was formed around it. Punishment would

17. Ibid.
18. Wood, *The Creation of the American Republic,* 83–90; Foner, *Tom Paine and Revolutionary America,* 107–144.
19. Thorpe, ed., *Federal and State Constitutions,* V, 3091.

cease to be an isolated or temporary ritual. Instead, it would spread out through society, constantly present before the eyes of the citizenry. In the new "punitive city," criminals would not merely undergo their punishments to avenge their crimes—their very presence would transform the social world into a giant schoolroom of legality.[20]

Indeed, the notion that the penal system could be turned into a giant orrery of order was one of the dreams of the European Enlightenment. Most famously developed in Cesare Beccaria's *On Crimes and Punishments* (1764), European philosophers and jurists debated the proper means to achieve deterrent terror without the excesses of exemplary pain and death. For Beccaria, the key was "certainty"—a term by which he connoted a penal quality that combined proportionality of penalty, assurance of execution, rapidity of juridical action, and visibility of punishment. By creating punishments proportional to the crime, by punishing all criminals according to the letter of the law, and by doing so in public, capital punishments could be avoided, and criminality would decrease.[21]

On one level, Beccaria articulated a vision of penal regularity and moderation. Rigorously opposed to all forms of capital punishment as both unwise and unjust, Beccaria suggested that legislators had for too long relied on the painful or fatal seizure of the body. Exemplary punishments, he believed, combined excess with inconsistency; they punished too much and too little. Beccaria, in a commonplace of Enlightenment penal thought, assumed that the severity of punishment caused officials to let the guilty go free. Just punishment demanded a precise calculation: "Such punishments and such method of inflicting them ought to be chosen, therefore, which will make the strongest

20. On New York's attempt, see *Pa. Packet*, Oct. 10, 1785, and David Jackson to George Bryan, June 12, 1785, George Bryan Papers, box 2, folder 1, HSP. On England, see Michael Ignatieff, *A Just Measure of Pain: The Penitentiary in the Industrial Revolution, 1750–1850* (New York, 1978), 80–82. In fact, there had been discussion of establishing public penal labor in 1751. See John Beattie, *Crime and the Courts in England, 1660–1800* (Princeton, N.J., 1986), 522–524.

On Jefferson's proposal, see Jefferson, "A Bill for Proportioning Crimes and Punishments," in Merrill Peterson, ed., *The Writings of Thomas Jefferson* (New York, 1984), 349–350. I have discussed Jefferson's proposal and its implications for understanding Pennsylvania's actions more extensively in my "Public Punishments, Reformative Incarceration, and Authority in Philadelphia, 1750–1835" (Ph.D. diss., University of California, Berkeley, 1987), 122–125.

On France, see Michel Foucault, *Discipline and Punish: The Birth of the Prison*, trans. Alan Sheridan (New York, 1977), 73–114; reference to the "punitive city" is on 113–114.

21. Cesare Beccaria, *On Crimes and Punishments*, trans. Henry Paolucci (New York, 1963), 47–49, 58 (from the original *Dei delitti e delle penne* [1764]). Beccaria's philosophy was in many ways an elaboration of suggestions found in Montesquieu's *The Spirit of Laws* (1748). See Charles Secondat, baron de Montesquieu, *The Spirit of Laws*, trans., Thomas Nugent (New York, 1949), I, 19–21, 84.

and most lasting impression on the minds of men, and inflict the least torment on the body of the criminal." It was not the severity, Beccaria suggested,
but the inevitability of punishment that prevented crime. Following Montesquieu, he argued, "The certainty of a punishment, even if it be moderate,
will always make a stronger impression than the fear of another which is
more terrible but combined with the hope of impunity." Certainty would
make moderate punishments possible. Beccaria's whole system depended on
achieving "certain" punishment.[22]

Beccaria thought that legislators should create a criminal code that analo-
gized punishments to crimes. Crimes against persons should be punished corporally, people convicted of smuggling should work in the public treasury,
and so on. He wanted punishments constructed so that anyone witnessing the
punishment would know instinctively what crime had been committed. At
the same time, Beccaria argued, delays in punishment undercut the efficacy of
penal sanctions. He hoped to strengthen the mental associations between
crimes and penalties through promptness in punishment: "When the length
of time that passes between the punishment and the misdeed is less, so much
the stronger and more lasting in the human mind is the association of these
two ideas, *crime and punishment;* they then come insensibly to be considered,
one as the cause, the other as the necessary inevitable effect." [23] In this manner,
punishments would prevent future crimes because the idea of the punishment
would be indissolubly linked to the thought of the crime.

If the criminal as object established a limit to the force of punishment, the
criminal as subject of crime played little role. It was an error, he declared, to
believe that "the true measure of crimes is to be found in the intention of the
person who commits them." "Sometimes, with the best intentions, men do
the greatest injury to society; at other times, intending the worst for it, they do
the greatest good." Intentions depend "on the impression objects actually
make and on the precedent disposition of the mind"; these vary between individuals and at different times in the life of an individual. To take these variations into account would necessitate the formation of "not only a particular
code for each citizen, but a new law for every crime." The intentions of others
were notoriously difficult to grasp and understand; it was not, Beccaria contended, within the power of human beings to understand truly the motiva-
tions of others.[24] Beccaria wanted a fixed, certain code of crimes, not a judicial
system that established rules anew for every criminal or every criminal action.
He was, after all, writing a treatise on the relationship between crimes (an abstract category), not criminals (particular individuals), and punishments.

22. Beccaria, *On Crimes and Punishments,* 42 (see also, 13), 58. For Montesquieu's assertion on the importance of certainty, see *The Spirit of Laws,* I, 84.

23. Beccaria, *On Crimes and Punishments,* 56, 68, 76.

24. Ibid., 65–66.

But if Beccaria sought to moderate and regularize penalties, his proposal also implied a dramatic alteration in the corporal and visual economies of punishment. Beccaria, in effect, split punishment into two distinct parts: on the one hand, the actual experience of the condemned; on the other, the perceived experience of the condemned. If exemplary punishments aimed to operate through a universal dread of pain and death, Beccaria's reformed system would open a distance between reality and imagination. In Beccaria's calculation, the prolonged and systematic display of convicts drove the spectators to multiply the terrors of the punishment. The "advantage of penal servitude," he maintained, was "that it inspires terror in the spectator more than in the sufferer, for the former considers the entire sum of unhappy moments, while the latter is distracted from . . . future misery by that of the present moment."[25] Beccaria, in effect, dissociated the pain of the convict from the terror of the spectator.

Beccaria hoped that states would create criminal justice systems that were "just" because they were nonarbitrary. Punishments needed to be "*essentially public, prompt, necessary, the least possible in the given circumstances, proportionate to the crimes, dictated by the laws.*"[26] The laws needed to be written so that no excess pain was inflicted on the condemned. Magistrates should be bound to impose the sanctions of the laws and only those sanctions. In sum, no discretion should render the practice of criminal justice uncertain. At the same time, Beccaria proposed intensifying the public nature of punishment. But this publicity of punishment was paradoxical, for the condemned would be visible and hidden simultaneously, their bodies present but their experiences shrouded by the imagination of the spectators. Beccaria presumed that the very publicness of the punishment would construct a wall between the convicts and their spectators.

The dream of certain public penalties, then, was extensive. But Pennsylvania moved with particular rapidity to put it into practice. In November 1784, "divers citizens," from the city and county of Philadelphia, petitioned the General Assembly to "enact such laws as may tend to the good purposes" of sections 38 and 39 of the constitution. In July 1785, the grand jury and justices of the Court of Oyer and Terminer represented the legislature in favor of penal labor "on the public works and highways." Finally, in October 1785, the grand jury of the city's Court of Quarter Sessions echoed the call for penal reform and public labor.[27] A consensus among Philadelphia's authorities had emerged in favor of penal labor in the streets.

25. Ibid., 48–49.

26. Ibid., 99.

27. Pennsylvania, General Assembly, *Minutes of the First Session of the Ninth General Assembly of the Commonwealth of Pennsylvania. . . ,* 1784 (Philadelphia, 1784), 21; *Pa. Packet,* July 18, Sept. 14, Oct. 10, 1785.

The Court of Oyer and Terminer argued that, under "regular" governments, punishments were neither acts of vengeance nor attempts to restore
some previous state of social order. Instead, punishments aimed to achieve
"the security of society from the mischiefs of repeated wrongs and injuries,
(not the atonement or expiation of guilt)." To achieve this goal, they should
"produce such strong impressions on the minds of others as to deter them
from committing the like offence." [28] Punishments, although inflicted for acts
already committed, were concerned, not with the past, but the future. They
needed only terror sufficient to prevent future crimes.

Pennsylvanians followed the arguments of European philosophers and argued that terror could be achieved only if punishments were certain. The
"certainty of punishments," according to James Wilson, was "of the greatest
importance, in order to constitute them fit preventatives of crimes." It is
a "maxim," wrote one commentator, "that the frequency of crimes ariseth
more from impunity" than from moderation in punishments. English jurisprudence, with the frequency of its pardons and the "great" number of its
crimes, offered Pennsylvanians examples of the danger of impunity.[29]

In addition to providing certainty and terror, the Court of Oyer and Terminer argued that one of the "principal views of society" in criminal justice
was to "correct and reform the offender." [30] Here was a departure from both
traditional penal practice and Beccarian philosophy. For Beccaria, inner character was unimportant; only outer behavior and obedience to the laws mat-
tered. The Court of Oyer and Terminer, however, distinguished the subject of
obedience from the act of obedience and brought the former within the concerns of the penal system. Even the inner character of criminal offenders concerned a republican jurisprudence.

Although principle guided the reform, fear of a decline in morals underlay
the movement for change. The October 1785 grand jury, citing the "uncommon number of bills for assault and battery, larceny, keeping of tippling
houses, etc." they had returned, expressed "great concern" over the amount of
"vice and immorality" in the city. The grand jury attributed these "melancholy proofs of the depravity of morals," in part, to "a constant influx of
vagabonds" from surrounding states. Philadelphia offered the "hope for a
more plentiful harvest of plunder" as well as a place where criminals hoped to
be "better concealed in their villainies." [31] The city operated like a magnet,

28. *Pa. Packet*, Sept. 14, 1785.

29. James Wilson, "Lectures on Law," in Robert Mcloskey, ed., *The Works of James Wilson* (Cambridge, Mass., 1967), II, 441; "Essay on Capital Punishment," *Freeman's Journal*
(Philadelphia), Sept. 7, 1785; *Pa. Packet*, July 19, 1785, Sept. 1, 1786; *Pa. Eve. Herald*, July 16,
1785; "Z," *Pa. Mercury*, Sept. 23, 1788, "A Citizen of the World," Nov. 27, 1788.

30. *Pa. Packet*, Sept. 14, 1785.

31. Ibid., Oct. 10, 1785.

drawing criminals to its wealth and safety. To the grand jury, it seemed as if Philadelphia was beginning a reign of vice, not virtue.

Philadelphians, then, took up the question of penal reform not only from the vantage point of "enlightened" moderation but also from a growing fear of criminality and immorality. The creation of the Bank of North America in 1781 led many to fear a new mercantile aristocracy in control of the city's commerce and economy, and conservatives thought that the revolutionary revocation of Philadelphia's corporate charter was a call for anarchy. Throughout the late 1770s and 1780s, the unprecedented wartime inflation accelerated the growth of social inequality, and the city became increasingly marked by luxury and poverty. In the summer of 1785, a writer in the *Pennsylvania Packet* asserted "our social happiness is now in danger . . . from the prevalence of vice and impiety, from our increasing luxury, extravagance, selfishness and injustice." This danger was just as great as that posed by the British and called for "the same united ardour" as did fighting the British. The "war" for the Republic was only beginning. Leading Quakers, in a December address to the Assembly, claimed it was "lamentably obvious, that intemperance, licentiousness, and profane swearing and cursing, have of late abounded among the people in a greater degree . . . than at any former period of time." [32]

Numerous incidents reinforced this vision of growing social disorder. In August 1785, the *Pennsylvania Packet* drew attention to the "vast increase of counterfeit coppers in this state" and argued that this trend would soon destroy Pennsylvania's currency. In October, the city was alerted to the destruction of public lamps used to illuminate the city streets at night. In November, "a Native of Philadelphia" argued that the city's jail dockets were disproportionately large compared to country ones. He shared the assumption that criminals were less likely to be caught in the city than in the country. Consequently, he implied, this disproportion manifested the extremely precarious state of social order. Finally, in December, a watchman assigned to light the remaining public lamps was assaulted. [33]

It seemed clear to city officials that criminal punishments no longer achieved their aims. The Court of Oyer and Terminer contended that "the punishments directed by the laws now in force, for felonies, as well as other atrocious and infamous offences, less than capital . . . have lost much of their efficacy." October's grand jury agreed implicitly, arguing that the "vagabonds" who were infesting the city came not only because of the availability of plun-

32. *Pa. Packet*, July 30, 1785; "The Address and Memorial of the People Called Quakers in Philadelphia," *Ind. Gazetteer*, Dec. 10, 1785. See also, John K. Alexander, *Render Them Submissive: Responses to Poverty in Philadelphia, 1760–1800* (Amherst, Mass., 1980), 73–74. On the importance of the city charter as a lightning rod for conservative unrest, see ibid., 42–44.

33. *Pa. Packet*, Aug. 2, Nov. 17, 1785, Jan. 4, 1786; *Pa. Gazette*, Nov. 2, 1785.

der and concealment but also because New York City was experimenting with public labor, which criminals "dread more than a thousand stripes."[34] Traditional punishments no longer held sufficient terror to deter. The legislature, they insisted, needed to institute new penal sanctions that were more efficient and better suited to the purpose of punishment.

IV

Corporal and capital punishments, critics charged, were not only ineffective in preventing crime but inappropriate for a republican polity. Such penalties, they insisted, inverted justice and law; the display of punitive corporality debased society while promoting violence. In making these charges, Revolutionary-era reformers forcefully redefined exemplary punishments as cruel and excessive. They linked the practice of capital and corporal punishments to the archaisms of tyranny and monarchy. Pennsylvanians fused the languages of radical Protestantism and civic virtue with the arguments derived from the Continental theorists for "moderate yet certain" penalties into a critique of capital and corporal punishments. Exemplary punishments, they acknowledged, might provoke sullen acceptance. But a republican society, they were convinced, needed more than passive obedience from its citizens.

The Revolutionary process itself had demonstrated the instability of public punishments. Throughout the resistance period, Philadelphians protesting British actions and colonial collaborators mimed the rituals of public punishments. Crowds engaged in carting, tarring and feathering, and hangings in effigy. These actions often were not controlled by upper-class resistance leaders but manifested the self-organization of the lower sorts. As such, they demonstrated the reversibility of public punishments—the state's reliance on violence carried its own social dangers. From another perspective, the exercise of governmental violence during the Revolutionary period might have stimulated growing opposition to capital penalties. The years following Independence saw the greatest number of executions in Pennsylvania's history. And many of these executions were clearly related to political conflicts. Whereas colonial penalties might have taken place within a rough consensus on the defense of persons and property, that consensus did not exist on the execution of political opponents. For Quakers especially, the Revolutionary era was traumatic, as several of their sect were sent to the gallows. It might have strengthened their will to reduce the number of crimes considered capital.[35]

34. *Pa. Packet*, Sept. 14, Oct. 10, 1785. On New York's experiment, see Jackson to Bryan, June 12, 1785, George Bryan Papers.

35. For one example of a tarring and feathering, see John Hughes to Customs Commissioners, Oct. 13, 1769, in Custom House Papers, X (May 1769–Nov. 1770), HSP. On

Critics of capital and corporal punishments, in effect, aimed to subordinate the practice of example to a law of regularity. Whereas exemplary punishments followed a logic of spectacular seizure, proponents of penal reform demanded a system of constant constraint. From their vantage point, the very singularity of penal spectacle diminished its deterrent effect; capital punishment in its very ferocity failed to provoke a general submission to the law. "To prove this," the *Pennsylvania Evening Herald* declared, "let it be considered that the place of execution in London . . . is perhaps a scene of as much villainy, picking pockets, etc. as the city affords." Despite large numbers of executions in London, "the late capital punishments do not appear to have any good effect. . . . There are now between four and five hundred wretches charged with felonies in the gaol of Newgate." One commentator drew attention to the case of Robert Elliot, executed at Chester, Pennsylvania, for burglary. Elliot's two older brothers had previously been executed, one in Ireland for robbery and one at Chester for murder. "We should suppose that these examples were brought as close home . . . as example can possibly be pressed," the *Packet* declared, "yet so feeble is the effect of this ever-failing experiment, that the execution of *two brothers* was insufficient to preserve from the same fate, the *third* to the twenty-seventh year of his age!" [36]

The very drama and definitiveness of the penalty, critics charged, turned the attention of the crowd from the nature of the crime to the performance of the condemned. "A Citizen of the World" claimed that audiences at London hangings were more concerned with the heroics of the condemned than the justice of the sentence. After the execution, "the populace depart, either applauding the criminal's hardness, or as they term it, his spirit, in dying 'like a cock'—or else condemning his weakness—'He died like a d——d chicken

---

the more general context and patterns, see Rosswurm, *Arms, Country, and Class,* 31–34, 46–48.

Quakers were particularly sensitive to the issue of reducing capital crimes owing to the execution of Quakers Abraham Carlisle and John Roberts in 1778. See the various materials and petitions in *Pa. Archives,* 1st Ser., VII, 21–58. For discussion of these executions, see Louis P. Masur, *Rites of Execution: Capital Punishment and the Transformation of American Culture, 1776–1865* (New York, 1990), 75–76; G. S. Rowe, *Thomas McKean: The Shaping of an American Republicanism* (Boulder, 1978), 114–120; Rosswurm, *Arms, Country, and Class,* 156–159; John T. Scharf and Thompson Westcott, *History of Philadelphia, 1609–1884* (Philadelphia, 1884), I, 394–395. There was also continual conflict during the 1780s about the outlawry and execution of the Doan family, whose crimes seemed clearly directed against the new political regime. For a discussion of the conflicts over the Doans, see Rowe, *Thomas McKean,* 202–209, 215–225.

36. *Pa. Eve. Herald,* July 16, 1785; *Pa. Packet,* July 20, Aug. 18, 1785, May 19, 1787. For a fuller comment on Elliot, see Negley K. Teeters, "Public Executions in Pennsylvania, 1682–1838," *Journal of the Lancaster County Historical Society,* LXIV (1960), 135.

hearted dog.'" Even the guards at the execution, it was charged, partook in the general lawlessness.[37] Capital punishments introduced disorder into society; the spectacle itself, and the procession to the gallows, disrupted the daily life of the community.

To their opponents, capital and corporal punishments were not merely unwise; they actively disrupted the certainty of the law. Rather than providing a scaffolding for the display of justice and mercy, exemplary punishments, they charged, joined brutality to instability. The very presence of capital punishments undermined the laws themselves. "The morals of states," one Pennsylvanian argued, "greatly depends on preserving a due equilibrium between the enormity of crimes, and the punishments held out to deter from the perpetration of them." Although it would be dangerous to employ insufficient punishments, it was "a miserable impolicy" to prescribe capital punishments too widely. Capital punishments made lesser penalties ineffective and consequently encouraged, rather than deterred, criminality. Excessive use of capital punishments taught the community that all crimes were alike and encouraged criminals to commit greater crimes to escape detection for lesser ones. Criminals, moreover, were notoriously difficult to convict for capital crimes. Capital punishments, then, not only undermined the efficiency of other penalties; they also undercut the achievement of penal certainty. Instead of being a "striking engine for supporting society," capital punishment was a source of depravity.[38]

But more was at stake than merely unwise social policy. Critics charged that capital punishments were contrary to the spirit of Christianity. Benjamin Rush, in particular, insisted that "'The Son of Man came not to destroy men's *lives,* but to *save* them,' is a passage that at once refutes all the arguments that ever were offered in favor of . . . capital punishments."[39] Those who defended capital punishment remained tied to "Calvinistical" principles inappropriate to an enlightened age. They failed to recognize that the New Testament superseded the Old Testament passages on which they based their penal philosophy, just as progress of manners had superseded the barbarism of primitive societies.

Critics thereby viewed sanguinary punishments as unnecessary legacies from unenlightened, barbaric times. "Amongst unpolished nations, and during the prevalence of savage manners," the author of "An Essay on Capital

37. *Pa. Mercury,* Sept. 23, 1788, "A Citizen of the World," Nov. 27, 1788.

38. *Pa. Eve. Herald,* July 16, 1785; "Essay on Capital Punishment," *Freeman's Journal,* Sept. 7, 1785. See also *Pa. Packet,* Sept. 14, 1785. For the expression of similar concerns in England, see Randall McGowen, "The Body and Punishment in Eighteenth-Century England," *Journal of Modern History,* LIX (1987), 670–671.

39. Benjamin Rush to Jeremy Belknap, Oct. 7, 1788, in L. H. Butterfield, ed., *Letters of Benjamin Rush* (Princeton, N.J., 1951), I, 490.

Punishment" insisted, "punishment is the only means known for preserving public order. A rude legislator is acquainted with no other. When one proves ineffectual, he thinks of another more rigourous." "In some countries," the *Pennsylvania Evening Herald* declared, "the legislators, like Draco of old, seem to make a sport of human life, and declare it forfeit on the most trivial occasions." But if these punishments could be explained historically, there was no reason a republic should emulate them. The Court of Oyer and Terminer argued that if the aims of punishments "could be attained by certain but milder punishments, great advantage and honor would be thereby derived to the commonwealth." In a "new Country," according to Edward Shippen, a moderation of punishments (consistent with the "public safety") would be "particularly wise," and it would bring "honor" to "our rising Empire, to set an Example of Lenity, moderation and Wisdom to the Older Countries of the World."[40]

Public penal labor seemed to open up this possibility of personal redemption and national honor. Unlike capital punishments or "stripes," public labor, the *Pennsylvania Packet* argued, would alter the habits of the condemned and, "whilst it tends to reform the culprits, preserve life." Rather than "being hardened in habits of villainy and idleness," criminals subject to the new punishment might "by dint of hard labour, acquire such a spirit of industry and sobriety" as would enable them to regain "that place in the community, which their misdemeanours had forfeited."[41] This position drew on Protestantism's emphasis on the positive value of labor, moderation, and simplicity. The artisan community shared the belief in the moral and political virtue of labor, albeit in a more secular form. These various ideological strains combined in a vision of an almost redemptive power of labor and the dangers of luxury and dependence.

At the same time, unlike brief public punishments, the continuing presence of convicts would make a lasting impression on the citizenry. Public labor would "lessen the number of offenders, by proving a reasonable warning, and a durable example to others . . . perpetually reminding them of the dangerous consequences on an aberation from virtue, and a breach of the laws." Effective deterrence depended on constant impressions. This departure from the brevity of traditional public punishments drew on the conviction held in the late eighteenth century that habit formed character. Public labor would be "benevolent in its consequences, as it holds the offenders up *in terrorem* to other profligates, whom nothing short of a constant and efficacious memento can guard against giving a loose rein to their inordinate passions, perpetually

40. "Essay On Capital Punishment," *Freeman's Journal*, Sept. 7, 1785; *Pa. Eve. Herald*, Apr. 30, 1785; *Pa. Packet*, Sept. 14, 1785; Edward Shippen, Jr., "Grand Jury Charge," Philadelphia Court of Quarter Sessions, Oct. 24, 1785, Balch-Shippen Papers, II, 88, HSP.

41. *Pa. Packet*, Sept. 14, 1785; *Pa. Eve. Herald*, July 20, 1785.

goading them to transgress the laws."[42] Public labor not only would change the habits of the condemned but instill new habits among the populace. The mental association between crime and punishment would become habitual.

Proponents of public labor highlighted its educational nature. One commentator suggested that convicts labor with "*insignia* borne about by them" to ensure they were "subjects of abhorrence—lighted beacons for the virtuous to avoid—and living monuments of depravity and unrighteousness." In this way, by combining shame with labor, the criminal justice system could effectively draw on human nature "as mankind are more afraid of infamy, or slavery, than of death." "The punishment of the few" would become the "preservation of the many." True policy would be achieved.[43]

The arguments for public labor, then, joined revulsion of penal corporality to a utilitarian critique of punitive rationality. To their critics, capital and corporal punishments were symptoms of the cruelty and irrationality of archaic political systems. Seizing the body in a public display of sanguinary vengeance was, in effect, an admission of failure; rather than a dramatic reassertion of community and law, it was a spectacle of tyrannical excess and frustration. In its place, proponents of public labor proposed an entirely different order of constraint, one that put into play a new organization of visibility and embodiment.

V

Making the condemned public examples drew not only on traditional forms of punishment and Enlightenment theory but on Revolutionary practices of public spectacle. Throughout the early 1780s, Philadelphians participated in public displays that marked important moments in the Revolutionary struggle. Some were brief signs demonstrating public happiness over specific events. But others, designed as allegories, sought to educate the community through complex symbols. When city leaders thought that public laborers could be not only examples of the terror of the law but constant signs of the results of human depravity, they drew on a practice of public allegory familiar to their urban audience.

On September 28, 1780, Philadelphians celebrated the discovery of Benedict Arnold's treason. A procession was led by "several Gentlemen mounted on horse back," followed by "a line of Continental Officers," then "Sundry Gentlemen in a line," and, lastly, "a guard of City Infantry." "Drums and fifes playing the Rogues March" preceded a cart containing an effigy of Arnold

---

42. *Pa. Packet,* Sept. 14, 1785; *Pa. Eve. Herald,* July 20, 1785. On the 18th-century idea that habit forms character, see Jay Fliegelman, *Prodigals and Pilgrims: The American Revolution against Patriarchal Authority* (New York, 1982); Norman Fiering, "Benjamin Franklin and the Way to Virtue," *American Quarterly,* XXX (1978), 199–223. See also below, Chapters 4, 5.

43. *Freeman's Journal,* Aug. 31, 1785; *Pa. Eve. Herald,* Jan. 20, 1785.

("dressed in regimentals" with "two faces emblematical of his traiterous conduct") sitting on a stage. In Arnold's left hand was "a mask" and in his right a "letter . . . from Belzebub." A "figure of the Devil, dressed in black robes" stood behind Arnold. He was "shaking a purse of money" next to one of Arnold's ears and had "in his right hand a pitch fork, ready to drive him into hell" as "reward" for the crimes "his thirst of gold had made him commit."[44]

In front of Arnold's effigy hung a large lantern of transparent paper that "delineated" the results of Arnold's crimes. Arnold—"on his knees before the Devil, who is pulling him into the flames"—was saying, "'My dear Sir, I have served you faithfully'; to which the Devil replies, 'And I'll reward you.'" The other side of the lantern depicted two figures hanging under the inscription "The Traitors' reward."[45] The lantern's front contained a description of Arnold's crimes and concluded: "The treachery of this ungrateful General is held up to public view, for the exposition of infamy. . . . The effigy of this ingrate is therefore hanged (for want of his body) as a Traitor to his native country, and a Betrayer of the laws of honor." "A numerous concourse of people" accompanied the procession, and, "after expressing their abhorrence of the Trason and the Traitor," they "committed him to the flames, and left both the effigy and the original to sink into ashes and oblivion."

This display was a politicized version of American Pope Day rituals. The English commemorated a failed Catholic attempt at regicide by celebrating Guy Fawkes Day on November 5. New Englanders had transformed this holiday into Pope Day—a less specific yet still anti-Catholic event. In the New England version of the ritual, the cart contained the pope and the devil to symbolize Catholicism's threat to the Protestant empire of America. During Stamp Act protests, New Englanders replaced the pope with stamp collectors and hanged them in effigy. The Stamp Act crowds repoliticized the event and returned the threat of internal subversion to the ritual.[46]

Philadelphians now replaced the pope with the figure of Arnold. England, like Catholicism, was the devil's tool with which to destroy virtue and liberty. But the replacement of the pope first with stamp collectors and then with

44. The description of this display here and below can be found in Lillian B. Miller, ed., *The Selected Papers of Charles Willson Peale and His Family,* I, *Charles Willson Peale: Artist in Revolutionary America, 1735–1791* (New Haven, Conn., 1983), 354–355.

45. These figures represent Major John Andre, the English officer who gained Arnold's assistance, and Joshua Smith, who was accused of treason for aiding Andre.

46. On the general question of these popular rituals and political culture, see Peter Shaw, *American Patriots and the Rituals of Revolution* (Cambridge, Mass., 1981) 15–18, 178–180, 197–199; Alfred F. Young, "English Plebeian Culture and Eighteenth-Century American Radicalism," in Margaret Jacob and James Jacob, eds., *The Origins of Anglo-American Radicalism* (London, 1984), 185–212. Charles Willson Peale, who created the Philadelphia spectacle, witnessed such a Stamp Act demonstration in Newburyport. See Miller, ed., *Selected Papers of Charles Willson Peale,* I, 44.

Arnold demonstrated that the threat to America was not only external but internal. Arnold's two faces, "emblematical of his traitorous conduct," heightened this sense of danger. Americans needed constant vigilance lest corruption undermine the Revolutionary Republic.

The careful depiction of Arnold's crimes reinforced the display's political meaning. In the Pope Day ritual, the lantern contained poems expressing general antipapal sentiments. But in the case of Arnold, the lantern spelled out specific dangers and referred to specific events. The Philadelphia spectacle drew on the established cultural symbols of Pope Day but also instructed its audience in the specific significance and meaning of its depiction. Philadelphia's radical leaders—as had their Boston predecessors—transformed a traditional allegorical ritual to exemplify the threat to Revolutionary virtue.

At the same time, this spectacle modified traditional public punishments. The procession through the streets paralleled the procession to the gallows. The cart would have been familiar to the public from its use both in capital executions and in penal carting. But unlike actual hangings that depended on the cooperation of the condemned, Arnold's hanging delineated its own meaning. Through its transparent lantern, it contained within itself a commentary on its own symbols of infamy. In this way, it anticipated the attempt to make criminals at public labor constant signs of the result of breaking the laws.

Just as the effigy procession removed authority from its dependence on the condemned, it also separated the symbolism of punishment from its materiality. In Arnold's hanging, Philadelphia's elites (those "gentlemen" on horseback) responded to betrayal by one of their own and reaffirmed their ties to the people. The spectacle quite literally papered over the wound Arnold had caused, allowing the Revolutionary community to stand together against the dangers of corruption and seduction. But they did so in pantomime, hanging Arnold's effigy "for want of his body." Whereas the traditional public punishment powerfully merged exemplary display with material suffering, the very nature of the effigy procession operated in a space between Arnold's body and his imagined punishment. The careful imitation of the rituals of public punishment, like Beccaria's dissociation of the pain of the condemned from the pain of the spectators, made manifest the unbridgeable gap between the body under constraint and its reflection within the imagination of the spectators.

If Arnold's fictitious execution delineated the dangerous seductions of vice, three years later Philadelphians witnessed the imaginary space of Revolutionary victory. In the winter of 1783, Pennsylvania's General Assembly commissioned the construction of a "Triumphal Arch" to celebrate the signing of the Treaty of Peace with Great Britain. In the ancient world, communities

constructed triumphal arches for the departure or return of their armies.[47]
In Philadelphia, the arch did not physically welcome the army; instead, it
marked the arrival of peace. Symbolizing the passage to a republican form of
government, the arch, in both its form and content, indicated the hopes and
anxieties accompanying the republican experiment.

Charles Willson Peale designed the arch to awaken associations with the
classical world. The four pillars were in the Greek "*Ionic*" style, and the "whole
Edifice" was "finished in the Style of Architecture proper for such a Building
and used by the *Romans*." To honor the newly independent states, Peale "em-
bellished" the arch with thirteen "*illuminated Paintings and suitable Inscrip-
tions*." To strengthen the classical references, the Assembly instructed that
these be "distributed in to several Parts appropriated by the Antients to such
Ornaments." Painted figures, on the railings at the top of the arch, represented justice, prudence, temperance, and fortitude. In its moment of Revolutionary triumph, America would take its place among the world's great republics and empires.

Peale's "embellishments" also drew on classical imagery. Each contained a
drawing and explanation in Latin and English. Two made explicit reference to
classical mythology. Over the center arch was a drawing of the "Temple of
Janus shut." The Roman god of doors and passages, it seemed, was guarding
the transition to a peaceful republican society. Elsewhere, Peale used the image
of Hermes' staff to remind his audience of the connection between peace and
trade. Asserting the connection between the young American Republic and its
classical counterparts, Peale implied that America was the true descendant of
Greece and Rome.

Peale also used modern images for teaching more specific political lessons.
Two drawings referred directly to potential or actual conflicts between civilians and the military. In the first, Peale drew a "Confederated *America* leaning
on a Soldier, military Trophies on each Side of them," a reminder of the debt
the new nation owed to the army. But the commentary pointed out an equally
important lesson—that the army must remain loyal to the nation: "FIDES
EXERCITUS. *The Fidelity of the Army*." In the second drawing, Peale, mindful
of the struggles over the militia's burdens and duties, depicted "Militia exercising." The commentary explained the drawing in this manner: "PROTOGENTES
GAUDEBUNT. *Protecting they shall enjoy*." Militia were crucial to the preservation of republican liberties. But, as with the Continental army, the Republic
could survive, and soldiers could be rewarded, only if the military protected

---

47. The description of the arch and its regulations here and below can be found in Miller,
ed., *Selected Papers of Charles Willson Peale*, I, 398–401. On the construction of triumphal
arches in ancient times, see Jean-Christophe Agnew, "The Threshold of Exchange: Speculations on the Market," *Radical History Review*, XXI (1979), 102.

the community and remained loyal to the commands of the civil government. Other images referred to contemporary politics—a bust of Louis XVI, the flags of France and the United States, a pyramid-shaped tomb to honor those who died in the war—or contemporary society—a library, native Americans building a church in the wilderness, a plow.[48] By adorning the pillars supporting the arch with thirteen such images, Peale made implicit reference to the Republic and the sources of its security.

Peale's design for the triumphal arch drew on well-known cultural symbols. The urban audience was well acquainted with images of plows, libraries, and Louis XVI. The archway's representations provided symbols of the Revolution's success and examples the audience might emulate in preserving its legacy. The substance of the arch, therefore, demonstrated both joy over the successful conclusion of the war and concern over the future course of the Revolution. By drawing on exemplary images, the arch's creators joined in the late-eighteenth-century celebration of the power of example. But the arch did not depend entirely on the audience's understanding; each of the drawings possessed its own commentary. Peale took no chances with misunderstanding or misinterpretation; in building a structure that interpreted itself, he sought to ensure that all his audience understood its meaning correctly. As with its substance, the form of the arch manifested both hope and anxiety about the virtue of the people. If virtue was assured, it would not need to be explained—but every element of the archway was designed for instruction.

Peale's images did more than draw parallels between the "rising empire" of America and the glories of the classical world. They also linked together the Republic's fate, classical example, and the ordered male body. One drawing insinuated the importance of classical virtue and military loyalty:

> On the Dye of the Pedestal, on the right Hand in passing through the Centre Arch, *Cincinnatus,* crowned with Laurel, returning to his Plough— The Plough adorned with a Wreath of the same—The Countenance of *Cincinnatus* is a striking Resemblance of General *Washington.*[49]

As in ancient times, the liberty of the people was linked to military loyalty. The representation of Washington as Cincinnatus offered respect to the general's selflessness while reminding the audience that classical virtue played a crucial role in obtaining (and maintaining) its freedom from despotism. And the im-

---

48. Miller ed., *Selected Papers of Charles Willson Peale,* I, 399–401. During the Revolution, the militia had struggled for radical democratization, a struggle that culminated with the Fort Wilson incident. Peale himself had opposed the militia in its actions surrounding this incident. On Fort Wilson, see John K. Alexander, "The Fort Wilson Incident of 1779: A Case Study of the Revolutionary Crowd," *WMQ,* 3d Ser., XXXI (1974), 589–612; and Rosswurm, *Arms, Country, and Class,* 205–227.

49. Miller, ed., *Selected Papers of Charles Willson Peale,* I, 401.

age of Cincinnatus, forward looking, at labor, with honor on his head, pointed to the appropriate display and self-discipline of the republican male body.

This upright and orderly display was not limited merely to the example. The Assembly sought to determine not only the meaning of the arch but the nature of the celebration. First, it forbade other forms of celebrating the peace. Quakers refused to illuminate their houses for public celebration. The Assembly's prohibition was, most likely, designed to prevent attempts to force Quakers to do so and thereby avoid the conflict that their refusal might occasion.[50] The city would celebrate communally or not at all.

The authorities went even further, however. The broadside announcing the spectacle contained "Regulations" detailing how "Citizens" should proceed in order to see the arch. The instructions sought to assure an "orderly" audience at the "Exhibition."[51] Pedestrians and riders would be separate at all times. The pedestrians would be formed into distinct lines, each viewing a different portion of the arch. If the audience followed the instructions, the viewing would proceed with almost mechanical precision. The triumphal arch, a machine of ordered representation, imposed its own schema on the public and the public space it dominated. The regulations for the audience, the broadside explained, were to ensure that the citizens had the "Opportunity of viewing and examining the Exhibition with the greatest Convenience and Satisfaction to themselves."

The state hoped to display the triumphal arch in January 1784. But the event was somewhat delayed. Somehow, firecrackers were set off too close to the artwork, and Peale's illuminations went up in flames. Luckily for Peale, he was able to find gentlemen in the city to fund a re-creation of his art. As a result, the arch, with all of its pedagogical embellishments, finally was displayed in May.[52]

Yet, if the *Pennsylvania Gazette* suggested that the delay was the result of an "unfortunate accident," this outcome could not be said to have been totally

50. "As these Demonstrations of Joy are prescribed and regulated by the Directions . . . of the State . . . no Person or Persons . . . will presume . . . to require or to make any other Demonstrations of Joy upon the Occasion." Ibid., 399.

51. "1st. Persons walking will please to advance towards the Exhibition by the Ways on the Outside of the Foot-pavements, which lead in straight Lines from *Fifth* Street through the Side Arches. Those that advance on the South Side, after passing the South Arch, will turn on the left Hand down *Market* Street on the Foot-pavement to *Fifth* Street. Those who advance on the North Side, after passing the North Arch, will turn on the right Hand down *Market* Street on the Foot-pavement to *Fifth* Street. In this Manner they may pass and return as often as they chuse.

"2d. Persons on Horseback or in Carriages are to advance in the Middle of *Market* Street, and passing through the Centre Arch, continue on to *Seventh* Street; then turning to the right or left return by *Arch* Street or *Chestnut* Street to *Fifth* Street, and so pass and return as often as they please." Ibid., 401.

52. *Pa. Gazette*, Jan. 28, May 12, 1784; Miller, ed., *Selected Papers of Charles Willson Peale*, I, 401.

unexpected. In fact, the regulations for audience behavior drafted in December and published in early January all but anticipated the disruption. "Any Boys," the Assembly declared, "who disturb the Citizens by throwing Squibs or Crackers, or otherwise, will be immediately apprehended and sent to the Work-house."[53] The Assembly, thereby, incorporated the threat of unclassical boys within its vision of the public realm. Just as the proper examples of the arch were set off against the implicit threats to the Republic, so the ordered realm of the arch was constructed against the more unruly and chaotic practices of the urban world. And as the reference to the workhouse makes clear, if the Assembly failed to create a public exhibition that would maintain its own order, the power to punish remained.

Between Arnold on the one hand and Washington on the other, the effigy and the arch displayed the instabilities of Revolutionary space and authority. The bodies of the two generals symbolized the possibility and precariousness of public virtue. In presenting Arnold kneeling for his devil's reward, Peale made manifest authority and privilege gone wrong, the military hero seduced by the base strivings of wealth and power. Washington, to the contrary, could stand upright, confident in his own purposes, a model of the traditions of classical leadership and manhood. And while the effigy procession, with its mimicry of carting and its allusions to Pope Day, acknowledged a shameful stain, the arch itself embodied a vision of virtue.

Philadelphians, then, had participated not only in traditional public punishments but also in Revolutionary spectacles of infamy and order. They were well acquainted with rituals and displays depicting virtue and its enemies. They were equally familiar with the notion that such displays could prove educational, that, through the display of infamy, people could be led to virtue. Given these experiences, it was not surprising that the city would embrace Beccaria's dream of punishment as a well-ordered system of signs.

VI

The General Assembly moved rapidly to transform the relationship of the penal law to public display and the suffering body. In September 1786, it debated and passed a statute reshaping Pennsylvania's penal code, diminishing the state's reliance on capital punishment and instituting a system of public penal labor. Shortly thereafter, it strengthened the penalties for "vice and immorality." In this new penal system, the legislature hoped, the representational qualities of punishment would be regularized and linked to the constrained body. The state would simultaneously diminish corporal pain and increase deterrent terror.

53. *Pa. Gazette*, Jan. 28, 1784.

The legislature argued that punishment should serve a dual purpose. The preamble to the Act Amending the Penal Laws of This State declared: "It is the wish of every good government to reclaim rather than destroy." Society's "principal" aims in inflicting punishments were "to correct and reform the offenders, and to produce such strong impressions on the minds of others as to deter them from committing the like offences." "Experience" demonstrated that inherited penal practices failed to achieve these aims—they neither reformed nor deterred. The answer, the Assembly suggested, was, not greater severity, but a more rigorous enforcement of moderate penalties. "The cause of human corruptions" proceeded "more from the impunity of crimes than from the moderation of punishments." [54]

Consequently, the legislature dramatically decreased the state's reliance on capital and other sanguinary punishments. An Act Amending the Penal Laws of This State eliminated capital and corporal punishments for robbery, burglary, buggery, sodomy, horse theft, larceny, or any other felony "not capital" previously subject to corporal punishment. No longer would the government depend primarily on the whipping post or the gallows for the maintenance of public order; instead, the legislature decreed "servitude" at public labor. The law specified maximum sentences: robbery, burglary, sodomy, or buggery up to ten years, horse theft up to seven years, simple larceny (more than twenty shillings) up to three years, and petit larceny up to one year. Bigamy, being an accessory after the fact for any felony, and receiving stolen goods, "knowing them to have been stolen," were now penalized with up to two years' confinement with public labor. All offenses remained subject to fines and restitution. [55]

More than simply punishment, the law mandated that prisoners perform a wide range of activities for the "benefit" of the public. Criminals were to labor "not only in the manner pointed out by the [constitutional] convention" but at "repairing and cleaning" city streets, "making, repairing and amending the public roads or highways," and in "fortifications" and "mines." All work would be "hard and laborious," and for the "benefit" of the county where they were convicted. To ensure that convicts performed their labor, the law prescribed that two days be added to their "servitude" for each day's labor missed through escape or because a prisoner was "absent . . . without good cause." [56]

The legislature was determined that the example of the convicts make a "strong impression" on the community. Male prisoners were to "have their heads and beards close shaven" each week. All convicts were to wear "habits of

54. *St. at Large*, XII, 280.
55. Ibid., 280–284.
56. Ibid., 281, 284, 286. The legislature empowered the court where the prisoner had been convicted to determine when "good cause" existed. Ibid., 286.

coarse materials, uniform in color and make and distinguished from all others used by the good citizens of this commonwealth," and their uniforms were to "have some visible mark on the outer garment designating the nature of the crime" of which they had been convicted. These insignia would ensure that convicts "may be marked out to public note as well while at their ordinary occupations as when attempting to make their escapes."[57] As with Peale's arch and Arnold's effigy, the authorities aimed to direct the vision and understanding of the audience.

If convicts' uniforms pointed to their specific offenses, the punishment itself did not aim for a Beccarian correspondence. Instead, the Assembly proportioned punishments through the medium of time, which, in the penal system, would function as money did in the economy. Not direct exchange, but the abstract intermediary of money demonstrated the value of different commodities. Similarly, the proportionality of punishments in Pennsylvania would be guaranteed by the amount of time that punishments cost the convicts. Time, in effect, was the price paid for committing crimes.

The Pennsylvania Assembly, then, combined moderation, proportionality, and display in its new penal system. In a sense, it reversed both the corporal and visual economies of exemplary punishments. The legislature dispersed the temporal element of punishment. Instead of the brief, yet dramatic, spectacle of traditional punishments, public labor offered a regular, extended demonstration of the penalties for crime. Instead of a momentary, yet severe, infliction of pain and death, public labor operated through constraint and indirection, using the body as a medium to reform the character. Time and labor would replace pain and death for the condemned, and constant reflection would succeed brief terror for the public. The regularly laboring criminal would embody the practices and mechanisms of the law itself.

The new penal law's debt to, and differences from, European theorists of certainty was apparent in the debates surrounding the penal reform act. The rationality of more moderate punishments was not challenged. All participants accepted the wisdom of reducing sanguinary punishments and creating a greater correspondence between crimes and penalties. Nor did the legislators challenge the importance of penal certainty in the achievement of social order; instead, the debate ranged over how best to achieve that certainty. And certainty posed distinct problems for Pennsylvania's reformed penal system.[58]

57. Ibid., 284.

58. It appears that the discussion about certainty and discretion, which dominated the debate over the penal reform bill, was tied to party conflicts. Suspicion existed that the judges of the Supreme Court, especially Thomas McKean, had undue influence over the framing of the bill. Francis Hopkinson, judge of the state's Court of Admiralty and longtime foe of McKean, made this charge most explicitly, but it was echoed by members of the Assembly

The 1786 penal code invested judges with considerable sentencing discretion. Offenses had a stipulated maximum period of servitude, and the different components of secondary punishments (for example, restitution, fines) were spelled out. But there were no other sentencing guidelines. Judges, after examining the circumstances of the case and the offender's character, would determine the sentence. If, during their imprisonment, prisoners "evidenced by a patient submission to the justice of their punishment a sincere reformation," the judges could grant them a certificate of good behavior that would "operate as a discharge from all claims . . . of the party injured . . . as a pardon of the guilt and infamy of the offence, and give him or her a new capacity and credit."[59] In other words, judges were given not only wide latitude in determining sentences but the power to rejudge prisoners at a later date in order to distinguish different classes of criminals on their return to society.

Critics charged that this discretion would destroy the certainty of the criminal law and undermine the Republic. The penal code, they alleged, was "founded on very different principles" from certainty and would leave "everything . . . to the discretion of the justices." This discretion would defeat the purpose of punishment: "I think fixing the punishment deters men from the commission of crimes. . . . This clause destroys what I take to be the principle of all criminal laws." In addition, Francis Hopkinson suggested that placing both "the severity of the law and the high prerogative of mercy" in the hands of justices would allow them to favor their allies. Social standing and political connections, he implied, would assume a great and undesirable place in criminal justice; the law would become a tool of political despotism. "True despotism," Hopkinson asserted, "is nothing more than a power to punish according to will and pleasure."[60] The only way to prevent this judicial despotism was through a scale of certain and known punishments.

This criticism was rooted, in part, in Revolutionary experience and ideology. Problems of consent and authority had dominated the political debates of the Revolutionary era. Whether the issue was the accountability of the vice-admiralty courts, the legitimacy of virtual representation and the limits to parliamentary legislation, or, finally, the obedience (whether perpetual or conditional) owed to the king, debates raged over consent. The colonists, in

---

during the debate. These suspicions were encouraged by the role assigned to judges in the new penal system. See *Pa. Packet,* Sept. 1, 1786 (the *Packet,* here, was reproducing the legislative debates); Rowe, *Thomas McKean,* 237–238. Rowe's study offers a careful treatment of the process of establishing judicial authority in Pennsylvania during the Revolution to which I am indebted.

59. *St. at Large,* XII, 288.

60. *Pa. Packet,* Sept. 1, 1786; Francis Hopkinson, *Miscellaneous Essays* (Philadelphia, 1792), II, 108, 107.

defending the act of Revolution, ultimately arrived at the position that allegiance was volitional and could be withdrawn. Government, Revolutionaries insisted, was based on the rational consent of the political nation, and, for the political nation to give its consent rationally, it had to be informed.[61]

The political necessity of an informed public underlay the constitutional provisions providing for the freedom of the press and the public display and discussion of all legislative bills before they were enacted. Penal certainty would contribute to the same ends. Each individual could be punished only for a crime, or with a punishment, that was clearly and publicly defined, for, as one legislator argued, "I take it to be a principle in this country of freedom, that punishments should be fixed, and not left discretionary."[62] Certainty would ensure that magistrates remained within limits the legislature had established.

Opponents of judicial discretion faced certain problems, however. All acknowledged that discretion had to be lodged somewhere; only its location was in dispute. The authors of the bill favored the judges. Opponents recommended either the Supreme Executive Council or juries.[63] But, in any case, the principle of certainty would be compromised.

Ultimately, critics of the bill could not maintain a coherent defense of the principle of certainty against judicial discretion. In part, this deviation stemmed from the difference between Beccaria's notion of justice and its Anglo-American meaning. Beccaria treated justice as a utilitarian issue of social necessity. Justice, for him, was more a metaphor for, than an attribute of, the bonds of society. The Anglo-American connotation of justice was entirely different. Justice, according to Thomas Sheridan's *Complete Dictionary of the English Language,* was "the virtue by which we give every man what is his due." The English notion implied an evaluation of individual cases through the prism of universal rule. Courts were expected to examine circumstance, character, and intentionality, creating, in effect, precisely the "new law for every crime" that Beccaria adamantly opposed. According to this notion of justice, judgment, although constrained by an established set of rules, was a positive act of discretion. And where better to place the right of such a nonarbitrary discretion than in the hands of a justice, who, after all, was "a civil officer appointed to do right by way of judgment"?[64] "Certain" punishments, unfortunately, might not necessarily be just.

The idea of individual reformation further complicated the issue of cer-

61. James H. Kettner, *The Development of American Citizenship, 1608–1870* (Chapel Hill, N.C., 1978), chaps. 6–7.

62. *Pa. Packet,* Sept. 1, 1786.

63. Ibid.

64. Beccaria, *On Crimes and Punishments,* 13 n. 18, 65; Thomas Sheridan, *A Complete Dictionary of the English Language* (Philadelphia, 1789), s. v. "justice."

tainty. The logic of reformation conflicted with the logic of fixed and certain sentences. The ultimate purpose of punishment, Pennsylvania reformers agreed, was the "security of society," not "the expiation of guilt." Individuals should be punished only so long as they were a threat to society's security; any additional punishment was arbitrary and unjust. How then, could the state hold people in servitude after they had been reformed? Beccaria did not face this problem, having never claimed a reformative power for punishment. But Pennsylvania's penal reformers proclaimed reformation "the noblest object of punishment." [65] In doing so, they further undercut the logic of certainty and established the need for a discretionary power to evaluate the prisoners' transformation.

Despite these problems, certainty had an importance for Pennsylvania's penal reformers that it lacked for its Continental advocates. In Europe, certainty, although an aim of penal reform, was ultimately a means to achieve moderate punishments. In Pennsylvania, the relationship between moderation and certainty was altered. Beccaria presupposed Continental forms of inquisitorial justice and predicated his scheme on the development of an effective police led by vigilant magistrates. In Pennsylvania, this infrastructure of vigilance did not exist. Private individuals, not justices of the peace or constables, were the primary instigators of criminal prosecutions. A grand jury had to indict, and a petit jury convict, an individual. Popular consent to the laws was an extremely important problem. Severe laws might eliminate popular consent and undercut certainty: if one fixes a "severe punishment for a small crime, the criminal will frequently escape; for witnesses will not give evidence nor the jury convict." [66] Only by moderating sanguinary laws would enough certainty be achieved to assure deterrent fear. Certainty, in spite of its logical opposition to justice and reformation, retained its preeminent spot in the pursuit of terror.

The legislature was not content merely to reconstruct the penal system. It also tried to strike at practices of individual vice and immorality. Accepting the contention of Quakers and civic leaders that a serious decline of morals had occurred and that a 1779 statute to control vice and immorality had proven ineffective, they passed the Act for the Better Suppression of Vice and Immorality. In it, the Assembly increased the penalties inflicted for Sabbath violations, drunkenness, cockfighting, horse racing, keeping an unlicensed tavern, gaming, running a public billiard table, dueling, or putting on "theatrical entertainments." [67] In a brief flurry of legislative activity, the General

65. *Pa. Packet,* Sept. 1, 1786.

66. Allen Steinberg, "From Private Prosecution to Plea Bargaining: Criminal Prosecution, the District Attorney, and American Legal History" (paper presented to the Philadelphia Center for Early American Studies, Mar. 4, 1983); *Pa. Packet,* Sept. 1, 1786.

67. *St. at Large,* XII, 313–322.

Assembly, in its attempt to preserve virtue and diminish crimes, had brought the state's penal codes into accord with Enlightenment thinking.

The differences between the act to suppress vice and the penal reform bill further indicate the importance of opinion in the operation of criminal justice. Despite the great importance placed on vice as the root of both criminality and social decay, the legislature affixed relatively minor penalties to it. These penalties stood in stark contrast to the terms of servitude placed on infractions in the penal code, even lesser offenses such as petit larceny. Popular opinion, reformers suggested, necessitated these distinctions. One legislator argued that the penal code "proposed infamous punishments for crimes which were infamous; this only fined, because the generality of mankind did not consider the vice infamous, whatever its real nature might be." For an example, he pointed out that "swearing by the name of Almighty God affixed no infamy on the guilty person."[68] Therefore, it was proper to treat the offenses in the penal code and the offenses against morality as categorically different. No law could maintain popular respect that departed too greatly from popular opinion.

The problem of opinion was not limited to the generality of mankind, however. The punishment for instigating a duel was a one-hundred-pound fine or one year imprisonment, and accepting the challenge subjected an individual to a fine of fifty pounds or six months confinement.[69] Neither the challenge to, nor the acceptance of, a duel imposed on the participants a prison term equal to that for petit larceny. But the punishments were substantially greater than for any of the other offenses against public morality. The legislature acknowledged that dueling had long been an accepted means to settle differences among the better sorts of Anglo-America. It sought to discourage the practice through fines and short imprisonment, but it recognized that too serious penalties would prevent the offense from being prosecuted. Public opinion determined the extent of effective punishments.

Pennsylvanians, then, had translated the theory of moderate yet certain punishments into penal law. Linked to a republican public sphere, the new penal system based on moderation, certainty, and reformation would, its proponents argued, promote virtue. Public labor, with its notion of a constantly present embodiment of the law, spoke to Revolutionary hopes for a unified common good while its insistence on penal certainty spoke to fears of the fragility of Revolutionary virtue. At the same time, the new system's emphasis on labor reaffirmed the impact of mechanics on Philadelphia's Revolutionary

68. *Pa. Packet,* Sept. 23, 1786.
69. *St. at Large,* XII, 320.

culture. Convicts laboring in the streets would "perpetually" serve as "efficacious mementos" of the results of vice and criminality. Certain terror would be achieved.

Public labor was structured around penal servitude. Both the ideology of the Revolution and the culture of the middling classes stressed the connection between personal and national independence and virtue. Revolutionary leaders thought that individuals naturally possessed the desire for independence. In the eighteenth century, social independence was secured through achieving a "competency." The linguistic identification of "competence" and "independence" indicated personal as well as social characteristics. Those unable to manage their "independence" were not "competent."[70] To the Assembly, the deprivation of liberty might have seemed a rational and effective punishment.

Moreover, the social connotations of servitude were in transition. At mid-century, indentured servants and slaves accounted for almost 40 percent of the city's work force. This proportion declined precipitously during the Revolutionary era. On the eve of Independence, bound labor accounted for only 13 percent of the work force and, by 1783, for just over 6 percent.[71] At the same time, the nature of bound labor changed as artisans, formerly major purchasers of bound labor, increasingly employed journeymen wage laborers. Throughout most of the century, bound labor had been used primarily in the workplace and had often been skilled labor, but, by the mid-1780s, most servants were either domestic or unskilled labor. "Servitude" was identified increasingly with black slaves or domestic (primarily female) labor. When the Assembly characterized penal labor as "servitude," it equated it with a condition that many Pennsylvanians were familiar with (either as servant or as employer). But it also identified it with a situation increasingly limited to groups stigmatized as naturally inferior or dependent.

Yet, penal servitude was a contradictory notion in the context of the republican civic ideal. Republican theory presupposed the activity and vocality of the male population—the government, after all, represented the "voice of the people." The system of public labor reduced male citizens to the status of dependents in preparation for their freedom. The law aimed to reconfigure plebeian manhood by rooting out the habits and practices of alternative forms of life. But it did so by demanding a passive compliance that inverted the fundamental activity of republican virtue. To demonstrate a "patient submission"

70. For a discussion of the psychological components of "competence," see Ric Northrup, "Speculation and Competence: Case Studies in Capitalist Expansion, 1785–1815" (paper presented to the "Transformation of Philadelphia and the Delaware Valley, 1750–1850" project, Philadelphia Center for Early American Studies, May 15, 1985).

71. Sharon V. Salinger, "Artisans, Journeymen, and the Transformation of Labor in Late Eighteenth-Century Philadelphia," *WMQ*, 3d Ser., XL (1983), 65.

to the law meant being silent and obedient—in other words, the opposite of the active consent that framed the notion of the republican public sphere.[72]

Moreover, if patient submission signified reformation, then any act of opposition was the sign of viciousness. Independence while under sentence equaled insubordination. Prisoners who did not demonstrate total incorporation of the laws' mandates necessitated ever greater institutional control. The emphasis on reformation and submission would trigger increasing surveillance and regimentation. The emphasis on patient submission opened up an ever-expanding line of disciplinary intervention.

The system of public penal labor dramatically revised the nature of criminal punishments. Public labor transformed the forms through which the state attempted to seize and discipline the penal body, and it altered the relationship between the penal display of the body and the community of spectators. As such, it was a transformative moment for the politics of the body in the eighteenth century. Philadelphia's experiment in public labor condensed a set of Revolutionary hopes and fears about the public, the self, and the nature of communication. Although lasting a mere four years, public labor would trigger anxieties within Revolutionary society that stimulated the transition to discipline as we know it.

72. This ambiguity of speech and silence in public labor offered an inverted example of a central dilemma of Revolutionary culture. As Jay Fliegelman has argued, even those who claimed to express the "voice of the people" did so by claiming that they were representing not their own wills but historical necessity. In a sense, the silence of public labor merely brought to the fore the truth of this wider Revolutionary problem—that the claims rooted in the "voice of the people" (or in nature or virtue) were predicated on the effective silencing of some element of will. See Fleigelman, *Declaring Independence: Jefferson, Natural Language, and the Culture of Performance* (Stanford, Calif., 1993), 150–164. For a general reflection on the conditions of rhetoric in late-18th-century America, see Kenneth Cmiel, *Democratic Eloquence: The Fight over Popular Speech in Nineteenth-Century America* (New York, 1990), 23–54.

CHAPTER THREE

Mimetic Corruption

Public labor pushed the visual economy of public punishments to its limits. Whereas the traditional system of display had been limited to isolated, if repeated, times and places, the new penal system placed criminals regularly and consistently before the public. Presuming a shared understanding of vice and virtue throughout the city's population, proponents of public labor believed that criminal punishments would be more effective if coterminous with society itself. At the heart of their vision was vision itself. As they imagined it, the orderly progression of silent, repentant convicts throughout the city would make criminal justice manifest. Justice, in effect, would seize and recreate everyday life through the very presence of the condemned.[1]

The actual experience of public labor, however, belied these expectations. From its inception, the new system created disarray and violence. Inmates regularly escaped and frequently battled with their keepers. Crowds gathered to watch, taunt, converse with, or give alms to the prisoners while at their labor. Rather than a theater of tragic sobriety and submission, public labor appeared a black comedy, subverting the very distinctions of vice and virtue. The presence of the subjects of penal labor seemed to corrupt the city's already precarious social virtue.

The evident failure of public labor led to a thorough reconceptualization of the relationship between criminal punishments and society. Critics of public labor broke with the notion of a shared and transparent public realm, which was presupposed by the new penal law. Proponents of public labor presumed a shared understanding at the basis of society; those opposed to the new system argued that such understanding did not exist. Opponents of public labor

---

1. This conception was not limited to Philadelphia. Michel Foucault has pointed to a similar dream among late-18th-century French philosophers. See *Discipline and Punish: The Birth of the Prison,* trans. Alan Sheridan (New York, 1977), 109–114.

envisioned the public domain as a dangerously alluring arena of misrecognition and contamination. The presence of convicts laboring in the streets, they argued, triggered a spiral of mimetic corruption that threatened to undermine the republican community itself. The penal scene became a vortex of viciousness, ominously seducing and contaminating the larger society. The law, they insisted, could depend on neither the behavior of the condemned nor the sensibility or reasoned sympathy of the public.

Public labor highlighted the contradictions of eighteenth-century notions of "sensibility" and "sympathy." In the wake of Locke's arguments on the impressionability of the senses and the materialist roots of morality, eighteenth-century Britain witnessed a wide-ranging debate about the nature and import of physical and mental "sensations." A fundamental ambiguity haunted these debates. Locke's writings seemed to point in two directions: toward the possibility that sensibility resulted from a reasoned self-creation, and toward an environmental determinism. If sensibility was rooted merely in sensation, then the individual was simply an effect; but if sensibility was a quality acquired by will, then its possession became a source of distinction. To a large extent, eighteenth-century writers sought to stabilize this ambiguity by defining it according to sex—women were passively, and men were actively, sensible. Despite this attempted stabilization, the logic of sensibility suggested not only the possibility of the cultivation of new, more refined manners but also that society itself could swallow up individual character and "sense."

If sensibility articulated the unstable distinctions of body and mind, of activity and passivity, sympathy struggled with the difficulties of distance and proximity, of sociability and isolation. Sympathy made possible social bonds. Yet it reinforced the atomism of the individual. Constructed, in part, as a mechanism for denying the more corrosive possibilities of sensibility, sympathy, as Adam Smith put it, connoted an innate capacity for "our fellow feeling with any passion whatever."[2] Sympathy, always dependent on distance, was an essentially theatrical capacity. As Smith made clear, sympathy was rooted in a capacity to represent—to represent the emotions contingent on being in the place of another person. That is, people imagined how they might feel if placed in another's situation—or, more precisely, how they would want to feel in another's situation. One reached out to others through sympathy but always remained confined within one's own experience and sympathetic imagination. If sensibility was both quality and threat, sympathy was both capacity and limit.

These ambiguities generated a number of other problems. Sympathy and sensibility were less about identity than about identification. Yet, as actions that put one in (imaginative or nervous) contact with others, these processes

2. Adam Smith, *The Theory of Moral Sentiments* (Indianapolis, Ind., 1969; orig. pub. 1759), 49.

of identification could shape and reshape one's own identity. As David Hume put it, "The minds of men are mirrors to one another, not only because they reflect each others emotions, but also because those rays of passions, sentiments and opinions, may be often reverberated, and may decay away by insensible degrees."[3] Hence there was an uncertainty in the characterization of sympathy and sensibility. On the one hand, sensibility and sympathy seemed overwhelming external forces, diseases of the will and mind, while, on the other, they were acts of the will, conscious ways of reaching out to the other. Was sympathy contagion or commiseration? Eighteenth-century writers struggled to determine the proper relationship between self and other.

Sensibility and sympathy were not only gendered; they were characteristics of class. As both qualities and aims, sensibility and sympathy had to be cultivated as much as experienced. But this cultivation meant that they could not be simply unleashed upon the world; too much sensibility or misplaced sympathy could have dangerous effects for the individual and society. Only those with properly cultivated qualities could withstand the temptations of vulgar sympathy and sensibility.

Within such a context, the experience of public labor seemed to indicate a void at the heart of republican society, a void that made the display of convicts, and communication between the condemned and the community, alarming and problematic. Criminals in the streets appeared to be actively seducing the community away from virtue. As a result, the implications of public labor extended beyond the confines of criminal punishment. Public labor condensed a wider set of anxieties about the nature and stability of both public authority and individual character. Indeed, the conflictual history of public labor framed, and was framed by, debates about the nature of the individual, the origins of poverty, the danger of theatricality, and the sources of social solidarity. As republican Philadelphians confronted their post-Revolutionary realities, the very possibility of a shared common good seemed in abeyance.

I

Public labor dramatically altered the extent and organization of penal space. Most obviously, the new penal system broke punishment out of its old confines at the whipping post or specially indicated spaces.[4] But, simultaneously, the administration of the law imposed new gender divisions within punishment. Punishment presented a vision of a new society within society itself.

3. David Hume, *A Treatise of Human Nature* (1749), ed. L. A. Selby-Bigge (Oxford, 1888), 365. On sense and sensibility, see David Marshall, *The Figure of Theater: Shaftesbury, Defoe, Adam Smith, and George Eliot* (New York, 1986), 177–181; John Mullan, *Sentiment and Sociability: The Language of Feeling in the Eighteenth Century* (Oxford, 1988), 18–56.

4. In a way, the practice of carting anticipated the expansion of penal space under the

Male convicts became public examples and were put to work cleaning the streets. Known to contemporaries as "wheelbarrow men," with their heads shaved, their clothing consisting of "a mixture of dark blue and brown stuff" and multicolored "woolen caps," they moved through the streets with an "iron collar around their neck and waist" connected to a chain leading to "a heavy ball." The prisoners were combined into "gangs," each of which had its own guard. A mark on their clothing indicated their particular crime.[5] Convict labor, designed to serve the state and reform the criminal, made male prisoners function as constant signs of the correspondence between crime and punishment.

But, if male criminals were to function as signs, they could do so only silently and passively. Speech was devalued in the new penal system. The identification of crime was left to written insignia sewn onto the convicts' uniforms to indicate their specific offenses. Convicts were mobile transparencies, the medium through which public order could be represented. But their only activity was labor; unlike capital penalties, no public, oral acknowledgment of justice was sought during public labor. Ideally, the condemned would be automatons, silently moving through the city in groups. Truly living machines of the legal order, public laborers were to reinforce the distinction between virtue and vice while embodying the labor needed to construct the new society. Reformation and utility would be joined.

Female convicts, on the other hand, were not sentenced to public labor. Instead, they were confined (during the day) in the city's workhouse. Placed under "strict" oversight, they made "coarse linen, and articles of summer wear" for the male convicts as well as a "very considerable quantity of fine linen" for the public. In this way, one commentator suggested, even those who entered "prison with dissolute dispositions" were "reconciled to labour and industry" and "thus acquired a skill by which an honest livelihood may be obtained." The state not only profited by their labor, but the "noblest end" of punishment, "the reformation of the offender," would follow.[6] Like the labor of their male counterparts, if in a dramatically different manner, the labor of the female convicts would be doubly productive—not only of goods that would benefit the state but of individuals who would benefit society.

This treatment of female convicts marked a triple departure from colonial practice. During the colonial period, women had suffered the same public

---

wheelbarrow law. But carting had been an exception, not the norm, and carting was still primarily a mechanism to move a convict from one clearly demarcated space to another. It served as a supplement to the basic punishment addressed directly to the body.

5. Ann Warder, "Extracts from the Diary of Ann Warder," ed. Sarah Cadbury, *PMHB*, XVIII (1894), 61; *St. at Large*, XII, 284.

6. *Pa. Packet*, Jan. 3, 1788.

corporal punishments as men. Now, not only were women's punishments neither public nor corporal, but they were distinguished from the punishments inflicted on men.[7] Women were removed from the public stage of punishment and their labor used, at least in part, in support of the male prisoners.

The gendered nature of punishment was part of a post-Revolutionary strategy to construct a new reality. The new penal system not only changed the relationship between penality and everyday life but promoted an ideal gender system within penality itself. Altered penal practice did not merely express underlying social forms—it actively helped construct them. The penal system was one site for the imposition of new, more radical gender divisions. Interestingly, this newly gendered penality occurred unheralded. The law of 1786 had made no distinctions between men and women; the text had mandated that all suffer public labor. Yet, almost immediately, and without public debate, women were sheltered from the public gaze. One silent effect of public labor was to erase female convicts from public sight and banish them to the imagination. The system of public labor eerily anticipated the ideology of separate spheres.[8]

Despite the initial hopes of its proponents, public labor quickly generated disciplinary problems and violence. Onlookers crowded about the convicts while they were at their labor, some talking to the convicts, some ridiculing them, and some giving them charity. The wheelbarrow men obtained liquor with relative ease, often wandered away from their keepers to solicit money, and engaged in conversation among themselves and with onlookers. Prisoners fought with each other and, not surprisingly, given some of the harassment to which they were subject, with some of the spectators.[9]

Confrontations between guards and inmates plagued the new system almost immediately. On May 15, 1787, for instance, one of the keepers killed one of the inmates. The *Pennsylvania Packet* defended the guard, charging that the prisoner had behaved in a "riotous" manner and that the guard had acted to "prevent a general mutiny." The following day, inmates nearly killed one of their keepers. As the *Pennsylvania Packet* described the event, one of the pris-

---

7. This is not to say that, during the colonial period, distinctions in sentencing did not occur because of the sex of the offender. The number of stripes during whipping, for example, may have been affected, and women were granted pardons or reprieves because of pregnancy. But the nature of punishments inflicted on offenders was uniform relative to sex. Women were not generally spared public display, for example, because they were women.

8. On the larger struggle to redefine urban gender boundaries, see Christine Stansell, *City of Women: Sex and Class in New York, 1789–1860* (New York, 1986), 20–37.

9. On these issues, see, for instance, *Ind. Gazetteer*, Mar. 31, May 21, 1787; *Pa. Packet*, May 19, 28, Sept. 17, 1787; Negly K. Teeters, *The Cradle of the Penitentiary: The Walnut Street Jail at Philadelphia, 1773–1835* (Philadelphia, 1955), 27–28.

oners had thrown a "heavy stone" that struck the guard's head. When "chastized," the inmate tried to strike the keeper with a spade. The guard, having taken the spade from the inmate, knocked him down with it, at which time "several of the gang drew their knives, and called out to kill the keeper." The inmates, however, were "soon suppressed," and the authorities regained their control. Even more ominously, it appeared that the wheelbarrow men had not acted alone. The *Pennsylvania Packet* charged that several "associates and accomplices of these offenders, who are as yet at large," were present during the assault on the keeper, which "afforded strong ground of suspicion that the riot had been premeditated." One, in particular, a "woman of infamous character," had been discovered with a "cutteau knife, about 16 inches long," which the *Packet* "supposed" she intended to deliver to "one of the villains." Criminals, the paper implied, were using their numbers, their contacts, and their ability to move throughout the city streets to plot new "depredations" against the public.[10]

Escapes and attempted escapes also haunted the system of public labor. On March 1, 1787, eighteen men who had been "condemned to punishment at the *wheelbarrow*" broke out of the city jail. While free, they committed new crimes. Later in March, inmates "designed" a "general massacre or an escape." It took an armed force to suppress the attempt; one inmate was killed, and another was severely wounded. In September, "several of the convicts" attempted to escape through the city's sewers, although, after a "long and vigilant subterranean pursuit," they were recaptured. Despite the failure of this attempt, several of the inmates did escape the following week, and a general advertisement and reward for their recapture was posted. Escapes and attempted escapes—one consisting of thirty-three men—continued throughout 1788 and 1789.[11]

These struggles over internal discipline climaxed in 1789. On the evening of March 3, twenty-two of the inmates attacked and captured the jailer, John Reynolds, and one of his assistants while they were making their nightly rounds. After taking Reynolds's watch, money, and hat, and the turnkey's coat, hat, key, and pistol, the prisoners "confined them both in the dungeon." One of the prisoners, dressed in the turnkey's hat and coat, preceded the group to the outer doors where "as usual with the turnkey, [he] rattled the keys as a signal for the keeper of the outer door to come and let them out." Six

10. *Pa. Packet*, May 19, 21, 22, July 16, 1787; *Pa. Eve. Herald*, July 14, 1787.

11. The prisoners had been "condemned" to the wheelbarrow but had not yet suffered their punishment; they had been placed together while awaiting their term of servitude to begin. *Freeman's Journal*, Mar. 7, 1787, Mar. 25, 1789; *Pa. Eve. Herald*, Mar. 7, 21, 1787; *Ind. Gazetteer*, Mar. 3, 1787; *Pa. Packet*, Aug. 25, Sept. 17, 28, 29, 1787, Oct. 14, 1788, Jan. 28, Mar. 11, Aug. 1, Sept. 22, 1789; *Pa. Mercury*, Oct. 16, 1788.

of the inmates escaped before the guard realized the trick. During these events, Reynolds and his assistant had remained locked in the dungeon. But Reynolds's son, having noticed his father's hat in the possession of one of the inmates, "suspected something" and, discovering Reynolds in the dungeon, "liberated his father and his frightened companion." The jailer then organized the officers of the jail and, with the assistance of some citizens, pursued and recaptured the escaped prisoners.[12]

Despite the successful pursuit of the prisoners, the inmates had demonstrated their ability to plan collective actions, to act upon these plans decisively and in concert, and to obtain and conceal weapons. In addition, they had overpowered prison authorities with relative ease, and Reynolds had been forced to gain the assistance of private citizens in order to recapture the prisoners. The lesson seemed clear. The jail required "nightly watchfulness and daily penetration." To oversee such "rogues" was an extremely "dangerous office."[13]

Problems with internal discipline and control were not the only signs of the failures of public labor. Depictions of criminality run rampant began in November 1786. Early in the month, the *Pennsylvania Evening Herald* alerted its readers to the "audacity" of the "lurking sons of rapine." Criminals, the paper suggested, had become a constant threat, waiting for the slightest opportunity to commit "their depredations." "Many of them prowl about towards the dusk of the evening, and whenever an open door invites their entrance, they advance forward." Crime had become an "alarming evil" as "scarcely a night" elapsed "without one or more [robberies or burglaries] being committed." One house had been broken into three times in three weeks, and some of the leading figures of the city (including Francis Hopkinson and Charles Willson Peale) were among the victims of crime. These crimes struck at the peace and security of citizens' homes: "Hardly any degree of vigilance, or strength of locks, keys, bars, etc. afford protection."[14] The city and all of its citizens seemed at risk.

These images of encroaching criminality continued throughout the late 1780s. In June 1787, after a "boy" was arrested for picking a "gentleman's pocket" during a militia parade in honor of George Washington, the *Pennsylvania Packet* warned its readers that "instances of that species of crime begin to occur frequently in Pennsylvania." In September, the paper reported an "alarming encrease of robberies" in the city. The *Independent Gazetteer* pointed to the indictments for "disorderly houses, and committing assaults and battery" at the October 1787 session of the City Court as "proof of the de-

12. *Pa. Packet*, Mar. 11, 1789.
13. Ibid.
14. *Pa. Eve. Herald*, Nov. 11, 1786; *Ind. Gazetteer*, Nov. 21, 1786.

praved manners, and the contentious spirit of the times." Nor were crimes against persons limited to assaults and batteries. The following year, at the end of October, two men attacked a farming family on its way to the city market. One of the men raped the wife while the other held a gun to the husband and child. They then rode off.[15]

Many of these crimes apparently involved gangs rather than isolated individuals. In June 1787, *The Freeman's Journal* reported that a "nest of footpads" was in the suburbs and had "attacked and robbed several people on the highway." A few days later, the *Independent Gazetteer* informed its readers that, at the western edge of Market Street, a group of eight "footpads," "armed with blunderbusses and pistols," surrounded the carriage of one of the city's leading families (the Hamiltons), firing upon one of the drivers. Only quick thinking by those inside the carriage, the paper suggested, saved all from "being robbed, and perhaps murdered, by those atrocious" offenders. In November 1788, the *Pennsylvania Mercury,* professing that "our fellow-citizens cannot be too well apprized of the danger to which they are exposed, by walking in our streets," described another attack at Third and Lombard Streets. According to the paper, "eight or nine ruffians" had attacked a pedestrian, stabbing him in the back with a bayonet and cutting him under his chin with a knife. They robbed him of his shoe and knee buckles and his hat. Indeed, the possibility of collective criminality had been a continuing concern in eighteenth-century Anglo-America. Gangs, far more than wayward individuals, threatened the order and stability of a republican society.[16] The message of these events seemed clear: health, safety, and property could be lost in a moment of violence.

The internal and external instabilities of the penal system culminated in the autumn of 1789. On September 18, five wheelbarrow men escaped from jail. Later that evening, they entered a house at the end of Market Street, and, after beating one of the tenants "in the most barbarous manner," they "plundered" the house. The tenant was taken to the hospital but to no avail; he died on Saturday afternoon. On Sunday, he was buried, "attended by a large group of respectable citizens." The five wheelbarrow men were quickly retaken. Several of them, the *Pennsylvania Packet* informed its readers, had "very often been concerned in business similar . . . the merciful tenderness of the [wheelbarrow] law serving only to encourage their bloody depredations." A few weeks

15. *Pa. Packet,* June 9, Sept. 17, 1787, Nov. 10, 1788; *Ind. Gazetteer,* Oct. 29, 1787. For continuing descriptions of crimes and expressions of concern, see *Pa. Packet,* Feb. 20, Aug. 1, 1789; *Freeman's Journal,* Mar. 25, 1789.

16. *Freeman's Journal,* June 20, 1787; *Ind. Gazetteer,* June 22, 1787; *Pa. Mercury,* Nov. 1, 1788. For a discussion of fears over gangs, see Daniel A. Cohen, *Pillars of Salt, Monuments of Grace: New England Crime Literature and the Origins of American Popular Culture, 1674–1860* (New York, 1993), 138–142.

later, they were hanged in the public square near where they had committed the murder. The rigor of public execution had been called on to rectify the "depredations" that had resulted from the "tenderness of the law." [17]

Although expressions of fear of crime increased during 1785, they intensified during the period of the wheelbarrow law. In the fall of 1788, "O. T." criticized the failure of the authorities to recapture several escaped wheelbarrow men: It was inconceivable that "near forty of the most abandoned wretches ... should in a body be turned loose upon the poor defenceless country people, to steal, burn, plunder, wound and kill at pleasure." Nor, he claimed, was he alone in his anxiety: "With respect to our danger and apprehensions, I don't speak at random; I speak not only my own, but the sentiments of the neighbourhood I live in. We feel ourselves as in an enemy's country, keeping guard and losing our rest." By 1789, many believed that the city was under "attack" and that the root of the problem was the criminal law. James P. Malcolm, writing to London's *Universal Magazine of Knowledge and Pleasure*, argued that the number of convicts under the new penal code was "so much increased" that they "frequently" rose against the keeper and escaped in large numbers. The convicts "not content to rob the persons they attack . . . wound and strip them of their clothes." "There have been two or three instances of their leaving the objects of their plunder quite naked." The result was a city filled with fear: "No person . . . can venture to walk the streets or road, out of reach of the watch, after eight in the evening." Instead of securing social order on a new republican basis, the criminal law seemed to be generating ever greater criminality. [18]

17. *Pa. Packet,* Sept. 22, Oct. 13, 1789.

18. "O. T.," *Pa. Packet,* Oct. 23, 1788; *Universal Magazine of Knowledge and Pleasure* (London), July 1787, 18.

The expressions about anxieties over criminality had begun to surge during 1785. On this issue, see above, Chapter 2, and John K. Alexander, *Render Them Submissive: Responses to Poverty in Philadelphia, 1760–1800* (Amherst, Mass., 1980), 73–77, 85.

It is difficult to determine whether real criminality increased during the years of the wheelbarrow law. Dockets of the city and county courts do not exist for the period between 1787 and 1790, so it is impossible to determine whether criminal prosecutions, themselves an ambiguous indicator of actual crime, increased. But there does exist evidence suggesting that convictions were considerable (for Philadelphia) during the years of the law. One correspondent claimed that in Philadelphia courts alone nearly 160 individuals had been condemned to the wheelbarrow during the first year and a half of the law. Roberts Vaux, writing from the 1820s, claimed that prison records indicated that a high rate of commitments to the prison continued during 1788 and 1789. On the other hand, some newspaper descriptions of court sessions claim that there were relatively few convictions for those crimes that fell under the purview of the new punishment. Despite these contradictory reports, it appears that, compared to pre-Revolutionary figures, the number of those punished did increase during the mid- and late-1780s, whether or not there was an increase in real criminal activities. For evidence of a rising rate of criminality, see *Pa. Packet,* May 4, 1788; Roberts

Philadelphians responded to the evident failure of public labor and the continued presence of vice with calls for increased security and surveillance. The public papers consistently warned readers to take precautions to secure their homes and persons. The *Pennsylvania Mercury,* while reporting an escape from jail, suggested that citizens "obliged to go abroad in the evening would do well to arm themselves." Others called for an increase in the rewards offered for captured criminals. One correspondent suggested the city's residents adopt a popular English tactic and form a society for prosecuting criminals. This society would "raise a large sum of money by subscription" to be given to appointed individuals "to enable them to give adequate rewards for taking and prosecuting to conviction all house-breakers, street and highway robbers, for offences committed within certain districts, perhaps the city and liberties." Another wanted a law requiring "every housekeeper" in the city and liberties to report to a magistrate every stranger lodging with them. This increased surveillance "would do more towards the preservation of the lives and property of the citizens, than any other measure." The state used the militia on several occasions to police the city.[19] The late 1780s, then, had witnessed a search for ever-widening means to police and regulate a city increasingly divided.

II

Just as the daily practices of the wheelbarrow law overturned the imagined order of its proponents, so the practices of popular culture threatened the universalistic and rationalistic presumptions of republican culture. And just as the violence surrounding the penal scene indicated the fragmented and contentious nature of the post-Revolutionary city, so the leisure practices of many in the city—particularly plebeian men and boys—circumscribed the values of republican society. Public concern focused on the behavior of young men in taverns, at fairs, while idle, and during violations of the Sabbath. Much of male popular culture, it seems, perpetuated ancestral forms of manhood and operated outside the strictures of republican self-discipline. These behaviors, critics believed, revealed the existence of a regressive culture within the city, one that seemed to frustrate the republican experiment from within. In the realm of popular culture, individuals identified with values and practices that

---

Vaux, *Notices of the Original and Successive Efforts to Improve the Discipline of the Prisons of Philadelphia, and to Reform the Criminal Code of Pennsylvania: With a Few Observations on the Penitentiary System* (Philadelphia, 1826), 65. For skepticism about this perception, see, *Ind. Gazetteer,* Oct. 29, 1787; *Pa. Packet,* Mar. 6, 1788.

19. *Pa. Mercury,* Oct. 16, 1788; *Pa. Packet,* June 26, Aug. 2, 8, 1787, "O. T.," Oct. 23, Nov. 10, 1788, Nov. 3, 1789; *Ind. Gazetteer,* Aug. 3, 1787; *Universal Magazine of Knowledge and Pleasure,* July 1787, 18.

undermined not only the regularity of the community but the self-discipline on which republican social order was based.

Religious practice lay at the heart of the disputes over popular culture. The observance of the Sabbath, the *Pennsylvania Packet* argued, "humanizes by the help of conversation and society the manners of the lower classes; which would otherwise degenerate into a sordid ferocity and savage selfishness of spirit" while "it enables the industrious workman to pursue his occupation in the ensuing week with health and chearfulness." Religion turned laborers into citizens by "imprint[ing] on the minds of the people that sense of their duty to God so necessary to make them good citizens," a sense "which yet would be worn out and defaced by an unremitted continuance of labour, without any shared times of recalling them to the worship of their Maker."[20]

As the *Pennsylvania Packet*'s faith in religious practice indicates, post-Revolutionary reformers placed great stress on the prospect of civilizing "conversation" and "society" (in the eighteenth-century sense of a sphere where men and women would shape each other), providing mechanisms to soften manners and bind the public together. Religion would help transform workers into humanity, humanity into citizens, and citizens into a community. But the language of humanizing, imprinting, and defacing all point as well to the importance of metaphors and practices of literacy and print for republican culture. Locke had seized on the metaphor of print to describe the effects of ideas, and his suggestions that ideas and character are inscribed on the mind reverberated throughout eighteenth-century Anglo-American thought.[21]

Indeed, Benjamin Franklin's *Autobiography*, with its personal "errata" and inserted correspondence, had made the ambiguities of the notion of character—both personal and typographical—a central theme. Franklin's self-conscious treatment of his life as a text to be written, and rewritten, had demonstrated that neither the printed page nor the imprinted character was stable or constant. But, by writing the *Autobiography*, with its implicit advocacy of a mild and mannered conversational style to avoid conflict and violence, Franklin simultaneously suggested that proper conversation guided by written authority could create consensus.[22] In a similar manner, observance of the

20. "Sabbath Breaking," *Pa. Packet*, Feb. 2, 1788.

21. On this vision of "society," see G. J. Barker-Benfield, *The Culture of Sensibility: Sex and Society in Eighteenth-Century Britain* (Chicago, 1992), 91–92; Richard L. Bushman, *The Refinement of America: Persons, Houses, Cities* (New York, 1992), 46–51, 58–60; Paul Langford, *A Polite and Commercial People: England, 1727–1783* (Oxford, 1989), 99–116. On the uses of the metaphor of print, see Michael Warner, *The Letters of the Republic: Publication and the Public Sphere in Eighteenth-Century America* (Cambridge, Mass., 1990).

22. Christopher Looby, "'The Affairs Of the Revolution Occasion'd the Interruption': Writing, Revolution, Deferral, and Conciliation in Franklin's Autobiography," *American Quarterly*, XXXVIII (1986), 72–96; Warner, *Letters of the Republic*, 73–76.

Sabbath, with its humanizing effect, remained an oral activity linked implicitly with the condition of literate learning. The *Pennsylvania Packet*'s advocacy of a shared culture of reflection on the Bible suggested a vision of a restrained and authoritative conversation that could support a new republican stability.

Unfortunately, many displayed indifference to the importance of prayer. Sunday worshipers above Market Street, the *Pennsylvania Packet* claimed, were "continually disturbed by the rattling of one horse chairs and their carriages." But these displays of elite disregard were minor compared to the disrespect shown by young boys who spent their Sundays, not in dutiful worship, but "skating on the ice in winter, and swimming in summer in our river, and at all seasons playing in the streets on Sundays." These frolics, critics complained, were hardly innocent diversions: "It is a matter of certainty, that the seeds of many vices are sown in these Sunday frolicks, which bring forth abundant fruit in after life, to the discredit of themselves and relations, as well as to the injury of the state." Even apparently innocent play had its own dangers. On at least one occasion, a boy playing at the river fell in and drowned. But young boys did more than frolic irreligiously (and self-destructively) on Sunday. "Wicked boys" were also "fond of fighting" among themselves—fighting that could lead to injury and death. And, in doing so, they posed a danger to more than themselves. "It is not uncommon," the *Freeman's Journal* insisted, "to meet half a dozen unlucky boys, late in the evening, returning (sometimes intoxicated) with fowling pieces on their shoulders, charged with small shot, after an afternoon's diversion of bird-shooting." These meetings often worked to the disadvantage of "peaceful citizens," who, if they "should come in their way, it is very probable . . . will be insulted." And "many are the accidents that happen to women and children who may be riding in their carriages, as it is a certain rule with those lads of powder to fire away all the ammunition as they traverse the road to their affectionate mothers."[23] Here, the boys practically personified a parody of the classical republican notion of the importance of martial capacity to the exercise of virtue. Drink, idleness, and guns were brought together in these "unlucky boys" who brought all into danger.

In their lack of consideration for "women and children who may be riding in their carriages," these boys also reenacted the truculent qualities of English aristocratic male culture. As the literature of the rake recorded, aristocratic practices after the Restoration and through the eighteenth century contained more than their share of openly displayed violence. Groups of young "gentlemen," some organized into clubs, made pastimes of the open harassment of

23. *Pa. Packet*, Feb. 10, 1787, "V. M.," Nov. 28, 1788; "A. B.," *Ind. Gazetteer*, Mar. 2, 1787. Benjamin Rush, *Essays: Literary, Moral and Philosophical* (1806), ed. Michael Meranze (Schenectady, N.Y., 1988), 70; *Freeman's Journal*, Aug. 13, 17, 1791.

women they encountered in public thoroughfares. Although perhaps more sporadic, these practices made their way to Philadelphia. In 1761, for example, a group of young men—"sons and relatives of some of the most respectable citizens"—attacked women they met "by cutting their gowns and petticoats with a razor." In 1787, the *Pennsylvania Mercury* reported that "a young coxcomb who had made too free with the bottle," and had "staggered" in pursuit of "a lady of delicate dress and shape . . . laid hold of her hand, and peering under the large hat, told her that he did not like her as well *before* as *behind*, but not withstanding, he would be glad of a favour of a kiss." The lady, the *Mercury* reported happily, "replied, 'with all my heart, Sir, if you will do me the favour to kiss the part you like best.'"[24] When young plebeian boys went out, displaying themselves and imperiling others, they mirrored their social betters.

Even greater sources of contention were the taverns and disorderly houses dotting the city. Observers suggested that the number of taverns in the city was uncommonly great. These taverns, they claimed, corrupted the young and threatened to undermine the Revolutionary experiment. "Low taverns and tippling-houses," one commentator suggested, were "in all large cities, the bane of youth, and the nocturnal haunts of sharpers, robbers and ruffians of every description." Taverns were "the very root of vice."[25] They seduced the young from proper habits and encouraged the vicious in improper ones.

At the same time, taverns threatened to draw servants and laborers away from their duty to their masters and employers. The conviction, in City Court, of one tavern keeper offers an example of the concern these houses provoked. The owner ran a tavern that, according to the public papers, was "a place of resort for all the loose and idle characters of the city, whether whites, blacks or mulattoes." Even more dangerous, "frequently in the night gentlemen's servants would arrive there, mounted on their masters horses . . . and indulge in riotous mirth and dancing till the dawn when they posted again to their respective homes." To the *Pennsylvania Packet*, this conviction made clear "the growing nuisance of the cabins in the suburbs of the city, occupied by free negroes," and the paper urged that masters take greater care to "watch the conduct of their servants, who may in these nocturnal excursions, commit a greater outrage upon their property than the midnight robber." The tippling houses on the outskirts of the city, many believed, were the sites of an alterna-

24. Barker-Benfield, *The Culture of Sensibility*, 37–55; John F. Watson, *Annals of Philadelphia and Pennsylvania, in the Olden Time; Being a Collection of Memoirs, Anecdote, and Incidents of the City and Its Inhabitants, and of the Earliest Settlements of the Inland Part of Pennsylvania, from the Days of the Founders . . .* 2 vols. (Philadelphia, 1857), I, 310; *Pa. Mercury*, May 18, 1787. On issues of young male criminality, see Teeters, *The Cradle of the Penitentiary*, 23–26.

25. *Pa. Packet*, Oct. 30, 1788, "A Well-wisher to Sots," Feb. 4, June 30, 1789.

tive, interracial, lower-class culture that offered an escape, however temporary, from the demands of masters and employers.[26]

Like taverns, fairs offered opportunities for the laboring classes to remove
themselves from daily discipline and supervision. Traditionally, Philadelphians had celebrated fairs twice yearly, once in November and once in May. To
their critics, at least, fairs were breeding grounds for vice and disorder: they
"had such an influence in spreading vices of all kinds thro' our county. Drinking, gaming, swearing, etc. etc., are their usual attendants." Benjamin Rush
argued that fairs were particularly dangerous for a republic: "They tempt
to extravagance—gaming—drunkenness—and uncleanness. They are proper
only in despotic states, where the more a people are corrupted, the more readily they submit to arbitrary government."[27] Left dependent on their passions
and vices, citizens would fall into new forms of political dependence; taverns
and fairs encouraged excess, and such self-abandon, Rush and others suggested, laid the groundwork for political despots.

These attacks on taverns and fairs were rooted in a wider hostility toward
liquor. Drunkenness, critics charged, was "totally incompatible with every
idea of civilization." Drinking was not only self-destructive; it led to greater
and greater offenses against the community, the habit of drinking was inextricably linked to other habits of vice and crime. Dissolving the self-control necessary for virtue, drinking stimulated a continuing cycle of depravity and
deprivation and "to its own peculiar curse of incorrigibility, it adds the more
fatal and deplorable one of conferring strength and permanency upon every
criminal habit we have contracted."[28] Instead of remaining obedient to the
rules of propriety, drinkers became enslaved to their vice. Intemperance destroyed the virtue and discipline demanded of the republican citizen.

Just as important, drinking weakened the capacity for labor. One commentator went so far as to suggest that sobriety should be the primary test for employment: "Ask the man who offers to serve, or to work for you—not, are you

26. Ibid., Aug. 6, 1787; reprinted in *Ind. Gazetteer,* Aug. 8, 1787.

For studies of lower-class culture, see Eric Foner, *Tom Paine and Revolutionary America*
(New York, 1976), 19–56; Steven Rosswurm, "Arms, Culture, and Class: The Philadelphia
Militia and 'Lower Orders' in the American Revolution, 1765–1783" (Ph.D. diss., Northern
Illinois University, 1979), chap. 1; Billy Smith, "Down Those Mean Streets" (paper pre-
sented to the Seminar of the Philadelphia Center for Early American Studies, December
1984). For a wide-ranging discussion of the experiences of black Philadelphians with the
late-18th-century criminal justice system and the attitudes of white Philadelphians toward
the possibility and actuality of crimes committed by black Philadelphians, see G. S. Rowe,
"Black Offenders, Criminal Courts, and Philadelphia Society in the Late Eighteenth-
Century," *Journal Of Social History,* XXII (1989), 685–712.

27. Rosswurm, "Arms, Culture, and Class," 48–49; *Pa. Packet,* Oct. 9, 1789; Rush, *Essays,*
ed. Meranze, 68. On suppression of the fairs, see Rosswurm, "Arms, Culture, and Class," 49.

28. *Pa. Packet,* Aug. 15, 1789, May 25, 26, 1790. See also Rush, *Essays,* ed. Meranze, 67–68.

acquainted with the business you undertake to do—or have you a character or a certificate of your good behaviour—But simply ask him, '*Do you drink Rum?*'—and at the same time smell his breath. If you find that he is addicted to drinking rum, have nothing more to say to him." Here lay the critics' great fear. To them, drunkenness and idleness were not merely compatible; they were causally connected. Liquor was not only an unfortunate vice, it destroyed the everyday self-discipline necessary for productive labor.[29]

For critics of drinking, eliminating intemperance and diminishing the number of taverns were crucial steps in the establishment of a republican culture and polity. Drunkenness, they argued, was an unfortunate legacy from darker, less enlightened societies: "We should not expect to find a practice [drunkenness] continue among a civilized people, the tendency of which is to debase the man below the brute, to ruin his health, and to annihilate the faculties of his mind. We would naturally be led to look for such a vice, only in the darkest ages of ignorance." But sobriety was more than merely the negation of drunkenness. Its proponents saw it as a positive and necessary component of true virtue. "As a proneness to drinking," "Cato" argued, "leads a man into a variety of evils, which he never thought of, so an inflexible sobriety engages a man into good habits, which he could never have otherwise acquired."[30]

Not all agreed with Cato on the necessity of an "inflexible sobriety." Drinking, after all, had been, and continued to be, a central locus of gentlemanly sociability in Philadelphia. And, taverns and inns had been deeply tied to the spread of commercial networks and merchant activities. But tavern drinking, once a communal practice, increasingly was differentiated across class lines and, among elites at least, was domesticated. This differentiation made it possible to link plebeian tavern drinking with monarchical behavior and to see it as a threat to the Republic. Plebeian taverns were both far removed from genteel drinking and uncannily close. Like the young boys with their fowling pieces, plebeian taverns perpetuated earlier practices, practices rooted in the male culture of nascent capitalism.[31] But from the perspective of republican

29. *Pa. Packet,* July 24, Oct. 13, 1788, "A Well-wisher to Sots," Feb. 4, 1789.

Rush believed: Liquors "render the temper peevish and passionate. They beget quarrels, and lead to profane and indecent language. They are the parents of idleness and extravagance, and the certain forerunners of poverty, and frequently of jails, wheelbarrows, and the gallows." Rush, *Essays,* ed. Meranze, 67. See also Benjamin Rush to *Pa. Journal,* June 22, 1782, in L. H. Butterfield, ed., *Letters of Benjamin Rush,* 2 vols. (Princeton, N.J., 1951), I, 271.

30. "Cato," *Pa. Packet,* Jan. 30, 1788, "A Well-wisher to Sots," Feb. 4, 1789, May 25, 1790; Rush, *Essays,* ed. Meranze, 115.

31. For some examples of youthful genteel drinking, see Alexander Graydon, *Memoirs of His Own Time, with Reminiscences of the Men and Events of the Revolution,* ed. John Stockton Littell (Philadelphia, 1846), 80–82, 92–94. For broader discussions of the importance of drinking to patrician culture in the city, see Peter Thompson, "A Social History of Philadel-

values, drinking, especially unsupervised plebeian drinking, was a barbarous and antirepublican practice, yet another sign of the incompleteness of Revolutionary enlightenment.

The dynamic of example and identification, critics charged, meant that idleness, in turn, bred poverty and vice. For the idle, "Monitor" argued, the dangers of seductive vices were ever present: "A man void, of industry, is as it were empty, and vicious thoughts run in upon as air into an empty space, and make deep impressions on the heart." And, commentators argued, this emptiness was all too often filled with the image of, and desire for, luxury. The search for luxury helped expand poverty; individuals seeking to emulate the riches of their fellows were compelled to live beyond their means. It was in their gaming, their display of wealth, and their languid recreation that the wealthy reinforced the poor in their poverty. "In a free government, like that of Pennsylvania," asserted Cato, "nothing is so prevalent as example. The conduct of a few rich men, excite similar dispositions in others, who wish to imitate, because they judge them honorable and happy. This childish emulation has become so habitual, that, like an epidemic disorder, it pervades every part of the state."[32]

From this perspective, the power of imitation was powerfully expansive. Imitation seemed both seduction and contagion, the unthinking poor ("as it were empty") were overwhelmed by the power of vicious example. Luxury, critics charged, drew individuals into the pits of indolence and vice. As the *Pennsylvania Packet* saw it, the demands of luxury destroyed self-control, leading individuals inexorably to their ruin: "A man once engaged in this extravagant course of living, seldom is able to extricate himself in time. . . . He is now no more master of himself, but like a drowning man catches at every thing, even his dearest friend, though he should perish with him. To what extremities will not this melancholy situation lead a man; to poverty, shame, villainy, dependency, and disgrace." Luxury paradoxically linked the wealthy and the idle; the wealthy's example drew the poor into the snares of luxury and vice.[33]

---

phia's Taverns, 1683–1800" (Ph.D. diss., University of Pennsylvania, 1989), 30–54; Thompson, "'The Friendly Glass': Drink and Gentility in Colonial Philadelphia," *PMHB*, CXIII (1989), 549–573. On the ties between male tavern culture and the emergence of capitalist relations in early modern Britain, see Barker-Benfield, *The Culture of Sensibility*, 50–53.

32. "Monitor," *Pa. Packet*, Jan. 14, 1786, June 11, 1787; "Cato," *Pa. Mercury*, June 3, 1788. This was the same Cato who wrote the defense of capital punishments discussed below in Chapter 4. For another discussion of luxury and idleness, see "A. B.," *Pa. Packet*, July 11, 1787.

33. "The Fatal Consequences of Luxury," *Pa. Packet*, July 9, 1785, "A. B.," July 11, 1787, Nov. 11, 1789; *Ind. Gazetteer*, June 11, 1785. John K. Alexander contends that the argument linking luxury, viciousness, and the idle poor was a way of constructing the category of the

Luxury not only propelled mimetic corruption it also stood in ambiguous proximity to the normal structures of the capitalist economy. Consumption, after all, was actively promoted for the "better sorts," the purchase and display of appropriate commodities a crucial mechanism for performing gentility. The distance between luxury and the values of genteel society was always unstable; one passed easily from discrete gentility to extravagant luxury and vice. The linking of luxury, vice, and poverty was a rhetorical attempt to police the boundaries between acceptable and unacceptable desire, to make certain that the pursuit of pleasure remained within the bounds of appropriate gentility and within the hands of the genteel themselves. Excess on the part of the wealthy or the poor threatened to disrupt the precarious stability of genteel authority.[34] Like unruly conversation or plebeian drinking, luxury marked an inverted continuation of the practices of proper society.

Nothing indicated the tenacity of schisms within the city's culture more clearly than the assaults, in the spring and summer of 1787, on a woman accused of witchcraft. Beginning in May, "an antient woman residing near the New-market" was "upon a supposition she was a witch . . . cut in the forehead, according to antient and immemorial custom." These attacks continued, despite her appeals to the legal authorities. On July 10, "she was carried through several of the streets, and was hooted and pelted as she passed along." When a "gentleman" tried to help her, he was "greatly insulted," whereas those who accused her "were listened to with curiosity and attention." Nor did the attacks stop there. "Several outrages" were "most barbarously committed upon her by some white savages." On July 18, the woman died. Accusations of witchcraft, it seemed, were more credible to the city's "white savages" than attempts to prove its impossibility.[35]

Beneath the surface of enlightened republicanism lurked another, more mysterious culture. To the public commentators, these proceedings demonstrated the persistence of barbarous superstition. The belief in witchcraft was contrary to all reason; it was "ridiculous and abominable." Such beliefs could affect only a "certain class of ignorant people"; only "an ignorant and inhuman mob" would have attacked the elderly woman. The fear of witches was a "belief so horrid [it] is a picture of the greatest weakness in human nature,

---

"respectable poor" and of teaching the poor and middling sorts to remain satisfied with their lot. If Cato's connection between luxury and moral decay was true, after all, then luxury was something not to be sought after, and the rich, at least the idle rich, were not to be blindly emulated. See, Alexander, *Render Them Submissive*, 53–59.

34. On the links between gentility, luxury, and the authority of the genteel, see Bushman, *The Refinement of America*, 182–197.

35. *Ind. Gazetteer*, July 17, 1787; *Pa. Packet*, May 11, July 16, 17, 1787. The *Packet* reported that her death was a "consequence of the barbarous treatment [she had] lately suffered."

and can only source from a mind coiled up in its scanty orbit, replete with dormant prejudices, and thick with the grossest original ignorance."[36]

This alternative culture threatened the Revolutionary experiment. Republicanism presumed that the rational consent and freedom of the citizens were the foundations of any just social order. But, if witches could control the fate of others, the whole notion of consent and choice was meaningless. Witchcraft "would destroy our free agency and activity, the offsprings of the Divinity itself, and reduce man to a passive, inanimate, and stupid Being." It would deny the possibility of human progress: "In fine, it would controul the grand course of Providence, and abuse the sacred and sublime decrees of Heaven, which have directed man (if he chooses) like Mary of old, to take the better part, and be both sociable and happy!" The crowd's actions were "disgraceful to a country like this" and were "destructive of the peace of society, and that personal security, every man and woman have a right to look for, where laws are to govern and not barbarity and superstition." The belief in witchcraft, in effect, denied the reality (and, indeed, the possibility) of a law-governed world. It was a direct affront to the idea of a society governed in accord with the Enlightenment. Such superstitions had no place in a republican society; superstition was the monarchy of the mind. If men and women were enslaved to superstition (or were enslaved to their vices), they could not function as republican citizens.[37]

The public papers demanded that legal action be taken against the crowds. In part, these demands were made to protect (or, later, to avenge) the endangered woman. But the newspapers' concerns were more general. The papers argued that, if the authorities were not able to combat the fear of witchcraft, the credulity of youth would ensure that superstitions would be transmitted across the generations. The "illiterate and youthful" were especially prone to the dangers of corruptive influences. As the *Pennsylvania Packet* put it, they called for legal action "not merely for the sake of the wretched object herself . . . but for the sake of the illiterate and youthful part of the society, who will naturally imagine that the charge of sorcery must be just, when such persecution is publicly practiced with impunity."[38]

36. *Ind. Gazetteer*, July 17, 1787; *Pa. Packet*, May 11, July 16, 1787.

37. *Ind. Gazetteer*, July 17, 1787. This belief in witchcraft was also threatening because it denied the divine rationality of the world: "To suppose any man or woman should have absolute dominion to annoy and injure their fellow creatures, and make them miserable 'at will and pleasure,' is undoubtedly impious to an extreme, and at once removing God himself from his exalted station in the celestial system and arrangement of affairs!" The faith in witchcraft denied the efficacy of both divine and human laws. It implied that the world was arbitrary, subject to the whims and powers of the devil and his disciples. *Pa. Packet*, May 11, 1787.

38. *Pa. Packet*, May 11, July 16, 1787; *Ind. Gazetteer*, July 23, 1787.

The city, then, contained many worlds. At the October 1787 session of the City Court, a woman indicted for her part in the assaults on the alleged witch offered her defense. Before the judges, she "maintained the justice of that opinion" (that the old woman had been a witch) "and insinuated her belief that her only child sickened and died under the malignant influence of a *charm*." Confronted with this folk belief, one of the judges could not restrain his scorn, declaring it "an idle and absurd superstition" that a "poor wretch whose sorrows and infirmities have sunk her eyes into her head, and whose features are streaked with the wrinkles of old age, should therefore become an object of terror, and be endowed with the powers of witchcraft." Marking the distance between himself and the accused, he suggested: "If, however, some damsels that I have seen, animated with the bloom of youth, and equipped with all the grace of beauty, if such women were indicted for the offense, the charge might receive some countenance, for they are indeed calculated to *charm* and *bewitch* us." The justice's casual sarcasm condensed the entire struggle over the witchcraft incident. From the perspective of the defendant, it was the accused witch who represented the emergence of the uncanny in everyday life (her capacity to slay a child with a charm). But, to the judge and the public papers, who trivialized the notion of a powerful "charm," reducing it to the commonplaces of the language of genteel beauty, it was the popular belief in witchcraft that was uncanny. It was in this conflict, and this reversal of the uncanny, that the tragedy of the accused witch was transformed into a symptom of the state of Revolutionary society.[39]

39. *Pa. Packet,* Oct. 29, 1787. In speaking of the "uncanny" here, I am drawing on Sigmund Freud's analysis. Freud suggested that uncanny experiences—which combined a feeling of dread and unease with sensations of repetition and familiarity—occurred when one confronted "something familiar and old-established in the mind that has been estranged only by the process of repression." See Freud, "The Uncanny," in Ernest Jones et al., eds., 5 vols., *Collected Papers,* trans. Joan Riviere et al. (London, 1953), IV, 394. Freud understood this process primarily in terms of childhood repression. But in order to make his argument, he was forced to draw on both etymology and modern aesthetics—more precisely, the aesthetics of the early 19th century. Freud, in other words, drew from the effects of modern aesthetics and culture a transhistorical principle.

Although borrowing from Freud's sense of the uncanny, I propose to reverse that process and read the uncanny less as a universal psychological phenomenon than as a historically located sociocultural one. Certain forms of the cultural uncanny, at least, were rooted in the transatlantic movements of Enlightenment and Revolution that aimed to efface lingering practices of superstition and indiscipline. And, although Freud focused his attention on European examples, this threatening uncanny—as the battle over the meaning of this witch indicates—appeared as well in Revolutionary and post-Revolutionary America. Eighteenth-century Philadelphians, it is true, did not employ the language of "uncanniness" to describe popular social practices. But Philadelphia's popular culture did appear, to those seeking to expand republican self-discipline, to manifest something "old and familiar" that they wished to "estrange by the process of repression." In this context,

As with public labor, popular practices and beliefs raised questions about republican discipline and its limits. In the case of witch-hunting, the aggressiveness and violence of popular culture was directly, and fatally, imposed on an isolated old woman. As the continued ineffectivenss of the public papers indicated, at least part of the city was beyond the reach of literary suasion. And, as the images of "peaceful citizens" and "affectionate mothers" suggest, these discussions contained both class anxiety and a critique of plebeian womanhood: it was the tolerance of "affectionate" mothers that allowed boys to avoid the Sabbath, endanger their "peaceful" neighbors, and devolve into threats to society.[40] Implicitly, at least, these critics suggested that the failings of plebeian motherhood returned to endanger the existence of women.

At the same time, the dread of interracial comradery at taverns run by free blacks or the reduction of the "lower classes" to "white savages" marked by "sordid ferocity and savageness of spirit" mobilized images of racial inferiority. The discourse about public disorder framed the city's lower sorts as primitive savages, equating them with native Americans while linking their indiscipline to blacks. The city streets seemed dangerously to blur class, sex, and racial boundaries, a blurring that demonstrated the precariousness of republican civilization. The continuing presence of unsupervised youths indicated basic failings in the practice of domestic and civil government—particularly with regard to laboring-class boys.[41]

These criticisms of Sabbath breaking, taverns, fairs, and superstition were less responses to new social developments than signs of a larger devaluation of traditional social customs and assumptions. To take another example, the city's lower classes traditionally had "shot in" the New Year. Commentators viewed this activity with particular hostility. In 1787, the *Independent Gazetteer* declared it a "ridiculous custom" and a "mischievous practice." In 1793, Elizabeth Drinker echoed these sentiments in noting that some were "now practis-

---

social practices were redescribed as regressive or barbaric and constituted as what Freud would later call "uncanny." It was, in part, in their becoming uncanny that the practices of popular culture found their republican significance. On the centrality of early-19th-century literature and aesthetic theories to Freud's notion of the uncanny, see Anthony Vidler, *The Architectural Uncanny: Essays in the Modern Unhomely* (Cambridge, Mass., 1992), 17–44. Vidler also stresses the importance of the spatial to the uncanny, a point that I will return to in Chapter 5.

For a recent argument that the 18th century effectively "invented" the uncanny through its practices of rationalization, see Terry Castle, *The Female Thermometer: Eighteenth-Century Culture and the Invention of the Uncanny* (New York, 1995), 3–15.

40. *Freeman's Journal,* Aug. 17, 1791.

41. *Pa. Packet,* Mar. 3, 1787. For a discussion in the 1790s on the relationship between the government of youth and civil order and authority, see Mathew Clarkson, *An Address to the Citizens of Philadelphia, respecting the Better Government of Youth* (Philadelphia, 1795).

ing the foolish custom of firing out the old year."[42] To these critics, the perpetuation of "foolish," "ridiculous," and "mischievous" customs was a sign of the limits of Revolutionary enlightenment.

The city's popular culture, then, continued to mirror aristocratic and plebeian practices against which republican cultural criticism was directed. Whether gentry followed plebs or plebs followed gentry is not clear. But the uncanny inversions that accompanied the relationship of genteel to popular culture suggested a city whose communicative economy was producing, not self-discipline, but a spiral of dangerous frivolity. As high and low avoided the strictures of republican order, mimetic corruption seemed to haunt the Revolutionary vision.

III

Despite the violence and insubordination of the city's popular culture, the clearest example of mimetic corruption was the penal scene itself. Public labor appeared a moving and open wound on the social body. As convicts moved through the streets, drawing the interest and consideration of onlookers, as the wheelbarrow men planned and attempted their escapes, as fears of crime and criminality within the city grew, the excesses of the penal scene appeared to mark an ineffective law turning a world upside down. To its critics, public labor spawned a cycle of dangerous mimicry and contagion. Conversation, critics of the wheelbarrow law argued, counteracted the terror of the penalty, while the seduction and repulsion of the penal scene spread chaos throughout the city. Public labor, and the wheelbarrow men who embodied it, blurred social categories: mercy, justice, charity, and cruelty were all disrupted and inverted. Just as popular culture had offered a reversed form of religious practice, so the penal scene mirrored and subverted the genteel hope for sensible dialogue.[43]

The dangers of communication among criminals, critics charged, began within the scene of punishment itself. Companionship, the *Pennsylvania Evening Herald* insisted, destroyed the power of the punishment, rendering the criminals "unaffected" by their condition: "They laugh, sing and swear in their chains." Even worse, communication and association, critics charged, enabled prisoners to organize insubordination and escape. Although many incidents of resistance to penal discipline and authority were individual or spontaneous, others, critics of public labor believed, were "designed" or "premeditated." They linked the inmates' capacity for planned collective action to

42. *Ind. Gazetteer*, Jan. 3, 1787; Drinker, cited in Rosswurm, "Arms, Culture, and Class," 52.
43. For the hopes that 18th-century genteel society placed on proper conversation to enliven and enlarge the mind, see Bushman, *The Refinement of America*, 83–89.

their communication while at labor in the streets. During public labor, "many" prisoners, "being employed together," had the opportunity of "further corrupting one another, and entering into combinations to do mischief."[44] The freedom to communicate and organize within the prison or while in the streets appeared to make collective action possible.

Criminals' speech not only increased the opportunity to resist penal discipline; it expanded criminality itself. Reformers assumed that vice and criminality developed from "diseased" habits. Criminality, according to the *Pennsylvania Packet,* was a "contagion of villainy" spread by "evil communication." A too "promiscuous" association among inmates assured the "corruption" of "young sinners." In fact, one commentator wrote, though the "vices of the lower class of people" could be "contracted" in the streets and the taverns, it was the indiscriminate confinement of criminals that brought it to its greatest degree of "perfection." The "finished villain and the half sinner associate, and the latter profits by the example of the former."[45] The new system, critics argued, actually reinforced criminality.

But communication among inmates was only one danger; when citizens gathered around the prisoners and joked with them, or spoke with them, they destroyed the terror of the punishment. Public labor sought not only to impose hard labor but to break the moral habits of the inmates, to eliminate not just "indolence" but "vice" and "licentiousness." Toward this goal, prisoners were expected to endure a "spare diet and hard labour." But the communication and charity that accompanied the public display of the laborers prevented this transformative process. The "effect" of punishment was "greatly lessened by many unthinking people who converse with these felons in the streets." The "great disadvantage" of the crowds of onlookers, the *Independent Gazetteer* suggested, was that "a number of well disposed persons (from mistaken humanity)" not only conversed with the laborers but also gave the prisoners money that "enabled" them "to procure liquor." Conversation and association, as it were, had replaced labor as the dominant experience of the condemned. "Begging, drinking and conversation" were the "prevailing employments" of the prisoners. It was "more common," one commentator complained, "to see these wretches staggering with intoxication, than with the weight of their burthens," thereby eliminating "all hope of reformation or example."[46]

44. *Pa. Eve. Herald,* Mar. 21, Apr. 28, 1787; *Ind. Gazetteer,* Mar. 22, 1787; *Pa. Packet,* May 22, June 26, 1787.

45. *Pa. Packet,* May 14, June 26, July 14 (reprinted from *Glasgow Mercury,* Mar. 10, 1787), Sept. 4, 1787. The criticism of the indiscriminate mingling of inmates within a prison was a call for better classification, not an attack on the idea of imprisonment.

46. *Pa. Eve. Herald,* July 14, 1787; *Pa. Packet,* May 5, 21, "Dennis K——Y," Aug. 3, 1787; *Ind. Gazetteer,* Mar. 31, 1787. For a discussion of the statute itself, see above in Chapter 2.

This charity, commentators argued, encouraged the very habits that the penal system hoped to destroy. With the prisoners "living in the exercise and gratifications of those very dispositions [from] which they are . . . to be reclaimed," there was no hope of reformation. Even the violence surrounding the scene of punishment was, in part, attributed to this charity. Supplying the criminals with liquor was an action that "never fail[ed]" to lead to "riot," and made "severity" toward the inmates "unavoidable." Corruption and contamination of the prisoners continued; it was no surprise that the streets were filled with "horrid scenes."[47]

This disruptive and unthinking sympathy extended even into the administration of justice. One correspondent charged, that of ninety-eight individuals convicted during the law's first year of offenses of the "base kind," because of the "lenity of government, and by escape," almost half had avoided their punishment. This executive laxness had to be pernicious: "The extreme facility with which pardons are obtained [by destroying the certainty of punishment], must have invited to crime." Even worse, he insisted, these numbers only represented those who had been prosecuted successfully. Although he could not determine how many "favoured by the tenderness of prosecutors, want of evidence, non-attendance of witnesses, artful defence of counsel, and mistakes and reluctance of jurors, had eluded justice," it "probably" exceeded the number of those convicted under the new punishment. "Ill-judged favors, mistaken lenity, or groundless fears" had "too often superseded" the imposition of legal penalties. Government officials and the public had allowed themselves a "too great indulgence of humane feelings," thereby destroying the basis of moderate yet certain punishments.[48]

Critics of public labor argued that the government and public misunderstood the "true" relationship between mercy and justice under the reformed penal code. Under the old code, mercy had been necessary to mitigate the "cruelty" of punishment. But moderate punishments obliterated this need; mercy consisted, not in mitigating punishment, but in imposing it. "Deeper insight" established that the "impartial and strict execution of the moderate sentences under this law, would be the truest exercise of mercy." The effectiveness of moderate punishments presupposed "energetic government"; justice and mercy were joined.[49] Here was the classic case of a sympathy misguided by a thoughtless sensibility.

47. "E. G.," *Ind. Gazetteer*, May 19, 1787; *Pa. Packet*, May 21, 22, 1787.

48. The correspondent reported that 27 convicts had been pardoned, 17 had escaped, and 2 had died. *Pa. Packet*, May 14, Aug. 22, 1787, May 14, 1788. The May 1788 article was a summary of a report prepared for the General Assembly on the effects of the penal law.

49. *Pa. Packet*, Aug. 22, 1787, May 14, 1788. The frequency of escapes was also attributed to the lack of energetic government combined with the difficulties of controlling prisoners while they labored in public.

Commentators also claimed that the cruelty and indifference spectators displayed toward the convicts debased both criminals and citizens. The imposition of infamy through public labor, one argued, would neither reform nor reclaim. Every face, the *Pennsylvania Evening Herald* insisted, became hostile, the criminal "an outcast on the face of the earth, like Cain he is doomed to shun the day, and to associate, ever after, with the most depraved of the human species." Even worse, cruelty begot cruelty. The "dreadful spectacles of human misery and depravity" only hardened the citizenry and turned them away from virtue. The effect of the wheelbarrow act was to "plant and water [vice] everywhere." [50]

The wheelbarrow law, these observers argued, combined psychological cruelty with excessive material generosity. Instead of subjecting criminals to discipline and deprivation, the practice of public labor indulged them in their licentious desires. Public labor was an escape, not a punishment, for the poor; it encouraged criminality as a means to obtain food, clothing, liquor, and shelter. "It requires too much virtue," the *Pennsylvania Packet* declared, for a poor person "to preserve his integrity in want and wretchedness, when the conveniences of life may be purchased by the smallest deviation from the rules of honesty." [51] By drawing the poor toward criminality and subjecting them to degradation as punishment, critics suggested, public labor was not only cruel to its subjects, it also corrupted the general community.

Critics simultaneously sympathized with and were repulsed by the convicts. Some viewed the wheelbarrow men through the lens of Christian charity, seeing criminals as "unfortunate fellow creatures" still "related to us by the ties of a common Creator and Redeemer." But more common was another language of criminality. Here the prisoners were a threat, dehumanized and animalistic. They were "rogues," "villains," and "lurking sons of rapine" who "prowl[ed]" and "plundered." Their "dissolute dispositions" led to the "corruption" and "infection" of themselves and the community. From this perspective, criminality posed a threat to more than just the persons and property of individuals. The corruption of criminals, when combined with public display, threatened to infect the entire community. [52]

The critics, however, displayed equal ambivalence toward the general public. They accused the public of being both too sympathetic toward the condemned and too indifferent to their fate. So long as criminals were punished

---

50. *Pa. Eve. Herald*, Mar. 24, 1787; *Pa. Packet*, Sept. 18, 1788.

51. *Pa. Packet*, June 7, 1787.

52. Ibid., Sept. 18, 1788. See also The Philadelphia Society for Alleviating the Miseries of Public Prisons, *Constitution* (Philadelphia, 1787). The discourse of mimetic corruption was not limited to Philadelphia. For similar fears of the contagious example of criminality as expressed in England, see Randall McGowen, "The Body and Punishment in Eighteenth-Century England," *Journal of Modern History*, LIX (1987), 656–666.

in public, they would seduce and repel onlookers. Neither the realm of public meaning nor the virtue of the populace was stable enough to support a penal system based upon public display and example. As a consequence, the debates over public labor, although focused on the display and communication of criminals, implicated the very structure of post-Revolutionary society and post-Revolutionary identity. More than a mere problem of criminal justice, the significance of the wheelbarrow men and their public response radiated far beyond the penal scene; they posed in stark terms not only the form of the law but the nature of obedience and authority in the new Republic.

The critique of public labor and mimetic corruption pointed in two directions: toward the analysis of individual character and toward the organization of society itself. A letter purportedly from one of the wheelbarrow men, "Dennis K——Y," to his brother "Patrick" manifested clearly these contradictory perceptions. In the letter, which appeared in the *Pennsylvania Packet* in August 1787, Dennis described how he had been condemned to public labor, his convict experience, and the crowds that witnessed his punishment. In the telling, he attacked the system of public punishment for being too generous and too harsh to both the public and the criminal. Dennis spoke for the values of middling discipline that were so central to public labor. Attacking both indolence and financial manipulation, he positioned himself on the side of honest laborers and censured both high and low for threatening the Republic. From Dennis K——Y's perspective, the wheelbarrow law was symptomatic of a society that blurred the distinction between the poor and the criminal. Doing so from within the discourse of mimetic corruption, he acknowledged the failed attempt to transparently represent vice and virtue. And he explicitly linked the problems of crime and punishment to the fundamental structures of society.[53]

Dennis explained to Patrick that he had been unable to find honest labor when he landed in Philadelphia. He was unemployed, however, not from a lack of desire, but owing to the "decay of trade and business of all kinds since the peace." Left without any regular means to support himself (he was able "now and then" to earn "a shilling or eighteen-pence by piling wood"), he spent "many whole days . . . without eating any thing," and his "nights were passed under the shambles, or in hay-lofts" outside the city.

He soon learned that Pennsylvania had begun to punish theft with labor rather than with hanging or whipping. The provisions of the statute, he reported, provided that all "who suffered its penalties should be well fed, cloathed and lodged." These, he averred, were "all I wanted, and I had no objection to working for them." He "therefore joined a company of strolling

---

53. "Dennis K——Y," *Pa. Packet*, Aug. 3, 1787. The quotations in the following six paragraphs are taken from this source.

footpads" but found that his "conscience shuddered" at assisting them in a planned robbery, and he "declined" the opportunity. But when they returned with their "booty," he discovered that it consisted "in part of good eatables," and he "chearfully partook of it."

Soon after, the authorities seized him and his companions and condemned them to the wheelbarrow. But Dennis had no complaints about his fate. "I embraced my situation with thankfulness. I work, it is true, constantly in the streets of Philadelphia, but . . . our beef and bread are excellent, and our keepers are kind to those of us who behave as we ought to do." The women and children of the city conversed with the prisoners and gave them alms "to buy liquor and tobacco." Indeed, Dennis concluded, he had "never lived better in [his] life." He suggested that Patrick join him and bring all of their "cousins and play-fellows," if they could do so without "disgracing" themselves.

But Dennis countered this idyllic picture with another view of the penal scene. He urged his brother to hurry, because, otherwise, "the people of the country will get into place before you." Dennis believed that the spectators "follow and croud about so constantly, and listen with so much eagerness to our conversation"—which he was "sorry to say" was "both profane and absurd"—because they were "preparing themselves by idleness, and a familiarity with wickedness, to follow our example." He reported that some "visionary gentlemen have proposed that we should work out of light, to prevent our infecting the good people of the State, with our example." But he doubted that such a plan would be implemented. Pennsylvanians were "too jealous of their liberties" ever to "surrender the power of punishing" by their own hands. Even more important, the citizens would lose a cruel and pleasurable sport if convicts labored indoors:

> As bull-baiting and slavery are forbidden by the laws of the State the citizens of Pennsylvania would have no idea of the diversion of the former, or of the cruelty of the latter practice, should we be sentenced to work out of their sight; for in spite of the resentment and morality of their laws, they show by the delight they take in looking at us, that cruelty and chains are not repugnant to their feelings, and that they enjoy the *hating* and degradation of their species with a malicious pleasure unknown to any other beings but a *free people*.

In Dennis's hands, the wheelbarrow law continued the cruel theatricality that structured popular culture. But it was more. As Dennis saw it, the cruel display of public labor was not an incidental excess; rather, it lay at the heart of the exercise of the wheelbarrow law. Rather than a sign of the growing sensibility of Revolutionary society, public labor revealed the malice and degradation that accompanied republican character.

By casting Dennis as an honest individual unable to find work, the letter implied that crime could stem from enforced poverty. It was the lack of work (and his resultant hunger) that led Dennis to jail in the first place. The state of the economy, more than personal corruption or moral weakness, seemed at the root of his criminality. The letter's postscript reinforced this sympathetic image of the petty thief. There Dennis cautioned Patrick that only certain kinds of theft led to jail. "Indirect roguery" would not suffice. Creditors could commit "theft or fraud" without penalty, for the law only punished the poor criminal. Dennis informed his brother, "You may cheat, and lie, and rob with paper money. . . . You may refuse to take any thing but specie from your debtors, and afterwards sell that specie to a broker for paper, which you may force a poor tradesmen to take from you at par with gold and silver, by swearing you received it as such." Only "literally" picking a pocket, breaking into a house, or committing a highway robbery would lead to the wheelbarrow. A class bias marred the law; while the poor suffered, the rich prospered. Under such circumstances, the communal display of the inmates was degradation piled on misfortune.

But the letter contradicted this image of the inmates. Dennis might be a virtuous unfortunate, but his companions were not. While his conscience "shuddered" at the thought of crime, those of the "strolling footpads" had no such compunction. Indeed, the imagery of "strolling footpads," with its connotations of professional (or at least continual) criminality, suggested collective depravity, not individual misfortune. Dennis's description of his fellow prisoners reinforced this counterimage. Their conversation, after all, was often both "profane and absurd," and they provided the spectators with examples of "wickedness." The criminals were "infecting" the public with their vices. From this perspective, the callousness of the punishment lay in its vicious effects on the spectators. To the author of Dennis K——Y's letter, the inmates were objects of both pity and fear.

The wheelbarrow law became, in Dennis K——Y's hands, a spotlight for revealing the instabilities and injustices of the post-Revolutionary order. The contradictions of public labor revealed a world of economic dislocation, class injustice, and confused sensibilities that crystallized in degradations that matched the hunting of witches. From this perspective, the wheelbarrow law was a symptom of a wider cruelty that pervaded the public and the economy as well as convicts. But that was not the only way to interpret the dislocation of post-Revolutionary culture and society.

IV

Simultaneously with the debates over public labor, the theatrical stage and the place of justice brought into question the stability of the Revolutionary public realm. Like public labor, the stage and the courts were important sites of public display and interaction. In each, the city's classes confronted and communicated with each other; like public labor, each could serve as media for representing and reinforcing the social order. But rather than sources of republican unanimity, the stage and the courts, like public labor, triggered debate and conflicts. Linking anxieties about corporality and public display, the debates over the theater and the scene of justice, alongside the turmoil surrounding public labor and the disruptive particularities of Philadelphia's popular culture, disclosed the social fissures and cultural fears that haunted the republican experiment.

Critics of the theatrical stage and the stage of justice told the story of mimetic corruption as one of the decline of authority, morality, and individual self-possession. In this narrative, theatrical displays and the dispensation of justice were linked to public labor as disseminators of unruly and vicious communication, and actors and justices of the peace assumed the devouring and foreboding qualities of the wheelbarrow men. Critics of the theater and of "trading justices" condensed social anxieties onto bodily presence. Indeed, from the perspective of their critics, players and trading justices embodied the disruption of morality and threatened to consume the republican project itself.

The campaign against the theater exemplified contemporary fears that public meaning and social order had become problematic. Struggles to define and institutionalize the difference between legitimate and illegitimate representation, after all, helped shape the Revolution itself. The theater debate continued these struggles. In posing the question of the social and psychological effects of "theatrical representations," opponents of the stage articulated the problematic character of public communication. Like the opponents of public labor, they evinced their lack of faith in the populace's ability to interpret signs correctly. Only properly ordered representations, they implied, should be publicly conveyed.

To many religious leaders, stage plays, like executions or whippings, were tied to aristocratic and monarchical decadence; they had always been, and always would remain, contrary to Christian principles and political virtue. Quakers, in particular, drew on Revolutionary hostility to the theater, citing the opposition of the Continental Congress to stage plays, and argued that Revolutionary wisdom (in this matter at least) should not be overturned. "We consider the sacred ties of virtue," they declared, "to be immutable and at all times obligatory, and therefore the people of all ranks are as loudly called upon as ever to revere and maintain them."[54] Given the long-standing associ-

54. *The Address and Petition of the People Called Quakers to the Senate and Assembly of the State of Pennsylvania* (Philadelphia, 1793), 1. For an analysis of Revolutionary strictures against the theater, see Ann Fairfax Withington, *Toward a More Perfect Union: Virtue and the Formation of American Republics* (New York, 1991), 20–47, 76–78, 90–91.

ation between the theater and the Royal Court, and the support of Pennsylvania's proprietary governors for the colonial theater, religious leaders may have seen their efforts as one more chapter in an attempt to stem the tide of secularizing and decadent monarchical power and symbolism. The danger of the theater to virtue was as strong, and the duty to oppose it just as demanding, as during the Revolutionary crisis.

Quaker anxieties helped instigate debate over the theater. When the General Assembly, in late 1785, began its discussion of the bill to suppress vice and immorality, leading Friends expressed their approbation of the proposals. But, despite their general support, they also expressed their "concern and sorrow" that the Assembly was considering legalizing "theatrical representations." This, they believed, would "defeat the measures you [the General Assembly] may adopt for the prevention of iniquity." [55] In response to this proposal, and in accord with their anxieties, the Quakers lobbied the legislature to continue the ban on plays.

Quakers grounded their opposition in Christian tradition. "The judgement of many wise and pious men, of ancient and modern times," and of different denominations, they insisted, had long opposed the stage. "However these sentiments may be censured by the libertine world, as proceeding from narrow bigotry, and gloomy superstition," hostility to the stage was the only viable Christian position. Not only did the stage contradict Christian doctrine, it seduced the young. The "amusements of the stage," Quakers argued, were "productive of the most pernicious evils." Plays ensnared the unwary in the coils of vice, thereby planting the seeds of future immorality; they debauched the "morals and principles of unguarded youth, and others." [56] As with the critique of public labor, the danger of youthful emulation of vice was of central importance. For the Quakers, stage players as well as wheelbarrow men carried the contagion of corruption.

Plays, the Quakers argued, were "delusive exhibitions." They were built around duplicity (the actors represented themselves as things that in reality they were not) and excess (their plots were taken from the extraordinary). The stage destroyed "that innocence and sobriety of conduct and conversation, which the spirit and precepts of the christian religion enjoin on its professors." The stage was a continual practice of seduction, an "incitement to dissipation, and [to] the depravity of the manners of the people." [57] A Christian commonwealth could not survive the theater.

The Quakers were not alone in their hostility to the stage. In Philadelphia,

55. "Address and Memorial of the People Called Quakers in Philadelphia," *Ind. Gazetteer*, Dec. 10, 1785. On the statute to lesson vice and immorality, see above in Chapter 2.
56. "Address and Memorial of the People Called Quakers in Philadelphia," *Ind. Gazetteer*, Dec. 10, 1785.
57. Ibid.

the city's other religious denominations shared the Quakers' hostility to the stage and agitated for its suppression. During the early years of the Revolution, the radical governments had joined the religious hostility to the theater and passed laws forbidding the staging of theatrical entertainments. Consequently, the Quakers found numerous allies when they struggled to continue the ban on the theater. In February 1789, Anglican bishop William White, Presbyterian minister George Duffield, Baptist minister William Rogers, Lutheran minister Henry Helmuth, and Methodist minister Joseph Pilmore led a committee to present a petition against the theater, signed by 3,210 inhabitants of the city and county, to the General Assembly. The petition echoed the anxieties of the Friends that the stage would be "injurious to the virtue, happiness, morals and property of the citizens and productive of many vices and mischiefs."[58]

That Protestant religious leaders were unified in their opposition to the theater was not unusual. Antitheatrical sentiments had been a defining characteristic of more radical seventeenth-century English Protestants. Puritans objected both to the plays (with their emphasis on the assumption of disguises and roles) and to the players (whose transience violated the notion of communal boundaries). The stage symbolized the dislocations in society and economy that radical English Protestantism sought to overcome. These sentiments accompanied the transfer of Protestantism to North America and took especially deep root in the settlements from Pennsylvania northward.[59] The Quakers and their allies drew on well-established arguments against the corruptive representations of the stage.

More than shared fears linked the movements against the stage and against the wheelbarrow law. The personnel of the two campaigns overlapped. Of the nineteen members of the delegation that presented the Assembly with the antitheater petition of February 1789, ten were also leaders of the Philadelphia Society for Alleviating the Miseries of Public Prisons.[60] This overlap (consist-

58. Samuel Hazard, ed., *The Register of Pennsylvania, Devoted to the Preservation of Facts and Documents, and Every Other Kind of Useful Information respecting the State of Pennsylvania*, 16 vols. (Philadelphia, 1828), I, 346; *Pa. Archives*, 8th Ser., VI, 4993–4994, 5288, VII, 5991; William S. Dye, Jr., "Pennsylvania versus the Theatre," *PMHB*, LV (1931), 331–372; *Pa. Packet*, Feb. 16, 18, 1789.

59. Jean-Christophe Agnew, *Worlds Apart: The Market and the Theater in Anglo-American Thought, 1550–1750* (New York, 1986), 131–143; Kenneth Silverman, *A Cultural History of the American Revolution: Painting, Music, Literature, and the Theatre in the Colonies and the United States from the Treaty of Paris to the Inauguration of George Washington, 1763–1789* (New York, 1976), 66–67.

60. *Pa. Packet*, Feb. 18, 1789. Membership of the Philadelphia Society for Alleviating the Miseries of Public Prisons was drawn from Negley K. Teeters, *They Were in Prison: A History of the Pennsylvania Prison Society, 1787–1937* (Philadelphia, 1937), 90–99.

ing primarily of ministers and Quakers) stemmed from the religious component in the alliance against public punishments. Religious leaders, frightened
by the threat of social corruption, had joined to fight on several fronts.

Like the theater and the scene of punishment, the site of justice itself came
under critical assault. Too many magistrates, critics charged, were "trading
justices"—those interested in governmental service solely to enhance their
personal wealth. These trading justices did not serve justice; instead, they
prostituted and debased its form and content. Critics of the character and
composition of the city's lower magistracy merged anxieties over display and
injustice through the language of mimetic corruption.

Financial considerations triggered the debate over trading justices. Justices
of the peace and constables received court fees, not salaries. Those accused in
criminal cases paid a number of court costs, including charges for witnesses,
juries, and so forth. Proceedings for debt or other civil suits generated fees for
writing and delivering writs, executing collections, and other duties. Those
detained temporarily for drunkenness or vagrancy also faced court charges.
The financial well-being of judicial officers depended on these fees. If too few
individuals appeared in court, or if the number of documents that accompanied legal actions was small, then the justices and their constables would not
earn enough money. From another perspective, an appearance in the courtroom could be a financial, not just a legal, burden.[61] Court costs could prevent
the poor from pursuing their interests through the judicial system or lead individuals to plead guilty or nolo contendere in criminal cases to avoid trial
expenses.

Although the fee system existed throughout the colonial period, it exploded
into public debate during the mid-1780s. From 1785 until 1789, criticisms of
magistrates appeared in the public press. Initially stimulated by the extortion
conviction of the city's high constable, Alexander Carlisle, the discussion of
trading justices focused on the impact of judicial fees on the poor, the attitudes of justices and constables toward the respectable citizens of the city, and
the manner in which justices of the peace were selected.[62]

Critics charged that justices manipulated their power to extract money. Un-

61. Alexander, *Render Them Submissive,* 81. For a colonial example of a statute regulating
fees, see *St. at Large,* V, 161–178. The fees charged to those convicted of crimes were sometimes greatly in excess of the fines actually meted out for their offense. *Pa. Eve. Herald,*
Mar. 24, 1787.

62. Alexander, *Render Them Submissive,* 71–73. The assault on trading justices coincided
with efforts to reincorporate the city. As a result, it seems likely that the criticism of trading
justices and the movement for reincorporation were intertwined—each designed to return
political power to the better sort and to curb the excesses of democracy. On these issues,
see ibid., 42–44, 71–73, and Chapter 4 below. For Carlisle's conviction, see *Ind. Gazetteer,*
Oct. 29, 1785.

scrupulous justices had two primary means to extort money. First, they could manipulate court fees and charge exorbitant and illegal prices for court services. The *Pennsylvania Evening Herald* claimed that, despite legal limits on court costs, "there are in this city, justices who . . . multiply expences on a most unwarrantable, illegal, and inhuman manner." Second, magistrates could unnecessarily multiply the witnesses called to testify. "A Friend to the Oppressed" alleged that when complaints were made to "Trading Justices," no matter how straightforward, the magistrate "makes it a point to call before him all those whom he can, with any degree of colour, summon to give evidence." "And though the nature of the case is such, as that justice might be administered without any witness but the parties, by the contrivance of the *Justice* and his *runners,* the defendant is mulcted with a long bill of costs." This multiplication of witnesses was, "a Friend" thought, especially dangerous because, unlike illegal fees, it was a "species of oppression . . . the law of the land does not reach."[63]

Critics also charged magistrates and constables with arresting innocent citizens to obtain extra fees. The poor were the main victims of this "species of villainy." Constables, "frequently, at unfashionable hours, recontre the sons and daughters of misery" who were "generally friendless, comfortless, houseless, destitute of a morsel to appease the most urgent calls of nature, and unprovided with any other canopy to shelter their dew-beaten heads, than the heavens." Seized, they were taken to the watchhouse and brought before the magistrate in the morning, where fees were "mounted up" against them. If unable to pay, they were condemned to the workhouse. The same treatment was accorded those of "unbridled festivity." These, "though perhaps inebriated," were "returning home peaceable." If they had "money enough to gratify their sordid captor," they would be let free. If not, they were bound over. Justices and their helpers, these critics believed, turned simple poverty or revelry into criminality. The "sons and daughters of misery" and those of "unbridled festivity" were not the only objects of these machinations. Judicial oppression extended to more established citizens. In the winter of 1786, indictments were returned against "several" watchmen for false imprisonment. Watchmen had seized one gentleman, "without his doing any injury or committing any offence, whatsoever, and at [an] early hour of the evening."[64]

The petty judiciary, critics also claimed, inverted the proper relationship between state and society, giving reign less to justice than to barbarous, and corporal, cruelty. In its practices, it regressed to a tyrannical infliction of pain

63. *Pa. Eve. Herald,* July 27, 1785; "A Friend to the Oppressed," *Ind. Gazetteer,* June 5, "A Dramatic Scene," Aug. 25, 1787.

64. "Official Injustice," *Pa. Eve. Herald,* Aug. 10, 1785; *Pa. Gazette,* Feb. 1, 1786. For other examples of charges that trading justices extorted money from the poor—and, in doing so, drove the poor further into vice—see "A Citizen," *Ind. Gazetteer,* June 6, 25, 1787.

and despair. Too often "good inhabitants" had "groaned beneath the pressure" of the watchmen. Watchmen, the *Pennsylvania Gazette* asserted, needed to learn "the lesson of gentleness and civility, and that they are not to do as they please with freemen and established citizens." The *Pennsylvania Evening Herald* argued: a justice, "unless he be a man of strict integrity, and of sufficient sensibility to feel for the calamities of the woe-begone part of the community, is a nuisance to the state; and becomes as cruel a despot within the circle of his authority, as an imperious Turkish bashaw." Trading justices and constables were "scourges," whose "diabolical exercise of power" left them "lost to every principle of humanity." "Leonatas" averred that the appellation of trading justice "conveys such a detestable and deadly image, that it exceeds all human invention to aggravate it." The most horrific analogies only mitigated its severity: "It improves by the worst comparisons you can make. Your terror lessens when you assimilate them to *crocodiles* and *Cannibals*, who feed for hunger on human bodies."[65] Once again, anxieties about social relations transmuted into bodily fear; the seeming insubstantiality and instability of social order was articulated as a threat to the body's substance. If the injustice of society, in Dennis K——Y's eyes, pushed the honest poor to crime for survival, the injustice of the judiciary went even further. Like crocodiles, cannibals, and "Turkish bashaws," trading justices would consume not only virtue but the very bodies of the citizenry.

Trading justices, then, seemed to reinforce the dangers of public labor. The example of criminals in the city streets, critics charged, dissolved the distinctions between virtue and vice. The great danger of the wheelbarrow law lay in its potentially corruptive effects on the wider society; it not only failed to reform those under sentence, but it threatened to deform those who witnessed its charges. Trading justices dissolved the difference between justice and self-interest; they not only oppressed citizens but destroyed the image of authority itself.

In the theater of justice and the theatrical stage, critics charged, duplicity was embodied and disarray reigned. In their dissemination of vice and debasement of virtue, actors and trading justices undermined the very spirit of a republican society. Yet these criticisms also point to encrypted fears about selfhood and bodily integrity.[66] It was the bodily presence of stage players and

---

65. *Pa. Gazette*, Feb. 1, 1786; *Pa. Eve. Herald*, July 27, 1785; "Leonatas," *Ind. Gazetteer*, Sept. 10, 1785, "A Friend to the Oppressed," June 25, 1787.

66. For important accounts of the ways in which the socioeconomic instabilities engendered within capitalistic social relations helped structure anxieties about bodily integrity and fears of being devoured, for both artisans and merchants in late-18th- and early-19th-century Philadelphia, see Ric Northrup, "Decomposition and Recomposition: A Theoretical and Historical Study of Philadelphia Artisans, 1785–1820" (Ph.D. diss., University of North Carolina, 1989), 166–172, 227–241; Toby L. Ditz, "Shipwrecked; or, Masculinity

trading justices that threatened—the one by corporally representing duplicity and vice as playful possibilities, the other by seizing and implicitly devouring the bodies of the citizens to satisfy gluttonous desires. The seductive and devouring body haunted the stage and justice, just as justice and the stage impressed their effects on the bodies and characters of those they touched. And nowhere was this interplay between the spirit, justice, and the body clearer than in the scene of punishment itself.

V

Unquestionably, Benjamin Rush offered the most sustained and theoretically elaborate criticism of the wheelbarrow law. Rush, raised in an evangelical Presbyterian household, was educated at Princeton, finished a medical apprenticeship in Philadelphia, and pursued an advanced medical education in Edinburgh, where he met such dignitaries of the Scottish Enlightenment as David Hume. A fervent supporter of American Independence and an opponent of monarchy, Rush remained a social conservative. Rush's search for a disciplined republic rooted in Christian love underpinned his long public activity: from signing the Declaration of Independence, through a long opposition to Pennsylvania's constitution of 1776, to his continuing participation in a wide range of social reforms in Philadelphia, and in his career as the city's leading doctor. Rush took a public stand against the wheelbarrow law in the spring of 1787. His *Enquiry into the Effects of Public Punishments upon Criminals, and upon Society,* delivered to the Society for Promoting Political Inquiries in March 1787, then published in the *American Museum,* finally appeared independently in pamphlet form.[67]

Imperiled: Mercantile Representations of Failure and the Gendered Self in Eighteenth-Century Philadelphia," *Journal of American History,* LXXXI (1994), 51–81. As Ditz and Northrup show, artisans and merchants imagined the social insecurities that accompanied engagement in the market as the instabilities of both body and soul. They experienced social dislocation as psychological and corporal dissolution. Their very selfhood seemed, in Ditz's formulation, "imperiled."

67. Benjamin Rush, *An Enquiry into the Effects of Public Punishments upon Criminals, and upon Society, Read in the Society for Promoting Political Enquiries, Convened at the House of His Excellency Benjamin Franklin, Esquire, in Philadelphia, March 9th, 1787* (Philadelphia, 1787). For a thorough and stimulating treatment of Rush's life and thought, see Donald J. D'Elia, *Benjamin Rush: Philosopher of the American Revolution,* American Philosophical Society, *Transactions,* N.S., LXIV, Pt. 5 (Philadelphia, 1974). I have treated the strategy of Rush's reformist vision more extensively in my introduction to Rush, *Essays,* ed. Meranze, i–xxi. For Rush's experience in Edinburgh, see Rush, *The Autobiography of Benjamin Rush: His "Travels through Life" Together with His Commonplace Book for 1789–1813,* ed. George W. Corner (Princeton, N.J., 1948), 42–52. Rush's meeting Hume is on 49.

Whereas most critics focused on practical difficulties surrounding public labor, Rush transformed the difficulties of public labor into a full-scale assault on public punishments in general. Rush insisted that all public punishments were inherently unstable and dangerous to social order. Rush suggested that spectators, confronting the debasement or dignity of the condemned, too often sided with the criminal rather than the criminal law. To Rush's mind, disruption and disorder did not incidentally plague public punishments—public punishments actively produced turmoil. The result, Rush thought, was that "all *public* punishments tend to make bad men worse, and to encrease crimes, by their influence on society."[68]

The destructive effects of public punishments began with the condemned themselves. Rush argued that public punishments destroyed the sensibility of those subject to them. Contending that public punishments were "generally" too short for the reformation of character, he argued that even their extension would serve no purpose. The public display of criminals, Rush noted, was intrinsically tied to infamy. But, however horrible the imposition of infamy— and Rush claimed human beings feared infamy more than death—it did not improve character. Instead, it destroyed the "sense of shame" that was "one of the strongest out-posts of virtue" while eliminating one of the external bases of virtue—the criminal's reputation. "A man who has lost his character at a whipping-post," Rush insisted, "has nothing valuable left to lose in society." Without reputation, a criminal was cast adrift within society.[69]

As a result, Rush argued, public punishments turned criminals into irredeemable enemies of society: "Pain has begotten insensibility to the whip; and shame to infamy." Criminals, left "infamous," "shameless," and "insensible," would "probably" possess a "spirit of revenge against the whole community" under whose laws they had suffered. This spirit "stimulated" criminals "to add to the number and enormity" of their "outrages upon society." Those who believed that prolonged public punishments (like public labor) eventually improved the character of the condemned were mistaken. A "long duration" of punishment "when public, by encreasing its infamy, serves only to encrease the evils that have been mentioned."[70]

If public punishments destroyed the sympathy criminals felt for society, the effects of public punishments on spectators, Rush argued, were even more dangerous. He delineated the problem of penal display within a logic of iden-

68. Rush, *Enquiry into the Effects of Public Punishments*, 4.

69. Ibid., 4–5.

70. Ibid. Rush believed that England's experiment of condemning criminals to labor "in the presence of the City of London" along the Thames had proven the error of the theory behind public punishment. This experience, he argued, had "prepared" the criminals subject to it, for "every crime, as soon as they were set at liberty." Ibid.

tity and identification. If criminal punishments were designed to remake the condemned while re-sensitizing both convicts and crowds to the evils of law-breaking, then, Rush insisted, public punishments were self-defeating. And the essential aspect of their inherent failure lay in their theatricality. As Rush presented it, spectators engaged in a series of mistaken, incomplete, and dangerous identifications. Rather than achieving the distance necessary to view the public punishment in its entirety, they were drawn sympathetically into affiliation with the condemned. As he catalogued the penal display, the behavior and reactions of the condemned set in motion an almost irresistible sequence of spectatorial delusion and misplaced sympathy. Rush found that sufferers of punishment manifested three reactions: "Fortitude, insensibility, or distress."[71] Each of these reactions, he argued, undermined the effectiveness of punishment; the danger of mimetic corruption haunted the penal scene.

For one thing, public punishments could stimulate crime itself. The display of fortitude "seizes so forcibly" the "esteem" of the spectator that it, literally, seduces the audience and "never fails to weaken, or to obliterate" the "detestation of the crimes with which it is connected in criminals." The display of fortitude transformed the villain into a hero; the scene of punishment, rather than making crime and criminals detestable, made them objects of emulation. The misplaced "admiration which fortitude, under suffering, excites, has in some instances excited envy." Insensibility could have similar effects. The criminal's insensibility established the weakness, not the strength, of the law. It might therefore "excite a desire" in those "made miserable" by debt or guilt to commit crimes so they could end "their distresses in the same enviable apathy to evil" displayed at the scaffold.[72] The effectiveness of public punishment presumed terror in the spectators. But fortitude and insensibility, Rush insisted, mocked terror.

Distress, on the other hand, undermined legal authority. Pity for the distressed criminal alienated the audience from the state: "While we pity, we secretly condemn the law which inflicts the punishment." This secret condemnation eventually leads to a "want of respect" for the laws "in general" and thus to "a more feeble union of the great ties of government."[73] If the law appeared to engage in acts of cruelty, its legitimacy would disappear.

At the same time, public punishments threatened to unravel society itself. In this matter, the display of distress was a particularly grave danger. Rush argued that it was an "immutable law" of human nature that distress "when *seen*, produces sympathy, and a disposition to relieve it." This sympathy was not diminished in "generous" minds because the distress resulted from crim-

71. Ibid., 5.
72. Ibid.
73. Ibid., 7.

inality. Instead, when the criminal manifested distress, indignation over the punishment replaced indignation over the crime. The sympathetic spectator mitigated the responsibility of the offender, and "even the crimes themselves are often palliated by the reflection, that they were the unfortunate consequences of extreme poverty—of seducing company—or of the want of virtuous education." The spectators, once again, assumed the position of the criminal. But here they identified, not with the strength of the condemned, but with their weakness. In assuming this masochistic identification, Rush's analysis suggested, spectators turned their backs on morality and virtue—their painful affiliation overrode all considerations of the necessity of justice. This distressing identification unleashed an ascending frustration that threatened society itself because the offender's distress was the result of legal authority and could not, according to Rush, "be resisted." This situation rendered sympathy "abortive" and forced it to return "empty to the bosom in which it was awakened."[74] The ritual of public punishment simultaneously demanded and denied human sympathy.

For Rush, this production of frustrated sympathy threatened to eliminate sympathy itself. He believed that sensibility, of the mind as well as of the body, divided into components both active (involving both motion and sensation) and passive (involving only sensation). Habit (in physical terms, "the repetition of impressions") strengthened active and weakened passive sensibilities. Public punishments, habituating the audience to the sight of distress they could not alleviate, would eliminate both: "The principle of sympathy, after being often opposed by the law of the state, which forbids it to relieve the distress it commiserates, will cease to act altogether; and, from this defect of action, and the habit arising from it, will soon lose its place in the human breast."[75]

And, if sympathy were destroyed, the damage to society would be incalculable. Sympathy was "intended to bind up all the wounds which sin and death have made among mankind." The human capacity for sympathy produced charity; without it, charity would disappear. "Misery of every kind," Rush suggested, "will then be contemplated without emotion or sympathy—The widow and the orphan—the naked—the sick, and the prisoner, will have no avenue to our services or our charity." Moreover, sensibility judged actions to determine whether they were good or evil—it served, according to Rush, as the "sentinel of our moral faculty." Without sensibility, there would be nothing left to "guard the mind from the inroads of every positive vice."[76] The erosion of sympathy would leave everyone vicious and warring each against all.

74. Ibid., 6.
75. Ibid., 6–7, 7.
76. Ibid., 6, 7.

Yet, as with sympathy more generally, overidentification with the condemned was only one danger. Sympathy was inextricably tied to distance, and spectators could identify with the distance between themselves and the condemned. Rush suggested that the "characters or conduct of criminals" could elicit "indignation or contempt" instead of pity. Under these circumstances, there was no problem of mimetic corruption. But spectatorial indignation or contempt corrupted the human mind from within. Since sympathetic identification, although natural, was capable of being denied and destroyed, those "passions" (such as indignation or contempt) that habituated individuals to see the pain of others with indifference were extremely dangerous. Indignation or contempt would have the same effect on charity as frustrated sympathy. It would prevent the fulfillment of the "obligations to *universal* benevolence." Even everyday sociability would suffer. "If a spectator should give himself time to reflect on such a sight of human depravity," Rush argued, "he would naturally recoil from the embraces of friendship, and the endearments of domestic life."[77] The association of ideas—the identification of "depravity" with humanity—would eliminate the trust necessary for sociability. As with the eradication of sympathy, contempt destroyed the very fabric of social interaction.

Finally, spectators could identify, not with the condemned or with their anger at the transgression, but with the physical act of punishment itself. In addition to those "generous" minds who possessed "sensibility," Rush suggested, there existed another class of spectators who were "hardened with vice . . . too young, or too ignorant, to connect the ideas of crimes and punishments together." To them, the criminals' deeds were unimportant; only the punishment drew their attention. Lacking a larger moral or legal framework, they saw punishments as "mere arbitrary acts of cruelty" imposed by the state on a criminal whose "passive behaviour . . . indicates innocence more than vice." Under these circumstances, the punishment, in effect, legitimated cruelty itself. The spectators became increasingly disposed "to exercise the same arbitrary cruelty over the feelings and lives" of others. Here the process of mimetic corruption occurred in its starkest form. Designed as a symbolic lesson in the necessity and justice of obedience to the law, the punishment became an example of a seemingly arbitrary infliction of misery. Instead of reclaiming those immured in vice or still maturing, the public display of criminals provided new lessons in viciousness.[78]

As Rush saw it, then, the dynamics of sympathetic identification undermined respect for, and commitment to, the law. Like critics of the theater,

---

77. Ibid., 7–8.

78. Ibid., 8. Rush also believed that it might bring to the attention of the crowd crimes of which otherwise they would have remained ignorant.

Rush argued that spectators were drawn too much to the characters on display—the visual spectacle itself overwhelmed its larger moral meaning. Rush's analysis suggested that public punishments were too embodied, that the displayed and speaking body of the condemned communicated too forcefully to the viewing spectator. Spectators, in sympathetic communion with the condemned, were unable to imagine the ritual as a whole; the intent of the punishment was submerged in the sensations of the spectacle itself. The very visuality of the punishment meant that the infliction of suffering overwhelmed its own context. The penal sanction, designed as a moment in a larger drama, subordinated that larger story to itself. Rush thereby pushed the ambiguous logic of sympathy to its limit. In his account of public punishments, the individual spectator had little defense against the seductions of the exhibition, whereas the condemned could lose themselves in the supportive gaze of the multitude.

All of these problems plagued public punishments. But public labor faced a special, additional difficulty. Its proponents contended that forced labor would reclaim criminals from indolence and viciousness while providing economic benefits to the community. Rush disagreed. The association of ideas, he argued, would link labor with criminality in the public mind. The situation, he suggested, was similar to slave societies where it was "a well-known fact" that whites refused to labor "because the agriculture, and mechanical employment of those countries, are carried on chiefly by Negro slaves." Instead of uplifting offenders, public labor degraded labor itself, especially labor done for the "improvement" of the state. It would bring into disrepute the very notions of public virtue and patriotism and eventually remove more wealth from the state because of the "idleness [laboring criminals] will create, by alluring spectators from their business," than it could hope to create through the "industry" of the condemned.[79] The wheelbarrow law would make Pennsylvania poorer in virtue and in wealth.

Rush, therefore, condensed the anxieties about the dangers of mimetic corruption into a full-scale assault on public punishments. Although cast in transhistorical language, Rush sought to delegitimize public labor by linking it not only with failed sensibility but with wider anxieties about public order and self-discipline in the new Republic. Public labor, Rush implied, combined the most destructive and seductive aspects of popular culture and theatricality, and opened the door to idleness and an ensuing spiral into poverty, viciousness, and criminality. In his hands, mimetic corruption offered the extreme case of the logic of sensibility and sympathy. Mimetic corruption made clear what sensibility and sympathy only implied: the self, formed through sensation, was drawn as much to vice as to virtue, to cruelty as to charity, to luxury

79. Ibid., 9.

as to law, and the moral faculty was an insecure defense against the temptations and seductions of society's spectacles.

In this way, Rush, in effect, rewrote Adam Smith's famous representation of the mind of the murderer in his *Theory of Moral Sentiments.* As Smith depicted it, the individual who kills was almost inevitably struck down by the awareness that he was excluded from the sympathy of those around him. "The remembrance of his crimes," Smith declared, "has shut out all fellow-feeling with him from the hearts of his fellow-creatures . . . Every thing seems hostile, and he would be glad to fly to some inhospitable desert, where he might never more behold the face of a human creature, nor read in the countenance of mankind the condemnation of his crimes." But such flight is impossible because it is, in fact, the murderer's internalization of the gaze of "his fellow-creatures" that produces such suffering. And, so, driven back into society, "astonished to appear before them loaded with shame and distracted with fear," the murderer seeks "some little protection from . . . those very judges, who he knows have already all unanimously condemned him." As Smith imagined it, this mirroring of the gazes of the transgressor and the community helped produce what he called an "impartial spectator." This impartial spectator, in turn, compelled remorse in the murderer. Rush shared Smith's commitment to the production of remorse. But he reversed the perspective of the analysis. Smith imagined himself within the mind of the murderer, Rush within the minds of those in the crowd. Smith's discussion sought to demonstrate the emergence of an impartial spectator out of the dynamics of theatricality; Rush's argument pointed to the impossibility of an impartial spectator within the theatrical setting. In his telling of the scaffold story, the place of punishment became an escape not only from the powers of conscience but from the condemnation of the crowd. In a striking sense, the very publicness of the public punishment meant that the open space of punishment enabled the condemned to escape from his conscience.[80] Some other mechanism for the production of remorse was needed.

By the late 1780s, then, the experiment with public labor was in evident disarray. To its critics, public labor had become a machine of mimetic corruption.

80. Smith, *The Theory of Moral Sentiments,* 162, 164. Smith was aware of the possibility that public punishment could allow the condemned to escape from his conscience. See, for instance, his discussion of the ways in which the scaffold was far more desirable for a "brave man" than was the pillory (ibid., 124–125). Nonetheless, as Jean-Chistophe Agnew noted, "Images of pillories and scaffolds abound in the *Theory* as examples of isolation and mortification; there is little sense of the occasional bond felt between crowds and criminals as occurred, for example, when Defoe was pilloried for one of his satires." Agnew, *Worlds Apart,* 251 n. 104.

The penal site, they argued, was a scene less of self-discipline than of chaos; the behavior of the convicts was less virtuous than violent. Public laborers and the crowds that watched them, they insisted, engaged less in silent remorse and reflection than in sympathetic communication and charity. The wheelbarrow men appeared as players in a drama of discord and vice, their presence in the streets dissolving the very authority and legality they were supposed to represent.

The significance of public labor was not limited to criminal justice but helped reconfigure the language of the public realm. Rather than a public domain unified through republican values and a shared sense of justice, the contradictions of public labor and the continuation of vice and immorality had revealed fissures within Philadelphia's culture and society. Critics of public labor reimagined the city itself as a hall of mirrors where vice and criminality spread through mimicry and contagion. Public labor seemed so threatening because, in its inversions of proper dialogue and its denigration of appropriate demeanor, it mirrored and reinforced a wider range of popular cultural practices. In response, critics of public labor analyzed the public realm anew, focusing on the problematic nature of public communications and the radical instability of individual character. Arguing that contemporary practices of punishment, of everyday life, and of the theater of justice instigated a vicious circle of mimetic corruption, they urged a dramatic break with the logic of public penal display. Their suspicions about the public sphere and the character of the citizenry would lead, in turn, to a new strategy for social discipline and a new practice of punishment.

PART TWO

Imprisonment

CHAPTER FOUR

The Origins of Reformative
Incarceration in the City

The contradictions of public labor did not halt penal reform: they intensified it. Elite Philadelphians saw Revolutionary society as menaced from all sides and sought to reaffirm social distinctions while establishing social authority on a new basis. If the failure of public punishments resulted from the promiscuous effects of seductive communication, then the answer was to establish new boundaries between vice, criminality, and the public. By the mid-1790s, Philadelphia reformers formulated a philosophy of private punishments. Drawing on English experiments with reformative incarceration, they offered a positive alternative to public labor, one built on private penitence.

Advocates of reformative incarceration rejected the public display of criminals and proposed severing any direct links between convicts and the public. Within the walls of a prison criminals could be reformed and returned to the path of legality and virtue. Proponents of penitential punishments acknowledged the conflicts surrounding public labor, but they defined criminality as a problem of character. The post-Revolutionary order was consolidated under the sign of individual deficiency, not social conflict. And, in the end, Pennsylvania installed a penal system based on institutional segregation and representative authority rather than public display and direct, popular participation.

Penal reformers and their allies argued that reason and humanity demanded the transformation of punishment; the reformation of punishment signified the growing enlightenment of their society. As a result, they sought a system of penality that would continue the spiritualization of punishment begun with public labor but that repudiated the public display on which the wheelbarrow law was based. A fundamental paradox haunted this spiritualized retreat: at the same time as humanitarian sympathy expanded, so did the submissions demanded of its recipients. Humanitarian reform was a two-edged sword.

I

Rush's critique of public punishments not only condensed widespread anxieties over theatricality and mimetic corruption; it also imagined a new relationship between state and society. In his plan, the penal apparatus would assume a less direct, more distanced, relationship to the public. Rush's analysis suggested that it was, above all, the body of the condemned that seized the sympathy of the crowd. Altering the economy of penal visibility to remove punishment from the gaze of the public, he insisted, would bind the community to the meaning of the penal process rather than to the experiences of the condemned. He thus proposed replacing the theater of the scaffold with the plot of penitence in order to allow the idea of punishment to emerge in all its significance.

Whereas public labor made prisoners physical indicators of the correspondence between crimes and punishments, Rush hoped to make individual corporal signs superfluous. He proposed changing the "*place* and *manner*" of imposing punishments.[1] Instead of punishing criminals in highly visible public rituals (as in public labor), he suggested removing them from the community and placing them in a "house of repentance." In his scenario, the silent, immobile house of repentance, not groups of marked convicts laboring throughout the city, would establish the connection between criminal acts and their legal punishment. Distancing punishment from its display, Rush argued, would displace the medium of terror from public visibility to private imagination. With the penal scene shrouded in darkness and strengthened by the powers of the imagination, the dangers of sympathetic identification would no longer shadow punishment.

Rush, then, proposed reversing the visible economy of penal sanctions by removing the displayed body and subordinating it to imagined space. As he saw it, distance and uncertainty heightened fear and terror. Sympathetic identification depended on bodily presence: "*Active* sympathy can be fully excited only through the avenues of the eyes and the ears." Without such corporal contact, the true import and horror of punishment would emerge. Rush argued that the human mind tends to "exaggerate" everything that is distant and "ascribes the extremes in qualities" to something unknown.[2] Through

1. Benjamin Rush, *An Enquiry into the Effects of Public Punishments upon Criminals, and upon Society; Read in the Society for Promoting Political Enquiries, Convened at the House of His Excellency Benjamin Franklin, Esquire, in Philadelphia, March 9th, 1787* (Philadelphia, 1787), 10.

2. Ibid., 10, 11. In late-18th-century England, similar arguments were made in favor of withdrawing punishments from the direct gaze of the public. There, the theory was based in part on the allegedly greater terror produced by the mysterious and the sublime. See Steven Wilf, "Imagining Justice: Aesthetics and Public Executions in Late Eighteenth-

these dispositions, combined with curiosity, the popular imagination would associate the prison with the most horrifying qualities. The successful terror of the prison would depend on public ignorance of its reality. If visibility blinded the audience, obscuring the meaning of punishment behind its display, Rush believed that concealing punishment would allow its true purpose to be effected.

This strategy presumed that a diffuse horror had greater effects than a singular, if striking, fear. For similar reasons, Rush argued, the nature and duration of punishments should be fixed by law, yet remain secret. Publicizing the nature and duration of specific punishments diminished their effectiveness because criminals who knew their punishment could steel themselves against terror. But if the duration of punishments was kept secret, the convicts' "imagination, when agitated with uncertainty, will seldom fail of connecting the longest duration of punishment, with the smallest crime." Rush did not ignore the theory of certainty in punishment, "since the *certainty* of punishment operates so much more than its severity, or infamy, in preventing crimes." [3] But, although it was necessary to prevent people from imagining they might escape unpunished, it was equally important that they imagine themselves suffering the worst degrees of punishment.

The prison, in Rush's imagination, would be a system of totally ordered representations and techniques. Nothing should be left to chance. "Let the avenue to this house," he urged, "be rendered difficult and gloomy by mountains or morasses. Let its doors be of iron; and let the grating, occasioned by opening and shutting them, be encreased by an echo from a neighbouring mountain, that shall extend and continue a sound that shall deeply pierce the soul." The prison's governors should embody the house's discipline and "be strictly forbidden ever to discover any signs of mirth, or even levity, in the presence of the criminals." Even the institution's name should be designed to "encrease the horror of this abode of discipline and misery." [4]

Century England," *Yale Journal of Law and the Humanities*, V (1993), 51–78. I am grateful to Daniel Cohen for this reference.

3. Rush, *An Enquiry into the Effects of Public Punishments*, 11, 14.

4. Ibid., 10–11. When Rush rewrote this essay for inclusion in his *Essays,* he altered this geosocial vision in ways that brought his argument more in line with the experience of the Walnut Street Jail. In this later form, he urged that the prison contain "a number of apartments" with one "large room for public worship" and cells built for those with "refractory temper[s]." Within the prison proper, he pictured facilities for "carrying on such manufactures as can be conducted with the least instruction, or previous knowledge." Outside the building, but within the walls, he proposed a garden, which he suggested would be not only healthful but improve morality by leading inmates to "a familiarity with those pure and natural objects which are calculated to renew the connection of fallen man with his creator." The prison's name, he now insisted, should "convey an idea of its benevolent and

Conjuring up a gothic world where the unknown and mysterious depths of punishment achieved a mythic horror, Rush completed his inversion of traditional assumptions about penal visibility and display. The creation of mystery, rumor, and horror would compensate for the loss of direct terror. Fear and ignorance would become tools of the law. "I cannot conceive," Rush declared, "any thing more calculated to diffuse terror thro' a community" than removing criminals and subjecting them to fixed but unknown penalties. Storytellers would convey the meaning of punishment throughout the community. "Children will press upon the evening fire in listning to the tales that will be spread from this abode of misery. Superstition will add to its horrors, and romance will find in it ample materials for fiction, which cannot fail of encreasing the terror of its punishments."[5]

And, if isolating the penal scene allowed the narrative body of punishment to emerge, it would, in turn, cause the physical body of the condemned to achieve a new, clarified visibility. Once placed within the house of repentance, the process of punishment should be individualized "to the constitutions and tempers of the criminals, and the peculiar nature of their crimes." Rush argued for a variety of punishments, consisting "of BODILY PAIN, LABOUR, WATCHFULNESS, SOLITUDE, and SILENCE." These would be "joined with CLEANLINESS and a SIMPLE DIET." Rush saw criminality as essentially a medical problem. Accepting the proposition that humanity possessed a "Moral Faculty" (that is, an instinctive sense of right action), he believed that it, like sympathy or sensibility, could be debased. Although God ultimately determined morality and moral actions, Rush argued that "secondary" material or environmental causes affected an individual's moral faculty. One's physical habits and medical condition (including idleness, cleanliness, diet, and disease) affected one's moral behavior.[6]

To Rush, the importance of this psychology for punishment was clear. Pe-

---

salutary design." Punishment's oversight, he hoped, would be entrusted to "persons of established characters of probity, discretion, and humanity, who shall be amenable at all times to the legislature, or courts of law." Benjamin Rush, *Essays: Literary, Moral and Philosophical* (1806), ed. Michael Meranze (Schenectady, N.Y., 1988), 87.

5. Rush, *An Enquiry into the Effects of Public Punishments,* 11. It should be noted that, in 1787, Rush believed that this house should be constructed in a "remote" part of the state. Ibid., 10.

6. Ibid., 12, 13. Benjamin Rush, *An Inquiry into the Influence of Physical Causes upon the Moral Faculty* (Philadelphia, 1786). A similar medicalization of punishment was occurring to English reformers as well. See Randall McGowen, "The Body and Punishment in Eighteenth-Century England," *Journal of Modern History,* LIX (1987), 675–676. For a broad-ranging discussion of the importance of habit and education to the 18th century, see Jay Fliegelman, *Prodigals and Pilgrims: The American Revolt against Patriarchal Authority* (New York, 1982).

nal officials, operating with knowledge of "the principles of sensation, and of the sympathies . . . in the nervous system" and in accord with "the laws of the association of ideas, of habit, and of imitation," could create individualized programs to reform prisoners.[7] The penal system would employ pain, solitude, and silence to break down habits of vice and isolate the prisoner from new sources of evil. Then, through cleanliness, diet, and labor, a new morality of discipline and health coud be achieved. No longer an overwhelming object of almost sacred importance nor an undifferentiated part of a penal mass, the individual inmate, subject to such discipline, would be remade.

This medicalization of punishment, in the end, created a narrative of recovery and recuperation. Reverting to the distinction of active and passive sympathy, Rush insisted that the knowledge that punishment was designed to reform would stimulate passive sympathy in the community, sympathy akin to that produced by the physical suffering of surgery. Having subordinated their sympathies to the larger meaning of punishment, the community would welcome back the lost figure of the condemned. One of the glories of private punishments, he insisted, was that they would leave no "scar" on criminals but rather remove the "stain" of their crimes. Rush envisioned "the inhabitants of our villages and townships counting the years" until the reformation of the condemned. After that, "I behold them running to meet him on the day of his deliverance.—His friends and family bathe his cheeks with tears of joy; and the universal shout of the neighbourhood is, 'This our brother was lost, and is found—was dead and is alive.'"[8]

Rush proposed placing narrative over sight as the source of penal terror. Separating the public from punishments done in its name, Rush opened up the space for new forms of imaginary identifications. Despite his distrust of novel reading, Rush presumed the very structures of imaginary communion that novelists from Samuel Richardson onward had sought to cultivate. Like eighteenth-century authors who hoped to create a new public through the reading and discussion of novels, a public joined together through acts of imagination, Rush suggested that stories and imagined suffering would seal together the community. Like proponents of the novel, Rush presumed that these narratives would convey moral instruction. But, whereas the stereotypical eighteenth-century novel conveyed moral messages through sentimental identification with characters in distress, Rush, in effect, imagined a system where the audience identified with the overall moral process itself.[9] Given the eighteenth-century identification of novel reading with women, the assump-

7. Rush, *An Enquiry into the Effects of Public Punishments,* 13.
8. Ibid., 11–12, 14.
9. On Rush's aversion to novels, see Rush, *Essays,* ed. Meranze, 47–48. For a discussion of the production of community through novel reading and writing that focuses on the

tions that active sensibility was male and passive sensibility was female, and the presumption that women possessed greater charity than men, Rush's transvaluation seems naturally to have a gendered quality. In effect, Rush was proposing that the public assume a feminine position relative to the punishment done in its name—one that was simultaneously passive and sympathetic while paradoxically imaginary and impartial.

Rush's *Enquiry,* then, articulated a number of modifications in the discourse on punishment. Inverting the basis of terror from public display and humiliation to mysterious horror and private fear, and delegating supervision of punishment to the discretion of men of truth, it opened the space for a feminine sympathy. Having maintained that the theatricality of public punishments undermined the moral faculty (and thereby implicitly precluded the emergence of a Smithian impartial spectator), Rush deposited the moral faculty in the apparatus of the state and circumvented public theatricality through the mechanism of a collective imagination. Rush assumed that, ultimately, it was the visible punishment, not the remembered crime, that prevented the acceptance of the condemned in society. The absence of the condemned made possible their ultimate welcome, and the shared narratives of horror and loss bound the community together. In proposing this reversal of visibility and invisibility, of display and concealment, Rush was true to the logics of sensibility and sympathy. Sympathy and sensibility presumed the danger of unrestricted example, the importance of genteel knowledge and understanding, and the necessity of social hierarchy. And the institutionalization of private punishments, in turn, would not only address the crisis in public communication but establish new forms of authority.[10]

---

admittedly special case of Samuel Richardson, see Terry Eagleton, *The Rape of Clarissa: Writing, Sexuality and Class Struggle in Samuel Richardson* (Minneapolis, Minn., 1982).

John Bender has made the strong argument that the novel enabled the turn to penitentiary structures by constructing the individual as a narrative object. It was the presentation of individual lives through (narrative) sentences that paved the way for individuals to be subjected to (penal) sentences. At the same time, he suggests, the novelistic space made possible the reconfiguration of penal space through its emphasis on a more detailed realistic representation. This individual and spatial attention led to a reconceptualization of time and space that made possible the notion of reform through controlled environment. Although I think that the strong version of this argument—with its emphasis on the transformative power of "writing"—is overstated, I do think that Rush's justification for the privatization of punishment presumes the same sort of imaginary community that the novel does. It is the different mechanisms for identification and the different objects of identification that are at stake, mechanisms and objects that the novel shares with the prison but not with public punishment. See John Bender, *Imagining the Penitentiary: Fiction and the Architecture of Mind in Eighteenth-Century England* (Chicago, 1987).

10. Rush expanded his critique of capital punishment in a second essay entitled *Considerations on the Injustice and Impolicy of Punishing Murder by Death* (Philadelphia, 1792).

II

Rush first presented his arguments against public punishments to the Society for Political Inquiries. Members of Philadelphia's elite had formed the Society in 1787 as a tool for their self-education, a means to explore new modes of governance in a republican setting. Although the Society cut across the state's political factions, a majority was drawn from Pennsylvania's anticonstitutionalist faction, including such political leaders as George Clymer, Tench Coxe, Francis Hopkinson, Jared Ingersoll, Thomas Mifflin, Gouverneur Morris, Robert Morris, and James Wilson. Here, before an audience including Benjamin Franklin and James Wilson, Rush presented his philosophy and psychology of private, penitential punishments.[11]

According to the Society for Political Inquiries, politics, culture, and morality were inseparable. Its constitution argued that the "moral character and Happiness of Mankind" were "interwoven with the Operations of Government," and the "progress" of the arts and sciences were "dependent" on the "nature" of "political institutions." As a consequence, reflection on the forms of government was "essential" for the "Advancement of civiliz'd Society." There could be no virtuous people without a virtuous government.[12]

These universal rules were especially true for the American republics. Americans, the Society asserted, had "retained with undistinguishing reverence" the practices of those countries from which they were descended. They had "blended with our Public Institutions the Policy of Dissimilar Countries; and . . . grafted on an Infant Commonwealth the Manners of ancient and corrupted Monarchies." Although "having effected a Separate Government," the United States had accomplished "but a partial Independence." The Revolution would not be "complete" until Americans had "freed" themselves "no less from the influence of Foreign Prejudices, than from the fetters of foreign power." Only in "breaking through the Bounds, in which dependent People have been accustomed to think and act," would Americans "properly comprehend the character" they had "assumed, and adopt those Maxims of Policy . . . suited to" their "new situation."[13] Political independence necessitated intellectual independence.

11. Society for Political Inquiries, Minutes, Feb. 9, 1787, HSP. The committee that approved the presentation of papers included William Bradford and Francis Hopkinson. In other words, many of the major legal thinkers in Philadelphia (with the important exceptions of Thomas McKean and George Bryan) either heard or had encouraged Rush in presenting his arguments. For the connection between the Society and the state's political factions, see Michael Vinson, "The Society for Political Inquiries: The Limits of Republican Discourse in Philadelphia on the Eve of the Constitutional Convention," *PMHB*, CXIII (1989), 188–189.

12. Constitution of the Society for Political Inquiries, Preamble, HSP.

13. Ibid.

The Society's members hoped to rethink methods of government in a republican society. To do so required collective effort by "learned and ingenious Men." Although "Objects of subordinate Importance" had been the subject of the "associated labors" of such individuals, the "arduous and complicated Science of Government" had remained in the "Care of practical Politicians, or the Speculations of Individual Theorists." The Society for Political Inquiries took on the task of "Supplying this Deficiency and of promoting the Welfare of our Country." As a step toward these aims, its members agreed to meet periodically to hear and discuss papers relating to the "Knowledge of Government" and the "Advancement of Political Science." The first paper read to this gathering was Rush's *Enquiry*.[14]

The Society for Political Inquiries was an appropriate arena for questioning whether the people's virtue and wisdom could maintain (or even survive) a system of public punishment. Both republican (in the general sense) and elitist, its members sought to become intellectually independent from England and Europe and distance themselves from inherited modes of thinking among the American population.[15] Rush's message and his forum were well suited for each other.

III

Support for penal reform spread rapidly. Rush presented his ideas to the Society for Political Inquiries in March. By April, the *Enquiry* had been published in pamphlet form. In June, the *Pennsylvania Packet* printed the sections critical of public punishments. The *Enquiry* rapidly became a crucial reference in the continuing debate about the organization of the penal system.[16] Rush did not agitate alone, however. Demands for private punishments emanated from a variety of locations and voiced disparate concerns. But all thought the creation of an enclosed, disciplined scene of punishment was essential to an enlightened, republican society.

Some cited the experiences of prisoners awaiting execution to justify their support for solitary labor. The *Pennsylvania Mercury* informed its readers that the greatest burden for "Durham," a Newgate prisoner sentenced to death, was the time spent alone: "The hour he is locked up he describes as superlatively horrible." His impending execution would provide welcome relief from

14. Ibid.; Society for Political Inquiries, Minutes, Mar. 9, 1787.

15. For a discussion of the general practices and characteristics of the Society for Political Inquiries, see Vinson, "The Society for Political Inquiries," *PMHB*, CXIII (1989), 185–205.

16. Rush to John Dickinson, Apr. 5, 1787, in L. H. Butterfield, ed., *Letters of Benjamin Rush* (Princeton, N.J., 1951), I, 416; *Pa. Packet*, June 11, 1787; "M," *Pa. Eve. Herald*, Apr. 28, 1787. Dennis K——Y's reference to "visionary gentlemen" seems most likely an allusion to Rush and his allies. See above in Chapter 3.

a solitude "infinitely worse than the most agonizing death, to which he looks forward as a kind of relief from the worst of human evils—his own reflections." The paper concluded that Durham's experience "confirms the late adopted opinions, that solitude and confinement would operate very powerfully on the minds of men, and strike a greater terror than mere sanguinary punishments." "A Citizen of the World" agreed. The evident inefficacy of capital punishments justified experimenting with private labor: "It is certainly worthy of the present era, to try whether very hard and solitary labour for life, would not strike a greater terror, than the gibbet, as it would certainly better answer the ends of reparation and reformation."[17]

Others tied their responses directly to the experience of public labor. Pennsylvania's Supreme Executive Council joined the call for "alterations" in the penal system and declared that "the benefits from the penal law hav[e] not equalled the benevolent wishes of its friends and framers." It suggested that only by imposing "temperance and solitude of labor" could punishment become a "means of reformation, and the labour of criminals of profit to the state." Petitions from 488 of the city's inhabitants proposing "divers" amendments to the law were presented to the General Assembly. By the fall of 1788, the movement for private punishments was so strong that Rush could inform a correspondent: "Truth has at last prevailed upon the subject of our *penal laws* . . . Private punishments by means of solitude and labor are now generally talked of."[18] The experience of public labor had abetted a revolution in penal strategy.

These arguments, however, did not proceed merely from an aversion to public punishments. The commitment to reform stemmed from a growing faith in the possibility of individual reformation within incarcerative institutions. Proponents of private punishments were convinced that penitential imprisonment would succeed where public labor had not. This conviction was based on the theory and practice of institutional discipline and philosophy of penitential punishments then emerging (or reemerging) in Britain and on the Continent. The most significant British advocate of penitential discipline was John Howard. Both his life and his writings provided crucial support for Philadelphians who wished to replace the wheelbarrow law with "more *private* or even *solitary* labor."[19]

17. *Pa. Mercury,* May 3, "A Citizen of the World," Nov. 27, 1788.

18. *Freeman's Journal,* Feb. 27, 1788; *Pa. Mercury,* Mar. 8, 1788; Rush to Jeremy Belknap, Nov. 5, 1788, in Butterfield, ed., *Letters,* I, 496.

19. Minutes, Jan. 29, 1788, PSAMPP; "M," *Pa. Eve. Herald,* Apr. 28, 1787; *Pa. Mercury,* May 3, 1788. David Rothman suggested that it was only during the 1820s that a positive vision of reformative incarceration emerged. Earlier penal reform was driven by concerns to rationalize and humanize the law, not to seriously reform the inmate. See *The Discovery of the Asylum: Social Order and Disorder in the New Republic* (Boston, 1971), 61–62.

Little in John Howard's life before 1773 separated him from his peers in the English gentry.[20] The son of a nonconformist warehouseman who had achieved personal wealth, Howard chose the life of a country squire. He lived the life of a philanthropic landlord creating model villages for his tenants and engaging in moral supervision. Howard's election as sheriff of Bedfordshire in 1773 changed all that. A sheriff's duties included examining and overseeing county jails. English sheriffs traditionally neglected the task; Howard did not. From his first visit to Bedford jail in 1773 until his death in 1790, Howard devoted his life to prison and hospital reform. Through his writings and personal behavior, Howard was the focal point of a wider British movement to improve institutional discipline.

Howard published his great work, *The State of the Prisons in England and Wales*, in 1777. Based on wide-ranging observation of British and Continental prisons and hospitals, *The State of the Prisons* provided a detailed description of prison conditions, a critique of their management, and proposals for their improvement. Howard advocated a disciplinary regime similar to that of Dutch workhouses. Renovating the prison environment and controlling prison abuses, he argued, would enable the regeneration of criminals. Penitential discipline would cure the moral diseases that created criminals as well as the physical diseases prisons spawned. No longer did the state need to lose members through excessive executions or unnecessary jail fevers.[21]

The wealth of documentation and detail in *The State of the Prisons* helped gain support for institutional reform.[22] But Howard's personality was equally important. To his contemporaries, Howard exemplified the self-sacrificing individual. He embodied a new approach to social problems, one that combined Christian duty with secular institutions to overcome the social dislocations of the age. When prison reformers imagined the ideal person to guide the penitentiary, they imagined John Howard.

Rothman seriously underestimates 18th-century efforts to reform inmates. For other discussions that document the 18th-century philosophy of reform, see Adam J. Hirsch, *The Rise of the Penitentiary: Prisons and Punishment in Early America* (New Haven, Conn., 1992), 57–60; Louis P. Masur, *Rites of Execution: Capital Punishment and the Transformation of American Culture, 1776–1865* (New York, 1989), 71–88; Negley K. Teeters, *The Cradle of the Penitentiary: The Walnut Street Jail at Philadelphia, 1773–1835* (Philadelphia, 1955), 29–62.

20. I have drawn the following discussion from Michael Ignatieff's treatment of Howard and his career in *A Just Measure of Pain: The Penitentiary in the Industrial Revolution, 1750–1850* (New York, 1978), 44–113.

21. John Howard, *The State of the Prisons in England and Wales* (London, 1777).

22. On the importance of this minute description and empiricist analysis for English prison reform, see Robin Evans, *The Fabrication of Virtue: English Prison Architecture, 1750–1840* (New York, 1982), 10–12.

This image was not limited to England. Philadelphians eagerly followed his labors and travels. In an era when civic elites prided themselves on the depth of their philanthropy, John Howard's labors seemed heroic. According to the *Packet:* "If ever there was a man who did good *for the sake of doing good,* that man was Howard. In this respect, we know not, in this age, a man more perfectly disinterested." The Philadelphia papers held him up as an indefatigable servant of the Gospels; nothing, it seemed, deterred him from the pursuit of his reforms. "His confidence in Divine Providence was strong, and the *utility* of his labours so powerfully impressed on his mind, that he permitted no amusement, nor any social pleasures to interfere with them." Almost inevitably, his labors led to his death, a death his admirers portrayed as an act of divine relief.[23] Howard represented the possibility of merging the sacred and the profane in institutions for the transformation of human personality.

When the American Revolution interrupted transportation, and the prison hulks on the Thames developed problems of health and discipline, Howard's arguments helped transform English penal policy. In 1779, Howard, William Blackstone, and William Eden drafted, and Parliament enacted, the Penitentiary Act. The act mandated the construction of two London prisons with internal regulations modeled on Dutch workhouses. Prisoners would labor constantly, and their diet, clothing, and communication would be strictly controlled. Britain would transpose the (reformed) prison from the margins to the center of penal practice.[24]

Howard's conception marked a departure not only from English practice but from his Continental models. As Michael Ignatieff has pointed out, the Continental institutions Howard's committee copied were not known as "Penitentiaries."[25] "Penitentiary" indicated the element of personal penitence the English reformers wished to add to the workhouse structure. The Penitentiary Act marked the intersection of the practice of coercive, institutionalized labor with monastic traditions of penitence and self-transformation.

The direct practical impact of the Penitentiary Act was limited. The committee overseeing the prisons' construction split internally, and neither of the two mandated prisons was built. Resistance of local elites to this centralized

---

23. *Pa. Packet,* Apr. 19, 1787, "Mr. Howard," June 16, "To the Memory of Mr. Howard," July 31, 1790; *Ind. Gazetteer,* Feb. 27, 1788; "The Humane Howard," *Freeman's Journal,* June 9, 1790. For an English equivalent of the effort to commemorate Howard's life in poetry, see Walter Lisle Bowles, quoted in Ignatieff, *A Just Measure of Pain,* 57. Howard's death from duty also resonated with the increasing sentimentality of death in British culture. On this issue, see G. J. Barker-Benfield, *The Culture of Sensibility: Sex and Society in Eighteenth-Century Britain* (Chicago, 1992), 223.

24. Ignatieff, *A Just Measure of Pain,* 93–96; John Beattie, *Crime and the Courts in England, 1660–1800* (Princeton, N.J., 1986), 573–576.

25. Ignatieff, *A Just Measure of Pain,* 94.

initiative prevented the development of any coherent national implementation of the act. Finally, the subsequent opening of transportation to Australia
reduced the pressures on the criminal justice system, suspending development of a national prison structure in England.[26]

Nonetheless, the Penitentiary Act encouraged experimentation on the local
level. Individual counties reorganized their jails along "Howardian" lines,
providing examples of apparently successful programs of reformative incarceration. On both sides of the Atlantic, these attempts helped legitimate the
belief in the reformative power of penitential prisons. Howard's writings and
the Penitentiary Act he coauthored were nodal points in a wider movement
for institutional reformation throughout England.

Howard's vocation and asceticism had led him into an alliance with other
nonconformists attempting to create new institutional arrangements. Howard's
circle was involved in activities ranging from hospital administration to industrial organization, from urban hygiene to political reform. The materialist
psychology of Locke and David Hartley provided the intellectual underpin-
nings for experiments in institutional discipline during the 1770s and 1780s.
British reformers, convinced of the unity of mind and body, created new institutional environments to root out the moral diseases then corrupting Britain, most especially, of course, among the British poor.[27]

Philadelphians duly noted these local experiments. The public papers reported on the construction of a new prison in Manchester, on T. B. Bayley's
efforts to implement Howardian plans in county institutions, and on the
spread of these techniques to the United States, most notably to Massachusetts. The Philadelphia Society for Alleviating the Miseries of Public Prisons,
as part of its agitation for solitary labor, issued a pamphlet reproducing the
rules and effects of Thomas Beevor's penitential regimen at the jail in Wy-
mondham, Norfolk. These ideas and techniques also spread through private
correspondence. English physicians John Fothergill and John C. Lettsom were
close allies to Howard, and they each had close ties to Benjamin Rush and
other religious and civic leaders in the city. It was within this international
context of institutional reform as well as the local context of public labor
that Rush developed his *Enquiry* and the debate over private punishments
occurred.[28]

26. Ibid., 91–93; Beattie, *Crime and the Courts,* 594–601; Evans, *The Fabrication of
Virtue,* 119–131.

27. Ignatieff, *A Just Measure of Pain,* 59–68; Evans, *The Fabrication of Virtue,* 74–75,
115–117. On the influence of the materialist psychology of Locke and Hartley in England,
see Ignatieff, *A Just Measure of Pain,* 66–71; Barker-Benfield, *The Culture of Sensibility,*
1–36.

28. On Howard's connections with Fothergill, see Ignatieff, *A Just Measure of Pain,*
59–60. On Rush's connections with, and attachment to, Fothergill, see George W. Corner,

Locally, the Philadelphia Society for Alleviating the Miseries of Public Prisons led the agitation for further penal change. Thirty-seven Philadelphians founded the Society in May 1787; membership grew to 175 by the spring of 1788. Although ministers dominated the Society's early leadership, merchants and professionals dominated its early membership. Of the first 175 members, 87 were merchants or professionals, 15 were clergy, 19 were probably artisans, 8 were governmental officials, 6 were gentlemen, and the occupations of 30 were of uncertain status. The membership of the Society embodied the commercial, professional, and religious alliance that pushed for the new system of punishment.[29]

This Society fused Christian charity with political advocacy. Declaring that "the obligations of benevolence . . . founded on the precepts and example of the author of Christianity" prompted its efforts, the Society argued that these "obligations" were not "cancelled by the follies or crimes of our fellow-creatures." The opposite was the case: the "miseries" that beset "that part of mankind" confined in jails called on the charitable to "extend" their "compassion." The organization set itself three goals: first, to prevent the "undue and illegal sufferings" that often accompanied imprisonment; second, to ensure that "the links, which should bind the whole family of mankind . . . be preserved intact"; third, to discover and suggest "modes of punishment" that "instead of continuing habits of vice," would be the "means of restoring our fellow-creatures to virtue and happiness." Like the Society for Political In-

---

ed., *The Autobiography of Benjamin Rush: His "Travels through Life" Together with his Commonplace Book for 1789–1813* (Princeton, N.J., 1948), 54–55; Rush to John Coakley Lettsom, Nov. 15, 1783, in Butterfield, ed., *Letters,* I, 312; and Donald J. D'Elia, *Benjamin Rush: Philosopher of the American Revolution,* in American Philosophical Society, *Transactions,* N. S., LXIV, Pt. 5 (1974), 36. Lettsom, a follower of Fothergill, was a longtime correspondent of Rush's. Among their topics were Howard and penal reform. See Rush to Lettsom, May 18, 1787, Rush to Lettsom, Sept. 28, 1787, and Rush to Lettsom, June 8, 1789, in Butterfield, ed., *Letters,* I, 417, 441, 515. See also Lettsom to Rush, July 15, 1787, Rush Papers, Library Company of Philadelphia.

29. William White, Episcopal bishop and Robert Morris's brother-in-law, was the first president. Other early leaders included George Duffield, a Presbyterian minister, William Rogers, a Baptist minister, and John Oldden, a merchant. Both Benjamin Rush and Caleb Lownes, a Quaker ironmonger who later became a key figure in administering the reformed Walnut Street Jail, were also early members (Negley K. Teeters, *They Were in Prison: A History of the Pennsylvania Prison Society* [Philadelphia, 1937], 90–99). Many of the early members of the Society were Quakers. Their exact number and influence, however, are unclear. Peter and Elizabeth Jonitas have identified at least 17 of the 37 charter members and at least 69 of the first 175 members as Quakers. See Peter Jonitas and Elizabeth Jonitas, "Members of the Prison Society: Biographical Vignettes, 1776–1830, of the Managers of the Philadelphia Society for Assisting Distressed Prisoners and the Members of the PSAMPP 1787–1830," I, 50, 147–152, II, 1–2, 34–35, Department of Special Collections, Haverford College Library, Philadelphia, Pa., 1982.

quiries, then, the Philadelphia Society saw itself as a mechanism for the reasoned interrogation of political forms. Despite its considerable, continuing charitable work, the Philadelphia Society struggled to do more than ameliorate prison conditions; it hoped to transform punishment itself.[30]

The Philadelphia Society quickly opposed public labor and supported private punishments. Addressing the General Assembly, the Society expressed its "pleasure" over the attempts to reform the penal laws but suggested that "the good ends thereby intended, have not hitherto been fully answered," a problem that could be solved by "means of some Amendments." Most important was replacing "hard labor *publickly* and disgracefully Imposed" with "more *private* or even *solitary* labor." Such labor could be "conducted more steadily and uniformly," permit the "Kind" and "Portion of labor" to be correlated precisely "to the different Abilities of the criminals," eliminate "the Evils of familiarizing young minds to vicious characters," and prevent begging. Private punishment possessed two great advantages. First, it would prevent corruption of the community by the criminals and the criminals by the community. Second, it would allow for consistent and individualized programs of reformation. The elimination of corruption and the possibility of reformation were the beauties of the prison.[31]

Proponents of private punishments both perpetuated and repudiated the goals of public labor. Like the wheelbarrow law, the Philadelphia Society and its allies believed that punishment could be made more spiritual and less corporal, that it could not only penalize but reform. In their plans, the ambiguous individualism of penal reform—its emphasis on individual responsibility and redemption—was intensified, their stress on individuation increasing both the hope of individual amendment and the demands on individual prisoners. But if they aimed to intensify the corrective power of punishment, they retreated from a vision of an open and vibrant public penal sphere. Public labor, like the constitution of 1776, had presumed that public discussion and representation should take place in the open with the participation of all citizens. The movement for private punishments represented faith in enclosed institutions, not in open, public communication.

Both the Philadelphia Society and the Society for Political Inquiries exemplified what Jürgen Habermas has described as the "bourgeois public sphere." In Europe, as Habermas has argued, the opening of the space for a public

30. Philadelphia Society for Alleviating the Miseries of Public Prisons, *Constitution* (Philadelphia, 1787).

31. Minutes, Jan. 29, 1788, PSAMPP. As another commentator stressed, reformation would proceed, at least in part, from regulated conversation. "Would it not be better they should be confined to hard labour in separate apartments, and none be permitted to speak to them but persons of good character, than to employ them in cleansing the streets?" *Pa. Packet,* June 26, 1787.

sphere where "private people come together as a public" to rationally contest and analyze governmental policy was a central development of eighteenth-century bourgeois society.[32] At the heart of this public sphere were the independent press and the social spaces of coffeehouses, reading clubs, debating societies, and moral reform associations. In these arenas, he stressed, bourgeois males could gather in an atmosphere of open conversation to discuss current developments. As part of the transatlantic republic of letters, Philadelphia was home to both a highly contentious press and numerous clubs, societies, and coffeehouses.

Within the context of this wider public sphere, the Philadelphia Society and the Society for Political Inquiries took shape. Composed of middling- and upper-class men who came together to debate public policy and social philosophy, both societies aimed to bring political power under the sway of reason. Each created clearly defined rules and regulations to ensure open debate and participation among members. Under these rules of debate, members would not merely clarify issues of pressing concern but establish themselves as individuals capable of engaging in reasoned discourse. Both groups were more than devices to affect policy; they were training grounds for rational individualization.[33] Representing themselves as the voices of reason, they epitomized the Enlightenment desire to regulate society through reason and the state through society.

The Philadelphia Society and, as the site of Rush's reflections, the Society for Political Inquiries, present the paradoxical case of a self-dissolving public sphere. Within their exercise of open debate, they implicitly defined what constituted rational conversation and who might engage in it while explicitly redrawing the map of legitimate public speech. Groups like the Philadelphia Society and the Society for Political Inquiries proposed that certain speech was too corruptive to flow freely and publicly. For those who met the discursive standards of the public sphere, open debate could continue. For those who did not, silence or discipline was the answer. The Philadelphia Society and its allies simultaneously developed out of the organized public sphere and repudiated its universalistic claims.

32. Jürgen Habermas, *The Structural Transformation of the Public Sphere: An Inquiry into a Category of Bourgeois Society,* trans. Thomas Burger (Cambridge, Mass., 1989), 27.

33. For the general structure of the Philadelphia Society for Alleviating the Miseries of Public Prisons, see their *Constitution,* and for their rules of discussion, see Minutes, Apr. 14, 1788, PSAMPP. For the structures of the Society for Political Inquiries, see their *Rules and Regulations of the Society for Political Inquiries* (Philadelphia, 1787), 2–5, and, more generally, Vinson, "The Society for Political Inquiries," *PMHB,* CXIII (1989), 185–205. For a stimulating reading of artisanal culture and fire companies that suggests that formalized and ritualized debate structures helped individuate male artisans through mutual recognition, see Ric Northrup, "Decomposition and Recomposition: A Theoretical and Historical Study of Philadelphia Artisans" (Ph.D. diss., University of North Carolina, 1989), 198–206.

By 1788, then, a transatlantic discourse was arguing that the solution to the problem of criminality lay in a penal system based on private, individualized punishments. Proponents of private punishments insisted that removing prisoners from the community and subjecting them to labor and controlled conversation would transform their character and save the community from social contamination. Leading figures on both sides of the Atlantic had adopted this discourse and had, in certain places, incorporated it into public policy. Practical local experiments had been implemented in both England and America. Reformative incarceration had emerged as an important tactic of governance and authority.

IV

Reform spoke the language of humanity. The Society for Political Inquiries viewed itself as contributing to the "Advancement of civiliiz'd Society." The Philadelphia Society, in turn, hoped to fulfill, "universal obligations," and, through their charity, to reaffirm "the links, which should bind the whole family of mankind." To its defenders, the Philadelphia Society was a true monument of the city, inheriting traditions of civic accomplishments that stretched back to the classical world. The *Pennsylvania Mercury* declared the Philadelphia Society among the "most valuable" of the societies "for charitable and literary purposes" that had emerged in Philadelphia. Quoting Edmund Burke and invoking Howard, the *Mercury* aligned the Society with transatlantic images of liberal and genteel sentiment. The paper imagined the Society's members employing "their attentive zeal to prevent, as much as in them lies, the accumulation of human sufferings, in their most common receptacles." But that was not all: "They will come in aid of the merciful designs of their country in its late lenient mitigations of sanguinary punishment, and will probably lay the foundation of a charitable system whose utility and fame will spread and increase with the progress of society." All the city's "charitable and humane," the paper insisted, were welcome in the Society's labors and would thereby earn those "laurels" gained only by helping others and thus "more likely than any other, to blossom and to flourish through every revolution of the world, and of time." [34]

But neither the penal reformers' ideas nor their humanity went unchallenged. Although fragmentary, and with little apparent influence on the creation of public policy, a defense of traditional, capital punishments appeared

34. Constitution of the Society for Political Inquiries, Preamble, HSP; Philadelphia Society for Alleviating the Miseries of Public Prisons, *Constitution;* "Observations Recommendatory of the Philadelphia Society for Alleviating the Miseries of Public Prisons," *Pa. Mercury,* May 25, 1787; "A Citizen of Philadelphia," *Pa. Packet,* Aug. 30, 1787.

in the public presses. Defenders of capital punishments opposed the rationale for private punishments on almost every point, and their arguments help reveal the distinctiveness of the reform position. Advocates of capital punishment assumed that truth was eternal and self-evident (either through the immediacy of common sense or the Scriptures). Whether through a literal reading of the Bible or the assertion of a constant social contract, defenders of traditional punishments denied the reformers' faith in the progressive improvement of human institutions. At the same time, proponents of capital punishments continued to assume a unified, coherent public culture. They believed that authority and the public realm still represented divine or natural truths, truths shared and recognized by all. Capital punishments manifested these eternal truths, striking terror in the hearts of the wicked in ways sanctioned by tradition and the Bible.

Indeed, opposition to penal reform turned on the influence of humanity. Instead of relying on God, "Philochoras" complained, people now trusted themselves: "Humanity is the popular cry! Weak men join in the cry, to gain the gaping applause of the unthinking; but as understood it degenerates into nonsense." Insisting that he entered the debate on punishment because "Liberty in the United States" was "verging fast on licentiousness," he argued that the alleged wisdom of the age had led to the "magistracy" and the "gospel" being "treated with neglect and contempt," leaving "government in a relaxed and feeble state." Nothing demonstrated the problem with "enlightened" experimentation so well as the wheelbarrow law. The wheelbarrow law, he argued, was "a sporting with justice; and in its execution at least, a burlesque on the laws of society!" Philochoras assumed that the laws of justice were eternal; the wheelbarrow law was not only unwise; it was sacrilegious. While Rush and his allies sought to differentiate themselves from the experiment with public labor, Philochoras argued that the difficulties of public labor stemmed from the same source as the proposed improvements: "our author's [Rush's] boasted humanity."[35] The humanism of the Enlightenment and the Revolution was the culprit; departing from biblical injunction and inherited practice had led to the disaster in the first place. The disorders accompanying public labor were symptomatic of the broader effects of the secular experiments of the Enlightenment and the Revolution.

Pointing to biblical injunctions and theories of a constant social contract, defenders of traditional punishments also challenged the central assumptions of the reform movement: the progressive enlightenment of society and the possibility of individual reformation. As "Candidus" put it, the "political gov-

35. "Philochoras," *Pa. Mercury,* Sept. 27, Oct. 7, 1788. On the debate between Rush and Philochoras (Noel Annan) in the context of Revolutionary-era struggles over capital punishment, see Masur, *Rites of Execution,* 67–70.

ernment" of the Hebrews "was of a peculiar kind—God himself being their immediate legislator. The code of laws therefore which He enacted must be perfect." And in this code, he noted, "murder and several other crimes" were subject to capital sanctions. Candidus acknowledged that some of the Hebraic laws and customs were of a "typical nature." But he found no "reason" to believe that human nature was so different in the American republics that it justified a revolution in penal practice. "Cato" disputed the very justice of attempts to reform individuals. Cato argued that attempts to reform criminals violated two key strictures of the social contract: that property be defended (this justified the banishment or execution of those who transgressed society's terms) and that neither liberty nor property be taken except for the unquestionable good of the whole. Attempts to reform neither expelled nor eliminated criminals; instead, they forced the virtuous part of the community to support the "vicious" through taxes. As he saw it, the laws of the community broke the contract that formed society itself.[36]

Philochoras and his allies thus repudiated the Enlightenment notion that authority and discipline could be generated from within reason and society. Instead, they argued, some external vantage point (either an unchanging social contract or an unchanging divine order) had to anchor social life and public policy. Moreover, they remained committed to the traditional economy of visibility; this vantage point had to be displayed before the assembled multitude. Authority had to be both visible and external to social life. Philochoras, citing Paul's dictum on the necessity to "rebuke" sinners before the whole community "that others might fear," argued that this command applied equally to offenders against the law: "Apply the rule to civil government, and it is, them that commit crimes, punish before all, that others might fear." The deliberate creation of terror through rituals of public degradation was not contrary to Christianity; instead, Philochoras implied, it was rooted in saintly wisdom. "The Apostle I fancy understood human nature as well as [Rush] or I."[37] Unlike those who characterized public punishments as ignorant and cruel and argued that both reason and Christianity called for their elimination, these authors saw public punishments as socially necessary and rooted in gospel teaching.

Penal reformers, on the other hand, assumed humanity had undergone a progressive enlightenment. When they posited self-evident truths or asserted that there was nothing in revelation contrary to reason, they presupposed a refined intellect capable of grasping ideas correctly. As a consequence, a sys-

---

36. "Candidus," *Ind. Gazetteer*, Apr. 21, 1787; "Cato," *Pa. Mercury*, Apr. 1, Sept. 6, 1788. For another, although less philosophical, attack on the costs of penal reform, see "The Voice of the People," *Pa. Packet*, Nov. 12, 1789.

37. "Philochoras," *Pa. Mercury*, Sept. 27, 1788.

tem of punishment necessary for older, less mature societies was not needed in a Christian republic. Rush argued the existence of a counterintuitive reason that held common sense and everyday practice to the test of "truth."[38] The necessity of removing punishment from the public domain stemmed, at least in part, from the belief that it could be entrusted only to select individuals who could represent the community and withstand the corruption of criminal contact.

Rush, in particular, assumed that it was possible to internalize order. Even more radically, however, he also presumed that it was possible to eliminate any externality to social life. God, he believed, had inscribed morality within society, nature, and the soul. The beauty of discipline was that it could incorporate the social totality within itself. "The great art of surgery has been said to consist in saving, not in destroying, or amputating, the diseased parts of the human body. Let governments learn to imitate, in this respect, the skill and humanity of the healing art." Nature did not eliminate "offal matters." Instead, they were "daily converted into the means of increasing the profits of industry, and the pleasures of human life." Only the human soul, "when misled by passion," was "abandoned, by the ignorance or cruelty of man, to unprofitable corruption, or extirpation."[39] Whereas proponents of capital punishments believed that some always remained outside of authority, Rush disagreed. All could be brought under the sway of reason and order. By applying the rules of truth to government, society could be harmonized and disciplined.

Despite the evident problems with public labor, defenders of corporal and capital punishments made few inroads against reformist ideology. The initial experiment with public labor did not dampen the enthusiasm for moderate punishments. "One of the People," responding to pro-capital punishment arguments, insisted that the reforms had resulted from "the clearest conviction of the cruelty and impiety of punishing with death men who had been guilty of crimes which affected *property* only." The old system did not differentiate between the "petty thief who stole a loaf of bread, and the unnatural son who murdered his own father" and was "contrary to the first principles of that natural law which God himself has engraved in our hearts." Reasserting the late eighteenth century's vision of the inherent cruelty of punishments against the body and reiterating the arguments for proportionality in criminal penalties, proponents of penal moderation argued that humanity remained on their side. "E. G." recalled the high hopes accompanying the wheelbarrow law that moderation, reformation, and terror could be achieved and "the lives of thousands" of criminals be saved while they received "punishments adequate to

38. Rush, *Essays,* ed. Meranze, 151–153.
39. Rush, *An Enquiry into the Effects of Public Punishments,* 17.

their crimes, and, if not too much hardened by length and courses of iniqui-
ties . . . be reclaimed and become useful citizens."[40]

Moreover, they reminded their audience, there was no evidence that the
traditional "cruel" and "impious" system actually worked. In England, another commentator noted, the "constant and strict execution of the sentence
of death" for forgery had not diminished the crime. Instead, it "has latterly
been perpetrated in England by men in higher stations than formerly . . .
so little has the severity of punishment restrained from the commission of
crime." On the other hand, there remained "no doubt" that, if "executed with
due force and justice," the new law would have "the most salutary consequences, to the community."[41] For an "Enlightened," "Christian" republic,
moderate punishments, whatever their drawbacks, remained the only true
policy.

V

Humanity also marked the realm of charity—but the realm of humanity itself
was implicitly redrawn. As reformative incarceration emerged as the dominant strategy within penality, reformers reconceptualized the nature and obligations of charitable activity. Reformers simultaneously intensified their attempts to aid inmates and placed greater stress on determining which inmates
deserved such aid. The Philadelphia Society for Alleviating the Miseries of
Public Prisons stood at this intersection of charity and punishment. Beyond
their attempts to reform the structures of punishment, the Society engaged in
acts of individual charity and intervention. And, in these charitable efforts,
they strengthened the links between charity and personal character and reinforced the connection between sentiment and submission.

The Philadelphia Society was not the first privately organized effort to aid
inmates. Traditionally, Philadelphia's citizens had made charitable contribu-
tions to prisoners, especially during winter. In 1776, a group of Philadelphians
had formed the Philadelphia Society for Assisting Distressed Prisoners. This
organization offered general relief to those held in Philadelphia jails. But it
proved short lived, its tenure disrupted by the British occupation of Philadelphia.[42] The Philadelphia Society took up this task but with new purposes.

40. "One of the People," *Pa. Packet*, Nov. 11, 1789; "E. G.," *Ind. Gazetteer*, May 19, 1787;
Beattie, *Crime and the Courts*, 554–560; McGowen, "The Body and Punishment in
Eighteenth-Century England," *Journal of Modern History*, LIX (1987), 669–670.

41. *Pa. Packet*, Aug. 22, 1787, May 14, 1788; *Pa. Eve. Herald*, Mar. 24, 1787.

42. On the Philadelphia Society for Assisting Distressed Prisoners, see Negley K. Teeters,
"The Philadelphia Society for the Relief of Distressed Prisoners," *Prison Journal*, XIXX
(1944), 452–460, and *They Were in Prison*, 14–17. On the relationship of the Philadelphia

The Society's charitable activities fell largely into two separate categories. First, it endeavored to identify any inmates wrongfully confined or who remained confined merely for the payment of fees. Many of these the Society hoped to help liberate. Second, it sought to determine when inmates suffered material deprivation. In those cases, it provided assistance to prisoners in the form of blankets, clothing, food, and so forth.[43] The Society engaged in a continuing effort to ameliorate prisoners' conditions.

But, if the Philadelphia Society perpetuated practices of charity, it also altered their nature. Previously, it appears, charity was distributed among prisoners with little effort to distinguish among recipients. But the Philadelphia Society actively investigated the characters and situations of those whose cases it considered. Especially when its charity related to helping individuals held for fees or seeking bail, the Society sought out the details of the inmates' history, background, and current situation (sometimes corresponding with respectable people who might have known the inmates before their confinement). Only then would it distribute its charity to those whose characters seemed worthy.[44]

Eligibility was not, however, the only link between charity and character. If a vicious reputation could exclude an inmate from assistance, the assistance itself was designed to aid in the process of reformation. Indeed, the hoped-for tie between reformation and charity extended beyond individual cases. When Benjamin Rush donated some melons to prison inmates, he appended a note to request "that in receiving them they would consider that their merciful

---

Society for Alleviating the Miseries of Public Prisons to earlier charitable efforts, see Michael Meranze, "The Penitential Ideal in Late Eighteenth-Century Philadelphia," *PMHB*, CVIII (1984), 443–445.

43. For examples of early efforts to liberate inmates, either through funds—having their fines waved—or other official action, see "To the Supreme Executive Council of the State of Pennsylvania; The Representation of the Subscribers," Sept. 1, 1787, PSAMPP-Society; Minutes of the Acting Committee, Aug. 23, 1787, Minute Book, 1787–1793, PSAMPP; Joseph Bankson to William Bradford, n.d., PSAMPP-Society. For examples of the Society's giving material assistance to prisoners, see *Pa. Packet,* Nov. 15, 1787, Jan. 8, 1789; *Pa. Mercury,* Jan. 15, 1788. The Society continued to provide this sort of charity throughout the late 18th and 19th centuries.

44. See, for example, in the case of Mary Fisher, Mr. Cathbert to George Duffield, May 3, 1788, and George Duffield to John Oldden, May 8, 1788, PSAMPP-Society; in the case of Thomas Welch, George Duffield to John Oldden, May 8, 1788, ibid.; in the case of Barney Hughes, Minutes of the Acting Committee, Aug. 23, 1787, Minute Book, 1787–1793, PSAMPP. For cases of those deemed unworthy, see Minutes of the Acting Committee, Aug. 23, 1787, Minute Book, 1787–1793, PSAMPP. For a more detailed description of information leading to a refusal to aid one of these prisoners, see Dr. Enoch Edwards to George Duffield and John Oldden, Aug. 20, 1787, PSAMPP-Society.

Creator by disposing one of his creatures to remember them in their present bonds discovers himself still to be their friend and Benefactor, and ready to receive them into his favor on repentance and amendment of their lives."[45] To Rush, charity was more than the relief of suffering; it functioned as a positive tool in the transformation of character. Just as the penal environment should be disciplined and subject to knowledge, so should the practice of charity.

The transformative aspect of charitable giving manifested the ambiguous individualism of reformative incarceration. Reformative incarceration recognized the individual criminal in two ways. On the one hand, the possibility of reformation presupposed that individuals could alter their lives: criminals need not be permanently outcast or degraded. But, as the selective and instrumental aspects of charity indicate, reformation added another element to punishment: criminals were expected to assume responsibility for the course of their own punishment. It was, in part, the manner in which inmates accepted the framework of authority that determined their access to the bounties of Christian charity.

The import of this charitable individualism can be seen through the wider issue of poverty and poor relief in late-eighteenth-century Philadelphia. The linking of reformation, selectivity, and charity was not limited to the Philadelphia Society or relevant only to inmates in the jail. Instead, it reflected a newer conceptualization of poverty and poor relief that sought to transform the relationship between poverty and charity and put great stress on the separation of different sorts of poor people. Late-eighteenth-century charity became not only a necessary safeguard against the unfortunate vicissitudes of earthly chance but a tool for the active remaking of individuals.

Philadelphians took the first steps toward this understanding of poverty and poor relief during the 1760s. In 1766, owing to the rising numbers of the city's poor and the growing amount of the city's poor tax, the colonial Assembly passed legislation that created a semipublic organization to establish and oversee a "Bettering House" for the confinement and reformation of the poor. The Bettering House, directed largely by Quaker merchants, represented the belief that many of the poor owed their poverty, not to temporary misfortune, natural causes (aging, infirmity, loss of relatives), or social circumstance, but to their own social habits. Its design incorporated a new—for Philadelphia at least—philosophy of poor relief. The very existence of the Bettering House challenged the traditional emphasis upon supporting the poor in their homes.

The House's philosophical importance was not limited to this attack on outdoor relief. The House was to be divided into two sections. The first, a continuation of the traditional almshouse, would shelter those poor unable to

---

45. Corner, ed., *The Autobiography of Benjamin Rush,* 253.

work, and the second would be a workhouse for the able-bodied poor. It would, its proponents claimed, lessen the costs of poor relief not only by providing employment for the industrious but also by "subjecting the Indolent and Supine to the Necessity of labouring for their Support."[46] The House's managers assumed that labor could reform this latter group. The Bettering House presumed that poverty (and the poor) could not be controlled with the older techniques of individual assistance but necessitated an institutional approach.

The Bettering House did not escape opposition. The "industrious" poor resisted confinement in the House, and their productivity never met the managers' expectations. The Revolutionary upheaval made the always problematic task of collecting the poor tax even more difficult. The result was economic chaos; the Bettering House failed to support itself and was chronically debt-ridden.[47] At the same time, the city's overseers of the poor remained committed, through the 1780s at least, to preserving outrelief for the "deserving poor" and struggled to keep the political and economic power of the Bettering House managers in check.

Still, despite opposition, the movement against outdoor relief—and in favor of employing poor relief for the transformation of character—continued in the 1780s and 1790s. In fact, the dominance of this approach grew during the post-Revolutionary period. During the 1760s, not only the poor but the overseers of the poor had resisted the movement to suppress outrelief. Arguing that many of the poor could survive at home with small amounts of aid (and perhaps seeking to preserve the basis of their authority), the overseers had struggled against the imposed confinement of individuals in the Bettering House. But in the late 1780s and early 1790s, after gaining control over the Bettering House (and being incorporated as the Guardians of the Poor of the City of Philadelphia), the overseers modified their position. Although they ameliorated some of the harsher conditions within the house of employment, they assumed the program of the managers by severely curbing outrelief.[48]

This transformation in the overseers' position appears to have stemmed, at least in part, from changes in their socioeconomic status. In the pre-Revolutionary period, the overseers were mostly artisans. Thus, socially, they differed greatly from the managers, who were primarily merchants. The overseers may have had more day-to-day contact with the laboring poor and, con-

46. John K. Alexander, *Render Them Submissive: Responses to Poverty in Philadelphia, 1760–1800* (Amherst, Mass., 1980), 87–89 (quotation on 88), 89, 91; Gary B. Nash, "Poverty and Poor Relief in Pre-Revolutionary Philadelphia," *WMQ*, 3d Ser., XXXIII (1976), 14–16.

47. Alexander, *Render Them Submissive*, 97–104.

48. Ibid., 103–121.

sequently, may have been more sensitive to the wishes of the poor.[49] But, by the 1780s, the social composition of the overseers had changed dramatically. Although still composed, in part, of artisans, and never as wealthy as the managers, the overseers (and their successors, the Guardians of the Poor) were increasingly drawn from the mercantile sector of the community. As the social composition of the overseers changed, their defense of outrelief lessened.

The overseers' changing social status cannot explain entirely the transformation of their position, however. Their altered position reflected a wider reconceptualization of poverty and poor relief. During the mid-1780s, elite Philadelphians demonstrated an increasing concern to distinguish the "vicious" from the "deserving" poor.[50] This concern manifested itself most clearly in the argument that, in many cases, the roots of poverty lay in individual character and that wealth and power resulted from individual effort. "The superior industry, frugality and abilities of some," "An Essay on Hard Times" argued, "will ever procure wealth and respect, while the idleness and dissipation of others must beget contempt and indigence." It was these differences in effort and character, not social conditions or external constraints, that caused the poor to be poor. "Hence an unavoidable distinction will take place, not from the design of individuals, but is the consequence naturally resulting from the pursuit of different plans in life; and hence, in some measure, every individual is answerable for his want of respect, and frequently for his indigence." As poverty came to be seen as an individual flaw, the question of society's proper response was problematized.[51]

---

49. On the social composition of the overseers and the managers, see ibid., 111–115. That the overseers were more sensitive to the wishes of the poor does not imply that the managers were unconcerned about the well-being of their poor charges. That the managers believed confinement in the House of Employment would be beneficial to the inmates is not at question. But there is clear evidence that the poor resented their forced confinement and preferred outrelief as a means of assistance, which allowed them to retain their dignity in trying times. And it does appear that the overseers were more sensitive to this attitude on the part of the laboring poor. On these issues, see ibid., 90–96; Steven Rosswurm, *Arms, Country, and Class: The Philadelphia Militia and 'Lower Orders' in the American Revolution, 1765–1783* (New Brunswick, N. J., 1987), 28–29.

50. Alexander, *Render Them Submissive*, 51–54, 73–74, 84–85.

51. "On the Misery Attending Idleness," *Pa. Packet*, Oct. 12, 1785, "An Essay on Hard Times," June 8, 1787; "On the Meanness and Malignity of Indolence," *Freeman's Journal*, Oct. 5, 1785. Although many blamed the individual for his poverty, some disagreement remained over the causes of poverty. As Alexander has shown, there was a continuing discourse that attributed poverty not to flaws of individual character but rather to social conditions. But the emphasis on individual responsibility for poverty predominated in the discourse about the poor and was the basic assumption behind the practices of the social institutions designed to respond to poverty. See Alexander, *Render Them Submissive*, esp. 77–79. See also, *Ind. Gazetteer*, July 18, 1787.

Critics charged that the idle, unlike those who labored consistently, were particularly susceptible to vice. The activity of business, "Monitor" argued, pointed an individual toward morality and virtue. For people who "engaged in business, its cares engross the attention, and there is not room for those vicious thoughts which might otherwise croud in upon the mind, nor leisure to attend to unlawful inclinations." They were "by this means kept out of the way of many fatal temptations which assault, and too often prevail over men." But, for those who failed to labor, the habits of idleness and viciousness intensified each other. One commentator bemoaned the fact that despite the "many resources which this period of the year [summer] presents to the poor, but industrious citizen, for the maintenance of his family . . . the number of vagrants and robbers [in the city] is not diminished." He believed that the root of this continued criminality lay in habits of indolence and its cure in the imposed discipline of the state: "When indeed the people have acquired habits of indolence and dissipation, there can be little hope of their reformation without the compulsory interposition of government." [52] The susceptibility of the idle to vice meant they could not be merely supported; they had to be transformed.

The redefinition of the nature and causes of poverty paralleled the effort that accompanied public labor to rethink the relationship between justice and mercy. As the numbers receiving poor relief grew, and as concern over criminality spread, some writers suggested that charity itself could cause vice and licentiousness. "Benevolus," although cautioning that he "would not be understood to discourage the charitably disposed from listening to the complaints of the vulgar poor," suggested that poverty "may have been the offspring of vice and imprudence." Like "excessive" pardons, a confusion of justice and mercy could lead to an "ill-timed charity." "We should be just, then generous and merciful." Delaying relief was "proper sometimes" so that "the subject, for his own sake," might feel the "bitter consequences that flowed from the seeming sweet draughts of vice." In this manner, "he might be taught, in the school of affliction, to correct in his future life . . . the errors of his past." [53] Assistance to the poor should only be distributed judiciously; it should not only relieve but transform.

Others went further. One correspondent suggested that, although both the "industrious" and "vicious" poor were worthy of public attention, only "the first [should be] supported as the orphans of the public." The "vicious," on

---

52. "Monitor," *Pa. Packet,* Jan. 14, 1786, June 28, 1787.

53. "Benevolus," *Freeman's Journal,* Sept. 24, 1788. Benjamin Franklin had made similar arguments. See Franklin, "'Arator': On the Price of Corn, and Management of the Poor," and "On the Laboring Poor," in Leonard Labaree et al., eds., *The Papers of Benjamin Franklin* (New Haven, Conn., 1959–), XIII, 512–516, XV, 103–107.

the other hand, "should be kept by authority to hard labour." The magistrates must be empowered to "compel the able and the idle to resort to their own labour for support." When the poor failed to labor industriously, they forfeited public sympathy; the vicious and idle poor, one critic charged, were no better than animals:

> Idleness, which is blameable in all persons, is insupportable in such as these; nor have they any claim to a maintenance from the public. The Scriptures have declared, that he who will not work, shall not eat; and it cannot be called an unmerciful severity to bestow nothing upon those who are able but not disposed to do any thing for themselves; who by obstinate laziness and perpetual foolishness become public nuisances; who prefer beggarly indolence to honest industry; who having two hands and two feet, expect to be fed like the fowls of the air, and to be clothed like flowers of the field, though they resemble not the one or the other, being neither useful nor ornamental in the creation. The only favor which suits such persons is compulsion; as among their relations, the brutes, those which will not be led must be driven.

From this perspective, the poor deserved no special sympathy.[54] In their indolence, they regressed to the level of beasts; they violated the laws of Scripture and of nature. The only way to avoid the spread of animality among the poor was to compel them to labor and to reform.

Not only were the idle poor a drain on the financial resources of the community, and the locus of criminality, their very presence, the *Pennsylvania Packet* charged, threatened to undermine the moral fiber of society. It was a "Vulgar Error" to assume that an idle individual did "hurt *to no one but himself.*" Because of the power of example, the idle threatened all who saw them: "The idle man, who, by a vulgar error, is supposed to be *nobody's enemy but his own*, is, in fact, the enemy of all his relatives, and the enemy of all who, seeing him, may follow his example." The example of an idle individual spread low and base habits through society: "He is something more than a blank in the creation, for he teaches others to neglect their duty as he has done. . . . The idle man, who is vicious, adds to the prevalence of bad example, and takes a part from the encouragement virtue ought to meet with."[55] The contagion of mimetic corruption emanated from the poor as well as the criminal.

The qualities of late-eighteenth-century humanity, then, were contradictory indeed. The very belief in reformation evinced faith in individual capacity. And the discourse of humanitarian concern seemed to indicate an expan-

---

54. *Pa. Packet,* June 7, 1787; "On the Meanness and Malignity of Indolence," *Freeman's Journal,* Oct. 5, 1785.

55. "Vulgar Error," *Pa. Packet,* July 14, 1789.

sion of the obligations of society to provide assistance and possibilities to the poor and the outcast. But, at the same time, the notion of humanity was practically, if implicitly, tied to certain laboring, submissive behaviors. If the obligation of humanity was extended, it was not extended to all of humanity. And, although reformation meant the increasing recognition of individual inmates, it was paradoxically linked with the collective concealment of the criminal and the poor. For inmates to be extended the possibility of subjective transformation, it seems, they had to be subjected to objectifying isolation.

By the late 1780s, then, the discourse and policy on poverty were remarkably similar to the critique of public labor. The fear of mimetic corruption permeated perceptions of the poor and criminal. Unlike the defenders of traditional modes of public punishments, these reformers believed that the contradictions of public examples could be overcome by fragmenting the public domain and isolating sources of social contagion. They argued that poor relief and criminal justice should be structured around segregative and reformative incarceration to remove inmates from potential corrupting influences (in order to reform them) and prevent inmates from corrupting the wider community. In this way, the dangers of uncontrolled public communication could be averted.

VI

The redefinition of poor relief intersected with the continuing attack on the qualifications of the city's magistrates. Critics tied the emergence of trading justices to the democratization of officeholding and the decline in the social status of the magistrates. Nonelite magistrates, critics asserted, lacked the sensibility to uphold authority effectively. Through their criticism, they formulated a definition of appropriate authority and virtuous masculinity. As the reorganization of poor relief had operated to impose differences among the poor, the debate over trading justices served to promote the claims of social distinction.

Critics of trading justices argued that restoring the better sort to public office would end judicial abuse. Only those with sufficient property should serve as magistrates, for only they would be sufficiently disinterested to recognize justice. A proper magistrate, "A Freeman" suggested, was an individual "who will not exercise the office for the sake of the profits arising therefrom; who has a competent estate, and will undertake it from a noble and disinterested affection for his country; who has knowledge sufficient to enable him to administer justice with impartiality; and integrity, to enable him to perform his duty with uprightness." "Zenophon" echoed this position. He argued that a magistrate had to possess both wealth and knowledge. To his mind, the qualifications of the magistrate were clear:

1. He should be a man of real untainted probity and honesty. . . .

2. His situation and circumstances in life ought to be substantial and independent of his office. . . .

3. A competent knowledge of the law and constitution of the country is also proper for him to possess. . . .

4. Management and courtesy in the exercise of business.

In a word, he had to possess sensibility. The ideal magistrate was a male with substantial property and education.[56]

From this perspective, judicial democracy was dangerous because it had changed the social composition of the judiciary. Elections had opened judicial office to nonelite men. A self-perpetuating corporation had governed colonial Philadelphia. After Independence, Revolutionary leaders withdrew Philadelphia's charter and altered the way city officials were chosen. Instead of members of the city corporation (drawn from the city's Quaker social elite) choosing justices, now they were selected by the public. It was this change that led to the abuses of the trading justices: "The mal-practices of our Justices have but one origin: They all spring from the *manner of their being elected*." Not only were "improper and unfit persons" elected, but they were "men who flagrantly abuse and invert every principle of their duty, and make a meer trade and commerce of justice."[57] The election of magistrates, critics charged, was at the root of the "trade and commerce" of justice. It was an unwise excess of democracy.

At stake in the debate was the right to govern the city. To critics of trading justices, the democratization of office holding was another example of the dangerous blurring of social distinctions within the city. Indeed, the apocalyptic tone of the critique turned on the fact that trading justices were not gentlemen. The "justices of the peace for the city of Philadelphia have been chosen from among that class of people, who have very little property." In former

56. "A Freeman," *Pa. Eve. Herald,* May 6, 1786; "Zenophon," *Pa. Mercury,* June 26, 1788; "Aristedes," *Ind. Gazetteer,* Sept. 17, 1785. Some did believe that problems could be lessened by increasing judicial accountability. The *Pennsylvania Evening Herald* suggested printing a list of legal fees to enable people to protect themselves from judicial extortion (*Pa. Eve. Herald,* July 27, 1785). Some lawyers proposed a legal aid society for the poor. This society could aid the poor in pressing complaints about judicial abuse. "A Hint," ibid., Aug. 22, "A Young Lawyer," Aug. 23, 1787.

For other descriptions of the proper magistrate as a gentleman of sensibility, see "Leonatas," *Ind. Gazetteer,* Sept. 10, 1785, "A Well-wisher to the Community," May 6, 1786; *Pa. Packet,* Aug. 23, 1787; "Senex," *Pa. Mercury,* June 17, "Socrates," June 24, 1788.

57. "Leonatas," *Ind. Gazetteer,* Sept. 10, 1785, June 18, 1787. For similar criticisms, see *Pa. Packet,* Sept 9, 1785; *Pa. Eve. Herald,* July 27, 1785, "A Freeman," May 6, 1786; "A Citizen," *Ind. Gazetteer,* June 6, 1787. The final choice in selecting judges lay with the president and his council. But they were to choose between the two individuals who received the greatest number of votes.

times public offices were sought only for "honor," but "of late Mechanics lay by their tools and become Constables to attend at the door of office to facilitate the destruction of some industrious and needy family, with less compassion than a crocodile." According to "Astrea," constables were even worse. They were "men taken from the lowest order of citizens; without property, character, honesty, humanity, or conscience; wretches destitute of every principle and sentiment that dignify human nature; fellows as dogishly cringing, and pitifully subservient to the magistrate, as they are insolently, haughty, and cruel to those in their custody." [58] Metaphors of animality linked the issue of trading justices to the discourse of poverty—casting the poor as brutes and figuring the justices and their assistants as predators and jackels. Each embodied the dangers posed by mimetic corruption run amok.

At the same time, the assault on trading justices was part of a larger effort to redefine elite manhood. A transatlantic "culture of sensibility" placed great emphasis on educating manners and cultivating empathy and sympathy. Rush's attack on public labor had presupposed the possibility of the formation, and deformation, of sensibility. The institutions of the bourgeois public sphere themselves were, in part, places to train and discipline the manners of men.[59] Yet, instead of displaying the sensibility and empathy of the "man of feeling," trading justices were devouring and cannibalistic. Instead of nurturing a peaceful society, they sowed the seeds of discord. Trading justices embodied the danger of an external and consuming political power.

To their critics, trading justices and wheelbarrow men signified the disruptive and destabilizing effects of Revolutionary democratization. Despite its nostalgic overtones, the assault on trading justices was rooted in concerns generated out of the post-Revolutionary order. Trading justices, like wheelbarrow men, revealed fears about the instability of the individual personality. They were each depicted in the public press as animalistic or subhuman, as vicious and violent, as humanity gone horribly wrong. They each served as sites for depositing the anxieties that swirled around the fear of mimetic corruption; they provided mechanisms for acknowledging yet containing the incomplete universality of the republican public sphere. If the dangers of trading

58. "A Well-wisher to the Community," *Ind. Gazetteer,* May 6, 1786, "Astrea," May 21, 1787. The narrowness of class prejudice, critics believed, blinded voters to the true qualities of candidates, causing them to vote only for those of similar status in the hopes of greater sympathy. See "A Freeman," *Pa. Eve. Herald,* May 6, 1786.

Some critics proposed making the magistracy salaried. See "A. B.," *Pa. Packet,* Sept. 9, 1785; *Pa. Eve. Herald,* July 27, 1785; and Alexander, *Render Them Submissive,* 72, 203 n. 35. It should also be noted that there was a long-standing political objection to salaried justices derived from a fear that such a salary would increase the possibility of judicial oppression.

59. Joan Landes, *Women and the Public Sphere in the Age of the French Revolution* (Ithaca, N.Y. 1989). I am borrowing the phrase "culture of sensibility" from Barker-Benfield's, *The Culture of Sensibility.*

justices and wheelbarrow men were to be overcome, the elite would have to reconstitute its own behavior on a new basis—that of sensibility. And new institutions would have to be developed that would diffuse the danger of mimetic corruption.

VII

The desire to return sensibility to the scene of justice found its counterpart in the sentimentalization of the theater. Defenders of the theater responded quickly to the Quakers and their allies. Opposing the association of the theater with corruption, advocates of the stage linked theatricality with distinction, culture, and virtue. In their vision, the importance of example and communication necessitated, not theatrical silence, but controlled speech, speech that (like a sermon) would teach the audience the way to survive in the world while improving their manners. Just as the courts would be returned to men of sensibility, sentimental speech would correct the stage and make it appropriate for the new Republic. Refined theatrical speech would help overcome the dangers of mimetic corruption.

Initially, the Quakers and their allies were successful. The legislature continued the ban on theatrical entertainments in 1786. But this action, and the Quakers' agitation for it, stimulated a counterattack by the stage's defenders. Their efforts led to legislative reconsideration of the ban on the stage and, eventually, in 1789, to passage of a bill allowing theatrical performances in Philadelphia.[60] The theater passed from an illicit enterprise, limited to the outskirts of the city, to an officially approved form of urban entertainment.

The defense of the theater highlights the social basis of the prison reform and antitheater movements. Although religious leaders were important advocates for the organized prison reform movement, substantial support also came from the city's commercial classes. In the case of suppressing the theater, however, religious leaders found their allies mainly among rural Presbyterians.[61] Many of Philadelphia's elite sought to enhance their social distinction (within the city and in the eyes of outsiders) through patronizing the theater.

The defenders of the theater sought to establish the stage's importance for obtaining social distinction and culture. Whereas opponents of the stage drew on long-standing Christian (and especially Protestant) suspicions of the stage as a source of social duplicity and transgression, advocates of the stage concentrated on its civilizing and enlightening effects. They argued that the stage

60. *Pa. Packet,* Feb. 9, 1789; *Freeman's Journal,* Feb. 11, 1789; *St. at Large,* XIII, 184–186.
61. Robert Brunhouse, *The Counter-Revolution in Pennsylvania: 1776–1790* (Philadelphia, 1942), 184. See above for a discussion of the membership of the Philadelphia Society for Alleviating the Miseries of Public Prisons.

could be both a source of cultural prestige for the city and a tool for a virtuous education. A well-regulated theater would educate the commonality to distinguish virtue from vice while providing the city's elites with stimulating and refreshing diversions. Defenders of the theater did not deny the increasing social differentiation in the city, nor did they subsume their defense under a vision of a relatively homogeneous virtuous citizenry. Instead, they built the defense of the theater on a recognition (and indeed validation) of social distinctions within the community. The glory of the theater lay in its alleged ability to operate differentially on its viewers and provide incentives for virtue appropriate for the different classes of its audience.

Proponents of the stage saw it as a tool for refining social manners, a "school of *manners, sentiment,* and *virtue.*" Displaying the benefits of virtue and the dangers of vice, stage plays inculcated moderate and republican dispositions. The theater was the "most effectual mode of painting vice and virtue in their different colours, and lashing the growing evils and follies of the time." The result of these dramatic paintings was a general rise in sensibility and culture. Refinement was not a sign of aristocratic decadence, as the Quakers and their allies feared, but rather an indication of the progressive enlightenment of republican society. "Dramatic Pieces," a legislative committee suggested, "tend to the general refinement of manners and polish in society, than which nothing can be more favorable to the growth of the virtues." [62] Refinement went hand in hand with virtue.

The stage, its defenders claimed, was "the great Mart of Genius." The encouragement of a native theater was "a natural and necessary concomitant" of political independence. The failure of Americans to patronize their own theater had left them dependent in thought and manners on the Old World: "We have cast off a foreign yoke in government, but shall still be dependent for those productions of the mind, which do most honor to human nature, until we can afford due protection and encouragement to every species of our own literature." The theater taught skills of communication—skills particularly important in a republic. Both leaders and citizens needed eloquence and the ability to discuss issues. The republican Revolution depended on the transformation of culture and manners. [63]

62. *Pa. Packet,* Nov. 13, "Anti-Persecutor," Dec. 27, 1788; "Impartial," *Ind. Gazetteer,* Feb. 25, 1786.

63. *Pa. Packet,* Nov. 13, 1788, "Candidus," Feb. 16, 1789. For thoughtful discussions of the place of eloquence and rhetorical skills among both speakers and listeners during the Revolution, see Jay Fliegelman, *Declaring Independence: Jefferson, Natural Language, and the Culture of Performance* (Stanford, Calif., 1993), esp. 35–49; Kenneth Cmiel, *Democratic Eloquence: The Fight over Popular Speech in Nineteenth-Century America* (New York, 1990), 39–54.

If the theater was essential to republican culture in general, it was especially important to the glory of Philadelphia. Philadelphia's elite hoped to secure the national government for

Proponents of the stage inverted the Protestant identification of the theater with base and vicious character. Rather than a haunt of the vicious, they argued, the theater was a haven for Philadelphia's better sorts. One commentator, discussing a theater audience that he estimated as between six and seven hundred people, claimed that many "were, in point of consequence, the first our city or counties could produce." To identify the theater solely with depraved or vicious people was mere prejudice. The better sort not only attended theatrical performances; they were its strongest proponents. The "principal support" of the theater "arises from the wealthy and enlightened part of mankind, who have every endearing tie to society, that can excite a love of virtue, and a desire for the prosperity of the rising generation." The wealthy would not support an institution harmful to the peace and security of society. The fears that the theater would undermine republican virtue were based on groundless superstition.[64]

The stage, its advocates claimed, refined manners in a particularly pleasing way. Elites supported the stage because theatrical performances were appropriate entertainment for their families. The theater provided opportunities for men of business to relax and enlighten themselves and their families. "Observator" painted a portrait of a father who had "fulfilled the office of a parent, with tenderness and care, and in doing a good action." It was the theater that enabled him to do these good deeds:

> After the necessary business of the day is over, the mercantile man, or even the man in a more elevated situation, will, to the great satisfaction of his family, carry them with him to the play-house, in order to see a good Tragedy, or perhaps a comedy performed; in which is contained a variety of the noblest sentiments of the humane mind; and on the other hand, laying open to the most undiscerning, the frailties of nature; and drawing the comparison between good and evil. Picture to yourself the pleasure he must feel, when he returns home, to see his little family elated with what they had heard, and repeating those parts which most engaged their attention.

---

the city. The theater's proponents, pointing to the attachment of many, including Washington, to the stage, argued that the city needed a fully flourishing culture to attract the national elite. The stage was necessary not only for the city's internal refinement but for its national and international distinction as well. See Kenneth Silverman, *A Cultural History of the American Revolution: Painting, Music, Literature, and the Theatre in the Colonies and the United States from the Treaty of Paris to the Inauguration of George Washington, 1763–1789* (New York, 1976), 593–594.

64. "Vice and Immorality," *Pa. Packet*, Dec. 12, "Anti-Persecutor," Dec. 27, 1788, Feb. 10, 1789.

The theater could be a crucial tool in social reproduction—a school where the young and old of elite families would learn sensibility and manners.[65]

The stage, rather than corroding domestic ties, reinforced them; it refreshed the family through collective relaxation and moral education. The theater provided a "rational" and necessary amusement for women who otherwise would be trapped in the home. Just as important, the theater drew men away from other, truly vicious, pursuits. Since the theater was "fascinating," "Candidus" suggested, it would keep men from gaming or taverns. Echoing these concerns, "Observator" argued that, if the theater were eliminated, the young "will naturally turn their minds to other amusements, more destructive to their health, and perhaps to their pockets." Nor was the danger limited merely to the young; their elders would also fall prey to ill-considered amusements. "Those more advanced in years, will probably go to a tavern, there to repeat the occurrences of the day, spend at least as much, if not more, than would have taken him to the theatre, return home, not so well entertained, and I am convinced, not in so good a habit of body next day."[66] The theater, by providing families with rational and refined amusements, reinvigorated their bodies and minds. Its elimination, rather than curbing vice, would only help to spread it further.

Defenders of the theater also argued that the stage could teach the poor and illiterate the lessons of virtue. Candidus emphasized the social benefits the community would obtain by using the theater to educate the lower orders: "Benevolence, justice, heroism, and the wisdom of moderating the passions, are plainly pointed out, and forcibly recommended to those savage sons of uncultivated nature, who have few opportunities, and would have no inclination for instruction, if it did not present itself under the form of a delightful amusement." The stage, he argued, could provide instruction to those "who cannot acquire it by *reading;* to relax and give their minds fresh vigour; to soften their manners, by inculcating the sentiments of humanity, honour, and all the moral virtues; to acquaint them with historical facts—and above all, to inspire them with a love of their country, is not only rendering them service, but essentially benefitting the community."[67] Plays and players were tools that the community should seize to help educate the poor and the illiterate. Properly handled, the stage would not incite its audience to vice; instead, it would dispose them toward virtue.

65. "Observator," *Ind. Gazetteer,* Aug. 3, 1787. These critics presumed the successful transformation of the stage in the direction of sensibility, a process that continued throughout the 18th century. On the sentimentalization of the British stage, see Janet Todd, *Sensibility: An Introduction* (New York, 1986), 32–48.

66. "Impartial," *Ind. Gazetteer,* Feb. 25, 1786, "Observator," Aug. 3, 1787; *Pa. Packet,* Feb. 10, 1789.

67. "Candidus," *Pa. Packet,* Feb. 4, 1789.

Proponents of the stage followed the Lockean emphasis on the importance of example in education. Locke had maintained that children should be taught, not through the memorization of precepts, but through discussion of concrete examples. It was the educator's task to ensure that students were familiar with only proper examples. For "Civis," the stage's employment of example made it an appropriate tool for teaching republican virtue: "Example is more powerful than precept, and representations on the stage have the effect of example." The fictions of the stage should not be feared, they should be exploited in order to inculcate values; the power of the visual should be mobilized in the interests of the moral: "If the painter and historian, says Sir Richard Steel, can do much in colours and language, what may not be performed by an excellent poet, when the character he draws is presented by the person, the manner, the look, and the motion of an accomplished player? If a thing painted or related can irresistibly enter our heads, what may not be brought to pass by seeing generous things performed before our eyes?"[68] If Rush, in his critique of public punishments, had argued against display because of the spectator's lack of aesthetic and moral distance, the supporters of theater aimed to deploy that lack of distance for their own purposes.

The theater, moreover, allowed the display of social differentiation. Although plays brought together all "ranks and classes," the audience was not merged indifferently. The theater was open to all, but viewers were divided into social sections (box, gallery, pit) based on the price of their tickets.[69] The great could distinguish themselves, at least partially, by purchasing the more expensive seats. In this way, economic differentiation was reproduced socially and spatially. The theater, by bringing the community together in a controlled way, could help to teach all their proper place.

At the same time, however, the theater crowd allowed the merging of social groups. The theater experience simultaneously differentiated and merged the audience: "The gallery could not receive all that came with tickets, the pit was so full that the people were obliged in many parts of it to stand, and some laughable scenes exhibited themselves at the expence of the little folks. . . . The boxes were overflowing—'The cream, the *new,* and much of the *skim* milk'— all mixed together. Tho' the former now and then seemed to curdle with disdain."[70] Despite the "laughable scenes" occurring "at the expence of the little folks," it was not possible for the great to separate themselves completely.

68. Fliegelman, *Prodigals and Pilgrims,* 12–16; "Civis," *Pa. Packet,* Mar. 5, "XY," July 10, 1787.

69. On the bringing together of the community, see "Anti-Persecutor," *Pa. Packet,* Dec. 27, 1789. For an example of pricing and sections, see the theater advertisement, ibid., July 10, 1787.

70. William Bradford, Jr., to Susan Bradford, May 6, 1790, Wallace Papers, HSP.

Whatever disdain elites may have felt, the theater brought the whole community together in pursuit of entertainment.

In certain ways, the social relationships within the theater audience were quite traditional. They continued the processes of identification and differentiation that occurred during colonial public entertainments. But these continuities should not be overstated. Traditional entertainments had stressed the active social interaction between classes (in drinking, gambling, cockfighting, and so forth). In the theater, on the other hand, although the "cream" and the "skim milk" were both present, the seating structures minimized their contact. The theater audience symbolized a (partly fluid) social hierarchy increasingly determined by access to money. In calling the theater a "Mart of Genius," emphasis must be placed as much on "mart" as on "genius." The theater displayed a social hierarchy increasingly stratified according to monetary distinctions.[71]

Proponents of the stage, however, did not intend for the players to be "at liberty to exhibit what pieces they pleased." Instead, they sought a stage "under a proper regulation." In this way, the stage's defenders incorporated the fear of corruption within their position. Like the critics of public labor, they hoped to eliminate contagious and corruptive statements. Only those plays that met the approval of the city's better sorts would be allowed. The discourses of the stage would be limited to those that inculcated virtue.[72]

Here, then, was a complete reversal of the Protestant critique of the stage as rooted in aristocratic and vicious habits. It was the mercantile man or one of a "more elevated situation," not the courtier or the criminal, who took his family to the theater. The stage, rather than being a source of vice, would transmit lessons of virtue. It would draw men and women away from corruption and restore the minds and bodies of families. The theater would reinforce social distinction within the city and strengthen the city's claims to distinction. But it would accomplish these things by being strictly controlled. The city's elite would not depend merely on the qualities of plays and players; they would supervise and control the productions of the stage. The stage, rather than being the site of popular disorder and corruption, was reconceptualized as the locus for elite distinction and popular refinement.

In 1789, the legislature transformed these sentiments into law. On March 2, the General Assembly lifted the ban on theatrical exhibitions in and around

---

71. Rosswurm, *Arms, Country, and Class,* 27, 34–39; Eric Foner, *Tom Paine and Revolutionary America* (New York, 1976), 19–56. For a discussion of the links between a culture of theatricality and a culture of the market, see Agnew, *Worlds Apart,* 149–203.

72. "Civis," *Pa. Packet,* Mar. 5, 1787; "Observator," *Ind. Gazetteer,* Aug. 3, 1787. On the long-term domestication of the theater, see Peter Stallybrass and Allon White, *The Politics and Poetics of Transgression* (Ithaca, N.Y., 1986), 66–100.

Philadelphia. The Assembly justified its actions as a response to public demand, noting that "a great number of the citizens of Philadelphia and the neighborhood thereof have petitioned this house for a repeal of so much of a certain law . . . as prohibits theatrical exhibitions." But the Assembly also indicated its belief that the stage was an important tool for the elevation of society. The legislature's legalization of theatrical entertainments proceeded from its "being desirous of promoting the interests of genius and literature by permitting such theatrical exhibitions as are capable of advancing morality and virtue and polishing the manners and habits of society." The legislature also professed its conviction that theatrical speech (within limits) was entitled to the protection of a republican government.[73] The theater would bring together "genius and literature" to inform and improve the habits and hearts of the citizenry. The power of example and communication would serve the interests of virtue.

The legislature did not authorize an unregulated stage. Noting that "many respectable citizens are apprehensive that theatrical representations may be abused by indecent, vicious and immoral performances being exhibited on the stage, to the scandal of religion and virtue and the destruction of good order and decency in society and the corruption of morals," the legislature empowered the president of Pennsylvania's Supreme Executive Council, the chief justice of the state supreme court, and the president of the county court of common pleas to license only those plays that "shall in the opinion of him who shall grant such license be unexceptional." Anyone who performed "any tragedy, comedy, tragi-comedy, farce, interlude, pantomime, or other play or any scene or part thereof" without possessing a license was liable to fine, imprisonment, and bond for good behavior.[74] The Assembly did not intend to allow stage players full freedom of speech; political authorities were empowered to limit what could be said on stage. The government would protect the community from the dangers of mimetic corruption.

The question of the stage, then, like public labor and trading justices, had caused elite Philadelphians to express their perception of an unsettled public domain and the necessity for proper representations. Whether it was the Quakers' apprehension of delusive representations or their opponents' faith in theatrical enlightenment, both sides in the debate believed in the impressionability of spectators. But, for the theater's proponents, that unstable impressionability demanded regulation, not rejection. Their fears of unregulated speech and desires to reinforce social distinction merged in the advocacy of regulated theatrical speech. The drive for a well-regulated theater, the calls for more socially distinguished justices of the peace, and the attempts to separate

73. *St. at Large,* XIII, 184, 185.
74. Ibid., 185–86.

and control the vicious poor anticipated the eventual result of the debate over public labor—the institution of a structure that aimed to control the speech and example of convicts by placing them under the control of proper individuals representing the community.[75]

VIII

During the 1790s, the legislature transformed the penal system. The General Assembly created a new governing structure within the prison, authorized steps to limit communication among inmates and between inmates and the community, introduced private labor and solitude into the practice of punishment, and further curtailed the use of capital penalties. The legislature aimed to separate prisoners and punishments from the wider community. Segregating the sources of social contamination, they hoped, would overcome the danger of mimetic corruption.

In 1790, the state established a system of private punishments. A statute of 1789 had authorized some labor facilities within the jail, but the penal system had remained primarily based upon public labor. In 1790, however, the Assembly acknowledged the failure of public labor and blamed "the exposure of the offenders employed at hard labor to public view and from the communication with each other not being sufficiently restrained within the places of confinement." Consequently, the legislature ordered that servitude within the jail replace public labor. Those convicted of "robbery, burglary, sodomy, or buggery," or as accessories "before the fact" to those crimes, could be sentenced to up to ten years of labor in jail. Those convicted of horse stealing, or of being an accessory to horse theft, could serve up to seven years, those of larceny (or their accessories) up to three years, those of petit larceny up to one year, and those of bigamy, of receiving stolen goods, of being an accessory after the fact, or of any crime that prior to 1786 had not been capital, could be sent to the prison for up to two years. In addition, vagrants and those convicted of misdemeanors, who the year before had been sent to the workhouse, were now returned to labor in the reformed prison.[76] In the colonial period, the prison had been a minor support of the scaffold, whipping post, and pillory. Now the scaffold and whipping post were infrequent supplements to the prison.

---

75. This is not to say that the defense of the stage continued unchallenged. For examples of continuing opposition to the theater and attempts to link it to vice and corruption, see, for the 1790s, *To the Senate and House of Representatives of the Commonwealth of Pennsylvania; Address and Petition of the People Called Quakers* (Philadelphia, 1793); and for the 19th century, "A Friend of the Drama," *An Enquiry into the Condition and Influence of the Brothels in Connection with the Theatres at Philadelphia* . . . (Philadelphia, 1834).

76. *St. at Large,* XIII, 511, 511–514, 516. These penalties could be joined by fines and restitution.

The state also moved to refashion the jail itself. The Assembly ordered the county commissioners of Philadelphia to have "as soon as conveniently may be . . . a suitable number of cells to be constructed in the yard of the gaol . . . for the purpose of confining therein the more hardened and atrocious offenders." This building, known to contemporaries as the "Solitary Cells, or Penitentiary House," introduced solitary confinement into the penal process. Its cells were to be six feet by eight feet by nine feet and "separated from the common yard by walls of such height as without unnecessary exclusion of air and light will prevent all external communication." Solitude was first a tool of discipline. The keeper was empowered to punish prisoners guilty of assaults when no "dangerous wound or bruise" resulted, or guilty of "profane cursing and swearing, indecent behavior, idleness or negligence in work or wilful mismanagement of it or disobedience to the orders and regulations" of the prison, with confinement within the cells for up to two days. If the keeper considered such penalties insufficient, he or she could request the inspectors and the mayor to punish prisoners with whipping or confinement in the cells for up to six days.[77]

Finally, in the mid-1790s, the legislature expanded the use of solitude and further limited the use of capital sanctions. In 1794, the Assembly limited capital punishment to first-degree murder. At the same time, it declared that those convicted of formerly capital crimes were required to spend a portion of their sentence in the "Penitentiary House."[78] Solitary confinement, not death, now set these offenders apart from their fellow inmates. Solitude had assumed a crucial position in the design of punishment and prison order.

Benjamin Rush believed that solitude had two primary virtues. If prisoners were separated from all companionship and outside influence, their consciences would be reawakened and activated. Once "loose" on the criminal, the conscience would drive him back to the path of virtue. "For this reason, a bad man should be left for some time without anything to employ his hands in his confinement. Every *thought* should recoil wholly upon *himself.*" Turned in on themselves, criminals would be forced to confront their own "wickedness." This recognition of wickedness, which paralleled Protestant conversion experiences, was the first step toward reformation. The terror of solitary confinement strengthened reawakened conscience. "A wheelbarrow, a whipping post, nay even a gibbet, are all light punishments compared with letting a man's conscience loose upon him in solitude. Company, conversation, and even business are the opiates of the Spirit of God in the human heart."[79] Solitary cells were the ultimate expression of the philosophy of private penitential

77. Ibid., 515, 520–521.
78. This applied to all crimes capital before 1786. Ibid., XV, 174–181.
79. Benjamin Rush to Enos Hitchcock, Apr. 24, 1789, in Butterfield, ed., *Letters,* I, 512.

punishments. Solitary confinement effectively dissolved networks of collective support, forcing the inmates to confront authority alone. Authority, however, was not alone; it was aided by anxiety, conscience, and terror.

Solitary confinement was merely part of penal incarceration. Even more important was the imposition of labor. Most reformers were convinced that criminality resulted from idleness.Thus, labor was designed to root out idle habits and transform inmates into productive citizens. Prisoners were "to be kept as far as may be consistent with their sex, age, health and ability to labor of the hardest and most servile kind."[80] Although the discretion of prison officials controlled the specifics of the labor, the law attempted to ensure the constancy and amount of labor required of the inmates. If solitude deployed the conscience to break the inmates down, constant labor would discipline the body, teach new habits, and lead to a recovery of lost virtue.

The Assembly affirmed this flurry of reformation in 1795.[81] In less than a decade, then, Pennsylvania had transformed its penal system, substituting penitence through labor and private solitude for shame through pain and public stigma. Segregative institutions for the deviant and dependent had come to dominate social policy.

IX

Fear of mimetic corruption, then, had restructured the theory and practice of the public realm. Whereas Pennsylvania's Revolutionary constitution was designed to institutionalize a vibrant and universalizing sphere of debate and consent, theorists of mimetic corruption conceptualized the public realm as an arena of miscommunication and misunderstanding. In their view, the power of example meant that individual personality and public virtue were dangerously unstable; all sources of corruption had to be controlled and contained. The public sphere was no longer to be uniform and open. Now the government had to protect the public from itself.

But if the theorists of mimetic corruption rejected the notion of the classical public sphere, they did not reject all the ideological assumptions upon which it rested. In particular, they remained tied to the idea that social conflict was ultimately a sign of immaturity or individual failing. Proponents of the public sphere assumed that unanimity could be produced through free debate—the public sphere presupposed that all reason was uniform. Theorists of mimetic corruption, on the other hand, acknowledged that not all shared the same communicative assumptions. But while acknowledging these

80. *St. at Large,* XIII, 517.
81. In that year, the legislature renewed the act of 1790. Ibid., XV, 355–357.

differences, they interpreted them as psychological or cultural weaknesses, not as social divisions.

The interpretive transformation of division into deficiency was clearest in Benjamin Rush. Rush's representation of punishment focused on ignorance and error, not social experience. Misinterpretations marred public punishments, as they did culture in general; the desire and sympathy of citizens were tied to inappropriate and anarchic examples. But each of these problems derived from the audience's failure to understand the ceremony correctly. Rush argued that misinterpretation was inherent to public punishments. Public punishments were policy errors that led to erroneous understanding. His position effectively denied the importance of class (or other structural differences) for understanding public reaction to punishment. Rush avoided the possibility that individuals reacted differently to the spectacle of public punishment because their experiences of law and authority might be different. He reduced conflict to error and thereby denied the legitimacy of conflicting interpretations. Conflicting interpretations could be dismissed as merely lack of wisdom or maturity.[82]

In his emphasis on the possibility of reformation, Rush broke with the logic of traditional punishments. Whereas capital penalties assumed that society was irrevocably split between good and evil, reformation held out the possibility that all could be brought within a unified social order. But when Rush denied the unalterable division of society, he displaced that division onto individual character. What gave Rush his utopian confidence was the malleability of the human character—but malleability meant that human characters were dangerously unstable. There was no guarantee that they would reach moral adulthood. Each individual was prone to the seductions of mimetic corruption.

Rush was only the most rigorous example of a more widespread approach. As the language of humanity attests, Revolutionary-era reformers took seriously the calls of sympathy and the possibility for a utopian rationalization of society. Their hope of spiritualizing punishment and reconfiguring authority presumed not only transforming society but redeeming individuals. But as the proliferation of metaphors of animality to describe the poor and the criminal demonstrates, the discourse of mimetic corruption imagined a polity threatened on all sides by inferior, aggressive creatures. Yet more was at stake than mere violence. Mimetic corruption presumed not only that dangerous threats existed on the borders of society but that they could function as seductive examples. Earlier supporters of the public sphere had presumed that the power of reason would extend outward from debate to transform society.

82. I develop this argument in the case of Rush more fully in my introduction to Rush, *Essays,* ed. Meranze, xxvii–xxxi.

Mimetic corruption threatened to reverse this process. Instead of reason spreading outward, corruption would move from the margins to the center. The contagions of indolence and criminality would overpower rational discourse.

Deep suspicions about the reliability of individual character, then, structured the fear of mimetic corruption. Whether the topic was poverty, criminality, the theater, or the qualities of a magistrate, concerns over communication and example implicitly recognized social differences while denying their legitimacy. As reformers analyzed the social and political struggles of the Revolutionary period, they repudiated any belief in a transparent common good. But they did not disavow a belief in the common good itself. Instead, they deposited that notion in institutions of discipline and regulation designed to reform and reshape individual character. Reformers thereby transformed harmony from an immanent condition to a future prospect. Disciplinary institutions, they believed, could overcome the individual weakness that prevented the peace of society.

CHAPTER FIVE

The Dynamics of Discipline

The separation of inmates from the public was only the most visible moment in the reconstruction of penal authority. Simultaneously with the critique of public penality, public officials and private reformers recast the nature of prison structure and practice. Their vision of incarceration stressed labor, religious instruction, and improved classification. By combining a regulated life with constant work, cleanliness, silence, and religious instruction, prison officials believed, imprisonment could reform individuals and make them dutiful and dependable citizens.

This reformed system of punishment replaced the public symbol of the body with the concealed practice of discipline. Rush and his allies argued that the public display of the body effectively disrupted the process of reformation and terror. In both traditional public punishments and public labor, the presence of the penalized body overwhelmed the meaning of punishment; the penal body intruded disorder and excess into everyday life. But more was at stake in reform than merely stripping the condemned of public figurative power. The enclosed prison space had itself to be transformed. Reformers attempted to impose what Michel Foucault would call the "disciplines"—tactics and techniques of governing through the careful division and regulation of time and space. The disciplinary regime affected the prison's governors as well as its subjects. In place of the porous and informal traditional practice of prison authority, reformers substituted an increasingly regularized and, in the eighteenth-century sense of the word, ritualized form of oversight—one modeled on written rules and regulations.[1]

---

1. On the disciplines, see Michel Foucault, *Discipline and Punish: The Birth of the Prison*, trans. Alan Sheridan (New York, 1977), 141–169. On ritual in the 18th century, see Talal Asad, *Genealogies of Religion: Discipline and Reasons of Power in Christianity and Islam* (Baltimore, 1993), 56–58.

Discipline not only negated the public symbolism of the body, but it institutionalized a practice of habit as well. Evacuating the body of its symbolic
importance and opening it up to disciplinary training were two sides of the
same coin. Habit stood at the intersection of these two processes. The aim of
the new disciplinary regime was to inculcate new bodily dispositions. Consequently, prison officials repeatedly struggled to control inmates' hygiene, sexual behavior, labor patterns, and speech. Late-eighteenth-century reformers
assumed that fixing the habits of the body would, in turn, fix moral character.
Spirit followed the body.[2]

Proponents of reformative incarceration, then, reframed the scene of punishment and transformed, rather than eliminated, visibility within the penal
structure. Within the prison, officials strove to perfect their surveillance of the
inmates. Challenging the brief corporality of the public punishment and the
corporal promiscuity of the unreformed prison, they aimed to develop a discipline within the space of imprisonment. At the same time, as punishment
receded from public view, the distance between everyday life and the world of
penality was filled with mechanisms of observation, communication, and
imagination. By removing punishment from the direct presence of the public,
reformers placed it in the realm of the imagination. Indeed, the reformed
space of the prison was linked to the larger public through newly created governmental mechanisms, the representations of the Philadelphia Society for
Alleviating the Miseries of Public Prisons, pamphlets, and imaginative literature. The prison itself, it seems, took its place in the space opened by the absence of the penal body.[3]

2. Adam Jay Hirsch has demonstrated the importance of this philosophy of habit for
late-18th-century reformers. He argues that it represents a philosophy of "rehabituation"
(which he suggests "was an inherently superficial form of rehabilitation") as opposed to a
goal of "reclamation" (which aimed at a more thoroughgoing transformation of character). This distinction underestimates the expectations of late-18th-century reformers, in effect, reading their philosophy through lenses carved by proponents of solitary confinement. The discipline of habit was, in the late 18th century, a utopian practice. See *The Rise
of the Penitentiary: Prisons and Punishment in Early America* (New Haven, Conn., 1992),
14–18, quotation on 14.

3. In this way, they anticipated the fantasy that Sigmund Freud would later christen "A
Child Is Being Beaten." Freud described a process of deindividualization and withdrawal.
As he recounted it, his patients were originally present in their fantasies, witnessing an act
of personalized and singular punishment. But, unable to bear the contradictions of this position (whether they witnessed or were subject to the punishment), they reimagined the
punitive scene as institutionalized and distant. In this latter fantasy, although they were
witnesses, they were not present; they stood, in some way, outside the frame of the penal
site. Much the same occurred in the 18th century, except, there, it was not in fantasy, but in
practice. See, Freud, "'A Child is Being Beaten': A Contribution to the Origin of Sexual Per-
versions," in Ernest Jones et al., *Collected Papers,* trans. Joan Riviere et al. (London, 1953),
II, 172–201.

I

On both sides of the Atlantic, the idea that prisons were schools of vice and the source of disease, both physical and moral, had long been a truism. In late-eighteenth-century England, in particular, repeated instances of jail fever spreading from prisoners to the wider public increased the sense that prisons threatened public health and safety.[4] Prison reform was first of all a question of medical police.

The eighteenth-century prison was a far cry from any form of disciplinary authority. Jailers supported themselves through fees and by providing services (supplying food, liquor, and other necessities) to inmates. Informal governments composed of inmates helped run day-to-day life in the large English debtors' prisons, which limited legal authority over prisoners. On both sides of the Atlantic, informal, extrajudicial authority existed in institutions holding criminal prisoners for trial, sentencing, or actual punishment.[5]

Throughout the century, the prison's role was circumscribed. In the unreformed penal system, prisons were primarily places of temporary detention. With the exception of long-term civil prisoners or the rare individual whose sentence included a short term of incarceration, the prison held debtors, witnesses, prisoners awaiting trial who were unable to post bond, and convicted criminals awaiting execution of their sentences. Terms of confinement could be lengthy, but that resulted less from design than from the erratic nature of judicial proceedings (for example, infrequency of court sittings, difficulties with witnesses or prosecutors, administrative problems). Prisons were unavoidable devices to ensure that all the players appeared on the stage of justice, but they were not elements of the theater itself.[6]

In Pennsylvania, the wheelbarrow law radically altered the context and importance of imprisonment. The legislation of 1786 transformed punishment into a continuing process.[7] No longer was punishment compressed into a few

4. John Beattie, *Crime and the Courts in England, 1660–1800* (Princeton, N.J., 1986), 570–573; Robin Evans, *The Fabrication of Virtue: English Prison Architecture, 1750–1840* (New York, 1982), 9–46, 94–96, 115–117; Michael Ignatieff, *A Just Measure of Pain: The Penitentiary in the Industrial Revolution, 1750–1850* (New York, 1978), 44–45, 52.

5. Joanna Innes, "The King's Bench Prison in the Later Eighteenth Century: Law, Authority and Order in a London Debtors' Prison," in John Brewer and John Styles, eds., *An Ungovernable People: The English and Their Law in the Seventeenth and Eighteenth Centuries* (New Brunswick, N.J., 1980), 280–284; Ignatieff, *A Just Measure of Pain*, 39–42; Negley K. Teeters, *The Cradle of the Penitentiary: The Walnut Street Jail at Philadelphia, 1773–1835* (Philadelphia, 1955), 46.

6. Harry E. Barnes, *The Evolution of Penology in Pennsylvania: A Study in American Social History* (1927; reprint, Montclair, N.J., 1968), 63–71.

7. Despite this change, the prison's debtor population for the 1780s still outnumbered its criminal population. See *Pa. Packet*, Oct. 13, 1790; John K. Alexander, *Render Them Submissive: Responses to Poverty in Philadelphia, 1760–1800* (Amherst, Mass., 1980), 66–67.

hours. Nor was confinement incidental to the penal system. Now it constituted one of its central elements. Whereas public corporal penalties aimed to restrain criminal behavior through pain and shame, the law now hoped to reform the habits and manners of the prisoners through continual labor and reeducation. If the time spent in prison undercut the time spent at public labor, then the penal system was at war with itself.

Consequently, criticism of the internal structure of the prison emerged rapidly after implementation of the reform legislation of 1786. Attempts to alter the prison's structure did not await the overthrow of the wheelbarrow law; instead, during the late 1780s, public officials, the Philadelphia Society for Alleviating the Miseries of Public Prisons and even parts of the prison community agitated to discipline the prison space. The prison was the object of reform before it became the tool of reform.

These criticisms focused on the body of the prison and the bodies of prisoners. In September 1787, the grand jury of the Court of Oyer and Terminer complained that prison officials failed to segregate the sexes. The prison, the grand jurors alleged, unashamedly allowed a "general intercourse between the criminals of the different sexes." There was "not even the appearance of decency, with respect to the scenes of debauchery that naturally result from such a situation." Confinement, they avowed, had become "desireable" to the "more wicked and polluted of both sexes." At the same time, the grand jury charged that officials failed to separate the different types of inmates, especially debtors and criminals. The "Common Hall," originally reserved for debtors, had become a "resort for the criminals and debtors indiscriminately." Debtors did not "have the liberty of a place to receive the air" without being surrounded "by wretches who are a disgrace to human nature; together with the horrid noise of chains and disorder of every kind."[8] Contact with criminals was an unintended consequence of the wheelbarrow law. The lack of separation, the grand jury implied, added social distress and insult to the debtors' loss of civil liberty.

The grand jury's concerns, or at least the manner in which they were voiced, not only defended the image (and situation) of debtors but debased the image of criminals. The grand jurors reminded the court that among the debtors were "many worthy characters" who had "once seen better days" but had been "reduced by misfortune" to the debtors' apartment.[9] Their concern expressed their humanitarian sympathy toward imprisoned debtors. But the grand jurors implied that an unbridgeable distance existed between the "worthy characters" who might have been imprisoned for problems with debt, and the criminals, who were "wretches" and a "disgrace to human nature." In

8. *Pa. Gazette*, Sept. 26, 1787.
9. Ibid.

drawing these stark distinctions, the grand jury evinced much of the same ambivalence underlying the movement to eliminate public labor.

The Philadelphia Society for Alleviating the Miseries of Public Prisons echoed the grand jury's fears. In April 1788, the Society's Acting Committee (individuals assigned to visit the prison regularly) reported that prisoners had a "too free open and unrestrained Intercourse with the sexes." The following month, the Acting Committee expanded its criticism of jail life and argued that the mingling of the sexes was only part of a more general problem of discipline. Prison officials, they asserted, were "indulging the most flagitious characters with a free range of the Jail." In fact, "some notorious offenders sentenced to a term of servitude . . . [were] not placed among the felons, or put into uniform agreeably to their sentence." As a result, "dissipation and licentiousness diffused among all ranks in Confinement, in consequence of an improper Intercourse between the sexes." In August, the Visiting Committee claimed that most of the women in the debtors' apartment "appeared to be drunk; fighting and in general confusion." [10]

These complaints did not emanate from only outside the prison. Those imprisoned for debt shared the more general fear of their criminal counterparts. One group of debtors alleged that "unfortunate debtors" were "crowded daily with the Culprits condemned to the Barrow and other criminals to the great annoyance of ourselves and Friends." Another debtor expressed fear for his life: given the lack of separation, "a debtor dar not say his life is his own . . . [or he will be] momentarily sorounded, by those untryed as well as those under Condemnation (*hard Endeed*)." The same sentiment was addressed to the Philadelphia Society's Visiting Committee in August 1788, who reported: "The debtors informed us of their *wretched* situation, owing as they said, to the thieves being constantly amongst them—They requested that some measures might be taken to effect a separation." [11] The debtors, who viewed their imprisonment as resulting from unavoidable misfortune, believed that the lack of classification and separation was unjust; indeed, that it threatened their lives.

Moreover, the debtors complained, prison officials were arbitrary and oppressive. In November 1787, they protested to the Philadelphia Society that "our Friends and Wives etc., have been and daly are search'd in the most insulting and indecent manner for spirituous liquor," and two guards "now posted at the Gate . . . have in divers instances, not only insulted but struck prisoners for Debt in a cruel manner." The protesting debtors expressed fears that they were "in danger from representing the particular impositions" that

10. Minutes of the Acting Committee, Apr. 11, May 16, 1788, Minute Book, 1787–1793, PSAMPP; Report of the Visiting Committee, August 1788, PSAMPP-Society.

11. Representation of Prisoners in Jail, Nov. 10, 1787, Address from Jail, Jan. 30, 1788, Report of the Visiting Committee, August 1788, PSAMPP-Society.

they reported to the Society. They pointed out that "having ordinary debtors to be associated in a Room without discrimination . . . deters any from complaining . . . [because] sychophants to the great arbiter Reynolds [the jailor] are not wanting in almost every room." [12] The debtors argued that the prison was an engine of arbitrary authority; both the jailor and the felons terrified them.

The grand jury and the Philadelphia Society also challenged the power and independence of the keeper and his assistants. The grand jurors believed that "one reason" why debtors and criminals mingled in the Common Hall was that "liquor is sold at the door by small measure, by the gaoler, or by his permission, contrary (as they conceive) to the law of this commonwealth." In their minds, the mingling of different sexes and different types of inmates could be traced, at least in part, to the traditional perquisites of the keeper. The Society thought that prison officials engaged in more direct forms of corruption than the sale of liquor. Members of the Society's Acting Committee became convinced that the keeper, John Reynolds, accepted stolen goods from inmates or their accessories. They also believed that their informants' safety was seriously at risk from Reynolds and his assistants. [13]

Throughout 1788, the Philadelphia Society lobbied the government to reorganize the prison. In January, it reminded the Assembly of the importance of ensuring sexual separation within the prison and requested that steps be taken

12. Representation of Prisoners in Jail, Nov. 10, 1787, PSAMPP. The debtors reiterated their fear of being exposed to Reynolds's power in August of the following year. "Report of the Visiting Committee," August 1788, PSAMPP.

13. *Pa. Gazette,* Sept. 26, 1787. Apparently, Reynolds was prosecuted and fined for his marketing of liquor. See Representation to the Supreme Executive Council, Minute Book, Dec. 18, 1788, PSAMPP. It should be noted that the grand jury did suggest that part of the problem might lie in the inadequate salary of the keeper. For examples of concerns about the behavior of jailors in England, see Evans, *The Fabrication of Virtue,* 22–26; Margaret DeLacy, *Prison Reform in Lancashire, 1700–1850: A Study in Local Administration* (Stanford, Calif., 1986), 107.

The Philadelphia Society was led to the beliefs about John Reynolds by the allegations of inmates. See John Oldden to Thomas Wistar, July 24, Draft of the Acting Committee Report, Aug. 4, "Narrative of Elizabeth Emery," May 27, 1788, PSAMPP-Society. Although the inmates' allegations did not lead to the removal of Reynolds, they did increase the Society's hostility to him and strengthened the Society's conviction that the prison structure needed serious alterations. For other incidents that caused tension between the Philadelphia Society and Reynolds, see Teeters, *The Cradle of the Penitentiary,* 32–35. Reynolds was removed from his office when the prison was restructured in 1790 (ibid., 41). It appears that the state's Supreme Executive Council did attempt to remove Reynolds in 1788 in response to the charges of corruption, but the sheriff blocked the effort. See Draft of the Acting Committee Report, Aug. 4, 1788, PSAMPP-Society. The Draft of the Acting Committee's Report indicates that the chief justice opposed the Acting Committee's actions in this case. It is also clear that Reynolds was not without support among the city's elite. See *Pa. Packet,* Oct. 13, 1789. These letters appear to have been written in 1788, although they were not published until 1789.

to eliminate liquor among the convicts. In December, they reiterated their concerns over the "promiscuous" intermingling of the sexes, the sale of liquor in the jail, the failure to separate debtors and criminals, the inadequate provision of bedding (which they believed contributed to sexual contact), the lack of labor for inmates, the treatment of witnesses and those held only for trial, and the problem of jail and court fees. They called for an internal transformation of the Walnut Street Jail. They stressed the trade in liquor, to which they attributed "great irregularities an[d] even outrages" as prisoners sought money to buy liquor "by not only selling their own clothes, but forcibly stripping others on the first admission in Goal," a practice the Society admitted was a "custom of long standing by the name of Garnish" but one that they asserted was "often productive of great subsequent sufferings."[14]

The Society (like the grand jury) opposed the traditional social organization of the prison. They insisted to the Supreme Executive Council that "solitary confinement to hard labor and a total abstinence from spirituous liquors will prove the most effectual means of reforming these unhappy creatures, and that many evils might be prevented by keeping the debtors from the necessity of associating with those who are committed for trial as well as by a constant separation of the sexes." Here were the key elements of the emerging philosophy of imprisonment: discipline, labor, and separation. The Philadelphia Society believed that, for the prison to serve as a moral quarantine for its inmates, a new morality would have to be imposed on prison life. These attempts to reform the interior of the prison paralleled efforts to restructure the interior of the house of employment. There the critique of mimetic corruption also joined the expansion of disciplinary practice. A general attempt to reorder the institutions dealing with the poor, and, most especially, the "dangerous" poor, was under way.[15]

In 1789, the Assembly legitimated these efforts to reshape the corporal geography of the prison. In an act passed on March 27, 1789, the legislature ordered that increased efforts be made to divide convicted felons from civil prisoners, witnesses, prisoners awaiting trial, "vagrants and other disorderly persons," and those prisoners convicted of misdemeanors. Instead of confining these lesser offenders in the prison, the Assembly directed they be removed to the city's workhouse. The law instructed the city's officials to reorganize and expand the workhouse to enable it to receive these prisoners and keep them separate from those confined for poverty. Those convicted of felonies (or those accused of felonies) not covered by the reform act of 1786

---

14. Minutes, Dec. 18, Jan. 29, 1788, PSAMPP. On the Society's attack on public labor, see above, Chapter 4.

15. Minutes, Dec. 18, 1788, PSAMPP. For similar developments in the philosophy of imprisonment in England, see Evans, *The Fabrication of Virtue*, 118–194. On the reorganization of the poorhouse, see Alexander, *Render Them Submissive*, 94–95, 107–108.

were ordered to be kept separate from those whose penalties included hard labor. To effect this separation, city officials were instructed to divide designated "rooms [and] apartments . . . from the rest, and cells, sheds and other suitable buildings . . . be constructed for the purpose of separating, confining and keeping employed at hard labor all felons" who had been sentenced to hard labor. This increased division and segregation aimed to control communication: "Such apartments, cells and sheds as [well as] the residue of the said gaol where necessary shall be properly walled up and secured to prevent all communication among the same felons and with the persons abroad."[16]

In addition, the Assembly enjoined the keeper to limit prisoners' social contacts. Beyond the "care and custody of the prisoners," the keeper was instructed to:

> superintend the felons employed at hard labor . . . to prevent all communication between the men and woman felons and to separate the men felons from each other as much as the construction of the buildings and the nature of their employment will admit of; to admit no persons whatever except officers and ministers of justice or counsellors or attorneys at law employed by the prisoners, ministers of the gospel or persons producing a written license from one of the said inspectors to enter within the walls where such felons shall be confined.

The statute banned spirituous liquors except (in the case of sickness) with written approval of the prison inspectors. Lastly, the keeper was directed to "prevent profligate or idle conversation and demeanor and to preserve the utmost possible cleanliness in the persons and apartments of the prisoners."[17] As with the larger attempts to impose separation upon the prison space, these new directives spoke to the pervasiveness of the fear of mimetic corruption. Simply removing prisoners from the sight of the public was insufficient; instead, the prison space itself had to be purified, prison authority regularized, and inmates' contact reduced and constrained.

Whereas the wheelbarrow law marked a spiritualization of public punishments, the new structure of prison authority remained dependent on physical coercion for its ultimate enforcement. The law granted the keeper discretion to "punish the obstinate and refractory and to reward those who shall show signs of reformation by lightening or increasing their tasks and by increasing or lessening their food, as occasion may require." The courts were empowered to impose "additional confinement at hard labor" on prisoners who escaped as well as "such corporal punishment as the court in their discretion shall ad-

16. *St. at Large*, XIII, 243–45, 245. Similar instructions were given to the other counties as well, although the smaller facilities at the disposal of the rural counties meant that the physical separation of felons from nonfelons could not be so drastic.

17. Ibid., 247.

judge and direct." [18] The reliance on corporal punishments highlights the extent to which the critique of traditional penalties centered on their public nature. The legislature showed little reluctance to inflict punishments directed at the body, so long as the punishments were not publicly visible.

The Assembly also initiated mechanisms to enable external authorities to control and supervise the prison. Perhaps most important, they created the office of the Board of Inspectors of the prison. Philadelphia's mayor and aldermen were instructed to appoint "six suitable and discreet" individuals to serve as inspectors. The inspectors, in turn, were commanded to ensure that prisoners had adequate supplies for their labor, to dispose of the products of the convicts' work, to enquire into any abuse of authority within the prison, and to suggest modifications of prison structures. [19] In this way, appointees of the city government would ensure (and be held responsible for ensuring) that the new prison regime would be introduced. No longer would the keeper have unsupervised control of the prison; instead, socially acceptable Philadelphians would regulate the keeper's actions.

In addition, the legislature sought to tie the keeper more closely to the new prison regime. To end the keeper's dependence on jail fees and the provision of (sometimes illegal) services to inmates, the Assembly made the keeper a salaried officer. The law established a fine of ten pounds for any keeper or deputy who allowed the introduction of liquor into the prison (except for medicinal purposes), who allowed communication between male and female felons, or who "shall ask, demand, or receive of or from any person whatsoever by color of his office or under any pretence whatever any sum or sums of money or other fee, gratuity or reward" in addition to their salaries. [20] A system of rewards and punishments, thereby, would control the behavior of keepers and their assistants; no longer (so the Assembly hoped) would the keeper be able to profit from the traditional social economy of the prison.

The following year, the legislature moved further to transform the internal structure of the prison. The penal act of 1790 expanded the number of inspectors from six to twelve and increased their power over prison organization, prison keepers, and inmates. At the same time, their duties and responsibilities were more clearly defined. The law mandated a new system of record keeping to assure greater knowledge of the prisoners and greater surveillance of the prison itself by city and state officials. The Assembly ordered the inspectors to draw up in writing rules and regulations for the prison—rules explicitly defined to control the keeper and the keeper's deputies and to elimi-

18. Ibid., 247–249.
19. Ibid., 246, 246–247.
20. The legislature declared that the keeper should receive "full compensation for his services including the expense of hiring and retaining his deputies" as well as a commission of 10% of the profits from convict labor. Ibid., 248, 251.

nate arbitrariness in the jail—and required that these regulations be "hung up in at least six of the most conspicuous places in the said gaol" to ensure that prisoners knew both their duties and their rights. The act also commanded that prisoners be confined separately until certified by a physician in order to guard against the introduction of contagious diseases.[21] Finally, the act of 1790 clearly specified who was eligible to converse with inmates; once again, the Assembly considered it essential to limit inmate conversation to officially approved people.

These statutory mandates prescribed roles for all the actors on the penal stage. The legislature hoped to bring together in an ordered fashion the three elements of the "penitentiary": "one who prescribes the rules and measures of penance; one who does penance; the place where penance is enjoined."[22] The result, they hoped, would be greater reformative power. Prisoners would come to realize that the prison was a machinelike organization of reformation. Pennsylvania would implement John Howard's vision of a new form of penal authority, an authority that was both just (because nonarbitrary) and certain (because known).

The internal history of the unreformed Walnut Street Jail, then, had led to an increased attention to prison organization. As Caleb Lownes noted, the Philadelphia Society quickly concluded that, in addition to the problems posed by public labor, it was the "*want of government* in the prison; the admission of all kinds of characters to a *free communications with the prisoners;* the unlimited use of spirituous liquors; the indiscriminate mixture of all descriptions of prisoners, without regard to character, sex, or condition, and idleness in the house, [which] were among the principle causes of the evils complained of" in the penal system. The Acting Committee, in 1788, reminded its peers that the "objects of their institution" were "to alleviate the miseries of prisons, by procuring in them that reform in their policy so obviously necessary, before a Reformation can rationally be expected in the Morals or Conduct of any Criminal confined in them; as well, as by pecuniary donations to assist those of their fellow Creatures, who for trifling debts" remain in prison. Here the primary emphasis was on reforms in policy and only secondarily on individual charity to inmates. The emphasis of the Philadelphia Society's original constitution, where Christian charity had been preeminent, was thus effectively reversed.[23] The problem of the internal structure of the prison had become a central concern of penal reformers.

21. Ibid., 516, 523.

22. Thomas Sheridan, *A Complete Dictionary of the English Language* (Philadelphia, 1789), s.v. "penitentiary."

23. Caleb Lownes, *An Account of the Alteration and Present State of the Penal Laws of Pennsylvania, Containing Also an Account of the Goal and Penitentiary House of Philadelphia and the Interior Management Thereof* (Philadelphia, 1793), 78. This pamphlet was published

II

If the main lines of the new disciplinary attack were laid down in the 1780s, they were elaborated during the 1790s. Throughout the decade, the inspectors and their allies elaborated and intensified the double movement of discipline—placing inmates within more finely organized time and space while subjecting them to an increasingly complex system of rules and records. Each of these disciplinary tactics was concerned with deploying the body to affect the spirit. In the movement from public punishments to reformative incarceration, the body had not lost its importance. But instead of a symbolic representative, the body became a terrain of disciplinary reformation.

The first concern was with the body in penal space. The new disciplinary regime dissected the space of the prison. The Walnut Street Jail, built in 1773, was located at Sixth and Walnut Streets, across from the statehouse. Placed on a lot of four hundred feet by two hundred feet, the prison was two stories high with wings extending back from the front on Walnut Street. A stone building on Prune Street (at the back of the lot) had been designed as a workhouse but, by the 1790s, held debtors. The prison was divided into large rooms (approximately twenty feet by eighteen feet). As both the grand jury and the Philadelphia Society indicated, the spatial and social promiscuity of the unreformed prison appalled penal reformers. Consequently, the Board of Inspectors struggled to impose both greater regularity and separation upon the prison. Prison officials separated the sexes. The male convicts, for "security and air," were placed on the second story of the east wing of the prison, the female convicts were placed on the first floor of the west wing (the farthest from the male convicts), the female vagrants on the second floor of the west wing, and the male vagrants on the first floor of the east wing. The inspectors moved the debtors to an apartment distinct from the convicts. They removed Reynolds as keeper of the prison, replacing him with an individual more amenable to their authority, attacked the informal prison economy, established a salary for the keeper, banned liquor, and "instantly suppressed" the practice of "garnish."[24] In short, they began dividing the prison community while eliminat-

---

as an appendix to William Bradford, *An Enquiry How Far the Punishment of Death Is Necessary in Pennsylvania with Notes and Illustrations, to Which Is Added, an Account of the Goal and Penitentiary House of Philadelphia, and of the Interior Management Thereof. By Caleb Lownes, of Philadelphia* (Philadelphia, 1793). Draft of Acting Committee Report, Aug. 4, 1788, PSAMPP. This report summarized the behavior of the Acting Committee in response to the allegations against John Reynolds discussed above. On the importance of charity to the Philadelphia Society, see Michael Meranze, "The Penitential Ideal in Late Eighteenth-Century Philadelphia," *PMHB*, CVIII (1984), 443–445, and above, Chapter 4.

24. Jurisdiction over the vagrants had been returned to the prison in 1790. Lownes, *An Account*, 78, 78–79, 80–81; "The Report of the Board of Inspectors on the State of the

ing any extralegal sources of income—or alternatives to their power—within the prison.

The threat of sexual contact obsessed prison reformers; it more than any other issue seems to have represented the seductiveness of vice. Sexual activity also marked the most blatant example of the nature of the unreformed prison regime. The new disciplinary regime aimed to reshape and redirect the practices of the body; the sexually active body transgressed disciplinary limits and expressed ungoverned desires and individual wills that escaped the control of prison regulations. Sexual activity brought together both spiritual and physical transgression, the "scenes of debauchery" of which the grand jury had complained that offended both moral and disciplinary rule.[25] Sexual intercourse represented undisciplined space; sexual activity embodied the disruption of the new prison project.

If the body, then, had lost its public symbolic value in the penal system, it remained a prime signifier of the process of reformation itself. Take, for example, the issue of hygiene. Prison officials laid great stress on the cleanliness of the prison and its inmates. On first entrance into the prison, an inmate was segregated, "washed and cleaned," and kept separate from the other inmates until it was "deemed prudent to admit him among the other prisoners." The prison was whitewashed at least three times a year, and the rooms and cells were washed twice a week during the summer months and once a week during the winter. Each prisoner washed daily, their linen was changed once a week, the men shaved twice weekly, and their hair was cut once a month. Similar attention was paid to clothing and bedding. The male prisoners were "cloathed in woollen jackets, waistcoats, and trowsers in winter, and linen in summer, shirts, shoes, etc." Female prisoners, on the other hand, were "dressed in plain, short gowns, of woollen in winter, and linen in summer." Prisoners were supposed to have individual beds with sheets and blankets. Finally, the diet of the inmates was designed to be "plain, cheap, and wholesome." The prison's "Rules, Orders, and Regulations" specified the daily allowance of food, which consisted of various amounts of bread, potatoes, mush, and meat broth.[26] In all of these areas, the prison sought to ensure a simple and ordered regimen for the prisoners.

Prison for the City and County of Philadelphia," Dec. 7, 1791, HSP; Teeters, *The Cradle of the Penitentiary,* 41.

25. *Pa. Gazette,* Sept. 26, 1787.

26. Robert James Turnbull, *A Visit to the Philadelphia Prison; Being an Accurate and Particular Account of the Wise and Humane Administration Adopted in Every Part of That Building; Containing Also an Account of the Gradual Reformation, and Present Improved State, of the Penal Laws of Pennsylvania: With Observations on the Impolicy and Injustice of Capital Punishments, in a Letter to a Friend* (Philadelphia, 1796), 32–33; Lownes, *An Account,* 84; François Alexandre Frédéric, duc de La Rochefoucault Liancourt, *On the Prisons of Phila-*

In part, this emphasis on the cleanliness of prisoners addressed the danger of jail fevers. The legislature had emphasized the importance of preventing jail fever and other contagious diseases, a point observers echoed more generally. But the emphasis on hygiene had moral and political purposes. The segregation prisoners underwent on their arrival sought to impress them with their new situation and remind them that their total transformation was expected. Penal reformers assumed that physical habits were intertwined with moral behavior. Uncleanliness, like indolence, led to more serious vices; cleanliness, on the other hand, would lead the prisoner toward virtue. "From the connection of the body with the mental and moral faculties," as Robert Turnbull put it, "or rather from the influence which the disposition of the former must have on that of the latter, it is certain, that a man's morals must, in some measure, depend on the proportion of ease and comfort the body enjoys." The importance placed on the moral effects of hygiene was not limited to cleanliness, however. In clothing, Lownes reported, the inspectors sought to assure "*usefulness, oeconomy,* and *decency.*" But the need to control both disease and vice was most clear in the question of bedding, where the fear of disease and sodomy joined together: "We have found this regulation [prisoners sleeping in beds] greatly conducive to cleanliness and decency. The former practice of prisoners sleeping in their cloaths, and being crowded together without any regard to decency, was destructive to the health of the prisoners, and was attended with many other ill consequences, especially where men are collected in the manner they are in prisons."[27] Through hygiene, the body's surface was a locus of education. Cleanliness, clothing, and sleep were all mechanisms to act on the spirit through bodily practices and habits.

The regulation of space and time within the prison had a double movement. The inspectors sought to eliminate certain forms of contact and communication to help forge other bonds. They commanded that no one be "admitted to a communication with the prisoners" with the exception of the keeper, his assistants, the inspectors, judicial officers, attorneys "employed by a prisoner," ministers, or "persons authorised by two of the inspectors." Men and women were to work, lodge, and eat in separate apartments and to "have no intercourse or communication with each other." Prisoners who were "guilty of profane cursing or swearing, or of any indecent behavior, conversation or expression, or of any assault, quarrel or abusive words to or with any other person," were subject to solitary confinement. François Alexandre Frédéric, duc de La Rochefoucault Liancourt reported that "long conversa-

delphia (Philadelphia, 1796), 17; *Rules, Orders, and Regulations for the Gaol of the City and County of Philadelphia* (Philadelphia, 1792), rule XXV.

27. Ignatieff, *A Just Measure of Pain,* 101–102; Turnbull, *A Visit,* 33; Lownes, *An Account,* 84, 84–85.

tions" between the convicts were "forbidden." They were "allowed to ask assistance of each other, and to speak on the subject of their mutual wants; but not otherwise." The inspectors forbade all other types of speech. The prisoners were "forbidden to bawl after one another, or to converse on the causes of their detention, or to reproach each other, on any account; at table the same silence is prescribed."[28]

Undisciplined speech, the inspectors and their supporters believed, distracted inmates from recognizing their tasks and prevented the imposition of regular and sober habits. The prohibition on unnecessary speech combined an Enlightenment concern about the control of sensation with a Protestant belief in the importance of "soften[ing] the disposition of the heart." "This prohibition of all unnecessary converse," according to Turnbull, was "an essential point for the complete administration of the prison; and whoever will subscribe to the doctrine, that the less exertion which is given to the nerves and organs of sense, must calm the state of the system, and by an immediate consequence, soften the disposition of the heart, will as readily consent to the policy of the regulation."[29] All distractions from the task at hand, even those of conversation, had to be eliminated; the inmates' conversion depended on their immersion in an ordered environment.

Suppressing undisciplined speech aimed to create a new verbal disposition in the convicts. Each Sunday the prison sponsored religious services, of "a sermon and a lecture, on subjects suited to the situation of the convicts." Generally, one of the city's clergy directed these services. Prisoners were required to attend and were divided by sex and their inmate classes. No contact with members of the other classes was allowed. The prisoners, according to Caleb Lownes, were "generally desirous of attending, and always conduct themselves with decency and attention" "some appear to be benefited." In addition, "proper books" were provided for Sunday afternoon reading. Christian services, by inculcating notions of duty and obedience, were essential "for the restoration of such as have deviated from the paths of rectitude and virtue."[30]

The emphasis on proper communication was not limited to Sunday service but extended into the everyday practices of the prison. "At times the inspectors, in their tour of duty, make it a point to discourse with all the criminals, one by one separately, in order to assure them of their relative duties, considered as men, moralists and members of society. The exhortations, on these

---

28. *Rules, Orders, and Regulations,* rule I, V; La Rochefoucault Liancourt, *On the Prisons of Philadelphia,* 17–18. See also Turnbull, *A Visit,* 17.

29. Turnbull, *A Visit,* 26. See, also, La Rochefoucault Liancourt, *On the Prisons of Philadelphia,* 18.

30. Turnbull, *A Visit,* 53. Turnbull also reported that Quakers sometimes led the service. See also Lownes, *An Account,* 87. On the division of inmates into classes, see below, this chapter.

occasions, proceed from them with such a philanthropic calmness, so much warmth of heart, that their appearance among the convicts never fails to cast a fresh beam of comfort on every countenance."[31] These conversations combined the power of example with the inculcation of moral precepts. If the elimination of disorderly speech was a crucial step in destroying the habits of vice, then the orchestration of orderly, moral speech was crucial to the construction of the habit of virtue. Fear of mimetic corruption, then, had helped trigger a two-sided process. On the one hand, removal and isolation; on the other, constrained and controlled communication. Put another way, the disciplinary response to mimetic corruption was repressive and productive at the same time. As it sought to eliminate one set of communicative contacts, it sought to inculcate others.

But the ultimate element in the reshaping of bodily disposition was labor. All those sentenced to prison were compelled to labor (except on Sundays or during illness). Prisoners were employed in a large number of tasks. Male convicts were employed at shoemaking, weaving, tailoring, chipping wood, sawing stone, cutting nails, grinding plaster, picking oakum or cotton, and beating hemp, among other tasks. Male vagrants and runaway servants were set at picking wool, oakum, moss, and hair or at beating hemp. Women were engaged in, among other occupations, spinning, sewing, washing, picking cotton, and preparing flax. Although the specific tasks varied according to sex, age, and skill, all were subject to "labor of the hardest and most servile kind."[32]

Labor served a variety of functions within the prison. The labor program of the prison, according to its defenders, helped support the cost of maintaining the inmates, and prisoners' labor, in some cases at least, provided inmates with the funds to begin their new, postimprisonment lives. In addition, labor was seen as an essential part of the punishment for crimes—a punishment its proponents thought more effective than corporal sanctions. Lownes insisted that many of the convicts "deem the constant return of the same labour and coarse fare, as more intolerable, than a sharp, but momentary punishment."[33] Labor was the perfect punishment, one that combined economy, order, and severity.

But labor was more than merely an economic necessity or a fearful sanction; it fused the terror of punishment with the promise of personal reformation. "Constant and hard labour," Turnbull argued, "to which a criminal is sentenced in Pennsylvania, must be productive (and it has been) of the most

31. Turnbull, *A Visit,* 51.
32. Ibid., 16–18, 85. The language is from the statue of 1790. See *St. at Large,* XIII, 517. For Lownes's description, see his *Account,* 91. See also Teeters, *The Cradle of the Penitentiary,* 44–45.
33. Lownes, *An Account,* 90, 92.

beneficial effects. Although humane, it is a punishment, sufficiently dreadful and severe to excite terror into the minds of the depraved; and, besides affording an example of true justice, it is of all others the best adapted for the amendment of the convict himself."[34] By constant work, the prisoner would gain new habits of industry and orderliness. These habits, like those of cleanliness and religious reflection, were tied to the growth of virtue. It was within the context of this faith in the reformative power of labor that the inspectors decided that only those convicts who had earned their keep could be considered for pardons. It was only through the demonstration of orderly and productive behavior (tied, of course, to deference) that personal reformation could be demonstrated. Labor, as it was in the larger Protestant culture, was both the cause and the sign of the reformation of the inmate.

All of these techniques of government and reformation merged in the daily life of the inmates. Turnbull, who visited the prison in 1795, reported that the prisoners awoke at dawn, made their beds, washed, and began work. During the workday, they were forbidden to leave their places of work without the permission of the keeper. The more skilled laborers (carpenters, shoemakers, weavers, and so forth) were divided into shops of approximately seven individuals, "one of whom is appointed by the jailor, whose duty it is strictly to notice all offences, and in default of it is punished according to the rules." In addition, the keepers were "constantly parading" throughout the yard and the halls. A bell called the prisoners to both breakfast and supper. While at their supper, they were divided according to occupational classes. Even at supper, Turnbull reported, a rule of silence was maintained: "During the time of eating, we witnessed no laughing, nor even an indecent gesture; but a perfect and respectful silence reigned along the benches." They rose from the table only at a sign from the keeper's assistant and returned to their labor. Finally, "at the approach of dusk," another bell was rung signaling the end of the workday. At this point, the inmates

> must leave off labour, immediately repair to their rooms, and form themselves in such a manner, that the keeper may have a perfect view of every person belonging to each room. They remain thus formed, till he calls the roll and counts them: he then locks them up in their apartments, but without candle or fire, except in extreme cold weather. From this time half an hour is allowed them to adjust their bedding, after which they are not permitted to converse aloud or make a noise.

Observation and regulation marked the daily life of the inmates. The government of the prison was designed to eliminate all informalities, irregularities, and personal secrecy. As La Rochefoucault Liancourt argued: "The present state of the prisons holds out to the offenders no other scenes than those of

34. Turnbull, *A Visit,* 21.

annihilated liberty, the obligation to labour, and the injunction of regularity and silence."[35] A tight mesh of regulations and ordered practices, so the inspectors and their supporters believed, controlled and directed the inmates.

The numbers of prisoners committed to the prison helped support this sense of optimism. Whereas 594 individuals were sentenced to the prison from January 1787 to June 1791, only 243 were sentenced from June 1791 to March 1795. The greatest decline occurred in the number convicted of larceny. In the earlier period, 374 were convicted for this crime, but in the latter period, only 163.[36] Given the common assumption that citizens were now more willing to report crimes, and that jurors were now more willing to convict, these numbers appeared to prove that reformation was occurring, or that, at least, the prison was a sufficient source of terror to deter criminals from committing crimes. In either case, the reformed prison seemed to be decreasing criminality in Pennsylvania.

III

Yet, even during the 1790s, struggles over the new prison form disrupted the apparently placid surface of the prison and anticipated the dissolution of the inspectors' vision. John Reynolds, the old keeper, sought to subvert their authority and to mobilize opposition to the reform effort within the community. Although he failed to stop the establishment of the new regime, he was not alone in his criticism of the reforms. Some of the state's justices, as well as some Philadelphians, were skeptical of the proposed reforms. Prisoners sought to block the implementation of the new system—even attempting a general escape in response to the new system.[37] Despite their legal authority, the actual power of the inspectors was always contested.

In part, the limits to the inspectors' power were rooted in the structure of the prison itself. The prison's population was highly complex. The overwhelming majority of convicts were poor males sentenced for larceny. But the prisoners were not homogeneous. Women, although a minority, were constantly present within the prison. Blacks made up approximately one-third, and the Irish approximately one-eighth of the convicts sentenced to the prison in Philadelphia courts. Convicts covered a wide range of age groupings, with the largest number falling between the ages of twenty-two and forty-five. The prison contained not only felons (themselves a disparate group) but vagrants, debtors, prisoners awaiting trial, runaways, and the like. Those committed for

35. This account is based on Turnbull, *A Visit*, 27–29, 41–42; La Rochefoucault Liancourt, *On the Prisons of Philadelphia*, 27. See also Teeters, *The Cradle of the Penitentiary*, 45–46.

36. La Rochefoucault Liancourt, *On the Prisons of Philadelphia*, 42.

37. At least 15 inmates escaped. Turnbull, *A Visit*, 12–13, 20; La Rochefoucault Liancourt, *On the Prisons of Philadelphia*, 28.

vagrancy were, on average, inmates for slightly more than one month (thirty-five days). Prisoners for trial, or witnesses, would normally be held in the prison only until the meeting of the appropriate court—which generally met quarterly. Even the felons themselves did not tend to be long-term inmates. During the latter half of the 1790s, the mean sentences of inmates convicted in Philadelphia courts never exceeded 1.9 years. Approximately 75 percent of the inmates did not serve out their full term, because they were pardoned, escaped, or died.[38] The prison itself, like the city that surrounded it, contained a complex population with diverse habits, expectations, and attitudes—and prison inmates were highly transient.

Prison officials had little control over the size and composition of the inmate population. Courts sentenced convicts, and the governor, at least officially, pardoned them. The inspectors (from the 1790s through the 1820s) were engaged in a constant struggle with magistrates to control the numbers of vagrants, prisoners for trial, and so forth.[39] The prison was merely one node in the larger system of criminal justice; consequently, although relatively autonomous throughout its history, it was subject to decisions and pressures made by others.

Inmates also resisted the new discipline. In practice, for example, the convicts rarely labored as the inspectors hoped. Although the prison clerk reported, in August 1796, that the inmates had, "in the aggregate," earned more than their costs during the previous quarter, this productivity was not constant. By the mid-1790s, the inspectors and the inmates were involved in continuing battles to determine the pace and amount of labor. In 1795, the inspectors reported an allegation that the stonecutters did "not cut the quantity of stone they are capable of" and recommended that steps be taken to respond to the charges. The following year, the inspectors attempted to rationalize la-

38. Batsheva Spiegel Epstein, "Patterns of Sentencing and Their Implementation in Philadelphia City and County, 1795–1829" (Ph.D. diss., University of Pennsylvania, 1981), 58, 87, 97, 238, 241, 242, 246. Alexander found a substantially higher proportion of Irish sentenced in the Mayor's Court from 1794 to 1800 (*Render Them Submissive*, 181). Vagrants were an extremely large part of the prison population. From November 1794 to November 1798, 3,698 vagrants were committed to the jail compared to 490 felons (Minutes, Nov. 24, 1800, PSAMPP). The mean sentences of inmates convicted in Philadelphia were 1795 = 1.6 years, 1796 = 1.0, 1797 = 1.3, 1798 = 1.2, 1799 = 1.9 (Epstein, "Patterns of Sentencing," 142). Of a sample of 66 individuals (10%) convicted between the beginning of the prison sentence docket in 1794 and Jan. 1, 1800, only 16 served their total terms of confinement. See Philadelphia County Prison, Sentence Docket, Inspectors of the Jail and Penitentiary House of the City and County of Philadelphia, R.G. 38.36, PCA.

39. For some examples of this problem, see Minutes of the Acting Committee, Oct. 9, 1806, Jan. 10, 1820, Oct. 3, 1822, July 10, 1822, PSAMPP, in addition to the discussion of vagrancy and yellow fever below. The Philadelphia Society was active during the 1820s in opposing irregular commitments by magistrates.

bor in the prison's nail manufactory. While recommending that prisoners there "be tasked with [a] reasonable days work," the board also established a scale of penalties for failing to perform a "reasonable days work":

> For the first offense, be deprived of their Breakfast, and should they fall two days together, they shall be deprived of both breakfast and supper, and in case this deprivation should not convince them of the propriety of complying with the mild requisitions of the Board, they shall then be separated from the society of their fellow Prisoners, and confined in the cells at the discretion of the visiting Inspectors.

The imposition of punishment was never far removed from the imposition of labor. Labor discipline remained highly problematic.[40]

Contrary to the hopes of its proponents, inmate labor never made the prison a self-supporting institution. As early as 1799, the Philadelphia Society reported that, even after excluding the costs for vagrants, "the labor of the Prisoners falls very short of maintaining them." In fact, the prison needed infusions of funds from city officials to remain afloat. The Society argued that these facts demonstrated "some very material defect in the system or its management" and recommended steps to improve productivity and profit. Although they focused their recommendations on the role of the keeper and the mechanisms employed to sell prison goods, in retrospect it seems clear that the problems ran far deeper. The prison's chronic indebtedness exacerbated these economic difficulties. The prison's labor program was dependent on local contractors. Contractors provided raw materials to the prisoners and were expected to pay for the prisoners' labor. But, although the inspectors were able to procure supplies for the inmates' labor, they were less successful in receiving payment from the contractors after the labor had been performed. In addition, although the law required that Pennsylvania's counties provide funds for the upkeep of convicts they sent to Walnut Street, counties were notably reluctant to do so.[41]

The system of contract labor and supplying prison necessities might have enabled inmates to circumvent prison rules. As goods and services moved in and out of the prison, individuals from the community accompanied them.

40. Bd. of Insp., Minutes, Jan. 12, 1795. Aug. 23, 1796, PCA.

41. The Philadelphia Society used figures provided by the inspectors and county treasurer and compared the proceeds from prisoner labor for the period 1794–1798 with the costs of inmate upkeep for both convicts and vagrants (they found no evidence of productive labor among the latter). Minutes, Nov. 24, 1800, PSAMMP; Bd. of Insp., Minutes, Ap. 24, 1798, May 5, 1798. See, for example, the difficulty with receiving funds from Caleb Lownes, who was an inspector himself, and from the stone cutters. Bd. of Insp., Minutes, Oct. 31, 1797, Jan. 22, 1799. See the debts listed in Minutes, Nov. 24, 1800, PSAMPP; Teeters, *The Cradle of the Penitentiary*, 90.

Although prison officials screened those who employed convicts, no evidence suggests that they were able to control these economic visitors completely. It seems likely that these visitors were able to chat with inmates, perhaps smuggle goods into the prison, and transmit goods and information to those outside the prison walls. In other words, the authorities' ability to control the communicative economy of the prison was limited.

Labor was only one area of conflict within the prison. At least twenty-one inmates escaped between 1795 and 1800. On September 12, 1795, "one of the Keepers having the west yard open a rush was made by the Prisoners." Five successfully escaped and the rest "appeared in motion." On July 22, 1800, twelve convicts executed another group escape—this time through the sewers. The inspectors recognized the continuing threat of group activity. On May 30, 1797, the Board's minutes noted: "It appears that of late many Plans have been made by the Prisoners for rushing at sixth street Gate, which the Board consider in a weak situation."[42]

Even within the prison, inmates were able to restrain official oversight. Seth Johnson, a prisoner awaiting trial, escaped the day he arrived. Johnson was able to pile "the frames of the saws and other implements" next to the prison wall and then to climb over to the street. Apparently, Johnson had obtained a set of false keys that unlocked the doors of the apartment where he had been confined. Johnson's escape indicates two fundamental aspects of prison life. The first was the erratic nature of the keepers' oversight. Even more fundamentally, Johnson's ability to purchase a false key within hours of his arrival points to an underground economy operating within the prison. Whether others were able to smuggle money or other items into the prison is unclear, but it does not seem unlikely. The inspectors' authority was porous indeed.[43]

42. Bd. of Insp., Minutes, Sept. 22, 1795, May 30, 1797, July 23, 1800. I say at least 21 inmates, because my numbers are based on a 10% sample of the prison's sentencing docket in which 5 of 66 sampled inmates escaped combined with evidence of an additional 17 escaped inmates from notations in the inspectors' Minutes. I have eliminated one of the escapees from my calculation because the date of his escape indicates that he may have been included within the record of one of the escapes in the inspectors' Minutes. Because I only sampled, I may have missed other escapes. See Philadelphia County Prison, Sentence Docket, Inspectors of the Jail and Penitentiary House of the City and County of Philadelphia, Record Group 38.36, PCA; Bd. of Insp., Minutes, 1795–1800.

43. Johnson was able to obtain the key, prison investigators reported, because "a Rule for searching the Prisoners . . . was on the commitment of Johnson we believe neglected, hence it is probable that he must have had money with him, and perhaps by means of it, may have procured from some of the Convicts, the key" he used to escape. Bd. of Insp., Minutes, Dec. 29, 1795.

In general, the records for this period are very sketchy, and to do more than make tentative suggestions on the prison's underground economy is impossible. But that the prisoners were smuggling items into the prison was certainly the inspectors' conclusion. They resolved that "no prisoner of whatever description, be locked" in any of the prison's apart-

Violence also riddled the prison. Owing to the sketchiness of the official records, the extent of prison violence during the 1790s is impossible to determine with any confidence. But both Caleb Lownes and Robert Turnbull indicated that violent incidents did occur at Walnut Street. One inmate, at least, died at the hands of another inmate. On June 9, 1798, several prisoners set fire to the prison's manufactory. According to *Claypoole's American Daily Advertiser,* the "whole of the roof, all the windows, three fourths of the floor, and the greater part of the machinery, tools, materials, etc., used by the various artisans employed therein, were destroyed."[44] If violence was not a regular occurrence, its possibility was ever present.

Nor was the inspectors' authority effective outside the convict section. During the 1790s, the new system did not extend over debtors, vagrants, or prisoners for trial. The debtors, in particular, resisted the inspectors' attempts at reformation. As early as 1794, the inspectors concluded that the condition of the debtors' apartment necessitated new regulations. Throughout the late 1790s, the inspectors continually complained about the organization and condition of the debtors' section. In December 1797, the visiting inspectors reported that "the situation of the Prison wherein the debtors are confined is a reflection on the refined state of Moral rectitude, for which our state has hitherto been so conspicuous" and called for a revision of Pennsylvania's insolvency laws. The following month, the board received information "setting forth many disgracefull practices permitted and encouraged, by the present keeper," and determined to attempt to have the keeper removed. Finally, in January 1799, the Visiting Committee of the Philadelphia Society complained that "the improper Intercourse of the Sexes, so long a subject of Complaint was not yet prevented" in the debtors' apartment.[45] A decade after the inspectors had first moved to oversee the prison, the debtors' apartment, at least, still operated in a manner the authorities found repugnant.

Authority and insubordination confronted each other most solemnly in the prison's solitary cells. Prison officials imposed solitary confinement on those

----

ments until searched and "that Money, trincketts Buckles or implements of any description" be seized and given over to the keeper until the prisoner's discharge. They also instructed that "no convict shall be permitted on any pretence whatever to have any intercourse with the prisoners for trial." Ibid.

44. Lownes, *An Account,* 88; Turnbull, *A Visit,* 54, 61; *Claypoole's American Daily Advertiser,* June 11, 1798. See the entry for John Billins—who died Mar. 15, 1796—in Philadelphia County Prison, Sentence Docket, Inspectors of the Jail and Penitentiary House of the City and County of Philadelphia, R.G. 38, PCA.

45. Minutes of the Acting Committee, Jan. 12, 1799, PSAMPP; Bd. of Insp., Minutes, Oct. 27, 1794, Dec. 19, 1797, Jan. 23, 1798. In February 1798, the committee reported that they had "but little prospect" of removing the keeper and proposed the creation of rules to eliminate the "evils complained of." Ibid., Feb. 27, 1798.

sentenced for crimes that prior to 1786 would have been capital and as a punishment for violations of prison rules and regulations. In either case, solitude was the most extreme punishment in the prison. The solitary cells were a prison within a prison. They were located within the prison compound in a three-story building. Each floor contained eight cells, six feet by eight feet by nine feet, and two passages four feet wide. Windows at the end of the passages and a small window in the cell provided light. Stoves placed in the passages provided heat during the winter. Each cell had two doors, one wooden and one iron, and the cell window had a double grating. The prisoner was allowed a mattress but no other furniture. Prisoners received one meal a day. Those confined in the cells for violating prison rules were allowed no diversions, not even labor. The very structure of these cells was designed to encase the prisoner in an almost perfect silence. "No communication whatever between the persons in the different cells can be effected," Turnbull maintained, "the walls being so thick as to render the loudest voice perfectly unintelligible; and as to any other sound, excepting the keeper's voice and the unlocking of the doors, they seldom hear." Inmates could not even leave the cells to exercise.[46]

The inspectors argued that the combination of limited food and increased isolation helped to break the resistance and transform the character of the prisoners. "The inspectors of these prisons," La Rochefoucault Liancourt wrote, "have great faith in this discipline, and consider the regimen of the prisoners among the most powerful means of their correction, owing to the change it produces in their ideas and turn of minds." Turnbull reported that "several of the most hardened and audacious criminals, on whom all other modes of discipline were attended with effects the very reverse of what they were designed to produce, . . . have been, by the simple punishment of *solitary*

46. Lownes, *An Account*, 81; La Rochefoucault Liancourt, *On the Prisons of Philadelphia*, 10; Turnbull, *A Visit*, 54–56, 56; Bd. of Insp., Minutes, July 7, 1795. Those who were confined in the cells as part of their sentences could petition for reading materials (La Rochefoucault Liancourt, *On the Prisons of Philadelphia*, 10). Prisoners did have contact with the turnkey who brought them their food. It should also be noted that, in other prisons, prisoners condemned to solitude have sometimes been able to communicate with each other. I have not been able to determine whether they could in Walnut Street during this period, however.

On the statutory requirement of solitude as part of a penal sentence, see *St. at Large*, XV, 178. The number of prisoners confined to solitary cells was not large (Teeters, *The Cradle of the Penitentiary*, 41). The total amount of time these prisoners spent in the solitary cells was set by the courts, but the inspectors determined when, during their sentence, they would serve their solitude. The bulk of their time in solitude generally came at the beginning of their sentence (La Rochefoucault Liancourt, *On the Prisons of Philadelphia*, 11; Turnbull, *A Visit*, 57–58). For the use of the cells as a prison discipline, see ibid., 57. For those placed in the solitary cells for infractions of the rules, the keeper determined the extent of their time in the cells. These confinements were subject to the review of the inspectors. Turnbull reported that failure to work normally resulted in 48 hours in solitude. Ibid.

confinement, transformed into such a calmness of disposition, as to have become entire new beings, and the least troublesome afterwards among the prisoners." Lownes reported that the "cells are an object of *real terror* to them all [the inmates], and those who have experienced confinement in them, discover by their subsequent conduct, how strong an impression it has made on their minds." In fact, he argued, the "consequences resulting from this mode of treating offenders . . . have been the most agreeable order and quietness." [47]

Here, faith in the reformative powers of the conscience came to the fore. Turnbull argued, "There is not perhaps a physical cause, which has so powerful an influence on the moral faculty, as that of *solitary* confinement; inasmuch as it is the only one which can give a friendly communication with the heart. We become by it gradually acquainted with a true knowledge of ourselves; with the purity of the dictates prescribed to us by our consciences; and of course easier convinced of the necessity of conforming to them." Lownes described, in even more explicit terms, the mechanisms through which solitude worked its magic. One convict, sent to the cells for refusing to work, "spent many anxious hours" in "this chearless habitation," where he suffered "the reflections inseperable from guilty minds." There he remained "ignorant how long his present condition was to continue—he was without employment—nothing to amuse him—in a state of suspense and uncertainty." After his release from solitude, Lownes declared, "the utmost propriety of conduct has been observed by this man ever since." [48]

The inspectors were convinced that, whereas stripes or public degradation served only to inflame hatred of authority and contempt for order, solitude reconciled individuals to both discipline and authority. As an example, Lownes described the case of one woman "of an extreme bad character, an old offender, and very ungovernable, who had made an attempt to burn the prison." She lasted in her cell for "some weeks, with firmness" but eventually "finding that the Keeper was easy; no provocation offered to keep up her passions; no remedy; no prospect of resenting her treatment, at length submitted." Still, the inspectors kept her in solitude. In order to obtain her release, she made "many promises" of future good behavior. At this point, with her spirit broken by her term in solitude, prison officials moved to assure her future docility. They "informed [her] that the officers of the house had no object in view, besides the strictest attention to the rules of the house, and the real welfare of those whose lot it was to be committed to their care; that it was vain to oppose

47. Turnbull, *A Visit*, 56–57; Lownes, *An Account*, 89, 92; La Rochefoucault Liancourt, *On the Prisons of Philadelphia*, 11. La Rochefoucault Liancourt was talking about those sentenced to the cells as part of their sentences, but it applies equally to all those confined there.

48. Turnbull, *A Visit*, 58; La Rochefoucault Liancourt, *On the Prisons of Philadelphia*, 10; Lownes, *An Account*, 88.

the order of the place; that her disorderly conduct would only effect herself; and that if she would accept her restoration upon these considerations, she should have it." Under these conditions, he reported, "she accepted it."[49]

The cells, Lownes believed, made it "vain" to resist and deflected the responsibility for "disorderly conduct" away from the authorities and back on the guilty inmate—because the authorities were "easy," they avoided inmate hostility. Inmates, in this situation, would only blame themselves for their plight; under these conditions, authority would appear both irresistible and just. There would be no place for hidden resentment or anger.

Although solitary confinement had an important role in support of prison authority, it was not the linchpin of the prison order. Not all inmates suffered solitude. Not even all those who violated prison regulations were sent to the cells.[50] Solitude was the last, not the first, resort of discipline. Contact with and pressure from prison officers was the immediate response. Solitary confinement was only one technique within a wider economy of communication—an economy marked by conflict and insubordination.

IV

Conflict and insubordination, however, did not halt the elaboration of disciplinary practice. Throughout the decade, the inspectors reshaped the structure of prison government, developing increasingly precise tools to monitor, record, and intervene in the life of the prison's inmates. Discipline was as much about new models of authority as it was about practices of the body.

Central to the operation of the new regime was the imposition of the authority of written rules. The presentation of the rules was so important to the inspectors that an inmate, upon arrival at Walnut Street, was almost immediately "informed of and made fully acquainted with the rules and government of the prison." Prison reformers hoped that the prison community, by recognizing and obeying these rules, would develop disciplined and regular habits. As Lownes argued, "*Mild regulations, strictly enjoined,* will meet with little resistance."[51] In this way, the prison would become a carefully orchestrated site of discipline and reformation.

The inspectors fixed in writing the duties of all those who came to the prison—whether they were officials, visitors, or inmates. On February 26, 1792, the Board passed the *Directions for the Inspectors, etc. of the Gaol of the City and County of Philadelphia* and the *Rules, Orders, and Regulations for the*

49. Lownes, *An Account,* 89.
50. Turnbull, *A Visit,* 54.
51. Ibid., 50; Lownes, *An Account,* 83. For a discussion of a similar emphasis on rules in English reformed prisons, see Ignatieff, *A Just Measure of Pain,* 103–105.

Gaol of the City and County of Philadelphia.[52] In keeping with the desire to make public and certain the nature of prison rules, these documents were printed and distributed publicly. The inspectors had codified the new form of prison organization to curb the discretion of prison staff and the resistance of inmates.

The *Directions for the Inspectors* set down the duties and responsibilities of the visiting inspectors, the keeper, the turnkey, the keeper's deputies, and the watchmen. The *Rules, Orders, and Regulations,* on the other hand, elaborated on the legislature's guidelines for prison life. The *Rules, Orders, and Regulations* included twenty-five items, covering topics such as the separation of prisoners, inmate labor, prisoners' diet, prison hygiene, physicians' records, the duties of prison staff, treatment of servants and vagrants, actions and items that were either forbidden to or required of inmates and staff, and prison penalties. In effect, the *Directions for the Inspectors* and the *Rules, Orders, and Regulations* outlined acceptable everyday conduct, rewards for good behavior, and punishments for violations of prison rules.

At the same time, the inspectors emphasized the importance of written documents, especially record keeping, within the prison. The new prison regime sought not only to fix behavior within a net of regulations but to document all transactions of persons and money that occurred within the prison. One step was recording information on the circulation of persons through the prison. The inspectors kept voluminous records on the inmates. The prison's sentencing docket, for example, contained information on each criminal sentenced, including: the criminal's name and crime, the prosecutor's name, the sentencing court and the date, the length of the sentence, amount of the fine, whether restitution was required, the date the prisoner left the prison and under what circumstances (for instance, pardoned, escaped, or served out the sentence), and, when available, age (often listed), occupation (rarely listed), and distinguishing personal characteristics (race, ethnicity, or individual physical conditions). Similar, if less complete, records were kept for vagrants and those in prison awaiting trial or sentencing.[53] These records would have enabled prison (and city or state) officials to track the inmates in their travels in and out of prison.

52. *Directions for the Inspectors, etc. of the Gaol of the City and County of Philadelphia* (Philadelphia, 1792). These were reprinted with Lownes, *An Account.* Future references to the *Directions for the Inspectors* will refer to this edition.

53. *Directions for the Inspectors,* 98; Prisoners for Trial Docket 1790–1802, R.G. 38.38, PCA; Philadelphia County Prison, Sentence Docket, Inspectors of the Jail and Penetentiary House of the City and County of Philadelphia, R.G. 38.36, PCA. According to Alexander, age and occupation were determined when the prisoner was released (*Render Them Submissive,* 179). This fact would help explain the gaps in age records, as they generally occur in the cases of escapes and deaths. The gaps in occupation, however, are too frequent to be

These records put into play a complex system of accounting and account-ability. Perhaps most important in this regard were the records relating to in-mate labor. According to La Rochefoucault Liancourt, who toured the prison in 1795:

> Each convict has a book, in which he enters his bargain made with the out-door employer, and in which his earnings are also set down in order. The convict's out-goings, whether on account of his prosecution, his fine, the price of the instruments which he breaks, or injures, of his cloathing, and of his board, are likewise set down in this book; which is audited every three months in the presence of the inspectors. A double entry is made of this account in the general register of the prison, and balanced every quarter; the overplus remains in the county treasury; which thus becomes the treasury of the prisoners.

The inspectors wanted to be certain that prison labor was not only regular but well documented. These records enabled the inspectors to monitor the labor of individual inmates to enforce labor discipline. The inspectors ordered that no prisoner be recommended for pardon "unless he has earned his keeping." The records were also designed to encourage inmates in their labor. The penal act of 1790 had mandated that if the proceeds from an individual's labor ex-ceeded the individual's costs, then "one half of said excess shall be laid out in decent raiment for such convicts at their discharge or otherwise applied to their use and benefit" at the discretion of the inspectors. Finally, these records were intended to prevent exploitation of inmates by either the jailer or the outside employer. The detail of the records, La Rochefoucault Liancourt sug-gested, "prevents any suspicion falling upon the goaler; who is a mere agent between the prisoner and the merchant or manufacturer, employing him" and also made it "easy . . . for the inspectors to determine whether, and how far, the agreement [between inmate and contractor] is equitable." [54]

---

explained in this way and are probably an indication of the undeveloped nature of the record-keeping system.

54. La Rochefoucault Liancourt, *On the Prisons of Philadelphia,* 15–16, 16; Bd. of Insp., Minutes, Mar. 11, 1795. Records on inmate labor consisted of documentation of labor per-formed and costs incurred by the prisoners (*Directions for the Inspectors,* 99). Rates (of pay-ment and costs) were set by the inspectors. See Turnbull, *A Visit,* 24; Bd. of Insp., Minutes, Oct. 27, 1794, Mar. 11, 1795. The law mandated that these books be balanced regularly, so that prisoners could receive anything that was their due (*St. at Large,* XIII, 519; Turnbull reported that excess proceeds from a prisoner's labor were used to benefit the prisoner. *A Visit,* 22). The inspectors, however, were careful to see that no inmate received more than the law enjoined (Bd. of Insp., Minutes, Mar. 20, 1795). It is also unclear how often a prisoner actually earned more than his costs.

Labor records, then, merged two different meanings of "accountability." On the one hand, the records enabled an institutional monitoring; they were literally accounts between inmates, the prison, and private contractors. In this way, they were part of the disciplining of authority itself. But on the other hand, they were a device to hold inmates themselves accountable for their labor, and, by implication, for their own reformation. The legislature had stressed the importance of accounting for labor "to encourage industry as an evidence of reformation."[55] Labor was a means for enriching inmates and subordinating them to the logic of the institution. But, for it to work, it had to be recorded and displayed to the inmate. The records, like labor itself, externalized the transformation of inmate character; the success or failure of the prison was inscribed in the good book. The development of these records manifested clearly the double nature of the individualization of punishment. Although labor records were acknowledgments of the possibility of reformation, they also were a tool for governing inmates more thoroughly.

The prison's deployment of accounts to merge work and reformation resembles Max Weber's description of double-column bookkeeping in his *Protestant Ethic and the Spirit of Capitalism*. Weber read the Calvinist fascination with the daily details of work and life as a crucial moment in the rationalization of everyday life; seeking signs of individual salvation, Calvinists inadvertently exploded the world of redemption and laid the roots for a bureaucratic iron cage. Disciplinary records also linked individual salvation with labor but in an inverted fashion. Whereas Weber's Calvinists imposed a regime on themselves and thereby changed the world, in the prison the regime changed itself to transform the self. Here lies both the resonance and the difference between Weberian and Foucaultian notions of discipline. What Foucault called discipline was imbued with technical rationality from the start; Weberian rationality was rooted in the irrational hope of affecting the unaffectable will of God. Weber's discipline was that of a self that made the world a terrain of its action; it was a regime imposed by a self upon itself. Foucault's discipline, by contrast, turned the self into a target of social regulation; it was a regime that altered the practices of authority in order to reforge the self. And in each, the manifold senses of accountability made the self subject to authority.[56]

The ritualization of accountability was tied to the larger goal of obtaining knowledge about individuals. The judicial system generated personal histories of some prisoners; these histories accompanied the inmates on their arrival at Walnut Street Jail, helping to distinguish inmates from each other and pro-

55. *St. at Large*, XIII, 519.

56. See Foucault, *Discipline and Punish*, 135–228; Max Weber, *The Protestant Ethic and the Spirit of Capitalism*, trans. Talcott Parsons (New York, 1958). Weber introduces the significance of record keeping on 16–19.

vide indications about their character. "On the first entrance of a convict," Turnbull recorded, "the inspectors receive from a proper officer of the court, before whom the conviction was had, a brief report of the circumstances attending his crime; particularly such as tend to palliate or aggravate it, with other information respecting his behaviour on his trial, and his general conduct previous to and after receiving the sentence of the court." Turnbull believed that these records were produced for all inmates, but the law only mandated that it be done for those whose offenses, prior to 1786, would have been capital. In fact, the Board of Inspectors indicated that it thought it important to enlarge the law so that it could cover all inmates.[57] But, however limited, these records suggest the growing desire to generate individuated knowledge about individual inmates, knowledge that could then aid prison officials to control and transform their charges.

Documentation of the sentencing court's "knowledge of the prisoner's character and disposition" served, at least, two purposes. First, it enabled the inspectors to "form an opinion of the prisoner and to conduct themselves toward him as the case requires." Thus informed, they would be able to determine what would "be requisite for the annihilation" of the prisoner's "former bad habits." But its presentation before the prisoner had a second effect. The delivery of these documents was part of the inculcation of prison discipline: "it early evinces to the criminal the strictness with which he may afterwards expect to be treated."[58] The presentation of knowledge was a prison ritual demonstrating the thoroughness of official oversight. As with the other forms of documentation about inmates, these records not only helped prison authorities determine how to treat individual inmates; they were part of the apparatus for maintaining authority.

All of these sources enabled the inspectors to construct a grid for the government of inmates. Lownes argued that a prison should be "so constructed as to effect a complete separation of the sexes—and of *characters*—the former, however important, is not more necessary than the latter." His fellow inspectors agreed. In 1795, the Board, increasingly frightened by contact between males of different characters and criminal backgrounds, took steps to

---

57. Turnbull, *A Visit,* 49–50; La Rochefoucault Liancourt, *On the Prisons of Philadelphia,* 12; Bd. of Insp., Minutes, June 28, 1796. Because the law required personal histories for only those convicted of capital offenses, it excluded the largest number of inmates, those committed for larceny. I think it unlikely that the courts began to provide personal histories for all inmates.

58. Turnbull, *A Visit,* 50. François Alexandre Frédéric Duc de La Rochefoucault Liancourt, *Travels through the United States of North America, the Country of the Iroquois, and Upper Canada, in the Years 1795, 1796, and 1797; With an Authentic Account of Lower Canada . . .* (London, 1799), II, 339.

increase separation not only between the sexes but within them as well. Initially, the inspectors offered a plan to create three classes of nonconvict male inmates: first, the prisoners for trial, sailors, and deserters; second, the servants, apprentices, and slaves; and third, the vagrants and "disorderly persons." All these groups were to be lodged and employed separately.[59]

This drive for separation took on increasingly elaborate forms. In June 1797, the Board implemented a classification system for convicts structured according to guilt and perceived capacity for reformation. The inspectors divided the convicts into four classes, "who shall neither lodge, eat, or associate together." The subdivision of convicts would, in theory at least, preclude the more "vicious" from affecting the lesser offenders.[60] The system of classification was both a way to order the inmates and a scale to evaluate their progress toward reformation.

The system differentiated convicts according to their history, their offenses, and their moral character. The first class was "composed of those prisoners who are sentenced to confinement only." But the basis for defining the remaining three categories was far more elaborate. The second, or "select class," was to include those

> whose characters and circumstances both before and after conviction induce a belief that they are not habitual offenders, those who may have committed an offense of considerable magnitude in the eyes of the Law; yet evince a disposition to demean themselves in an orderly and exemplary manner, and generally such as on account of their Youth or other circumstances the Visiting Inspectors with the concurrence of the Board may deem proper characters for this selection.

The third class were those

> whose characters being unknown, or being known are not considered proper to be among those of the former description—those who have nothing to recommend them either by their past life—society or connections but have received sentence without recommendation or any alleviating circumstance being forwarded either from the court—[or] the

59. Bd. of Insp., Minutes, May 19, 1795; Caleb Lownes to Thomas Eddy, Apr. 19, 1796, Philip Schuyler Papers, Rare Books and Manuscript Division, New York Public Library. On Eddy and his early efforts in New York, see W. David Lewis, *From Newgate to Dannemora: The Rise of the Penitentiary in New York, 1796–1848* (Ithaca, N.Y., 1965), 3–5, 29–35.

60. Bd. of Insp., Minutes, June 16, 1797. I have not found a similar, consistent concern with internally dividing the female population, perhaps owing to the smaller number of female prisoners. For a discussion of classification and housing, see Teeters, *The Cradle of the Penitentiary*, 58–60.

neighborhood they came [from], or other respectable quarter, and have not evinced any remarkable disposition since their confinement—this may be stiled the "probationary class."

Finally, the fourth class included:

Prisoners who are well known to be old offenders, either in this or another state or county, or those not being of this description, are men of depraved morals, dangerous Characters, unruly dispositions or disorderly conduct, whilst in prison, and generally those who are objects of more particular care and watchfulness.

These categories combined traditional moral judgments with an individuated knowledge. The successful classification of inmates, and its contribution to their reformation, presupposed the production of knowledge about individuals.[61] The inspectors assumed that they would be able, either through observation or prior history, to judge their inmates' characters and make reasoned choices about their future behavior. But the amorphous character of the moral categories left a wide degree of interpretive freedom for the inspectors. Classification decisions, although ordered by knowledge, were ultimately discretionary.

At the same time, the classification scheme allowed an ordering across time and space. The categories situated an inmate not only physically but spiritually as well. If classification enabled the inspectors to separate inmates spatially, it also documented prisoners' reformation across time. Prisoners could move across categories (in both directions presumably) depending on their demeanor and progress toward reformation. Classification constituted a grid of moral progress inscribed on prison space. And, just as important, separation did not immobilize the prisoners, it directed and produced acceptable movements.

The production and use of these documents occurred within a system of personal authority. Although prison officials hoped that more efficient record keeping would enable them to control the inmates more effectively and the promulgation of written records would eliminate arbitrary authority, the prison was not a fully developed bureaucratic entity. Instead, records were used within the context of personal interaction between prison officials and inmates. They were a supplement to, not a replacement for, the inspectors' discretionary evaluation and personal management. The interaction with officers, as much as the submission to written rules, would maintain prison

61. Bd. of Insp., Minutes, June 16, 1797. For a discussion of the significance of knowledge about the individual and the construction of the "case" within discipline, see Foucault, *Discipline and Punish*, 189–192.

order and lead to personal reformation. Authority in the prison was exercised as a hybrid of personal government and impersonal regulations and records.

Lownes laid great stress on the importance of effectively combining certain regulations with proper, personal authority. He believed that most people were far too worried about the danger posed by a prison population. Writing to New York's Thomas Eddy about the construction and organization of a prison, he argued: "As to security—*don't be alarmed about it*—let a well digested plan of Building be adopted—good regulations be formed—men of principle be appointed as Keeper or overseers—and Respectable citizens to inspect it, and you will have little occasion to fear from your prisoners."[62] Here the connection between rules and proper personal authority was made clear. If convicts were properly managed, both by wise regulations and by wise governors, there would be little problem.

Personalized oversight was not just lauded in theory; it was institutionalized in the structure of prison government. Prison authority depended on levels of personal observation. All of these levels employed the power of opinion and observation to control the prison. First, prisoners were observed by specially designated inmates, then by prison officials ascending from the watchmen, then the keeper, to the visiting inspectors, and from there to the entire Board. Finally, periodic visitors from the government examined the actions of all those connected with the prison, from the inmates to the Board.[63] Unremitting observation and the judgments based on it would serve to ensure that no one, neither prisoner nor prison official, behaved improperly.

Perhaps the clearest example of the combination of certain regulation and personal discretion lay in the granting of pardons. Despite the deep suspicion of pardons (combined with the moderation of penalties that, supposedly, made them superfluous), pardons emerged as a major tool of prison order. Prison officials held out the pardon as a reward for proper behavior. One requirement for a pardon was clearly spelled out: only those prisoners who had "earned their keeping" could be freed before they had completed their sentence. But, in addition to this rule, the inspectors had to evaluate prisoners in less fixed, more interpretive ways. The inspectors' language, from their minutes, was consistent on this point. Prisoners were recommended for a pardon when they displayed "good conduct and orderly behavior." As Lownes explained the system: "If the prisoners conduct with propriety, they attract the attention of the Keepers and Inspectors; who make enquiry into their circumstances; encourage them to bring forward recommendations from respectable citizens that they have lived with, or have had a knowledge of them; and, if it

62. Lownes to Eddy, Apr. 19, 1796, Schuyler Papers.
63. Turnbull, *A Visit,* 49, 52, 64.

should appear proper, or prudent, they are recommended to the Governor for a pardon."[64] The rule of self-supportive labor, then, provided a non-discretionary guideline to supplement the essentially personal evaluation of character.

Lownes believed that the inspectors' authority, both over pardons and over inmates, was tied to the larger system of personal observation. He argued that the periodic visits of the governor, mayor, judges, and grand juries were:

> a circumstance which greatly promotes the success of the plan, as it strengthens the hands of the officers, and encourages the prisoners to a propriety of conduct, and thereby claiming their attention and obtaining a remission of their sentence; for they well know if they have conducted improperly, that they have no encouragement *to hope;* but on the contrary, great cause *to fear;* those especially of the worst characters are thus influenced to a careful attention to preserve a propriety of conduct, in order to have some plea for their application for a pardon.

Effective prison government depended on the continuing presence of elite, proper individuals.[65]

Prison authority, then, combined detailed written regulations and records with personal oversight. Through this combination, prison officials believed they could control their charges and bring them to proper obedience and participation in the continuing prison regime. But even where obedience and participation did not occur, where what Foucault termed a "productive body and a subjected body" was not produced, prison officials continued to transform and expand the structures of disciplinary authority.[66] The written body of the prison was elaborated on the observed bodies of the prisoners.

V

Just as disciplinary government subjected prisoners to a new regime of visibility, so the prison itself became the object of a mediated public gaze. In part, this scrutiny occurred through official channels of observation and oversight, channels themselves separate from the everyday life outside the prison's walls. But Benjamin Rush's dream of storytellers bringing tales of prisons and prisoners to the community was not entirely misconceived. As punishment faded from the public presence, it took its place within the world of print and the imagination.

64. Bd. of Insp., Minutes, Mar. 11, 1795, May 15, 1798, Feb. 12, 1799; Lownes, *An Account,* 85.
65. Lownes, *An Account,* 82.
66. Foucault, *Discipline and Punish,* 26.

To some extent, contact between the public and the prison occurred within the prison structure. Both the prison's economy and the system of governmental oversight ensured that people moved in and out of the prison space. Moreover, the prison did not forbid visitors entirely. It is likely that information and descriptions of prison life found their way orally into the city at large.

But even more interestingly, the prison became the subject of written descriptions, analyses, and depictions during the 1790s. In them, the presence of punishment was displaced rather than excised; removed from the public gaze, punishment returned to the world through print. These writings, in effect, enacted punishment's new structures of distanced perception. In the place of immediate visibility, their authors offered imaginary connection. Presenting the world of punishment to the community at large (or at least to those segments of the community that consumed pamphlet and book literature), they simultaneously maintained and overcame the distance between the public and its punishments.

On the one hand were manuals of Enlightenment reform. Lownes's *Account of the Goal and Penitentiary House of Philadelphia* depicted the intentions and strategies of prison reform, providing context and justification for the actions of prison officials and defenses of the state's program to revitalize the incarcerative regime. La Rochefoucault Liancourt's *On the Prisons of Philadelphia* and Turnbull's *Visit to the Philadelphia Prison,* provided extensive descriptions of the new prison regime, the structure of daily life, and the attitudes of officials and inmates, and evaluated the prison's effects. Lownes, La Rochefoucault Liancourt, and Turnbull framed the prison within the context of expanding reason and humanity. They depicted the prison and prisoners in sober prose; their representation of the prison itself mirrored the meticulous regulation of prison discipline. These were all, in one way or another, authorized representations: Lownes himself was an important early inspector and La Rochefoucault Liancourt and Turnbull made clear that their descriptions represented the views of the inspectors, indeed, that they were rooted in official knowledge.[67] This pamphlet literature reflected back on its public a sense that this public and its reforms were enlightened and humane.

But the language of humanitarian reform was only one way to represent the realm of confinement. If reformative incarceration could be figured as Enlightenment practice, it could also be linked to gothic horror. The gothic, with its repetitive invocation of crypts and dungeons, mysteries and murders, secrets and sadistic practices, titillated and teased readers in late-eighteenth-century Anglo-America. In the frame of the gothic, confinement represented

---

67. See La Rochefoucault Liancourt, *On the Prisons of Philadelphia,* 46; Turnbull, *A Visit,* iv.

less a stable and stabilizing retreat than a dangerous and seductive realm of corruption and decay. The gothic offered another world of confinement, a world that, from the vantage of everyday life, appeared archaic but that, seen from another perspective, lay at the heart of the world at large.[68]

In Charles Brockden Brown's *Arthur Mervyn,* confinement takes its place within the paradoxes of the gothic space. *Arthur Mervyn,* like all of Brown's novels, offers a bewildering narrative of mistaken identities, misunderstandings, uncanny mirrorings, moral ambiguities, and social and personal dangers. Its protagonist, the novel's namesake, is a country boy who arrives in Philadelphia in time for the yellow fever epidemic of 1793. The novel traces Mervyn's fortunes both forward and backward in time, as Arthur reveals his past to his benefactors Doctor and Mrs. Stevens, is dogged by his ties to the mysterious Welbeck, escapes death several times, leaves and returns to the city, makes and breaks connections with women, until, finally, he surmounts his travails, becomes a doctor like his benefactor, and marries Ascha Fielding, whom he met for the first time in a brothel, and who may or may not be wealthy. Although Arthur himself is the thread that holds the narrative together, he is also its point of greatest potential dissolution. Despite his self-proclaimed high moral standards and desire to do good, doubt and deceit haunt young Arthur, as conflicting representations of his past and his ties to clearly villainous characters threaten to destroy him and condemn him to the prison life. Critical controversy has raged over Arthur's character—should we believe him, or his critics? Was he the prototypical con man, or a misunderstood innocent? But more to the point, *Arthur Mervyn* is, above all, a representation of the crisis of value and meaning that plagued the new Republic and that took conceptual shape in the discourse of mimetic corruption.[69]

68. For a discussion of the connections between gothic literature and the world of confinement in late-18th- and early-19th-century Anglo-America, to which I am indebted here, see Karen Halttunen, "Gothic Mystery and the Birth of the Asylum" (paper presented to the Annual Meeting of the American Studies Association, New Orleans, La., November 1990). On the structure of the gothic, see Eve Kosofsky Sedgwick, *The Coherence of Gothic Conventions* (New York, 1980), 8–40.

69. Charles Brockden Brown, *Arthur Mervyn; or, Memoirs of the Year 1793, First and Second Parts,* in Sydney J. Krause et al., eds., *The Novels and Related Works of Charles Brockden Brown, Bicentennial Edition* (Kent State, Ohio, 1980); Norman S. Grabo, "Historical Essay," in Brown, *Arthur Mervyn,* ed. Krause et al., 474–475.

The literature on *Arthur Mervyn* is enormous. But, for a sampling of recent criticism of the novel (by both historians and literary critics), see Daniel A. Cohen, "Arthur Mervyn and His Elders: The Ambivalence of Youth in the Early Republic," *WMQ,* XLIII (1986), 362–380; Cathy N. Davidson, *Revolution and the Word: The Rise of the Novel in America* (New York, 1986), 236–253; Shirley Samuels, "Plague and Politics in 1793: *Arthur Mervyn,*" *Criticism,* XXVII (1985), 225–246; Jane Tompkins, *Sensational Designs: The Cultural Work of American Fiction, 1790–1865* (New York, 1985), 62–93; Michael Warner, *The Letters of the*

Repetition and mirroring are central to *Arthur Mervyn*. Brown creates a world of dazzling doubles where not only characters but spaces repeat and mirror each other. Arthur's movements are consistently obstructed by confinement, sometimes in closets or cellars, and his narrative reaches its greatest tension in sealed rooms and hiding places. In the novel, morality is inscribed in space itself.

This repetition is clearest in experiences of imprisonment. Early in book 2 of the novel, Mervyn's benefactor Doctor Stevens finds himself summoned to the debtors' prison by a mysterious note. Knowing that his friend Carlton had debts that he was unable to discharge, Stevens goes with a certain dread, convinced that it was Carlton who had summoned him, "so prone is the human mind to create for itself distress." Entering the prison, Stevens found that it "was filled with pale faces and withered forms. The marks of negligence and poverty were visible in all; but few betrayed, in their features or gestures, any symptoms of concern on account of their condition." Within the debtors' chamber, context and character reinforced each other. "Ferocious gaity, or stupid indifference," Stevens continued, "seemed to sit on every brow. The vapour from an heated stove, mingled with the fumes of beer and tallow that were spilled upon it, and with the tainted breath of so promiscuous a crowd, loaded the stagnant atmosphere. At my first transition from the cold and pure air without, to this noxious element, I found it difficult to breathe." Here the atmosphere does double duty, the "vapours" a medium of both moral and physical contagion, the air a symbol of the very promiscuous denial of boundaries that shaped the entire prison space. Like some mesmeric fluid, the air of the prison materialized the very threat of mimetic corruption, carrying its poisonous depravity from prisoner to prisoner, and possibly infecting those who had entered the prison temporarily: "I found it difficult to breathe." Stevens had entered another world, an underworld, where the "stagnant atmosphere" and the "promiscuous crowd" stood as an inverted reminder of the "pure air" without, an ironic quality in a novel set in a city suffering a plague. "Almost every mouth" had a "segar" and "every hand . . . a glass of porter." Many inmates were talking, some playing "whist," while "others, unemployed, were strolling to and fro, and testified their vacancy of thought and care by humming or whistling a tune."[70] Stevens's spirit was only further dampened when he did discover Carlton, who had been seized by his creditors and thrown into his confinement.

Republic: Publication and the Public Sphere in Eighteenth-Century America (Cambridge, Mass., 1990), 151–173; Steven Watts, *The Romance of Real Life: Charles Brockden Brown and the Origins of American Culture* (Baltimore, 1994), 101–115.

70. Brown, *Arthur Mervyn*, ed. Krause et al., 253, 253–254.

But Stevens's visit was merely the entry into another case of temporal and spatial repetition. For the note had, in fact, come, not from Carlton, but from Mervyn, who was in the prison attending to Welbeck, previously arrested for fraud. Mervyn had gone to the prison on hearing rumors that Welbeck was held there. "Having enquired for Welbeck," Mervyn tells Stevens, "I was conducted through a dark room, crouded with beds, to a stair case." His descent into horror continued. "Never before had I been in a prison. Never had I smelt so noisome an odour, or surveyed faces so begrimed with filth and misery." As Mervyn enters the space of confinement, he confronts a world spiraling out of control and away from humanity, its residents oblivious, it seems, to the reality in which they lived, faces "distorted" or "void," representing either depravity or emptiness. "The walls and floors," Arthur continued, "were alike squalid and destestable. It seemed that in this house existence would be bereaved of all its attractions; and yet those faces, which could be seen through the obscurity that encompassed them, were either void of care or distorted with mirth."[71] As with Stevens, Mervyn reported a deliriously doubling effect, where persons and places seemed interchangeble.

Brown, through Mervyn, constructs the entrance into the prison as a passage of moral and physical descent. Reflecting on Welbeck's fall, Arthur could not but compare the past and the present, the dichotomy between the prison space and the space of everyday life. "What contrasts are these," he mused, "to the repose and splendor, pictured walls, glossy hangings, gilded sofas, mirrors that occupied from cieling to floor, carpets of Tauris, and the spotless and transcendent brilliancy of coverlets and napkins" that filled Welbeck's former house. In the prison, "brawling and the shuffling of rude feet are eternal. The air is loaded with the exhalations of disease and the fumes of debauchery." Welbeck, he concluded, was "cooped up in airless space, and, perhaps, compelled to share [a] narrow cell with some stupid ruffian."[72] In Brown's hands, the space of confinement, like some Piranesi prison brought to life or a Hogarthian progress put to words, offered an inversion of the clearness and purity that gave Enlightenment reform its self-image.

These scenes of a debauched prison, in turn, took their place within a wider network of cruel, sometimes fatal, confinements. In the hidden passages and tunnels of Welbeck's house, Mervyn had briefly imagined himself buried alive while he himself was helping Welbeck bury the murdered Watson. And, in the clearest precursor to the prison scenes, Arthur had listened in horror as young Wallace recounted his own confinement in the hospital set up for those infected with yellow fever. "I lay upon a mattress whose condition proved that an half decayed corpse had recently been dragged from it. The room was large,

71. Ibid., 334.
72. Ibid.

but it was covered with beds like my own. Between each there was scarcely the interval of three feet. Each sustained a wretch, whose groans and distortions, bespoke the desperateness of his condition." As in the debtors' prison, the state of the individuals mirrored the larger atmosphere, "loaded by mortal stenches." "A vapour, suffocating and malignant, scarcely allowed me to breathe. No suitable recepticle was provided for the evacuations produced by medicine or disease." And even more than the prison, Brown's hospital manifested not only depravity and desperation but moral cruelty. "You will scarcely believe," Wallace affirmed, "that in this scene of horrors, the sound of laughter should be overheard." The staff, "wretches who are hired, at enormous wages neglect their duty and consume the cordials, which are provided for the patients, in debauchery and riot." One woman, "bloated with malignity and drunkenness, occasionally looked in" but did nothing to succor the inmates.[73] In the hospital, once again the atmosphere materializes the double threat of contagion; both moral symptom and physical threat, the poisonous "vapour, suffocating and malignant," affected not only the bodies of the inmates but the characters of the staff. As the attendants embodied the horror of the fever, the fever itself externalized the evil of the attendants.

In *Arthur Mervyn*, then, the prison takes its place among horrifying and dangerous spaces. Confinement haunts the novel: it is the constant threat facing Arthur, the final fate of Welbeck, and, in the form of the yellow fever hospital, the ultimate site of the moral and physical miasma that was the yellow fever epidemic itself.[74] True, Brown is describing the debtors' section, not the convicts' area, and the Board of Inspectors had been less successful in imposing its authority on the debtors than on the criminals. True, Brown's depiction of a malignancy materialized in the space of the prison seems a far cry from the mundane realities of the debtors' apartment.

But this exaggeration is precisely what is important; the imaginative frame rather than the empirical content is at issue here. Through the repetitive presentation of horrific spaces, spaces that circulate around the prison and the hospital, Brown, in effect, makes terrible confinement the spatial and contagious equivalent of the yellow fever. In a way, Brown does little more than reactivate older discourses of infernal space and unreformed prisons.[75] But he

73. Ibid., 109–110, 173. Brown is repeating a factually dubious charge against the staff at the Bush-Hill hospital. On the Bush-Hill hospital and the racist politics that it engendered, see J. H. Powell, *Bring Out Your Dead: The Great Plague of Yellow Fever in Philadelphia in 1793* (Philadelphia, 1949), 100–107.

74. For an extended reflection on the ways in which the plague can be said to mark the intersection between moral and physical contagions, at least in *Arthur Mervyn*, see Samuels, "Plague and Politics in 1793," *Criticism*, XXVII (1985), 225–246.

75. As John Bender has shown, unreformed prisons figured crucially in the 18th-century English novel. As Bender sees it, these unreformed spaces exemplified the combined personal

does so in a postreform context. In *Arthur Mervyn,* the space of confinement, rather than being a place of reformation and virtue, is an otherworld containing the excesses and effluvia of the enlightened city. But, as its repetition indicates, it is a space separated from everyday life by only the slightest barriers, one lying concealed behind many doors and around many corners. The constant repetition of confined spaces erodes the clear-cut barriers between virtuous and debauched places; they implicitly undermine as they consciously affirm the distance separating the world of confinement from the world of morality and freedom. Their uncanny return stages the fragility and instability not only of virtue but of Enlightenment reform itself.

Brown's *Arthur Mervyn,* then, offers a distinctly different image of imprisonment than did the pamphlets of reform. The point is not, however, to choose between them. Brown did not aim for sober description; Lownes did not strive for horrific effect. Instead, they should be read together as two ways that imprisonment could fill the imagination. Each in its own way brought the prison back before the public eye, each connected the public to the world of confinement through the distance afforded by print.

Rush's dream of a spiral of terror emanating from the enclosed prison was not without prescience. In the narratives of the 1790s, Enlightenment sobriety may have led the way, but "romance" found "ample materials for fiction." The prison assumed its place as both site of discipline and space of horror, enlightened reform and uncanny dread. In print, at least, it joined the world of the gothic to the century of light, evincing that ambiguous distance that structured the project of reformative incarceration itself. Images of horrible crypts haunted the Enlightenment project.[76]

VI

Brown was not the first to link disease with the prison. When John Howard began his travels, prison disease had been one of his prime concerns, and when the reforms of the 1790s began, health had been at their heart. Ironically,

and spatial promiscuity against which English bourgeois society defined itself. The ideological work of the novel, and the institutional work of prison reform, consisted precisely in subjecting this promiscuity to the regulating power of ordered narratives of personal progress. On the unreformed prison in the English novel, see John Bender, *Imagining the Penitentiary: Fiction and the Architecture of Mind in Eighteenth-Century England* (Chicago, 1987), 43–61, 139–163.

76. Benjamin Rush, *An Enquiry into the Effects of Public Punishments upon Criminals and upon Society; Read in the Society for Promoting Political Enquiries, Convened at the House of His Excellency Benjamin Franklin, Esquire, in Philadelphia, March 9th, 1787* (Philadelphia, 1787), 11; Halttunen, "Gothic Mystery and the Birth of the Asylum," 11–14.

the effects of yellow fever would strike a stunning blow against prison government. In August 1798, the inspectors noted, "The influx of vagrants, servants,
etc., from all parts of the city being much greater than usual, the situation of
the prisoners, keepers, etc. has become very alarming in consequence, lest by
that means the prevailing disease should be introduced among them," and
they proposed meeting with city and county magistrates in order to "earnestly
request them to avoid sending in more of the aforesaid Classes" and to find a
temporary place to receive these prisoners. At some point in the next few
months, the city did obtain a place of temporary detention. The following
summer, the Board took steps to do the same if the problem of contagion
should reappear. Although the inspectors successfully persuaded city officials
to provide a temporary bridewell, their persuasiveness did not conceal the
flawed state of the prison. Despite the optimism of early visitors, the health of
prisoners in Walnut Street was extremely precarious.[77] Had city officials not
responded to their requests, the prison would have suffered even more severely from the yellow fever than it did. Rather than eliminating the threat of
jail fever to inmates and society, the new prison regime was threatened by diseases from society itself.

The yellow fever epidemic of 1798, combined with the fire at the prison
manufactory, shattered the internal structure of the prison. After the Acting
Committee of the Philadelphia Society inspected Walnut Street in December
of 1798, they reported that "they [had] observed much apathy to prevail and a
considerable derangement of the usual order of that place." This situation
prevailed in all of the apartments of the prison:

> On entering in at the Iron Gate we observed some of the Convicts Idle,
> sauntering about the Yard, and in the main passage of the House. In the
> ward allotted to the women Vagrants and such as were confined for tryal,
> we found many Idle, some dirty, and some ragged. In the Women Con-
> vict ward were also many Idle, and in the Hospital of the female Vagrants
> were two sick, one that appeared extremely Ill, miserably accomodated
> and so far Neglected as not to have received a visit from the Physician for
> three weeks.
>
> In the Ward allotted to the men vagrants we found upwards of One
> hundred persons, a large Proportion of them Black, some confined for

---

77. Bd. of Insp., Minutes, Aug. 24, Nov. 13, 1798, July 17, 1799, Aug. 14, 1799. For early indications of disease, see ibid., Oct. 6, 1795. For prisoners' complaints, see ibid., Jan. 8,
Jan. 22, Feb. 12, 1799. These complaints are an instance of prisoners combining together to
achieve a reform within the prison. Foucault suggested the origins of the disciplines lay in
fear of the plague (*Discipline and Punish*, 195–200). On the ways that the dangers of jail
fever stimulated efforts to devise new prison architectures, see Evans, *The Fabrication of
Virtue*, 94–117.

tryal, some as Runaways, some as Vagrants and some as Convicts in a
very dirty and generally ragged Condition without a Bed and/with only
one exception that came to our knowledge/but one Blankett per man;
the apartment dirty and offensive to the smell.

In sum, the Acting Committee concluded, the prison displayed "a state of
Idleness, Dirt and Wretchedness exceeding any thing of the kind which they
have observed there for some years past." The Philadelphia Society had no
doubt that the yellow fever and workshop arson had disrupted prison discipline.[78] The events of the spring and summer of 1798 had dissolved the always
tenuous discipline of Walnut Street.

Prison officials themselves might have increased the impact of the yellow
fever. Between August 24 and October 13, 1798, there were no meetings of the
Board of Inspectors. The Philadelphia Society's Acting Committee did not
meet from July 16, 1798, until January 1799. The prison doctor was quite lax in
attending to his charges—a laxness that undoubtedly contributed to the ill
health of some inmates.[79] But, for whatever reason, the yellow fever disrupted
the exercise of authority and oversight—by both prison officials and prison
reformers—as well as the everyday life of the prison.

By the end of the eighteenth century, the disciplinary project had advanced
from imagination to practice. Not only had penal reformers distanced the display of punishment from the public, but they imposed a new regime of government and regularity upon the prisoners. Within the prison, they placed the
penal body under a new scrutiny, seeking to create the dispositions of virtue
and self-discipline, and they sought to bring prison officials under greater
oversight and external control. Facing resistance from within the prison and
from the outside world, they expanded the mechanisms of disciplinary authority—particularly in asserting the importance of written regulations and
documentary records. Removed from sight, the new prison regime merged a
Protestant faith in personal reformation with Enlightenment notions of the
beneficial effects of a totally ordered environment. The 1790s marked a decisive moment in the elaboration of disciplinary government. Whatever set-
backs prison authorities faced, the result was a return to disciplinary methods
and practices; the failures of discipline led to the intensification of the disciplines. Late-eighteenth-century penal reform both extended the claims of humanity and tied them more closely to subordination.

78. Minutes, Jan. 14, 1799, PSAMPP; Minutes of the Acting Committee, Jan. 12, 1799,
PSAMPP.

79. Bd. of Insp., Minutes, Aug. 24, Oct. 13, 1792; Minutes of the Acting Committee, Jan. 10,
Jan. 12, 1799, PSAMPP. From the reports discussed above, clearly some members of the
committee did visit the jail during December 1798.

At the same time, the reformed prison assumed a place before the public and in its imagination. If penal reform aimed to overcome the symbol of the suffering body, the prison itself took on symbolic shape. The Walnut Street Jail, located within the urban community while defining its margins, provided a space to imagine both utopian possibilities and uncanny horrors. Liberal humanitarianism, with its hope for ordered and orderly progress, evoked a vision of recuperation, whereas its images of corruption and contagion evinced nothing so powerfully as the desire for, and the anxiety over, distance. The prison condensed these two moments, assuming the character of a spiritualized space of punishment and a distant, almost gothic realm of terror. Looming threat and hopeful retreat, the prison embodied the ambiguities of the discourse of mimetic corruption itself. And the fateful doubling of the body of the inmate and the space of punishment would generate a continually renewed dynamic of discipline.

PART THREE

Penitence

CHAPTER SIX

Boundaries, Architecture,
and the Reconstruction
of Penal Authority

During the 1790s, public authorities and private reformers had envisioned a utopian taxonomy of discipline, but their dream collapsed under the pressures of population growth and economic transformation. As a result, Pennsylvanians moved to transform their penal apparatus during the 1820s. The state restructured the penal program, replacing a system based on labor and classification with one centered on solitary reflection. This move to curb the disorder of the jail condensed wider concerns over the collapse of social boundaries and the dangers of public space. Faced with the disruption of Enlightenment taxonomy, reformers expanded and reinvigorated their efforts to control and order social space. The turn to solitary confinement, in fact, marked the ascension of a strategy of spatial control—one rooted in architecture and designed to reinvigorate social space itself. It would be the first step in a new, more intensified disciplinary intervention in urban life.

I

On the afternoon of March 27, 1820, a skirmish broke out between two convicts, Harry Powell and Peter Hedgman. During the course of an argument, Powell struck Hedgman "with a knife or piece of Iron" on the forehead. Fleeing to the blacksmith's shop with other prisoners in angry pursuit, Powell found himself under attack. Inmates broke windows and threw stones, seeking to revenge themselves for Powell's assault on Hedgman. Neither the keepers' commands that inmates return to their rooms nor the ringing of prison bells had any effect. Eventually, only the intervention of one of the prison inspectors quieted the situation, and the inmates were, at least temporarily, dispersed.[1]

This conflict revealed hidden fissures within the prison. Powell was black, and the violence directed at him might have been racially motivated. He was also suspected of being an informer, a "favourite" of the keepers. His initial conflict with Hedgman had resulted from the latter's suspicion that Powell had revealed a plan for a prison uprising.[2] The authorities' dependence on informers, the rapidity with which other inmates entered the fray, and the keepers inability to control the situation pointed to the fragility of day-to-day authority in the prison.

The following day, the prison exploded into general insurrection. Between eight and nine o'clock on Tuesday morning, the inspectors attempted to isolate and punish the participants in Monday's conflict. During this attempt, prisoners rebelled and "in a tumultuous riotous manner broke off the locks of the other rooms and released the other prisoners—A general Insurrection ensued." Making their way into the prison yard, with ladders prepared for scaling the walls, the prisoners attempted to escape. Some sought to break into the Prune Street apartment, some to climb the walls to freedom, and some to enter the women's section. According to the *Franklin Gazette:*

> The revolt was general; and every man confined in the cells was released by the ringleaders, to enable them to join in the insurrection. Almost every bar inside the prison was wrenched from its proper position; all the locks of the doors and cells were broken; and one of the doors at the southeast corner of the yard, communicating with the department for untried prisoners, was forced open by a large *Jack* used to raise stone, in order to let in about 200 men to their aid.

Unable to control the situation on their own, prison officials called on the support of both armed civilians and the local militia. Civilians on the wall fired into the prison yard while prisoners continued to throw bricks. One prisoner was killed, and three were wounded. After several hours, the authorities regained their tenuous control over the prison.[3]

Even after the state suppressed the uprising, the prison remained tense. The inspectors called in the United States Army, purchased large numbers of

1. Bd. of Insp., Minutes, Mar. 27, 1820.

2. Ibid., Mar. 27, Apr. 10, 1820; "The State Penitentiary," *Franklin Gazette* (Philadelphia), Mar. 30, 1820.

3. Bd. of Insp., Minutes, Mar. 28, 1820; *Franklin Gazette,* Mar. 28, 1820; *Union; United States Gazette and True American* (Philadelphia), Mar. 29, 1820; *Relf's Philadelphia Gazette, and Daily Advertiser,* Mar. 28, 1820; *Poulson's American Daily Advertiser* (Philadelphia), Mar. 29, 1820; *Niles' Weekly Register* (Baltimore), Apr. 1, 1820.

weapons, installed a new warning bell, and hired additional (if temporary) deputy keepers. A month later, forty-five inmates remained in the solitary cells as punishment for participating in the riot.[4] The limits to prison discipline had never been so evident.

The riot shattered the prison's public image. The city's newspapers covered the uprising in sensationalist and lurid terms. "Insurrection in the Prison," declared *Relf's Philadelphia Gazette*, a headline echoed in the *Union*. The prisoners were filled with "desperation," they were a "mob" containing a "spirit of discontent," "thundering" against the gates. Even the suppression of the revolt—dependent as it was on outside force—caused alarm. It was a "heart-appalling sight," opined the *Democratic Press*, "to see a body of regular soldiers marching with military music into a prison in the heart of a quiet city like ours." The inspectors and city officials were obliged to publish notices assuring the community that they were taking steps to secure prison order. Public papers debated prison safety. The city began an official investigation of the causes of the riot and expanded its police force. Nevertheless, doubts over the security of the prison and the safety of the community remained.[5]

II

The prison riot made manifest the collapse of prison discipline. Following the yellow fever epidemic of 1798, prison officials had restored some control over prison life. But this discipline was always fragile and never complete.[6] The inspectors never solved the prison's economic difficulties, and prison labor was neither fully productive nor sufficiently profitable. These difficulties only increased over time. By the late 1810s, overcrowding, combined with the prison's structural problems, helped to cause a general collapse of prison order. From 1815 onward, the inspectors' Minutes were filled with a litany of discouragement and failure. The prison order, never fully stable, dissolved. The end result was disease, violence, riot, and death.

4. Bd. of Insp., Minutes, Mar. 29, Apr. 10, 24, May 1, 1820.

5. *Relf's Philadelphia Gazette*, Mar. 28, 1820; *Union*, Mar. 29, 1820; *Dem. Press*, Mar. 28, 29, Apr. 3, 8, 1820; Bd. of Insp., Minutes, Apr. 10, May 1, 8, 1820.

6. Many of the problems that plagued the prison after 1815 (health, labor difficulties, insubordination, overpopulation) were present from the late 18th century onward. But the timing of the penal transformation suggests that the implementation of reform stemmed as much from the intersection of prison difficulties and external conflicts as from the condition of the prison itself. For this reason, I have stressed the years after 1815 here. For discussion and analysis of prison conditions during the early years of the 19th century, see my "Public Punishments, Reformative Incarceration, and Authority in Philadelphia, 1750–1835" (Ph.D. diss., University of California, Berkeley, 1987), 420–430; Negley K. Teeters, *The Cradle of the Penitentiary: The Walnut Street Jail at Philadelphia, 1773–1835* (Philadelphia, 1955), 86–100.

Throughout the nineteenth century, the prison population grew steadily. The number of convicts committed to the prison nearly tripled during the first twenty years of the nineteenth century. Although the annual committal rate of approximately 128 prisoners for the period 1795–1799 fell slightly to 125 (1800–1804), it then rose steadily to 171 (1805–1809), 251 (1810–1814), and 362 (1815–1819).[7] This growing population affected all aspects of prison life and practice.

Inmate health was particularly precarious. Death and disease were threats from the inception of the reformed regime at Walnut Street. But in the years after 1815, they became almost constant occurrences. In the winter of 1816–1817, smallpox broke out among the convicts and continued to cause concern for several months. In January 1818, the prison doctor reported that 97 inmates had been admitted to the hospital with "malignant fever," of whom 12 had died and 42 remained under care. Between May 25, 1818, and April 26, 1819, eighty prisoners died in the prison. In 1820, 469 inmates needed medical care and 30 died.[8] Disease and death were constant companions of the prison population.

Difficulties with the labor program increased. Although employment before 1815 was often intermittent, thereafter high unemployment became the rule. In 1816, the inspectors expressed their belief that truly adequate labor would never be achieved within the confines of Walnut Street. Commentators were continually worried about the level of employment within the prison. In December 1819, the visiting inspectors reported that "a great number of convicts are unemployed in each of the branches of manufacturing in the yard—among those usually employed at Sawing Stone very little is doing," a point echoed by the Philadelphia Society for Alleviating the Miseries of Public Prisons throughout 1820 and 1821. Thomas Bradford, Jr., one of the leading inspectors, complained in 1820 that there was "now very little hard labour for the convicts."[9] The combination of population growth and the limits of the prison's physical plant had undermined the labor program at Walnut Street.

The inspectors' authority collapsed in more subtle ways as well. Prisoners created their own systems of economic exchange outside the effective authority of the inspectors. In 1816, visiting inspectors discovered a "system of trades

7. Roberts Vaux, *Notices of the Original, and Successive Efforts, to Improve the Discipline of the Prison at Philadelphia, and to Reform the Criminal Code of Pennsylvania: With a Few Observations on the Penitentiary System* (Philadelphia, 1826), 66–71.

8. Meranze, "Public Punishments, Reformative Incarceration, and Authority," 415–419, 426–427; Bd. of Insp., Minutes, Nov. 11, 25, Dec. 9, 1816, Jan. 6, 1817, Jan. 12, 1818, Jan. 15, 1821.

9. Thomas Bradford, Jr., "Observations on the Penal Code," Prisons, Bradford Papers, HSP; Meranze, "Public Punishments, Reformative Incarceration, and Authority," 407–409, 427–428; Minutes of the Acting Committee, Apr. 10, 1820, Jan. 8, 1821, PSAMPP; Bd. of Insp., Minutes, Jan. 8, 1816, Sept. 27, Dec. 6, 1819. The Board believed that sawing of stone was the most profitable to the institution. Ibid., Jan. 9, 1815.

Coextensive with the number of prisoners." Through this widespread, illegal prison economy prisoners provided themselves with extra foodstuffs and luxuries. Despite the inspectors' discovery, prison officials were unable to curb this commerce among the inmates. In 1819, the Board reported that "large quantities of flour" were being "pilfered and converted into Bread and Cakes and disposed of by the Convicts" daily, in addition to "many other . . . equally improper" practices. A committee of the Board, assigned to investigate prison conditions, discovered "to their great astonishment but far greater disgust" that "almost every shop [was] amply supplied for a winters campaign with provisions and even luxuries viz Pork in abundance, Turkies, Fowls, Geese, Fish, butter lard, pies, eggs, sugar, coffee, tea, and spices." [10] The inmates had successfully created a society within Walnut Street and effectively limited the inspectors' authority over their day-to-day lives.

Even the boys confined in the prison's Prune Street apartment defied the inspectors. In April of 1830, the visiting inspectors reported that they had inflicted "severe punishment" on the Prune Street inmates. On appointing a new keeper for the section, the inspectors discovered that the boys had developed their own version of customary rights—rights that the inspectors wished to crush:

> The boys shewing a reckless independence of their keeper totally incompatible with good government—and on laying down rules to restore order Mr Roberts [the new keeper] was surprized and mortified at the resistance on their part of what they conceived to be an infraction of priviledges grafted on custom—Blue Monday was no working day—the liberty of going in and out of the shops at pleasure was by no means to be meddled with—Assembly in groups in any part of the Yard or building was a matter of right not to be disputed.

The boys resisted all attempts to impose a new discipline and the keeper responded by increasing the severity of his actions. "These repeated aggressions and the entire 'staunchness' of the boys induced the Keeper to put the greater portion of them in cells." But even the infliction of punishment was not enough to break their spirit. While confined they "kept up a continual howling and shouting" and then forced their way out of their cells. It was only with the aid of a nearby fire company armed with muskets that the prisoners were subdued. Even then, they continued to resist the keeper and to demonstrate a "refractory spirit." [11] The boys had developed their own system of behavior with its own rules, rights, and obligations.

10. Bd. of Insp., Minutes, Apr. 1, 1816, Feb. 15, 1819, Dec. 31, 1824.
11. Ibid., Apr. 26, 1830. A month later, the visiting inspectors reported that they still had not curbed the resistance within the Prune Street apartment. Ibid., May 24, 1830.

Keepers and members of the community also participated in the creation of this inmate economy and culture. Each time the inspectors discovered a flourishing prison economy, they also discovered the collusion of at least one of the keepers. The role of the keeper could vary from actually providing or storing illegally circulated goods to ignoring the evidence of the trade. In addition, citizens with business in the prison provided contraband to the inmates. The situation was so extreme that the inspectors concluded that "any article which the prisoners may be desirous of can be procured with ease owing to the hourly communication with the street by the passing in and out of persons having business with the prison." [12] Through the keepers and the community, inmates circumvented prison restrictions and provided themselves with some slight comforts during their confinement.

The keepers' accommodations with the inmates were embedded in the daily functioning of the prison. In exchange for relative peace, the keepers often enforced the rules sporadically, allowing inmates great leeway to organize their own lives. In 1821, for instance, the inspectors complained that the enforcement of prison discipline and the imposition of prison punishment was highly erratic, varying greatly from deputy keeper to deputy keeper. In 1824, they discovered that, "amongst other outrageous practices," the keepers were "allowing the Boss's of the different shops to have sole charge of those places and locking them up without the inspection of the keepers," thereby freeing the workplaces from effective oversight.[13] Between the inmates' desire to circumvent prison rules and the keepers' reluctance to enforce prison rules, prison discipline withered away.

Even more noticeable signs of the collapse of penal discipline were the numerous escapes, attempted escapes, and acts of violence that marked prison life. Escapes and attempted escapes increased strikingly after 1815. Inmates sought to break prison singly and in groups, over the walls, through the sewers, and from the cells. Not all of these attempts were successful, and many inmates were quickly recaptured. But the incidence of escapes and attempted escapes was too great to ignore. Nor was the prison free of violence. Some of the incidents of violence were tied to escape attempts. Other affrays among prisoners occurred for personal reasons or as acts of retribution toward suspected informers. In addition, prisoners battled with keepers. In general, the prison appears to have been a cauldron of discontent.[14]

12. Ibid., Apr. 1, 1816, Feb. 15, 1819, Dec. 31, 1824, Aug. 22, 1825, Apr. 26, 1830.

13. Ibid., Feb. 12, 1821, Dec. 31, 1824. The Board also complained that deputy keepers left their posts, and even the prison, without proper reason or authorization. Ibid., June 19, 1820, Feb. 12, 1821.

14. For planned escapes that were either discovered or halted in progress, see ibid., June 9, July 17, Sept. 29, 1817, May 11, 1818, Mar. 29, Apr. 25, June 11, July 19, 1819, June 5, Sept. 11, Oct. 23, 1820, Oct. 22, Dec. 5, 1821, July 29, 1822, Feb. 24, Mar. 24, June 2, July 22, 1823, Jan. 24,

Equally evident was a rise in recidivism. In 1816, Caleb Cresson and Roberts Vaux, writing to an English reformer on behalf of the Philadelphia Society, estimated that one-quarter of those sentenced to Walnut Street returned after their release. The inspectors, writing to the legislature in 1817, confessed that "in the present state of the prison of this County, we look in vain for a radical change in the characters of the prisoners—an Instance may occasionally occur—but it is rare." Others agreed. Although figures for the number of recidivists are lacking, both the Board and the Philadelphia Society were convinced that association among prisoners led to the increased corruption of inmates. The Society's acting committee reported that "the records of the prison prove . . . that lads of tender years and those of mature age committed as vagrants or for slight offences, for a few weeks from connexions with those of the most depraved characters . . . imbibe such a relish for vice, that when discharged they remain but a short time out before they are guilty of aggravated offences against the laws." The prison, in their eyes, once again had become a "school for depravity, and nursery for vice." [15]

Both the Philadelphia Society and the Board of Inspectors had long sought to expand and intensify the prison system—but with limited effect. As early as 1801, and periodically thereafter, they pressured the city and state to build new prison space. These efforts were not without success. The state did construct both the Arch Street Prison, ultimately used to house debtors and some prisoners for trial, and the State Penitentiary for the Western District of Pennsylvania, in Pittsburgh. But because of financial restrictions, building difficulties, and architectural problems, neither institution effectively restrained the growing pressures on Walnut Street. Prior to the 1820s, however, support for massive expansion of the penal apparatus was minimal. This situation changed after the prison riot of 1820. The uprising sent shock waves throughout the city that would not subside quickly. Prison and city officials as well as Philadelphia's newspapers sought both to reassure the city's population and to evaluate the condition of the prison.[16] In the face of this concern, the state moved rapidly.

Aug. 9, 1824, July 25, 1825. For actual escapes, see ibid., Mar. 3, Sept. 15, Oct. 27, 1817, Feb. 2, Mar. 2, July 6, 1818, Mar. 15, 1819, June 2, 1823, June 28, Aug. 9, 1824, Nov. 12, 1827. For prison violence not tied to escapes, see ibid., Oct. 27, 1817, Mar. 29 (an attack on a suspected informer), Aug. 2, 1819 (an attack on an informer), May 8, 1820, Apr. 1, 1822, Feb. 26, Apr. 5, 1824, Oct. 31, 1825, Aug. 7, 1826, Apr. 2, 1827 (this attack apparently was racially motivated). See Teeters, *The Cradle of the Penitentiary*, 100–101. For occasional attempts to set fire to the prison, see ibid., Dec. 25, 1815, Feb. 14, 1820, Feb. 22, 1824, July 25, 1825, Aug. 21, 1826.

15. Caleb Cresson and Roberts Vaux to William Allen, Oct. 19, 1816, Minutes, 1810–1832, PSAMPP; Bd. of Insp., Minutes, Dec. 29, 1817; Minutes of the Acting Committee, Jan. 10, 1820, Jan. 8, 1821, PSAMPP.

16. Minutes, Dec. 14, 1801, Jan. 25, 1803, PSAMPP; Bd. of Insp., Minutes, Jan. 8, 1816, Apr. 10,

III

In the aftermath of the riot, a wide range of public and private organizations called for a transformation of the penal system. In June of 1820, the grand jury of the city's Court of Oyer and Terminer expressed its belief that reformation could not be achieved in "the present state and construction of the prison" and called for the government to take steps to correct the situation. The governor, in his annual message, called for penal reforms, and both houses of the legislature convened committees (which operated jointly) to examine the situation at the prison. These committees investigated the condition of Walnut Street, conferred with the prison inspectors, and, ultimately, advocated a major reconstruction of prison organization.[17] The Board of Inspectors and the Philadelphia Society for Alleviating the Miseries of Public Prisons argued the case for radical reform. In addition, James Mease, a student and friend of Benjamin Rush, published a series of essays attacking the existing prison system and calling for solitary confinement. As a result of these efforts, the legislature and the governor mandated the construction of a new prison to impose solitary confinement on all prisoners.

The urgency of these efforts was tied to the prison riot of March 1820. The Senate committee noted with alarm that "in the course of last winter or spring, an insurrection broke out among the convicts, which threatened the destruction of the lives of the jailors and the escape of all who were confined. . . . Since that period a scene of discontent has constantly been exhibited, and a second revolt has been perpetually apprehended."[18] The riot demonstrated the absence of prison discipline in the present and foreshadowed even more threatening events. The viability of the entire system as well as the safety of inmates and the public, reformers believed, were in danger.

The main problem, the inspectors charged, lay in the physical capacity of the Walnut Street Jail. Constructed in 1773, prior to the reform of the penal code, it "was not properly constructed for such a system [of solitary confinement]." Yet Walnut Street's difficulties extended beyond the inability to provide solitary confinement for all inmates. Given its role as the state prison and given the increase of Pennsylvania's population, the numbers of inmates had soared. Serious overcrowding had led to the collapse of prison classification. The inspectors' capacity to separate inmates or control their communication, they concluded, was insufficient; the physical limits of Walnut Street denied

---

May 1, 8, 1820; *Relf's Philadelphia Gazette,* Mar. 28, 1820; *Niles' Weekly Register,* June 24, 1820; *Dem. Press,* Mar. 29, Apr. 3, "X," Apr. 18, 1820; *Poulson's Daily Advertiser,* Mar. 7, 1820.

17. *Niles' Weekly Register,* June 24, 1820; Pennsylvania General Assembly, Senate, Committee of the Penitentiary System, *Report on the Penitentiary System* (Harrisburg, 1821), 3.

18. Pennsylvania, Committee of the Penitentiary System, *Report on the Penitentiary System,* 6.

them the power to regulate and discipline prison life properly. As a result, the prison, with its mingling of prisoners, its inmate culture, and its lack of discipline only spread criminality and made revolt possible:

> For want of room to separate them, the young associate with the old offenders, the petty thief becomes the pupil of the highway robber; the beardless boy listens with delight to the well-told tale of daring exploits and hair-breadth escapes of hoary headed villainy, and from the experience of age derives instruction which fits him to be a pest and terror to society. A community of interest and design is excited among them, and instead of reformation, ruin is the general result.

Here lay the paradox of the prison. Far from affecting reformation, the inspectors realized that the prison had created a criminal "community"—a veritable countersociety within its walls. The prison, the inspectors declared, had been transformed into a "school of vice." [19]

At the same time, some pointed to the lack of independence of the Board of Inspectors themselves. James Mease, in particular, emphasized the problems resulting from the authority of the mayor and City Council to appoint inspectors. The political nature of appointment to the Board ensured a high degree of turnover and a low degree of competence. New inspectors, he charged, lifted penalties that old inspectors had imposed or were ensnared by the pretense of reformation. For Mease, the penal apparatus needed greater insulation and more independence from the larger political system. Should this happen, prison officials would develop greater administrative expertise, expertise that would expand their power to direct prison life. Thomas Bradford, Jr., echoed his concerns. In his private papers, he claimed that "party spirit has been the bane of this institution [the prison]." Bradford thought that the frequent turnover and large numbers of inspectors had undermined their authority. Inspectors needed to be men of "respectability" who served voluntarily and "as long as they [were] willing and capable." Experience was necessary because "deception always assails a new Inspector." [20] Only after the careful study of inmates could inspectors separate the reality from the appearance of reformation. For Bradford, independence, class, experience, and knowledge were joined. Like Mease, he believed it necessary to grant the inspectors (and the prison system as a whole) greater autonomy and authority.

These issues merged, symbolically at least, in the problem of pardons.

19. Ibid., 7, 8.

20. Bradford, "Observations on the Penal Code," Prisons, Bradford Papers; James Mease, *Observations on the Penitentiary System, and Penal Code of Pennsylvania; With Suggestions for Their Improvement* (Philadelphia, 1828), 10–12. This pamphlet was originally published in the winter of 1820–1821 in city newspapers.

The critique of pardons, after all, had been one of the central themes of late-eighteenth-century penal reform, and penal certainty had been one of the central elements of the strategy and legitimacy of the reformed system. Revolutionary-era theorists had argued that pardons were an effect of excessive, sanguinary punishments and that the transition to reformative incarceration would make them superfluous. Instead, given the growth of the prison population, pardons became one of the few tools open to the inspectors to limit overcrowding or induce inmates to discipline their behavior. To critics, this continued exercise of pardons, combined with the evidence of recidivism, signified the limits of the prison authorities' power. The inspectors' dependence on pardons indicated that the prison system had become internally contradictory. Not only had the prison ceased either to reform inmates or to provide deterrent terror, but the management of the institution destroyed penal certainty. Whether critics blamed the high rate of pardons on the structural situation of the prison (the inspectors) or on the inexperience of the inspectors (Mease), they agreed that the situation demanded radical change.

In addition, the inspectors maintained, the prison labor system had failed. Here, as elsewhere, they interpreted this failure as a lack of the power of authority. The inspectors' ability to secure work for inmates was always fragile. Because it was secured through contracts with private businesses in the city, the demand for prison labor was tied to the performance of Philadelphia's economy. The spread of mechanized production, the inspectors argued, had undermined the demand for some of the prison's more lucrative pursuits— most particularly, the cutting of nails. Economic depression during the late 1810s, coming at a time of population increase within the prison, had further curtailed the demand for labor and increased the number of idle prisoners. In a report to the legislature in 1822, the inspectors argued that they would never be able to ensure that all inmates constantly worked at Walnut Street. They listed a number of reasons for this: the large number of aged and diseased prisoners; the effect of weather conditions on stone cutting (the major form of inmate labor); the short working hours imposed for security reasons; and the large number of farmers "unacquainted with the branches of business carried on in the institution" who were inmates. But they also acknowledged their dependency on the participation of inmates, a dependency that marked the outer limits of their control. In part, they marked this problem as an instance of the moral failings of "many of the prisoners," whose "vicious habits . . . require[d] considerable punishment in the cells." But they also suggested that the problems lay in the structure of imprisonment, that the distinction between free and prison labor went beyond the question of moral habits. Indeed, they suggested that the difficulties of prison labor lay in the nature of man: the man, who is free, and is paid for the sweat of his brow, labours with a willing mind, to the extent of his power—the prisoner, in bondage, who toils for others, works with a dejected mind, and spares himself so far as he can.[21]

Ultimately, prison labor failed not merely because of the intrusions of the outside world but because of the inability of the prison authorities to engage the desires of the inmates. Here, at the subjectivity of the prisoners, the inspectors' rule ended.

I V

The inspectors proposed, and the legislative committees endorsed, a "pure solitary system." For the inspectors, the logic behind this proposal seemed clear. Human beings were social creatures who found pleasure in society. It was fitting, therefore, that, after breaking the law, an inmate "should suffer in that point in which he will feel the most keenly, the loss of social enjoyment." Central to this regime was enforced silence. Inmates would "be shut up in a cell for days, weeks, months, and years, alone," would "be deprived of converse with a fellow being," and having "no friendly voice to minister consolation, no friendly bosom on which to lean or into which to pour . . . [their] sorrows and complaints," would be forced "to count the tedious hours as they pass, a prey to the corrodings of conscience and the pangs of guilt." The result would be "almost to become the victim of despair." Such despair reopened the possibility of personal reformation. Even the "most hardened criminal," Mease believed, would be affected. And on the young, not yet hardened in their ways, the effects would be even greater. "I will venture to say," wrote Mease, "that one year passed in this way would have more effect upon criminals, than ten years passed in the continual society of numerous fellow convicts, where reflection is prevented by the bustle of work in the day, and drowned at night by idle or wicked conversation."[22] Silent solitude was the ultimate device for the imposition of terror and remorse.

State officials thereby displaced labor from the heart of the reformative program. The Senate committee argued that "employment diminishes in a very great degree the tediousness of confinement and thus mitigates the punishment" and asked "whether labor ought not to be abandoned altogether, ex-

21. Bradford, "Observations on the Penal Code," Prisons, Bradford Papers; Pennsylvania Committee on the Penitentiary System, *Report on the Penitentiary System,* 8; Pennsylvania General Assembly, Senate, *Journal of the Senate of the Commonwealth of Pennsylvania, 1821–1822* (Harrisburg, 1822), 383, 384.

22. Pennsylvania, Committee on the Penitentiary System, *Report on the Penitentiary System,* 9; Mease, *Observations on the Penitentiary System,* 17.

cept as an *indulgence* to penitent convicts, and as a relaxation from the *much more painful task of being compelled to be idle.*" Clearly skeptical of the reformative potential of prison labor, governmental committees took the collapse of Walnut Street's labor system as an indication that labor was counterproductive. Instead of instilling habits of discipline, labor (at least labor in groups) enabled prisoners to avoid the burdens of guilt and reflection. They intended to force inmates to turn inward, to extend the sway of authority beyond external behavior to internal desire. They were even prepared to sustain the economic burdens of idle inmates. In the long run, the legislators thought, the effectiveness of the new system would save the state money. Solitary confinement was so powerful that prison sentences could be shortened and prison costs (as well as property loss through crime) would decline.[23]

The proponents of solitary confinement reordered the basic techniques of reformative incarceration. At Walnut Street, labor had anchored the system. Solitude was only a part of the program, as well as being a tool of prison discipline. If solitude helped to break down the layers of vice, it was labor (with religious instruction) that would inculcate new habits of productive virtue. But, in the separate system, solitude became the basis of everyday life. Terror resided in solitude, and reformation took place through solitude. In this way, the inspectors and their allies proposed reversing the communicative economy of the prison. Whereas, in the Walnut Street Jail, communication between inmates had been free and constant, now communication *within* inmates would be free and constant. Whereas, before, the voice of conscience had been drowned out by the voices of others, now, without other voices, conscience would speak freely. The only intrusion of outside voices would come from the authorities. And these voices would supplement, not contradict, the effect of silent reflection.

Isolation and the control of communication, then, were the linchpins of the proposed new penitentiary system. Solitude would eliminate inmate communication and enable the authorities to control and reform prisoners. The imposition of solitude would dramatically increase the terrors of imprisonment, and individuals stripped of the collective networks of support would be driven to remorse and possibly reformation. The possibility of working on the souls of prisoners would increase.

V

The state, then, moved forcefully to expand its penal apparatus. Yet none of the prison's problems was new. Why had they seized the public consciousness

23. Pennsylvania, Committee on the Penitentiary System, *Report on the Penitentiary System,* 9–12, 12.

after the prison riot? Why was the prison no longer debated only by those in-volved with penal practice? Why did the state of the prison became a concern of the public papers and city officials? The answers lie in the condition of the city at large. In the aftermath of the riot, the prison became linked to other is-sues of public order and health; the debate over prison form, in turn, helped stimulate a wider reorganization of social discipline in the city. Prison vio-lence in general, and the riot in particular, fed elite concerns about the lack of social discipline among the poor and the young; the riot and its roots—far from being an isolated phenomenon in a marginal institution—mirrored and condensed the fundamental chasms of the urban world.

The penal uprising took place against the backdrop of economic disloca-tion. Following the War of 1812, European, especially British, manufactures flooded the American market. Demand for American foodstuffs initially mit-igated some of this European challenge. But, during the 1810s, both the num-ber of relief recipients and the expenses of poor relief grew dramatically. Whereas, in 1814, roughly 3,100 individuals received public poor relief, by 1819 the number was over 5,000. Then, in 1818, increased European agricultural production, combined with financial disarray in England, created a credit cri-sis in America. Economic depression resulted. In the summer and fall of 1819, a committee of Philadelphians appointed to investigate the extent of jobless-ness reported that in thirty branches of manufacturing for which reliable numbers could be generated, employment had dropped from 9,072 in 1816 to 2,137 in 1819. Mathew Carey, who helped lead the investigation, estimated that more than 11,000 were unemployed in the city's manufacturing sector. "The enlivening sound of the spindle," he reported, "the loom, and the hammer has in many places almost ceased to be heard. . . . Our cities exhibit an unvarying scene of gloom and despair." The slump was short but severe, continuing through 1820, after which the city's economy recovered in 1821 and 1822. But, despite the return of economic expansion in the early 1820s, the gap between rich and poor Philadelphians continued to grow. The fragmentation and divi-sion of the urban fabric (economic, spatial, and emotional) continued well beyond the end of the depression.[24]

Social tensions and fears intensified during the Panic of 1819. Throughout

24. Priscilla Ferguson Clement, *Welfare and the Poor in the Nineteenth-Century City: Philadelphia, 1800–1854* (Rutherford, N.J., 1985), 50–52, 178; Tom W. Smith, "The Dawn of the Urban Industrial Age: The Social Structure of Philadelphia, 1790–1830" (Ph.D. diss., University of Chicago, 1980), 26–27, 150–166; Mathew Carey, *Essays on Political Economy; or, the Most Certain Means of Promoting the Wealth, Power, Resources and Happiness of States: Applied Particularly to the United States* (1822; reprint, New York, 1968), 10; Susan G. Davis, *Parades and Power: Street Theater in Nineteenth-Century Philadelphia* (Philadel-phia, 1986), 24–25; Bruce Laurie, *Working People of Philadelphia, 1800–1850* (Philadelphia, 1980), 11–13.

the summer of that year, the city's newspapers warned of possible social calamity, arguing that the combination of poverty and the growing numbers of Irish immigrants posed grave dangers for social safety. In August, the *Independent Balance* reported on "the foreign mendacity stalking our streets, craving a morsel of bread . . . having no means of employ to earn it." If no improvement was forthcoming, a correspondent for the *Aurora* argued, then "*Look out ahead!*" The Panic of 1819 reinforced deeply held class fears—especially about the Irish and blacks. The post-Revolutionary dream of an orderly and open republican city, a dream that, although never including the Irish, had initially included free blacks, collapsed. Increased class tensions over the uses of the streets, combined with growing racial hostility, helped structure perceptions of the Panic and its effects.[25]

The fragility of the social order became clear in the fall of 1819. On September 8, a balloonist, one Mr. Michel, attempted to treat the citizens of Philadelphia with a balloon ascent from Vauxhall Gardens, near Centre Square. Balloon ascensions were popular spectacles in the late eighteenth and early nineteenth centuries. Even as doubtful an observer of public rituals as Benjamin Rush commented on seeing a balloon ascension in 1793: "Every faculty of the mind was seized, expanded, and captivated by it. 40,000 people concentrating their eyes and thoughts at the *same* instant, upon the *same* object, and all deriving nearly the *same* degrees of pleasure from it," making it "a truly sublime sight." Evidently, the city's population shared his enthusiasm. During the summer of 1819, they followed intently the news of balloon ascensions in New York and New Jersey. Although some of these efforts had proved unsuccessful, Philadelphians awaited the eighth with eager anticipation.[26] The unity that Rush had felt in the 1790s, however, would not be repeated in 1819.

25. *Independent Balance* (Philadelphia), Aug. 18, 1819; "To the City Councils," *Aurora; General Advertiser* (Philadelphia), Aug. 28, 1819, both quoted in J. David Lehman, "Political Economy and the Response to Unemployment during the Panic of 1819" (paper presented at the Organization of American Historians, Annual Meeting, Louisville, Ky., April 1991), 2. I would like to thank J. David Lehman for suggesting the significance of these developments. For a fuller discussion of the Panic of 1819 in the city, see his "Explaining Hard Times: Political Economy and the Panic of 1819 in Philadelphia" (Ph.D. diss., University of California, Los Angeles, 1992). For post-Revolutionary hopes of blacks, see Gary B. Nash, *Forging Freedom: The Formation of Philadelphia's Black Community, 1720–1840* (Cambridge, Mass., 1988), 88–135. On the constant exclusion of the Irish from any appearances of post-Revolutionary equality, see John K. Alexander, *Render Them Submissive: Responses to Poverty in Philadelphia, 1760–1800* (Amherst, Mass., 1980), 27, 78–79. I am borrowing the notion of class and gender struggles to define appropriate "uses of the streets" from Christine Stansell's study of working-class women in 19th-century New York. See chap. 10, "The Uses of the Streets," in *City of Women: Sex and Class in New York, 1789–1860* (New York, 1986), 193–216.

26. L. H. Butterfield, ed., *Letters of Benjamin Rush* (Princeton, N.J., 1951), II, 627; *Niles' Weekly Register*, Sept. 11, 1819; *Dem. Press*, Sept. 3, 4, 7, 8, 1819.

On the afternoon of September 8, more than thirty thousand individuals gathered to witness Michel's attempt. Although Michel had announced that the effort would begin between three and four in the afternoon, it was not until after six that the balloon was ready to ascend. But, at that point, events took another course. The crowd outside the gardens, who had waited for hours and were aware of the failure of other attempts in New Jersey, began to throw stones into Vauxhall, one of which struck the balloon, ripping its skin. At the same time, a boy, who had attempted to climb over the fence without paying the dollar fee, was struck with a stick by one of the event's guards, and rumors circulated that he was killed. "Horror was quickly converted into Rage," reported the *Democratic Press,* "and a cry of vengeance was no sooner uttered by one voice, than it was re-echoed by thousands." The crowd surged forward, breaking down the fence around the gardens, when, according to *Niles' Weekly Register,* they "went *deliberately* to work, breaking the lamps, summer houses, windows of the temple, etc. They broke into the bar-room, broke the bottles, glasses etc. spilled and drank the wine, and other liquors. *When they had destroyed all they conveniently could,* they SET FIRE TO THE TEMPLE, *which being composed of wood, was entirely consumed."* Samuel Breck, one of the city's leading citizens, reported in his diary that his family could see the fire all the way from their country estate.[27]

Beyond the physical damage done by the fire, the violence at Vauxhall panicked the city, stimulating fears and fantasies of social disgrace and destruction. The riot, in the eyes of *Niles' Weekly Register,* was "a scene, disgraceful to the city of Philadelphia" marked by the "wanton and illegal destruction of the property of an unoffending individual." Samuel Breck, from his vantage point in the suburbs, could barely restrain his disgust. The rioters were "a daring mob," a "party of base villains," and "a gang of unprincipled rascals." *The Union* was appalled by the "mobbing spirit," and the grand jury of the Mayor's Court could only look back with sorrow on the "late riotous and disgraceful event at Vauxhall Gardens."[28] In the eyes of Philadelphia's elite and its spokesmen, the rioters were a foreign presence within the city.

Following the riot, the city's papers sought to identify and isolate the culprits, thereby minimizing the meaning of the event. The disturbance, they insisted, was contrary to the history of the city; recourse to violence, they implied, an alien practice. The *Union* declared that "a mobbing spirit has not been a characteristic of Philadelphia," and *Niles'* assured its readers that the riot was "a scene the like of which never before occurred in this city, and

27. *Dem. Press,* Sept. 9, 1819; *Niles' Weekly Register,* Sept. 11, 1819; Nicholas B. Wainwright, ed., "The Diary of Samuel Breck," *PMHB,* CII (1978), 497.

28. *Niles' Weekly Register,* Sept. 11, 1819; Wainwright, ed., "Diary of Samuel Breck," *PMHB,* CII (1978), 497; *Union,* Sept 9, 1819; *Dem. Press,* Oct. 23, 1819.

which, we trust, never will again." The *Democratic Press,* while expressing its horror at the event, claimed that fewer than one hundred individuals actually had been involved. Its editors expressed their conviction of the city's "deep regret" over the event and their confidence that this "feeling will not only lead to the prosecution, conviction, and punishment of the principal rioters, but to a liberal subscription to indemnify the heavy and ruinous losses" suffered by the aviators and the owner of the gardens.[29] The riot and the rioters, then, had to be separated from the city as a whole. As an irrational irruption, the fire at Vauxhall was both deeply threatening and limited.

These attempts to interpret and contain the meaning of the Vauxhall riot, however, revealed an explosively fractured public sphere. Occurring during both the downturn of 1819 and an election campaign, the riot highlighted not only fears of the poor but ethnic and political divisions. The *Union,* in the first flush of the event, blamed the city's Irish, "recently come among us, who were disappointed in not finding dollars in the streets, and were ripe for vengeance in any shape." Here anti-Irish feeling meshed with anxieties over the state of idleness. The *Union's* assault drew scathing criticism from the *Democratic Press* and its Irish editor, John Binns. Binns objected to the depiction of the Irish, accusing the editor of the *Union* of attributing to the Irish "the most brutal ignorance, the worst motives, and the most depraved dispositions."[30]

Although the *Union* backed off from its claim that Irish had led the riot, the battle between the two newspapers over the characteristics of the Irish continued throughout September. At the same time, The *Democratic Press* engaged in verbal warfare with the *Franklin Gazette* over the proper response to the riot. This disagreement, like the disagreement with the *Union,* was politically charged, Binns's paper being Democratic while the *Union* and *Franklin Gazette* were Federalist. The *Democratic Press* was not above playing racial politics. Binns's paper systematically opposed the efforts of Philadelphia's black community to organize itself and implied that blacks were threats to the city's public health. Despite their shared efforts to contain and isolate the riot as an event, the newspapers' responses built on—and reinforced—the class, ethnic, racial, and political fractures of the city's public sphere. The conflagration and its aftermath revealed a highly combustible city.

Indeed, in the months following the Vauxhall riot, Philadelphia exploded physically as well as ideologically. Throughout the first third of 1820, a series of arsons traversed the city. The wave of fires led to both publicly announced rewards and the forming of extra evening patrols to smoke out the culprits. Still, the arsons continued for months while the newspapers railed against the "lurking villains" and "incendiaries" behind the fires, and the *Philadelphia*

---

29. *Union,* Sept 9, 1819; *Dem. Press,* Sept 9, 1819; *Niles' Weekly Register,* Sept. 11, 1819.
30. *Union,* Sept. 9, 1819; *Dem. Press,* Sept 9, 1819.

Gazette bemoaned the fact that "the city is at present infected with a desperate set of wretches, who for the purpose of plunder, would commit our dwellings to the flames." In April, the *Union* went so far as to wonder aloud whether hanging should not be reinstituted as the punishment for arson. Perhaps most ominously, prison and city officials, as well as some commentators, feared that the fires and the riot in the penitentiary were connected. The coincidence of the prison riot in March and arsons throughout the winter and spring increased the perception that the prison had become a staging ground for crime, leading to calls for increased police vigilance and the detention of all "suspicious" people.[31] Between the two riots and the arsons, the city appeared riddled with social conflict and threatened from within and without.

V I

Issues of social discipline and public health mediated these fears. Yellow fever and smallpox struck the city recurrently throughout the early nineteenth century. The ever-present threat of epidemic heightened concerns about physical and moral sources of disease. The city's ponds, cemeteries, streets, wharves, and docks all posed potential health threats. Dogs and pigs, some complained, ran loose throughout the city. Street vendors and hawkers were criticized for their behavior and their threats to the city's health.[32] As the city entered the 1820s, issues of public health and popular morality were inseparable.

Debates over the city's squares indicate the logic of these anxieties. As planned by William Penn, Philadelphia was structured around a series of open public squares. Penn envisioned five such squares: four in the corners of the city, originally called Southeast, Northeast, Northwest, and Southwest Squares, and one in the middle, Centre Square (the names of the squares were later changed to Washington, Franklin, Logan, Rittenhouse, and Penn Squares respectively). By the nineteenth century, however, these squares—far from being the center of urban life as originally intended—had become sites for urban excess. Washington was long in use as a burial ground for the poor; Logan and Rittenhouse were refuse dumps; Franklin had been taken over by the German Calvinist Society; and Centre, the home of the city's first attempt at a waterworks, was unkempt and unpoliced. Beginning in the late 1810s and continuing throughout the 1820s and 1830s, pressure built for transforming the condition and use of the squares.[33] Reformers sought to improve the physical

31. *Union*, Jan. 29, Feb. 19, Mar. 20, 25, Apr. 4, 5, 7, 1820; *Dem. Press*, Mar. 30, Apr. 3, 5, 6, 8, 1820; *Niles' Weekly Register*, Apr. 8, May 19, 1820; Bd. of Insp., Minutes, Apr. 5, 1820.

32. *Dem. Press*, Mar. 12, June 10, Sept. 9, 1818.

33. Minutes of the Common Council, May 2, 1799, PCA; Davis, *Parades and Power*, 30–31; John T. Scharf and Thompson Westcott, *History of Philadelphia, 1609–1884* (Philadelphia, 1884), III, 1842–1850; John F. Watson, *Annals of Philadelphia and Pennsylvania, in the Olden*

condition of the squares and alter the relationship between the squares and the citizenry. In this way, they hoped to make the squares sites for the generation of social order and individual discipline.

Fear of disease lay at the heart of this movement. In March 1818, a public meeting criticized city officials for the decayed condition of the public squares—particularly Southwest Square. Rather than being a source of fresh air and civilized relaxation, the city had used the square as a "receptacle for *filth of every description,*" thereby undermining what should have been the "chief object" of the authorities, "the preservation of the Health of the inhabitants." In July, "Z" charged that the "police" had "done less for the cleanliness and health of the city in the last two years . . . than their predecessors at any time the preceding twenty years."[34] The disorganization of public space, these critics claimed, threatened the very survival of the city's inhabitants. The city's streets and squares, far from being places to transfer goods and communicate ideas, were transmitting disease and circulating disorder.

More was at stake than physical disease, however. As early as 1816, "Civis," for example, called on the city government to reorganize Centre Square. Objecting both to the buildings in the square (deserted remnants from the city's earlier waterworks) and the trees that surrounded it, he argued that the square was unfit for "healthy and *innocent* recreation." "Much as I have travelled by night and often as I have crossed that polluted field, still, whenever I meet a solitary passenger, I can hardly avoid prying for the concealed weapon of the robber or assassin." Nor was it only at night that the square was objectionable. On Sunday afternoons, any "serious man" would be "annoyed by rude and profane noises, or by the disgustful spectacle of human bodies lying on the ground, in the state of torpid stupefaction." Indeed, to Civis, the square itself seemed a vibrant source of corruption and decay to the city—spreading its poisonous influences outward, threatening to undermine Christian morality itself:

> When we contemplate the present use and application of the Centre Square, we revert involuntarily to the licentious stories of the *Temples and Sacred Groves* of the Ancient Pagans, impure descriptions and allusions, in the perusal of which, some of us regret that we have partly

Time; Being a Collection of Memoirs, Anecdotes, and Incidents of the City and Its Inhabitants, and of the Earliest Settlements of the Inland Part of Pennsylvania, from the Days of the Founders* (Philadelphia, 1857), I, 405–407; John Binns, *Recollections of the Life of John Binns . . .* (Philadelphia, 1854), 194. There were, however, earlier efforts to clean up the squares. See Minutes of the Common Council, Mar. 19, Apr. 23, 1792, Sept. 26, 1796, May 2, 1799, Dec. 10, 1810, Mar. 28, Apr. 11, 1811, Feb. 12, June 18, 1812, PCA.

34. *Dem. Press,* Mar. 23, July 15, "Civis," July 17, 1818.

wasted the best years of our youth, in the monastic institutions of Education, to which we were unluckily consigned.

To Civis, at least, the conclusion was clear. The city must act to "remove, then, these nuisances and facilities of vice, by the demolition of that absurd edifice, and of that ugly darksome wood, the haunt of profligacy and the covert of danger and blood." [35]

These concerns led to attacks on public displays at Centre Square. In 1821, Zachariah Poulson, editor of *Poulson's Daily Advertiser,* dismissed Fourth of July celebrations in the square as being "disreputably distinguished." Poulson was particularly concerned with gambling "to which apprentice-boys and others are enticed." As with Civis, whom he published in his paper, Poulson viewed the activities on the square as a moral miasma, threatening to contaminate the young, who, seduced by the "harpies" of gambling, would at some "future period, trace their ruin to the deviations at Centre Square." Two years later, Mayor Robert Wharton banned booths and tents in the square on the Fourth of July. Wharton attacked "the scenes of debauchery, gambling, and drunkenness, with many other acts of excess" that took place on the holiday, noting that "his military brethren," who celebrated the Fourth in the square, paraded only briefly and could "obtain refreshments from sources less impure." Wharton, justifying his action, reminded his fellow citizens of the "propriety of banishing from our city limits causes of such ruinous effect to the morals and future usefulness of the rising generation." [36]

For both Poulson and Wharton, as for Civis before them, the square's activities were festering sources of corruption and moral contamination. Young boys, especially, were susceptible to the seductions of gambling and debauchery—ever vulnerable to the "harpies" and "excess" that accompanied "impure" sources of refreshment. The squares and the activities they spawned symbolized a world of gender monstrosity, where disorderly women and undisciplined boys combined to recreate the worst depredations of the pagan world. So long as they remained unreconstructed, the social order was in constant peril.

At the same time, the dramatic upsurge of poverty and the costs of poor relief following the War of 1812 stimulated new bourgeois reflection on the poor, their situation, and their characteristics. In February 1817, a public meeting was held "for the purpose of devising measures for their [the poor] present relief—as well as for preventing, in future, the occurrence of so great an extent of misery." The meeting assigned individuals to collect and distribute aid for

35. *Poulson's American Daily Advertiser,* Aug. 26, 1818.
36. *Poulson's American Daily Advertiser,* July 4, 1821, quoted in Scharf and Westcott, *History of Philadelphia,* III, 1844.

"the immediate exigencies of the poor" and created a "committee of superintendence" to investigate the causes of "mendicity."[37] The immediate experience of poverty was linked anew to reflection on the policy of poor relief.

In May, the committee of superintendence reported their findings and recommendations. As the gentlemen of the committee saw it, foremost among the structural factors underlying pauperism was the system of poor relief itself. They believed that a "radical" change was required in the system. The combination of public and private relief had produced a "dependence" that not only affected the poor of Philadelphia but functioned as a magnet to the "idle and worthless" of the other states of the Union. As a result, the city had become an "emporium of beggars." To rectify this situation, the committee proposed expanding the number of officials administering the poor laws while simultaneously limiting their jurisdiction, thereby assuring "an accurate knowledge of all persons under their care."[38]

The report went further than merely proposing an expansion in the personnel of poor relief. It also advocated concrete interventions in the lives of the poor: procuring "proper situations, and modes of employment," educating the children of the indigent in public schools, increasing public supervision of orphans to ensure their placement in families or to bind them to trades, and actively discouraging the use of liquor.[39] The committee's documentation (quotations from public and private dispensers of relief), however, focused largely on the habits of the poor. Although the problems of unemployment and illness were acknowledged, the main thrust of the committee's investigation centered on the ways that the poor contributed to their own poverty. Allegations of intemperance, laziness, and familial irresponsibility structured the committee's approach to the question of poverty.

The committee also proposed a new society to investigate poverty and agitate for the transformation of poor relief. The Pennsylvania Society for the

37. Pennsylvania Society for the Promotion of Public Economy, *Report of the Library Committee of the Pennsylvania Society for the Promotion of Public Economy, Containing a Summary of the Information Communicated by Sundry Citizens, in Reply to the Circular Letter of the Committee of Superintendence of February 21 1817* (Philadelphia, 1817), 3.

38. Ibid., 7–8. The committee had distributed a circular to public officials and private charities. This circular had a variety of objects. First, it sought to identify those groups who composed the poor—seeking to ascertain the proportion of the poor who were widows, single women, sick, sailors, "strangers," and blacks as well as determining which trades were most at risk of poverty. Second, the committee procured information on the causes of poverty—or at least those aspects of the lives of the poor that they deemed most likely to contribute to poverty: intemperance, abandonment, pawn brokers, laziness. And, lastly, they sought to determine potential ways to alter the system of poor relief and to attack poverty itself. Ibid., 4–6.

39. Ibid., 8. This discussion, in fact, helped stimulate the expansion of education discussed below.

Promotion of Public Economy resulted. Like the Philadelphia Society for Alleviating the Miseries of Public Prisons, the Pennsylvania Society was a gentlemen's organization. And, like its counterparts in other cities (New York's Society for the Prevention of Pauperism, for instance), it focused its attention on the failings of the poor. Organizing itself in the spring of 1817, the Society established a series of standing committees—on the poor laws, on public prisons, on domestic economy, on the suppression of vice and immorality, and on the public schools.[40] Each committee was designed to activate the power of the state and public opinion to intervene in the affairs of the poor.

As a component of the emerging bourgeois public sphere, the Pennsylvania Society sought to both influence public policy and shape the lives and culture of the poor. Indeed, the Society's very name indicates the nature of its intervention. "Public Economy" meant the economy of the poor. It was in their capacity as contributors to the public that the poor interested the Society's gentlemen; it was their contribution (or danger) to a growing economy that made them objects of study and government. As the preamble to its articles of association proclaimed, "the prosperity and happiness of a nation, depend upon the industry, the economy and the morals of its people." The Society believed that "to promote, to encourage, and to protect these three great essentials of national wealth and character" was of central importance to the "statesman" and the "philanthropist." Combining the aims of the statesman and the philanthropist by "ascertaining and pointing out" the "most profitable direction" for labor, teaching a "prudent and judicious expenditure of money" to the poor, "instructing the great mass of the community in the modes of economizing in their fuel and diet," while fulfilling "moral and religious obligation" by educating "the ignorant and the poor," would be "to strike at the root of poverty and vice, and to render the inhabitants of the land contented, virtuous and happy."[41] The Pennsylvania Society sought to redraw the relationship between the state, the economy, and the poor.

The Society did not believe that poverty was unavoidable. Its activism was

40. Pennsylvania Society, *Report of the Library Committee,* 43–44. There were more organizational committees on accounts, elections, and the library (to gather materials on public economy). On the Society for the Prevention of Pauperism, see Stansell, *City of Women,* 33–36.

41. Pennsylvania Society, *Report of the Library Committee,* 39. Jürgen Habermas argues that institutions like the Pennsylvania Society (or the Philadelphia Society for Alleviating the Miseries of Public Prisons, for that matter), as part of the public sphere, mediate between the state and civil society by virtue of their private deliberations on public matters. It is important to remember as well that the public sphere and its institutions were shaped in both form and content by its social position. For his extended argument, see *The Structural Transformation of the Public Sphere: An Inquiry into a Category of Bourgeois Society,* trans. Thomas Berger (Cambridge, Mass., 1989). See also my discussion above in the Introduction.

tied to its moral interpretation of poverty—intemperance and irresponsibility, not God's will or the workings of the economy, caused poverty—and, consequently, it believed public policy should be reconfigured to impose responsibility and discipline. The committee did recognize that the "want of employment" along with intemperance was at the "origin of the misery which has been so frequently witnessed."[42] The Society, then, had not yet made a total break from older attitudes and into a fetishism of the market. Its position remained transitional. The Pennsylvania Society believed that increasing morality among the poor and increasing knowledge of employment opportunities would solve the problem. As statesmen and philanthropists, their duty was to spread both that morality and that knowledge.

Initially, the Society's efforts had little effect on poor relief. Although minor alterations in Philadelphia's relief practices occurred, they were the handiwork of the city's Guardians of the Poor and not the result of public debate and legal transformation. But the Society did reopen a field of investigation and argument, and its positions—in somewhat modified form—would be taken up in the 1820s, when serious efforts to restructure the city's poor relief institutions took place.[43] Then the combination of moralism about the poor and amoralism about the economy would triumph.

But if the Pennsylvania Society had little immediate effect on the structure of poor relief, its efforts more directly shaped public education of the poor. In 1818, the city and county of Philadelphia organized a public school system led by Roberts Vaux. By 1820, more than five thousand students were enrolled. Boys were taught reading, writing, and arithmetic; in addition to these subjects, girls were taught sewing. A state Senate committee reported in 1822 that improvement in useful knowledge and morals had occurred. To their minds, "the utility of the system" was "beyond a question."[44] Philadelphia's school system appeared as a fixture of the city's enlightenment.

Still, the controllers of the city's public schools remained deeply troubled. Large numbers of children remained outside the effective reach of the schools. Some children attended but displayed a "shameful inattention to the advantages so freely offered to their acceptance." Others had parents who failed "to require, and ascertain, that their children attend regularly at school." And, lastly, there were those parents who, "preferring the temporary benefits they derive from the services of their children," chose to keep them out of school

42. Pennsylvania Society, *Report of the Library Committee*, 17–18, 37.

43. See below, Chapter 7.

44. Samuel Hazard, ed., *The Register of Pennsylvania, Devoted to the Preservation of Facts and Documents, and Every Other Kind of Useful Information respecting the State of Pennsylvania* (Philadelphia, 1828), I, 313. On Vaux and the formation of the new school system, see Roderick Naylor Ryon, "Roberts Vaux: A Biography of a Reformer" (Ph.D. diss., Pennsylvania State University, 1966), 60–67.

and "at home employed in domestic work." These children, and their parents, posed dangers that were, it seems, enormous. They helped "form an idle and dissolute class of beings who prowl about the wharves, and streets of the city, trespass upon the fields in its vicinity, pilfer the inhabitants, offend the feeling heart with obscene, and often profane language," leading, inexorably, "when they shall have arrived at maturer age, and become confirmed in depravity" to "the most serious and daring violations of the laws."[45] The schools, for all their apparent success, were surrounded by a sea of viciousness, a floating population of children being groomed, not in morals and useful knowledge, but in depravity and criminality.

The Controllers feared a city spinning out of control. Boys "wandering about the streets and wharves," parents ignorant of their duties, citizens vulnerable to the preying and prowling young—all indicated "a moral plague in the metropolis and its vicinity." From the perspective of the controllers, the schools were fortresses protecting the Republic from an invasion of immorality—one being unreflectively encouraged by unthinking parents and their vicious offspring. If, as they suggested, "the duration of the free institutions under which we are favoured to live, essentially depends upon the virtue and intelligibility of the People," then the presence of uneducated youths threatened the very existence of the Republic.[46] More dangerous, perhaps, than external threats, the dissolute and uneducated young were dissolving the future of "free institutions."

For the controllers, the existence of this class of children was a call to action. Recognizing that no legal means existed to compel parents to enroll their children, they called for more social weapons. The controllers aimed to mobilize the implicit and explicit powers the elite had over the poor in order to root out the culture of youthful dissolution. Urging all citizens to admonish the poor to send their children to school, they placed special stress on the Guardians of the Poor and the city's charitable institutions. These groups "could with singular propriety enforce the obligation they [parents] are under, to send their children to the public schools." They also urged the city's magistrates to "reprimand those boys who idly wander about the streets, and frequently collect in parties to the annoyance of the inhabitants, and to their own injury." Both girls withheld for domestic duties and boys engaged in public pilfering could be brought within the ambit of the schools. The implicit threat of withheld support, they believed, would convince parents to send their children to school.[47]

45. *National Recorder,* July 22, 1820.

46. Philadelphia, Controllers of the Public Schools, *4th Annual Report* (1822), 4–5, *5th Annual Report* (1823), 8, *6th Annual Report* (1824), 8, *7th Annual Report* (1825), 6, *8th Annual Report* (1826), 7.

47. *National Recorder,* July 22, 1820. In fact, the controllers proposed that the legislature

To the controllers, school and festivity—education and idleness, stood—in opposition. The system of public education for the poor would save the young from the culture of the poor; it would instill in children patriotism, useful knowledge, and morality. Public education was a countereducation; instead of the knowledge of the streets would come knowledge of rules and the state. In 1820, the controllers moved to save their charges from the dangers of the Fourth of July. One of the school sections (or districts) obtained the use of the Ebenezer Church for its own celebration. More than nine hundred children assembled in their schools at eight in the morning and were led to the church. The proceedings began with the senior classes singing a hymn written by one of the teachers, followed by a prayer, and the reading of the Declaration of Independence by one of the students. Then J. B. Sutherland, one of the controllers, gave an address "embracing the advantages of a good education, its influence upon society, the importance of a good example to children by their parents, the necessity of a punctual attendance at school, and other sensible observations upon the relative duties of parents and children." Then ensued another hymn, a prayer, and a closing benediction. The students were then taken back to their schools and sent on their way.[48]

This educational ritual operated in clear opposition to normal Fourth of July activities. Against the disorderly circulation of individuals stood children ordered in groups and isolated in a church. Against the festive popular celebrations stood a ritualized reading of the Declaration of Independence, solemn hymns, and edifying discourse. And against the evil influence of bad example stood the figures of teachers, parents, ministers, and governmental officials. The school district structured its Fourth through a rejection of street life. Arguing that "this method of celebrating our national independence, will be attended with the most salutary consequences," the committee organizing the event averred that, "besides its keeping children out of the public streets, in which examples of intemperance and temptation for imitation are exhibited, it will likewise produce an emulation among them, a desire to be distinguished in the manner the youth . . . [who read the declaration] . . . was." And, like children, the "attention and pride" of parents might "also be excited, and induce a more strict attendance of their children at school."[49] The committee thus reactivated the discourse of mimetic corruption, counterposing the "examples of intemperance and temptation for imitation" presented in the streets to the desire for "emulation" that might be established by the proper Fourth ritual.

---

consider the possibility that parents who failed to enroll their children be stripped of their poor relief. Ibid.

48. Ibid., July 29, 1820.

49. Ibid.

Both the criticisms of the squares and the advocacy of education, then, shared a set of assumptions about the dangers of public space, festivity, and the moral and physical health of the community. Each identified undisciplined social space and morally corrupt idleness as threats to the well being of the individual and society. Each sought to thwart these threats through the simultaneous transformation of space and its uses. Against the decayed, disease-ridden, and intemperate public square, they proposed revamped and cleansed parks of sober recreation; against the swarms of unwatched and menacing youths, they proposed the containing and uplifting rituals of patriotic and disciplined schools. This critique of idleness, however, was structured, not around a concept of labor, but of discipline. Sober leisure and ordered education, not increased labor, were the proposed solutions. Only the creation of zones of supervised and regulated activity, it seems, could maintain the social bases of free institutions.

In reality, attempts to eliminate the festive uses of public space were unsuccessful. The booths and stalls banished from Centre Square merely migrated across the street, where vendors continued to sell their wares. The city streets and squares continued to be sites of popular festivity.[50] And, as the controllers' complaints indicated, parents continued to withhold their children from the reach of the educational apparatus.

These efforts, and their limits, demonstrated the contested nature of authority and order in the city. Following the Revolution, and with increasing importance during the early nineteenth century, the Fourth of July—along with other holidays—had become central to working-class life and recreation. With changing work patterns, working-class festivity was concentrated in a smaller and smaller set of days—marked off from everyday life and marked with public revelry.[51] And, as the city's elite withdrew from popular festivity, its sense of distance from, and its sense of the danger of, those below them grew.

These attacks on public holiday behavior, however, were not projecting an abstract social order. They were defenses of particular class forms of appropriate social demeanor. The controllers' attacks on parents who kept their children employed signified different class perceptions of the necessities of life, and their hostility to children in the streets marked their increasingly privatized notion of moral space. The expanding importance of the bourgeois home was linked to the devaluation of the culture of the street. This valorization of the ordered home carried with it fears about the nature of public space and of the numbers of working-class families who existed in other domestic

50. Davis, *Parades and Power,* 42–43, 73–153; Scharf and Westcott, *History of Philadelphia,* III, 1844.

51. Davis, *Parades and Power,* 42–44; Laurie, *Working People,* 54–55.

relations.[52] Below the assertions of education and virtue lay anxieties about the citizenry of the Republic.

The debates over public space and education, then, condensed a number of class and gender anxieties. To the minds of the controllers and their allies, poor boys wandering the streets where they might be corrupted by "harpies" were an explosive danger to a properly ordered city. At the same time, poor girls, kept from school to work as servants or in manufacturing, threatened to undermine the family from within.[53] Given the greater textual attention to the problems of disorderly boys, it seems clear that they were feared most. But from the vantage point of the discourse of mimetic corruption, both dissolute boys and undomestic girls threatened the transmission of social discipline and moral perception that educators, commentators, and public officials deemed necessary for the state to survive.

The limited success of elite attacks on popular festivity, however, marked not only their challenge to popular culture but the capacity of the city's laboring poor to resist intrusion into their daily lives. In other words, as in the prison, attempts to reconstruct the desires of the poor to conform to the strategies of the elite proved difficult. But the plans themselves were not dropped. The desire that discipline did engage was the desire of private reformers and public officials to imagine an ordered society. As a result, they developed a strategy of urban reform and discipline—an activity repeated throughout the nineteenth century. As the streets and all that they signified grew ever more fearsome in the eyes of reformers, so the strategies of discipline grew.

VII

The possible links between the prison and urban excess were not lost on the city's governors. Two grand juries—one from the autumn of 1819, the other from the autumn of 1820—illustrate how fears about the prison meshed with other tensions within the social imagination. For each, the prison was merely one of a number of problems needing improved management. But, for each, the prison's problems spilled out of the jail, linking it with a wider dissolution of public morality and health.

The first grand jury sat during the September 1819 session of the city's Mayor's Court. After investigating the "late riotous and disgraceful event at

52. Stansell, *City of Women*, 63–75, 212–214.

53. A state examination from the 1830s discovered that roughly two-thirds of the children employed in the city's cotton manufactories were girls. See Pennsylvania General Assembly, House of Representatives, *Report of the Select Committee Appointed to Visit the Manufacturing Districts of the Commonwealth, for the Purpose of Investigating the Subject of the Employment of Children in Manufactories* (Harrisburg, 1838), 4.

Vauxhall Gardens," the grand jury noted sorrowfully that the citizens ("a vast concourse") who had gathered to watch the balloon's rise, "disappointed in expectations, industriously excited, and naturally, though perhaps unjustly ascribing their disappointment to intentional fraud," had gone home "only after having witnessed acts of outrage and violence, hitherto unknown among us." While expressing their unwillingness to comment on the behavior of individuals (aside from the indictments brought), the grand jurors still could not forbear from "observing that were some legal restrictions imposed upon those strangers who visit our city for the purpose of public exhibition, fewer opportunities for riot and uproar would occur." Although not denying the value of "rational amusement or philosophical experiment," they called for some examination of and security from those wishing to perform public exhibitions to "ensure order as well as enjoyment." [54]

If the grand jury, in its reflection on the Vauxhall riot, was concerned about the arrival of strangers to the city, with regard to the prison, it was the departure of former strangers that concerned them. It was the practice of releasing convicts, even those from other parts of the state, into the city that drew its attention: "These dangerous persons are gradually turned out upon our community to disturb its peace and to extend their depredations upon its property." The prison was a breeding ground for evil and "thus the city becomes in time a common receptacle for the crimes and vices of the whole state," with dire effects for both the reputation and the experience of the city's inhabitants. As the grand jury saw it, the process of release enabled the rest of the state to impose its criminal excesses on the city. Rather than supporting the commonwealth, the prison was subordinating the peace of Philadelphia to the narrow and unjust interests of the countryside. [55]

Finally, the jurors sought to curtail the number of prosecutions for assault and battery. They believed that far too many of these were "of a nature exceedingly trifling" or "scarcely sustained by any evidence." Magistrates, they argued, should not aid these cases; instead, they should seek to settle these cases out of court, "unless the criminal intent be flagrant or the injury severe." The grand jury believed that its time was too much taken up with trifling matters of interpersonal conflict, conflict that (unlike, say, crimes against property or public order) it wished to exclude from the court's problems. Aldermen colluded with these practices, it believed, allowing individuals to use public power to settle private concerns. [56]

In attacking these prosecutions, the grand jury, like those reforming the public squares or extending the educational system, was doing more than

54. *Dem. Press,* Oct. 23, 1819.
55. Ibid.
56. Ibid.

seeking a rational deployment of public resources. The system of private prosecution that underlay the cases for assault and battery was a vibrant form of popular conflict resolution that the city's poor employed to help police their own affairs and neighborhoods.[57] That many of these prosecutions were trifling and indeed vindictive, and that the aldermen colluded in the practice to secure fees, are true. But it is equally true that the system of private prosecution and the trifling indictments that raised the grand jury's ire were mechanisms that the poor used to mobilize the state in its own interests. When the grand jury called for their early suppression, it was also calling for the suppression of a deeply rooted form of popular justice.

Each of the grand jury's complaints, then, was linked to an affirmation of proper boundaries and a denigration of improper intrusion into the social order. The Vauxhall riot indicated the dangers of unsupervised strangers; the prison circulated increased crime and vice; and "trifling" indictments intruded merely private concerns into the majesty of the public court. Beneath the calm and balanced order of a properly run city, forces of motion and disruption, unless contained and controlled, threatened to explode. The prison, occupying the middle point in the grand jury's discourse, included the danger both of strangers and a legal apparatus at odds with the aims of order. Through its own practices, the most fearsome institution of state discipline engulfed the city in the excesses of criminality.

A somewhat different set of concerns emerged the following year during the October session of the Mayor's Court. Here, the penitentiary figured as the climax of a series of social problems: disease, uncleanliness, intemperance, conflict, and crime. Yellow fever had struck the city during the summer, and the grand jury was deeply concerned with the intersection between public health, personal morality, and governmental regulation of the city. The city it mapped was one in a state of fragility and impending disaster.[58]

Foremost in the minds of the grand jurors was the problem of disease. Although admitting that the yellow fever attack was "comparatively not so severe as hitherto," they urged the city government to take additional steps to prevent its recurrence and expressed their belief that "still greater vigilance" was demanded of the city's health officials. Medical science, they recognized, had not settled the question of the origin of the disease (whether domestic or foreign), but this indecision merely called for increased efforts on all fronts. Lack of knowledge should not stifle policy; instead, it was "the opinion of the grand jury, that it is a duty dictated by self preservation, to guard with vigilance every avenue to its approach." Consequently, the grand jurors urged

57. Allen Steinberg, *The Transformation of Criminal Justice: Philadelphia, 1800–1880* (Chapel Hill, N.C., 1989), 41–50.

58. *National Recorder,* Oct. 28, 1820.

that the quarantine laws be "strictly and rigidly enforced." But this defense against external threat only supplemented the practices of internal police. Given that it was "an uncontroverted fact, that cleanliness is healthful, and filthiness always a source of disease," they exhorted the government to pay greater attention to the city's streets, alleys, and wharves.[59]

Physical disease, however, was not the only threat the grand jurors saw to the city's well-being. They stressed the danger of tippling houses and pawn shops. In their minds, these seemingly trivial institutions unleashed a moral plague within the city. Licensed and unlicensed tippling houses, "almost innumerable," were spreading through "every quarter of the city," where they were the "resorts of drunkards and vagabonds." These houses, "overflowing fountains of misery and vice of every description," served not public and lawful purposes. Instead, they were "abused" and became the downfall of "the labouring poor, and . . . domestic servants." "To such houses they are tempted to resort, until the habit of intemperance becomes inveterate." In this manner, they were "corrupted by evil communications, and disease, extreme poverty, and crime, quickly and surely follow."[60] The tippling houses pulled the poor into a whirlpool of malignancy—intemperance, decay, and viciousness were the results. Through them, the grand jury implied, the uncleanliness of the city extended beyond the biological to the moral.

If tippling houses threatened to destroy the city through their seductive power, pawnshops figured as nodal points for the transmission of criminality. The grand jurors feared that the pawnshops, "which now lamentably abound," extorted from "the poor and distressed." But the heart of the complaint lay in their conviction that, because pawnshops provided opportunities for "converting stolen goods (of which they are notoriously the receptacles) into money," they functioned to encourage "the commission of larcenies, especially by domestics." Without pawnshops, the grand jury insisted, sales of stolen goods would become increasingly difficult "and the temptation to crime would not only be greatly diminished, but the chance of regaining his property would be greater for the plundered individual."[61] Pawnshops then, like tippling houses, drew the poor and the domestic away from morality and subordination. By unleashing intemperance and criminality, they threatened to undermine the social order by dissolving individual discipline.

If disease and immorality took the grand jury's concerns to the city's streets and shops, the unruly legal system pulled the grand jury's frustrations back to the courts. Like their predecessors, the grand jurors objected to the "many

59. The grand jury focused particularly on the dangers of the city's pest house and stagnant ponds. Ibid.

60. Ibid.

61. Ibid.

trifling vexations, and groundless prosecutions" that appeared before them. Once again, the grand jurors sought to establish a distinction between those cases where "public justice and the community" are concerned and those that were no more significant to the public than civil cases. From their perspective, most of these prosecutions were merely brought by "wrangling neighbours" whose "resentment," having been encouraged by aldermen, used the courts as a "means to prolong their quarrel." The result was a court system out of control; the dissolution of the proper boundary between public and private resulted in "great expense to the public, loss and inconvenience to the parties," while "producing a spirit of discord and litigation, adverse to the precepts of morality." [62] Popular recourse to the courts seemed to undercut public order itself.

Finally, there was the penitentiary. Here the grand jury struck an ambivalent pose, noting both the fame of Pennsylvania's prison philosophy ("imitated by not only most of our sister states, but in a degree by some foreign countries") as well as the "lamentable truth" that the physical situation at Walnut Street had "in practice greatly disappointed, if not defeated" its aims. Individual reformation ("its charitable purpose") was impossible under present circumstances. The prison's threat to public health "need only be adverted to" while the danger to public safety "must be obvious." The penitentiary and its future was a "subject of great interest and concern," and the grand jurors, confident that "their views are by no means peculiar to themselves," expressed their support for those who aimed to "remedy existing evils." To the grand jurors, the collapse of prison discipline was obvious, and obviously dangerous for the order of the city. Like the wharves, the tippling houses, and the pawnshops, the prison's evils overflowed its bounds; rather than being sites of health, lawfulness, and reformation, they were milieus of disease, decadence, and defiance. [63]

Both grand juries, then, spoke of a city under siege. For each, threats of internal dissolution and violence threatened the apparent order and orderliness of the citizens. Each presentment turned on the dangers of transgression and infiltration—whether the threat was strangers, external disease, the uncleanliness of the poor, internal immorality, insubordination, or the congregated mass of criminality in the prison. The grand jurors were highly sensitive to, and highly frightened by, the apparent confusion of social roles and the breakdown of proper discipline. The city, rather than fulfilling the desires of its founder and his enlightened heirs, had become a source of sickness and vice—and the continued presence of these urban seductions meant that sickness and vice were highly contagious.

62. Ibid.
63. Ibid.

VIII

The prison recapitulated the tensions of the society that surrounded it. From the boys demanding their customary rights in traditional working-class custom, through the structures of inmate culture that were counterweights to the inspectors' authority, to the psychic detachment of inmates from their labor, the Walnut Street prison reproduced the struggles and divisions that marked the culture and society of the city at large. Inmates, in fact, maintained the practices of the laboring poor despite their confinement. But what from the inmates' perspective might have been collective entitlements, from the vantage point of prison officials were signs of individual depravity. Committed to the project of individual transformation and rationalized authority, officials intensified their efforts. The failure of the prison, they implied, was a question of power. Whether discussing architecture, administration, or labor discipline, they pointed to structural conditions limiting the inspectors' ability to impose their will and directions on inmates and prison life. Until officials could control communication and individuate their subjects, the prison project was incomplete. If the penitentiary system was to be saved, reformers argued, a new form of prison organization and new strategies of discipline and power had to be created.

In 1823, construction of the Eastern State Penitentiary began near the northwest border of the city (the Spring Garden district of modern Philadelphia). After initial disagreements, the commissioners in charge of construction chose John Haviland to serve as architect. Haviland took great care to assure the circulation of air, the disposal of waste, and the supplies necessary for the continued healthiness of the prisoners.[64] The Eastern State Penitentiary, it was hoped, would not be a scene of disease, death, and resistance.

Haviland's design emphasized efficient surveillance and security. He shaped the central building radially. Seven wings extended outward from a central watchtower, each building containing thirty-six cells. The cells were twelve by eight feet, ten feet high. The walls between the cells and to the hallways were eighteen inches thick and extended three feet underground; the outside wall was twenty-seven inches thick and four feet below ground. The floor of each

---

64. *Poulson's American Daily Advertiser,* May 24, 1823; Committee to Superintend the Erection of the Eastern Penitentiary, Minutes, Mar. 26, Apr. 9, May 28, 1822, PHMC; [John Haviland], *A Description of Haviland's Design for the New Penitentiary, Now Erecting near Philadelphia, Accompanied by a Birdseye View* (Philadelphia, 1824). For more detailed examples of Haviland's thinking, see his "Day-Books," I, 19–29, 172–175, II, 147, 290, 293, John Haviland Papers, Department of Special Collections, Van Pelt Library, University of Pennsylvania. For a discussion of the history of the Penitentiary's construction, see Negley K. Teeters and John D. Shearer, *The Prison at Philadelphia, Cherry Hill, The Separate System of Penal Discipline: 1829–1913* (New York, 1957), 33–58.

cell was a layer of masonry covered by stone. Cell windows were placed high in a ceiling, out of reach of the inmate. Although there was no door to the inner passage, the connecting wall contained a peephole to allow a guard or warden to examine into each cell. In addition, a feed drawer was built into the inner door that, when shut, would prevent an inmate from seeing out of the cell. Each cell was linked to an outside exercise yard through two doors, an inner iron-grate door and an outer wooden one. The outside entrance to the exercise yard was another iron door. The watchtower had two stories, the first was designed to be used for a "general watch-house," and the second, in addition to providing the keepers with space for rest and relaxation, had an outside walkway to allow the guards to oversee the tops of the exercise yards. It also contained a warning bell.[65]

Haviland contended that his design allowed the guards to keep a continual watch over the inmates:

> By the distribution of the several blocks of Cells forming so many radiating lines to the Observatory or Watch-house, which is equal in width to one of those blocks; a watchman can, from one point, command a view of the extremity of the passages of the cells, or traverse under cover unobserved by the prisoners and overlook every cell; when they are exercising in their yards, the same watchman, . . . can see into every yard and detect any prisoner that may attempt to scale the minor walls.[66]

There were, however, certain limitations to this surveillance. Although the walkway allowed guards to see the top of the walls of the exercise yards, they could not see inside the yards themselves. Although a guard parading the hallways could look into each cell, the remaining cells would be free from inspection. Haviland, then, had not designed a true panopticon. Each individual could not be seen constantly from one central point. But, because the cell construction prevented the prisoners from being able to see out, they would be unable to know when they were or were not under observation (at least while within their cells). If constant surveillance was not possible, the threat of surveillance was ever present.

The general layout of the buildings served much the same purpose. The penitentiary was located on a ten-acre plot. The outer walls were thirty feet high and twelve feet thick at their base, two feet nine inches thick at the top. The front building was two stories high, containing the warden's compartments, the apothecary's room, and areas for cooking and washing as well as the rooms for prison officers. Over the apothecary's room was another warning bell. There was only one entrance to the building (the sole entrance to the

65. [Haviland], *A Description*, 3–7.
66. Ibid., 3–4.

penitentiary itself), a passageway at the base of the front building. This passageway was long enough to contain a horse-drawn wagon in order, Haviland noted, to allow the outer gate to be closed before opening the inner gate. Even the concentration of activities within the front building, he suggested, would help preserve order within the penitentiary. "A multiplicity of buildings scattered about the site," Haviland argued, was "objectionable, serving only as hiding places to assist escape." But his plan meant that the central building was "more solitary and secure." He believed the design also ensured that the "domestics" employed in the front building were kept far away from the cells (unless accompanied by a prison officer).[67] At the corners of the outside walls were four watchtowers.

The energy deployed to increase surveillance also was expended to prevent inmate communication. Because of their height, the windows, Haviland declared, would be "out of the reach of the prisoners climbing up to escape, or to converse from one cell to that of another." By using a feed drawer rather than an inner door, Haviland believed that he had provided a mechanism for feeding the prisoners without creating "the evil of the prisoners conversing from one door to another" and thereby "defeat[ing] in a great measure the object of solitary confinement." Even the prison's sewage system was created with an eye to security. Haviland proposed a complex system of pipes connected to a central reservoir, the pipes kept constantly filled with water to prevent inmates from communicating through them.[68]

Haviland clearly envisioned a withdrawn, enclosed life for his inmates. Each room contained a fold-out bed and blanket that would be hung on the wall during the day. The feed drawer, when extended, would serve as a table. Immured within their cells, inmates would be left to a life of quiet and solitude. The outdoor yards would allow necessary exercise. Haviland, as his attention to the apothecary's room, to waste disposal, and to ventilation demonstrates, was deeply concerned about protecting the inmates from disease. Implicitly responding to challenges about the healthiness of solitary confinement, Haviland aimed to control not only the escape of the inmates but the invasion of sickness. But the main theme of his design (and his printed explanation of it) was control through isolation. Throughout their existence in the penitentiary, the inmates would have only those contacts that the authorities intended. The building itself would prevent inmate communication and collective action.

The overall architectural style of the penitentiary was intended to reinforce its segregative mission. Haviland designed the front building and the corner towers in a medieval fashion, leaving the impression that Eastern State was a giant fortress transposed from the Middle Ages. Not only spatially but tempo-

67. Ibid., 4–5
68. Ibid., 4, 5, 6.

rally, the architecture signified that the penitentiary would be totally removed from the society around it. It would achieve what the reformed organization of Walnut Street could not—the penitentiary would be truly a world apart.

Haviland's design, and the prominence it achieved, marked a crucial development in the attempt to define and control penal space. Architecture had moved to center stage in organizing prison life. Throughout the eighteenth century, it is true, prison architecture had been a flourishing field of debate in Britain and on the Continent. But the first generation of Philadelphia prison reformers had placed their faith in the social regime of the prison. Caleb Lownes had gone so far as to deny the importance of architectural considerations if competent officials applied firm governance to the inmates.[69] Now the technical regulation of space became a central mechanism for controlling the prison and reforming prisoners. In effect, the turn to continual solitary confinement marked the replacement of a social with a spatial solution, the attempt to solve a crisis of authority through technical means.

Indeed, the tone of Haviland's pamphlet, *A Description of Haviland's Design for the New Penitentiary, Now Erecting near Philadelphia* reinforced the growing importance of a technical discourse. At no point did Haviland offer a justification for the importance of a system of solitary confinement. Instead, he assumed this importance as a given, using his textual space to describe the way he would organize the penitentiary's physical space. The ideological goals were not defended. Haviland's reasoning was deployed in solving a formal problem. Philosophical questions had no place in his argument.

The 1820 prison riot, then, highlighted the contradictions and tensions of the urban public realm. The prison and its problems represented the entire set of social issues haunting the imagination of the city's elite: unemployment, disease, racial tension, insubordination, crime, violence. The prison combined the fearsomeness of the parks and the streets with the presence of massed criminality; the transmission of criminal knowledge across generations reiterated the problem of schools, tippling houses, and pawnshops; racial violence within the prison yard mirrored racial hostility without; and the riot itself

69. My understanding of the emergence of architecture as a central element in penal life is indebted to the work of Robin Evans. Evans has traced the changing place of architecture and architects in transforming not only prison space but prison theory and prison life. As Evans demonstrates, one of the prime developments of the early 19th century was the increased faith placed in the purely architectural as a mechanism for transforming character, a development that received its fullest form in solitary-confinement prisons. For Evans's reading of Haviland, see *The Fabrication of Virtue: English Prison Architecture, 1750–1840* (New York, 1982), 320–328. For the debate on prison architecture in Britain and on the Continent, see ibid., 118–230. On Caleb Lownes and prison architecture, see above, Chapter 5.

echoed Vauxhall, only in an even more threatening form. The precarious nature of prison discipline—and its alleged connection to the arsons that were sweeping through the city—illumined the brittleness of authority.

At the same time, the turn to solitary confinement and the emphasis on spatial control marked the emergence of new tactics in the attempt to discipline the city. Nor were these tactics limited to the penitentiary. Throughout the 1820s and 1830s, public officials and private reformers would extend the deployment of disciplinary techniques to a continually widening circle of social realms. Intensified individuation, spatial reorganization, expanding targets, and increased autonomy of authority would become hallmarks of the disciplinary effort.

CHAPTER SEVEN

Discipline, the Family, and the Individual

The reformation of disciplinary techniques did not end with the turn to solitary confinement. Instead, the disciplinary project, conceived in the 1780s as a defensive enclave against the corruptions of public communication, became in the 1820s an expansive and expanding set of interventions in everyday life. The prison, rather than being the base of disciplinary practices, was repositioned as a local instance of a larger disciplinary apparatus. Beyond constructing the Eastern State Penitentiary, private reformers and public officials filled in the expanded disciplinary spaces that dotted the city with reinvigorated regimes of oversight, intervention, and training. The disciplinary realm thus achieved an expanded presence in the city as it freed itself from its moorings in the penal system proper.

Proponents of this institutional reformation articulated several related considerations. First, they continued to express fear of mimetic corruption—especially mimetic corruption within disciplinary institutions. Consequently, during the 1820s, they sought to classify inmates more completely and to intensify individualization. Second, proponents of new disciplinary institutions conveyed growing anxieties about the organization of working-class life—especially paternal authority within the working class. They therefore aimed to expand the regulation of labor and sexuality (particularly female sexuality). Third, private reformers and public officials increasingly conveyed their authority in terms of their own knowledge and expertise. They therefore redefined the relationship between disciplinary institutions and the family—and within the family to individuals. In so doing, they claimed greater authority for institutions of social discipline.

These efforts were paradoxical in their intent and effects. The reformation of poor relief, designed to strengthen paternal authority, subordinated the power of the father to the power of the market and the state. Private efforts to redeem prostitutes, while aiding some, also helped create the isolation of "fallen women" that they claimed to overcome. The juvenile House of Refuge, organized to salvage the young from the corruptions of the prison, ultimately incarcerated them regardless of actual criminal activity. And the prison form itself, designed to stabilize the entire disciplinary network, was the site of heated and angry conflict throughout the decade.

The disciplinary realm thus constructed its own excess. In claiming to shelter or supplement, disciplinary officials of the 1820s drew to themselves increasing authority and power. In offering refuge or restraint, the institutional strategies generated resistance. In seeking redemption or recovery, the asylums, refuges, and reforms affirmed the very social divisions they claimed to overcome. And whatever the initial point of entry, disciplinary efforts expanded in their import and meaning, implicating gender relations, the family, and sexuality. Each particular history of discipline encompassed a wide range of social meanings.

The 1820s witnessed what Michel Foucault termed the "swarming" of the disciplines. "While on the one hand," Foucault argued, "the disciplinary establishments increase, their mechanisms have a certain tendency to become 'de-institutionalized,' to emerge from the closed fortresses in which they once functioned and to circulate in a 'free' state; the massive, compact disciplines are broken down into flexible methods of control, which may be transferred and adapted."[1] Through the repetitive history of the expanded and intensified institutions of the 1820s, discipline, rather than simply being penal, extended further and further out into the wider social organization.

I

Although commissioned in 1821 and begun in 1823, the Eastern State Penitentiary was not opened until 1829. In the interim, conflict developed over proper penal form. By the late 1820s, two distinct strategies for reordering the prison existed in Pennsylvania. One, drawing on the experience of the Auburn penitentiary in New York, favored a system of congregate labor during the day and solitary confinement at night. The other, tied to the structure of Eastern State, sought a total separation of inmates and questioned the usefulness of prison labor. The conflict between the two programs turned on a number of issues: the importance of conscience and habit in the transformation of personality, the place of the body in punishment, the proper mechanisms for sustaining authority, the importance of labor, the nature of the threat to inmate health

1. Michel Foucault, *Discipline and Punish: The Birth of the Prison,* trans. Alan Sheridan (New York, 1977), 211.

and morality, and the limits and role of architecture in organizing penal practice. The debate over proper penal form contained highly charged disagreements over the nature of individual subjectivity and its relationship to social organization.[2]

This debate mirrored a wider transatlantic argument over penal forms. On both sides of the Atlantic, officials in the early nineteenth century sought to increase their control over the prison. By the late 1820s and 1830s, the models of Eastern State and Auburn came to dominate this discussion. Both the French and English governments dispatched commissioners to examine the two systems and report their conclusions, and prison reformers in the United States eagerly transmitted their experiences and expectations both at home and abroad. The result was the spread of the New York and Pennsylvania systems throughout Europe and the United States.[3]

The debate of the 1820s revisited the struggles of the 1780s but from within

2. New York, after initially modeling its prison organization on Walnut Street, had experimented briefly with a system of total solitary confinement and then, at the state penitentiary at Auburn, implemented a program of solitary confinement at night and congregate labor during the day. On the Auburn system and its implications and importance, see David J. Rothman, *The Discovery of the Asylum: Social Order and Disorder in the New Republic* (Boston, 1971), 95–101. On the larger history of New York's attempt to revise its penal system in the late 18th and early 19th centuries, see W. David Lewis, *From Newgate to Dannemora: The Rise of the Penitentiary in New York, 1796–1848* (Ithaca, N.Y., 1965).

On the system at Eastern State Penetentiary and its implications, see, for example, Franklin Bache, *Observations and Reflections on the Penitentiary System: A Letter from Franklin Bache, M.D. to Roberts Vaux* (Philadelphia, 1829); Charles Caldwell, *New Views of Penitentiary Discipline, and Moral Education and Reform* (Philadelphia, 1829); Edward Livingston, *On the Advantages of the Pennsylvania System of Prison Discipline* (Philadelphia, 1828); John Sergeant, *Observations and Reflections on the Design and Effects of Punishment . . .* (Philadelphia, 1828); Roberts Vaux, *Letter on the Penitentiary System of Pennsylvania . . .* (Philadelphia, 1827), and *Reply to Two Letters of William Roscoe, Esquire of Liverpool, on the Penitentiary System of Pennsylvania* (Philadelphia, 1827). On the implications of these two systems and the conflicts that they generated, see Foucault, *Discipline and Punish*, 235–240.

3. For the report of William Crawford, the English commissioner, see his *On the Penitentiaries of the United States* (London, 1835). Crawford was a proponent of the Pennsylvania system. For a discussion of Crawford's review, see Michael Ignatieff, *A Just Measure of Pain: The Penitentiary in the Industrial Revolution, 1750–1850* (New York, 1978), 195–197. For the French commissioners, Gustave de Beaumont and Alexis de Tocqueville, see their *On the Penitentiary System in the United States and Its Application in France . . .*, trans. Francis Lieber (Philadelphia, 1833). They, too, were smitten with the Pennsylvania system. On the transatlantic importance of the two prison models, see Robin Evans, *The Fabrication of Virtue: English Prison Architecture, 1750–1840* (Cambridge, 1982), 318–387; Foucault, *Discipline and Punish*, 235–256; U. R. Q. Henriques, "The Rise and Decline of the Separate System of Prison Discipline," *Past and Present*, no. 54 (February 1972), 61–93; Ignatieff, *A Just Measure of Pain*, 193–200; Rothman, *The Discovery of the Asylum*, 79–108, 240–247.

reformative incarceration itself. All sides recognized the failed and incomplete nature of discipline at Walnut Street, and all demanded a more individualized structure. They also returned to many of the late-eighteenth-century issues: the treatment of the body, the importance of labor, the place of conscience and habit, the nature of penitential authority. The repetitive quality of the debate points to the continued dominance of the discourse of mimetic corruption. And it also reveals, in an inversion of Rush's anxiety over the powerfully disruptive presence of the publicly displayed body, the continued dilemma of the relationship between penal corporality and the penitential imagination.

Still, the argument over proper penal forms did reveal important changes from the late eighteenth century. If Rush and his colleagues had evinced a growing recognition of inmate capability, reformers of the 1820s manifested greater skepticism of their subjects. Their concerns and their convictions focused on the proper model for penal organization. Their hopes resided less in the inmates than in their institutions. At the same time, both sides demanded that reconstructed penitentiaries reach deeper and deeper into the soul and character of their inmates. Out of their despair over the efficacy of Walnut Street and their increasing suspicions of convicts, they formulated a new and more demanding regime of penal discipline.

The debate over proper penitential forms, in Pennsylvania at least, was reopened by William Roscoe. Roscoe, a leading English proponent of prison reform well known for his *Observations on Penal Jurisprudence, and the Reformation of Criminals,* argued that Pennsylvania's plan marked the abandonment of the penitentiary system. For Roscoe, the proper organization of penitentiary life consisted of labor with "diligent" oversight during the day and separate sleeping quarters at night. Instead of seeing Eastern State as the fulfillment of years of humane legislation, Roscoe believed that it was a return to archaic and barbarous practices. The British visitor Basil Hall echoed this attack. He argued that solitary confinement, rather than leading to reformation, led instead to insanity.[4]

This English attack on solitary confinement was taken up within Pennsylvania by Charles Shaler, Edward King, and T. I. Wharton, who were appointed commissioners on the penal code in 1826. The legislature assigned Shaler, King, and Wharton the task of shaping a code of sentences to be implemented

---

4. Basil Hall, *Travels in North America during the years 1827, 1828, and 1829,* 3 vols. (London, 1829), II, 78; William Roscoe, *Observations on Penal Jurisprudence, and the Reformation of Criminals . . .* (London, 1819), 171; Roscoe, *A Brief Statement of the Causes Which Have Led to the Abandonment of the Celebrated System of Penitentiary Discipline, in Some of the United States of America . . .* (Liverpool, 1827). Roscoe possessed such international authority and respect that Roberts Vaux felt compelled to respond to his charges almost immediately. See Vaux, *Reply to Two Letters of William Roscoe.*

in the new penitentiaries at Philadelphia and Pittsburgh. But, instead, in December 1827, they returned with a long discussion of the varieties of punishments available to the state. The heart of their report was an extensive critique of total solitary confinement. Armed with the textual support of proponents of the Auburn system of penitentiary discipline, the commissioners directly challenged the design for Eastern State.[5]

Shaler, King, and Wharton argued that continual solitary confinement was unnecessary, ineffective, cruel, and unjustifiably expensive. They contended that it failed to distinguish adequately between daytime and nighttime organization, overstated the beneficial effects of solitary reflection, underestimated the likely physical and mental effects of solitude, and overlooked the legitimate fiscal concerns of the state. To their minds, solitude at night and congregate labor during the day would better accomplish the goal of ensuring prison discipline and individual reformation.

Crucial to the commissioners' position was a strict distinction between the dangers of nighttime and daytime. "All accounts agree," they claimed, that "night rooms" were the "means of the most corrupting communication, and the scenes of the most hideous depravity." These retreats from surveillance were an "asylum of free and unrestrained conversation, where the opportunity is eagerly seized to relate former exploits, to plan new adventures of villainy, to elevate the character of crime and to dissipate the suggestions of conscience." The night rooms were sites of an unrestrained and depraved sexuality, of "the nameless and unnatural crimes, which concurrent testimony proves to have been frequently perpetrated in these chambers of guilt and misery."[6] The impenetrable darkness of the night rooms, they believed, allowed seduction and corruption to take root and flourish.

The situation was quite different during the day. The commissioners conceded that daytime communication between inmates was also dangerous. But, during the day, "perfect silence, submission and order to the full extent of excluding all communication between [inmates], during the period of labor, may be enforced by the employment of a reasonable number of keepers, or superintendents, of common firmness and ability." With such superintendence, convicts could labor together during the day without spreading the contagion of criminality.[7]

The commissioners' defense of labor was linked to their skepticism of the power of solitary reflection. Admitting that solitary reflection might reform

5. Pennsylvania, Commissioners to Revise the Criminal Code, *Report of the Commissioners on the Penal Code, with the Accompanying Documents, Read in the Senate, January 4, 1828* (Harrisburg, 1828).

6. Ibid., 22, 23.

7. Ibid., 24.

individuals of "sensibility (although it might just as easily drive them mad), they denied that sensibility characterized most inmates. "The great mass of the tenantry of our penitentiaries, appeared to us, persons of coarse, brutal temperament, of stupid ignorance, and low cunning, or of sufficient intellectual capacity, and some cultivation, but an entire aversion to the inconvenient restraints of the law, and of a spirit to obtain a living in any other way, than by the pursuit of honest labor." For such individuals, it was unrealistic to suppose that reflection would lead to reformation and virtue. In fact, solitary reflection might only worsen matters. A system built on solitude neglected the importance of habit as it overstated the potential of conscience. Most convicts, they believed, were too "blunted" to be overwhelmed by their solitude. Instead of developing habits of labor, they would be reinforced in their habit of idleness.[8]

Moreover, the commissioners suggested, solitary confinement destroyed the physical, and possibly the mental, health of prisoners. Citing testimony from prison officials in New Jersey, New York, Virginia, and other states that had employed various forms of penal solitude, they argued that solitary confinement was counterproductive. Individuals confined to cells for full prison terms would be left enervated and demoralized at the end of their sentences. On their release, they would need medical assistance and probably be unable to perform labor to support themselves. Instead of creating model citizens, solitary confinement would only create new burdens for the public.[9]

Given these objections, the commissioners argued, the state should create a discipline that was sufficiently "severe" to ensure that prisoners would labor and thereby develop the habits of labor. They avowed "that unless the habits are radically affected; unless a course of industry is worked into the grain of the convict's life, the impression produced by the course of reflection on solitude for which so much good has been anticipated, will probably be of short duration." They thus declared their preference for congregate labor with continual oversight. Without labor, no good could come of the new penitentiary.[10]

The commissioners accepted not only congregate labor but Auburn's exercise of punitive whipping. Opposition to whipping, they believed, was an example of misplaced sympathy toward inmates. They denied that corporal punishment at Auburn was excessive; instead, it was only deployed when truly necessary. The commissioners aimed to continue the Revolutionary-era critique of arbitrary authority. But, whereas the defenders of solitude sought to

8. Ibid., 25, 29, 33.

9. Ibid., 39–46.

10. Ibid., 47. They also challenged the notion that one could combine continual solitary confinement with labor by arguing that such a system was impossible to monitor and economically impractical. Ibid., 47–55.

control authority by displacing the imposition of discipline onto architecture, the commissioners aimed to control it through visibility and surveillance.[11]

Although the commissioners on the penal code were not alone in their advocacy of the Auburn system, Eastern State's proponents were hardly silent. The new penitentiary, they insisted, would institute a program of "separate," not solitary, confinement. Not all human contact would be eliminated. Prisoners would be isolated only from corrupting influences; they would still have contact with the authorities and other approved visitors. Moreover, they argued, there was little danger to inmate health. Comparisons with other prisons failed to acknowledge that Eastern State would provide enough space, ventilation, and sanitation to preserve the inmates.[12]

To some extent, the defense of separate confinement was defensive, emphasizing its ability to prevent the expansion of criminality among inmates. "In separate confinement," Roberts Vaux noted, "every prisoner is placed beyond the possibility of being made more corrupt by his imprisonment."[13] At the very least, its proponents argued, prisoners would be no worse when they left prison than when they entered. The solidity of concrete would ensure that criminality would not spread.

But the benefits of separate confinement went beyond checking corruptive communication; the terror of solitude was so great that it rendered corporal punishments superfluous. The advocates of separate confinement were unwilling to accept disciplinary whipping. The lash, Samuel Miller declared, was "the most impolitic and pernicious system ever resorted to for the government and reformation of rational beings." He had seen but one case of refor-

11. Ibid., 62, 70–73. Shaler, King, and Wharton recognized, however, that the advanced state of the construction of Eastern State Penitentiary prevented a full employment of the Auburn model. Consequently, they proposed constructing manufacturing buildings on the lot of the penitentiary to supplement the completed structures. Such a move, they contended, would not only have greater reformative value but, in the long run, prove far more economical to the state than continual solitary confinement. Outlays for construction of the prison were enormous and continually growing. Given their doubts about the efficacy of solitary confinement, Shaler, King, and Wharton clearly believed that the decision to construct Eastern State along solitary lines was an unwise and unrealistic outlay of state funds. The sale of prison manufactures, they believed, would help to offset both the large construction costs of the penitentiary and to defray yearly operating expenses. Ibid., 76–77.

12. Pennsylvania, Commissioners to Superintend the Erection of the Eastern Penitentiary, *Letter Report and Documents, on the Penal Code, from the President and Commissioners Appointed to Superintend the Erection of the Eastern Penitentiary, Adapted and Modelled to the System of Solitary Confinement; Read in the Senate, January 8, 1828* (Harrisburg, 1828), 13–16. Mathew Carey shared in the commissioners on the penal code's suspicion of the new penitentiary discipline. See his *Essays on Penitentiary Discipline* (Philadelphia, 1829) and *Thoughts on Penitentiaries and Prison Discipline* (Philadelphia, 1831).

13. *Niles' Weekly Register* (Baltimore), June 16, 1827.

mation through corporal punishment; for the rest, "disgrace had destroyed their pride, damped their spirits, and generated habits of dissipation, from which they rarely recovered." Separate confinement, on the other hand, offered an exercise of authority freed from violence. Solitude, imposed through irresistible walls and ameliorated by the presence of authority, reformed without debasing.[14]

Corporal punishment, moreover, destroyed the character of those implementing the penalty. Charles Caldwell warned of the "deteriorating effect which [corporal punishment] produces on those who consent to engage in it, and become its ministers; its inhumanizing influence on all those who enlist themselves as punishers." The result of whipping was the simultaneous debasement of both the punished and the punisher. "Being exclusively the offspring of animal propensity," Caldwell insisted, "its unavoidable effect is to brutalize those who are daily concerned in it.[15]

Solitude, on the other hand, promised to create a space where the reconstruction of individuals' subjectivity could occur. Confidence in separate confinement was rooted in a continuing faith in the redemptive power of conscience. Proponents believed that inmates, trapped alone in their cells, would be forced to reflect on their past, to confront the actions that had brought them to their isolation. And, in this confrontation with themselves, their conscience would begin the task of reformation. "A new creation," Thomas Bradford, Jr., acknowledged, "must be effected by an almighty power." But "reflection and self examination are powerful agents in this work." Solitude would create the free space in which grace could work. Job Tyson pictured the inmate "in his solitary apartment, without a friend to sooth or an allurement to flatter," where "the felon [will] brood over the outrages he has committed on society, feel the compunctions of an offended conscience, and converse with that best admonisher—his heart." "Who will say," he asked, "that the expectations entertained of it [Eastern State] will not be realized?" An inmate, James J. Barclay, declared: "Freed from all that can excite his evil passions, unassisted by the vicious influence of his companions in profligacy, with no impure association . . . may be inspired with the spirit of benevolence that seeks to effect his reformation."[16] For all these writers, solitude acted spiritu-

14. Samuel Miller to Roberts Vaux, Jan. 1, 1828, in Samuel Hazard, ed., *The Register of Pennsylvania, Devoted to the Preservation of Facts and Documents, and Every Other Kind of Useful Information respecting the State of Pennsylvania* (Philadelphia, 1828–1836), I, 79. In this letter, Miller was describing his experience with military, not penal, discipline.

15. Caldwell, *New Views on Penitentiary Discipline,* 4.

16. Thomas Bradford, Jr., "Observations on the Penal Code," Prisons, Bradford Papers, HSP; Job R. Tyson, *Essay on the Penal Law of Pennsylvania* (Philadelphia, 1827), 59; James J. Barclay, "Review," 63, Philadelphia Society to Alleviate the Miseries of Public Prisons, Papers, 1797–1883, box 2, Department of Special Collections, Van Pelt Library, University of

ally—denying the contaminating effects of association through the irresistible compulsion of architecture and without direct or violent seizure of the body.

The reflection that accompanied solitude would stimulate transformative memory. As inmates relived the past that placed them in the penitentiary, their thoughts, especially if they were young and not too vicious, might move even farther back in time. Imagine a youth, Bradford suggested, "just entered on his career of vice," condemned to the penitentiary. There, alone and without fellow inmates for companionship, "left free to ponder on that folly and guilt which brought him to his cell . . . if in early life a parents tender care was employed to fill his mind with good advice and training up within [the] pattern of Nature and Religion; the recollection of these may be awakened in his soul and although anguish may attend them yet the result may under the divine blessing be a firm determination to walk the ways of righteousness the remnant of his life."[17] Solitary confinement would infantilize inmates, stripping away the layers of vice accumulated in adulthood. Then, having experienced a second childhood, inmates would be open to the possibility of personal reformation.

Separate confinement did not depend on only the efficacy of solitary conscience and memory, however. Religious leaders and prison officials, proponents insisted, would dispense the Bible and other religious materials, engage inmates in conversation, and provide religious services on Sunday. Confession and instruction would help bind inmates to virtue instead of vice. The commissioners appointed to superintend the erection of the Eastern Penitentiary envisioned the prison's religious instructor visiting inmates "as their counsellor, guide, and friend," thereby gaining "their confidence and attachment." After which "they would unbosom their souls with freedom; he would learn their history and character," and then tailor each inmate's lessons to their "dispositions and to their characters." Such intimate personal knowledge would allow the instructor to "constantly and patiently instruct them in the principles and doctrines of the christian religion, and in humble dependence on the divine blessing exert all his influence in fanning the feeble flame of virtue, and discouraging every appearance of vice; thus convincing them, he seeks their present and everlasting good."[18] In all these ways, the language of virtue would replace the language of vice in the inmates' hearts.

This process entailed inmates' rewriting, as it were, their own histories.

Pennsylvania. See also Francis Lieber to Roberts Vaux, Jan. 11, 1833, Vaux Papers, HSP. For a discussion of arguments made in England advocating solitude, see Evans, *The Fabrication of Virtue*, 318–344.

17. Bradford, "Observations on the Penal Code," Prisons, Bradford Papers.

18. Commissioners to Superintend the Erection of the Eastern State Penitentiary, *Letter Report and Documents*, 9, 24–25.

Solitude, supplemented by religious instruction, would force inmates to reconceptualize the meaning of their actions. Rather than seeing crime as connected to pleasure and criminality as tied to a sociable community, criminal actions would come to be seen as the causes of terror and isolation.

But even when reformation did not occur, solitude promised deterrent terror. Believing in the intrinsic sociability of humanity, defenders of separate confinement assumed that there was "no punishment which affects the mind so powerfully, as solitary confinement; none so much dreaded even by the most hardened." Solitude was so hard that it would "impress so great a dread and terror, as to deter the offender from the commission of crime in the state where the system of solitary confinement exists." [19]

The separate system, then, was a machinery combining traditional Christian assumptions about conscience with a more modernist, technical control of space. Each inmate would be placed in a limited area, cut off from peers, and would then engage in an individual and individualizing confession and education. Isolated, the inmates would be encouraged to talk of their past, to relive (both in speech and silent memory) the actions that had brought them to their cells, and then, with the help of the prison authorities, to restate their experiences through the language of Christian conscience. No hand (theoretically) would be raised against them in anger, and, gradually, they would recognize the mercy of their treatment and actively accept the justice of their sentence. Through this combination of confession, conscience, and concrete, individuals would be reborn and prepared to reenter the community at large.

This debate was not without effect. The new prison program did not eliminate the role of labor. When Eastern State opened in 1829, the prison implemented a system of separate confinement with labor.[20] Although labor was only a subsidiary part of the system, and although they failed in their effort to institute congregate labor, the commissioners on the penal code and their allies had successfully challenged an exclusive reliance on solitary reflection and conscience within the prison.

Still, the overall effect of the debate was to clarify, not displace, the penitential structure at Eastern State. The existence of the (partially completed) penitentiary established clear limits on the options open to Pennsylvania's lawmakers. When the commissioners on the penal code issued their report in 1828, the state had already expended a huge amount of money to construct a solitary confinement prison for Philadelphia, let alone the funds expended on the Western State Penitentiary in Allegheny.[21] Whatever modifications in the

19. Ibid., 7, 13.

20. Pennsylvania, Laws, Statutes, etc., *Acts of the General Assembly Relating to the Eastern State Penitentiary, and to the New Prisons of the City and County of Philadelphia* (Philadelphia, 1831), 7.

21. Commissioners to Revise the Criminal Code, *Report*, 74–76.

proposed program were to take place, the concrete realities of Eastern State ensured that they would be limited.

Moreover, both sides shared certain ideological commitments. The second generation of prison reformers was concerned, above all, to control what Franklin Bache termed "gregarious confinement." Any "association of convicts with each other," Roberts Vaux went so far as to say, "must inevitably yield pernicious consequences in a greater or lesser degree." The commissioners on the penal code echoed these concerns. "The intercourse between convicts," they wrote, "is an evil of the greatest magnitude; one which, as it taints and poisons the whole system of penal discipline, and, by its consequences, infests even the population outside the prison, no effort or sacrifice would be too great to destroy, and which any remedy, however severe must be adopted to cure." Furthermore, the association of inmates undermined the severity of criminal punishments. "Vicious company," Thomas Bradford, Jr., wrote, "is very acceptable to a vicious mind." [22] Company provided a distraction from the terrors of punishment; by preventing reflection and remorse, it halted the effects of conscience and precluded the possibility of reformation.

Linked to this fear of prison culture was a hardened attitude toward inmates. The effort to strengthen the hand of authority went hand in hand with a deep-rooted anxiety that some, perhaps many, of the inmates were too far beyond the power of penitential punishments to reclaim. James Mease, for instance, advocated limiting prison terms to first-time offenders. Those who had been subject to penitential discipline and were convicted of second offenses should be transported. Shaler's, King's, and Wharton's support for the Auburn system stemmed, in part, from their conviction that prison inmates, by their very nature, needed severe discipline. Only compelling them to labor, if that, would improve their characters. The men charged with directing the construction of Eastern State reminded their fellow citizens: The "inhabitants of the cells . . . will not be men of unblemished virtue, or moral habits, of high and honourable spirits, whose sensibilities are keenly alive. The subjects of this system of punishment will be generally criminals of degraded and vicious characters." Roberts Vaux, for his part, confessed that "all experience proves how difficult it is to make any impressions whatever upon the feelings of the benighted and unhappy subjects of criminal punishment." To Vaux, however,

22. *Niles' Weekly Register,* June 16, 1827; Commissioners to Revise the Criminal Code, *Report,* 20; Bradford, "Observations on the Penal Code," Prisons, Bradford Papers; Bache, *Observations and Reflections,* 3. Bache argued that the association of inmates had four main dangers; it led to mutual support for vice; it actually fostered "bad passions and evil propensities"; it made it impossible even for the "best disposed prisoners" to be free from their fellow inmates after release; and the resultant "notoriety of the prisoner's disgrace" to numbers of the "most depraved members of society" meant that the inmate's honest friends and relatives would refuse their "countenance and support." Ibid., 3–4.

the problems went even further. Prisons, he feared, would never eliminate criminality. "So long as men are constituted as we now find them to be," he wrote, "we have no reason to suppose any people will be exempt from the necessity of prisons and penal laws."[23] Prison was a permanent project.

These twin fears, of prison and of prison inmates, merged in an almost dystopian image of the unreformed prison. Proponents of both Auburn and Eastern State repeatedly evoked images of collapse when they discussed unreformed prisons: collapse of order, collapse of morality, collapse of the human personality. Beyond the threat to prison discipline posed by inmate communication, prison reformers imagined unregulated prisons as veritable bastions of transgression; as their fears of the dangers of "gregarious confinement" spiraled ever upward, so did the extravagance of their language. According to George Washington Smith, a devoted defender of the separate system, Walnut Street during the 1780s had been a "den of abomination" where there "mingled in one revolting mass of festering corruption, all the collected elements of contagion." Inmates of "all ages, colours, and sexes, were forced into one horrid, loathsome communion of depravity." In the end, he reported, "idleness, profligacy and widely diffused contamination, were the inevitable results." Or, in the more tempered words of Mathew Carey, the unreformed prison "was a mere pandemonium—exhibiting as complete an aggregate of human misery and corruption as probably ever existed."[24] For the second generation of prison reformers, the unreformed prison symbolized a total collapse of society and the individual. If the boundaries within the prison could not be reestablished, then the distinctions between vice and virtue would be permanently dissolved.

Underlying these agreements was a shared emphasis on an individualizing discipline. By the 1820s, prison officials and private reformers were increasingly suspicious of the prison population. Inmate recalcitrance, they reasoned, was a sign of individual failing or cultural miseducation. Consequently, the Philadelphia Society and its allies reconstructed the strategy of punishment. Their growing suspicion of inmates increased rather than decreased their commitment to a penal power both individualized and individuating—one that would reach into the deepest recesses of criminal character. The spiritual-

23. Commissioners to Revise the Criminal Code, *Report*, 24–26; Commissioners to Superintend the Erection of the Eastern Penitentiary, *Letter Report and Documents*, 13; *Niles' Weekly Register*, June 16, 1827; James Mease, *Observations on the Penitentiary System, and Penal Code of Pennsylvania with Suggestions for their Improvement* (Philadelphia, 1828), 19–23. This pamphlet originally appeared as newspaper essays during 1820 and 1821.

24. George W. Smith, *A Defence of the System of Solitary Confinement of Prisoners Adopted by the State of Pennsylvania, with Remarks on the Origin, Progress, and Extension of This Species of Prison Discipline* (Philadelphia, 1833), 11; Carey, *Thoughts on Penitentiaries and Prison Discipline*, 16.

ization of punishment evinced a faith less in the subjects of penitence than in the nature of penitential power and authority.

II

Philadelphia's governors also restructured the city's poor relief-system in the 1820s. Building on late-eighteenth-century notions of personal responsibility, elite Philadelphians defined the roots of poverty as inappropriate or uneducated desire. They suggested that the poor, both male and female, were misdirected—drawn toward the pleasures of the bottle, prone to promiscuous sexuality, trapped in the webs of indolence and debt. Poverty, short of the misfortune of accident or the ravages of age and illness, was rooted in personal habit. Pauperism was a state of mind as much as a state of being; its responsibility lay with the individual. It marked a disconnection from the reality of the social world—a failure to labor and productively engage in the marketplace.

The poor relief system, they argued, heightened these problems. Rather than strengthening the lure of the wage and the lessons of responsibility, it taught the poor that their vices would be forgiven and overcome through the practices of the state, not through their own actions. The poor laws expanded and entrenched pauperism, creating webs of dependence that drew the poor out of a necessary engagement with labor and discipline and into an unproductive reliance on the public bounty. It simultaneously undermined the individual, increased social conflict, and drained the economy.

Despite the efforts of the Pennsylvania Society for Promoting Public Economy, reform did not take place during the years of economic depression. Instead, political struggles over the administration of poor relief and a hardening of attitudes toward the poor stimulated transformation. In the years following 1820, control of the Board of Guardians (who levied the poor tax and distributed poor relief) increasingly fell to politicians in Philadelphia county aligned with the Democratic party, rather than politicians in the city of Philadelphia aligned with the Federalist party. The county politicians were closer to, and in greater sympathy with, their poor charges than were their city counterparts. In response to these developments, Federalist Philadelphia pushed for a revamping of the structure of poor relief.[25]

The most systematic attack on the poor-relief system came in 1825. In that year, a committee of the state House of Representatives chaired by William Meredith, a wealthy Philadelphia Federalist and lawyer, sought to delegitimate the very notion of public poor relief.[26] Focusing on discipline and cost,

25. Priscilla Ferguson Clement, *Welfare and the Poor in the Nineteenth-Century City: Philadelphia, 1800–1854* (Rutherford, N.J., 1985), 53–55.
26. On Meredith, see ibid., 54.

the committee aimed to limit the flexibility and independence of relief recipients. Female sexuality, male irresponsibility, and intemperance were at the heart of their fears. Although Meredith's committee was unable to remake the relief system as it hoped, it both inaugurated and set the tone for reformist arguments in the late 1820s.

Meredith and his committee situated their reflections in the context of Pennsylvania's changing economy. Pennsylvania's manufacturing sector was developing rapidly, and the experience of England, they insisted, had shown that manufacturing populations were most easily drawn into dependence on the state. Whereas agricultural peoples were "naturally more hardy and independent," and thereby more likely to resist the "temptations" posed by the poor laws, manufacturing peoples had no such resistance. Indeed, it was "on a manufacturing population, that the poor laws operate most deleteriously and fatally." The state, therefore, was at a turning point. The "effect" of the poor laws, the legislators argued, was "to increase the numbers of paupers; to entail an oppressive burthen on the country; to promote idleness and licentiousness among the labouring classes; and to afford to the profligate and abandoned, the relief which ought to be bestowed on the virtuous and industrious alone."[27] As a result, the committee's analysis and proposals focused on ways to ensure that working-class desire was tied to market incentives and coercions.

As Meredith and his allies saw it, public poor relief dissolved both class subordination and familial morality. Charity had "been wisely ordained by Providence to be a duty of imperfect obligation," dependent on "the operation of religious motives, and the sympathy for the distressed which is natural to the human heart." Voluntary obligation had three benefits. Its very uncertainty prevented the poor from assuming its availability, thereby inciting individual industry. It also promoted knowledgeable giving. When individuals gave charity, the committee avowed, they "generally take reasonable care that it is bestowed upon a proper object," ensuring that those whose poverty flowed from their own "abandoned and dissolute habits" would find "the access to relief hard and difficult." Finally, personal charity imposed a "feeling of humiliation" on its recipient, thereby stimulating the poor to avoid charity whenever possible. It provided a "pledge, that this mode of subsistence will generally not be resorted to, while any other remains open."[28] Private, voluntary charity provided for diligence, knowledge, and subordination.

Meredith and his allies insisted that public poor relief undermined these ef-

27. "'Report of the Committee Appointed to Inquire into the Operation of the Poor Laws,' Read, January 29th, 1825, Mr. Meredith, Chairman," in Hazard, ed., *Register of Pennsylvania*, II, 68.

28. Ibid., 50.

fects. By mediating charity through the government, public poor relief precluded the development of the "feeling of humanity, of kindness, of tenderness, on the one side" and the "sense of humiliation or gratitude, on the other." The poor, for their part, come to see relief as "a right," and the rich provide support "ungraciously" because they have no choice. Each group is left "dissatisfied and exasperated." The rich see the demands of the poor as a never ending process, and the poor, because what was given them was never enough, are left "uncomfortable, needy and dependent."[29]

Unlike private relief, structured by a knowing relationship between two individuals, public poor relief, the committee charged, was linked to ignorance. Public officials had neither the capacity nor the incentive to screen their recipients. The indigent were too numerous, and government officials had no personal interest in the money spent. Consequently, the "improvident, the dissolute, and the unworthy" compete for relief with those left poor by "unavoidable misfortune or calamity," and the "more clamorous and importunate demands" of the unworthy too often triumphed.[30]

An increase in idleness compounded these tendencies to hostility and waste. Meredith's committee believed that the laboring poor needed provocation to labor. If the state proclaimed that it would take care of a worker and his family, it could only lead to dissipation and destructive habits: "He soon falls into habits of idleness—idleness leads to profligacy—profligacy is sure to end in disease, and he becomes a wretched being, useless to himself, useless to his family and to society; and for the remainder of his miserable existence, an incumbrance—a dead weight upon the public bounty." By removing the common incentives to labor, poor relief only encouraged individuals to relax their self-discipline and partake in unreasonable indulgences. And by holding out the prospect of public satisfaction of private desires, public poor relief encouraged an indefinite expansion of the demands of its recipients.[31] The poor laws thereby established an unproductive economy of desire.

The committee's fears of unproductive desire were linked to its anxiety over the state of paternal authority. The gendered nature of their examples (the incessant repetition of the male pronoun) was not coincidental. Meredith and his allies focused their attention on the authority and responsibility of the male head of household. Poor relief did more than encourage men to laziness. By removing male obligation to support families, it destroyed the dependence of the family on the father. The legislators believed that "the sense of dependence in the members, upon the head of a family" as well as the "consciousness" of the father "that to him, and him alone, must those who are most dear

29. Ibid.
30. Ibid.
31. Ibid.

to him, look for protection and support" would normally "form strong and indissoluble links." The poor laws dissolved these links, "by removing all sense of necessary dependence on the one hand, and of indispensable protection on the other." To make matters worse, the poor laws made possible "improvident marriages" between individuals who could not support a family without aid. In this way, it helped create generations of "hereditary paupers." In effect, Meredith argued, the system of poor relief created a race of dependents who, left to their own resources to survive and reproduce, would have ceased to exist. The implications were clear. If steps were not taken to control this problem, the paupers' demands would overrun society.[32]

For Meredith's committee, then, poor relief was a social evil. The committee suggested a policy of imposed uncertainty for the poor. Stripping the poor of their governmental support would force them back to the market. Still, whatever the committee's beliefs, it did not propose the immediate abolition of poor relief. Perhaps recognizing both political realities and entrenched social expectations, it sought to strangle poor relief slowly instead. Calling for the accumulation of detailed knowledge about the operation of poor relief as well as fuller legislative investigation, the committee suggested transforming and reducing public poor relief—gradually throughout the state, more rapidly in Philadelphia and its surroundings. More immediately, they proposed limiting the level of money available for poor relief to its 1825 level. Given population growth, this action would inevitably decrease the amount of aid available to any individual.[33]

The committee's proposals met strong opposition, and the Guardians of the Poor were able to defeat the proposed freeze on poor rates. Still, despite this success, the Guardians were on the defensive. Pressures mounted for a reform of the poor laws, leading to a series of meetings, investigations, and reports on the system of poor relief and its flaws. In 1827, both the Guardians of the Poor and representatives from a public meeting to investigate the "pauper system" urged dramatic alterations in the practices and structures of poor relief.[34]

If Meredith's committee fretted over the problematic nature of paternal au-

32. Ibid.

33. Ibid., 68–69.

34. Clement, *Welfare and the Poor*, 54–56; Philadelphia Board of Guardians, *Report of the Committee Appointed by the Board of Guardians of the Poor of the City and Districts of Philadelphia, to Visit the Cities of Baltimore, New-York, Providence, Boston, and Salem* (Philadelphia, 1827); [Philadelphia], *Report of the Committee Appointed at a Town Meeting of the Citizens of the City and County of Philadelphia, on the 23d of July, 1827, to Consider the Subject of the Pauper System of the City and Districts, and to Report Remedies for Its Defects* (Philadelphia, 1827). Philadelphians were not alone in conducting such investigations into the connection between poverty and poor relief. See Rothman, *The Discovery of the Asylum*, 157–161.

thority, in 1827 attention rested on the issue of illegitimacy. The Board of Guardians, in particular, dwelt at great length on the issue of bastardy—its drain on the public fund, its threat to the public good, its affront to the public morality. The Board was particularly struck by the greater number of bastardy cases in Philadelphia compared to Boston or New York. It is hard not to see this anxiety as disproportionate. The proportion of women (and it was women who were outraging the Board's committee) receiving aid for illegitimate children was relatively small.[35] Yet illegitimacy remained at the heart of the Board's critique of the poor-relief system.

Unmarried mothers condensed the various anxieties that structured the drive for reform. The Board believed that the practice of granting outrelief to women with illegitimate children was "one of the most odious features in their whole system inasmuch as it is an encouragement to vice, and offers a premium for prostitution." The Board of Guardians treated working-class marriage as a form of economic exchange. If "extending relief" to unmarried mothers, "whenever the female cannot find a profitable father for her offspring," did not encourage illegitimacy, the Board asserted, then it was "ignorant of the meaning of words, and incapable of estimating the moral consequences of things." Yet beyond the encouragement to illegitimate sexuality lay the implications of outrelief for relations of authority and dependence. "Let any one whose convictions on this point are not sufficiently clear," the Board averred, come to the meetings when "the committee on bastardy pay the weekly allowances to their pensioners, and mark the unblushing effrontery, that some of them exhibit." These were women who did not know their place. "The thanklessness with which they receive their allotted stipend; the insolence with which they demand a further supply, arrogantly exacting as a *right*, what ought never to have been granted, even as a charity" all demonstrated a sex out of control, draining not only the public purse but threatening the social fabric as well.[36] Ultimately, the women's unruliness most affronted the committee.

At stake was the relationship between the family, the market, and the state. Both Meredith's committee and the Board of Guardians hoped to strengthen paternal authority and familial discipline by subordinating working-class families to the rigors of the market. Unlike, say, Roberts Vaux's school board, who defined themselves against an alliance of manufacturers and mothers, reformers of the poor laws sought to remove the barriers between the market and family survival. If Meredith's committee believed that poor relief posed especial danger to a "manufacturing population," its strategies did little to di-

35. Philadelphia Board of Guardians, *Report,* 6–7, 12, 13, 16, 18, 19, 28–29. Clement estimates that, between 1814 and 1826, anywhere from 4 to 20 percent of the women on the outdoor rolls fitted this status. See her *Welfare and the Poor,* 74.

36. Philadelphia Board of Guardians, *Report,* 29.

minish the relationships of subordination within the manufacturing economy itself. The committee believed it could reconstruct the working-class family (or at least its vision of the working-class family) by reasserting its dependence on market forces. In turn, the market would be sustained if families were compelled to labor. If poor relief destroyed the independence of fathers, it simultaneously made women too independent—of both market restraints and the authority of individual males (whether fathers or the members of the Board). As its critics saw it, the poor-relief system effectively inverted appropriate structures of independence and subordination between men and women and between poor families and the market.

At this point, confinement assumed center stage in the discussion of poor relief. The Committee to Consider the Subject of the Pauper System did examine a series of related issues: the limits of authority over the poor-relief system and the poor themselves, the inadequacy of the physical plant at the almshouse, the problems posed by immigrants, and the question of illegitimacy. But, both the guardians and the committee emphasized the confinement of the poor. If Meredith and his legislative allies hoped to abolish public poor-relief, public and institutional pressures within Philadelphia pointed to an expansion in the use of a house of employment. Both committees retained their faith in confinement: it was outrelief that they opposed. To their minds, outrelief constructed a degrading and nonproductive dependence from which there was no escape.[37] The answer lay in a renewed commitment to confinement. In effect, public officials acknowledged that the state needed to supplement market and family authority.

But it would be a reformed confinement. Both the Board of Guardians and the Committee to Consider the Subject of the Pauper System were highly critical of the organization and functioning of the house of employment. In large part, their concerns centered on the issues of classification and space. As the Board noted, "the great defect of our Alms House is, that from want of room, adequate accommodations for the employment of the paupers cannot be had; and from its imperfect construction, a suitable classification of the inmates cannot be effected."[38] As with the prison, inadequate space precluded continuing labor and sufficient classification. And, without labor and classification, no good could come of confinement in the city's almshouse.

These anxieties with labor and classification were linked to the danger of mimetic corruption. Both groups maintained that habits of idleness, intemperance, and irresponsibility were spread from the poor to the poor. "Under this promiscuous association," the Committee to Consider the Subject of the Pauper System declared, "it is not surprising that few escape the contaminat-

37. Ibid., 24; [Philadelphia], *Report of the Committee,* 17.
38. Philadelphia Board of Guardians, *Report,* 25.

ing influence of vicious example," a fact that led the almshouse to manifest "moral depravity, disgraceful to the age and community in which we live."[39] Congregating the poor could only diminish the sense of shame and desire for independence—at least if officials did not sufficiently control inmate communication and interaction.

But the arguments for classification moved to the grounds of knowledge and health. As the committee noted, the almshouse lumped together different classes of the ill indiscriminately. Especially within the hospital wards, inadequate classification threatened inmate health—those with more dangerous diseases infected those with lesser illnesses. Nor were the conditions of the hospital satisfactory. Both the extent and organization of medical space prevented adequate care. Thus, the dangers to inmates and the costs to the public of caring for continually ill inmates increased. Inadequate classification and medical space also inhibited the production of knowledge. The almshouse had long functioned as a teaching as well as a therapeutic arena. Medical students and young doctors provided services in exchange for access to patients. But the state of the surgical and clinical wards, whose "intention" was "to place at the disposal of the clinical lecturer, the most important and interesting cases of disease," were the "most objectionable of any in the establishment."[40] The space and equipment to turn the poor into proper objects of science was lacking.

This theme of knowledge was not limited to the scientific realm. Indeed, it helped justify expanding the surveillance of the poor and eliminating outrelief. Pointing to the possibilities of deception under the existing system, the Committee to Consider the Subject of the Pauper System advocated the creation of a new cadre of visitors of the poor to investigate more actively the claims for relief. These visitors would, when a request for aid was received, examine the claimant and report "in writing" to the next meeting of the Board of Guardians the "name, residence, age, sex, colour, birth-place, cause of impoverishment, and number of children" of the applicant. The Board, if they felt the claim justified, would determine the form and extent of aid. But this aid, beyond admission to the almshouse, could only be temporary—and could not consist of money.[41] The committee not only advocated moving confinement to center stage of the poor-relief system; they also sought greater discrimination among applicants. Each step meant that "deception" would become more difficult and that a greater governance of the poor would be possible.

Yet, more was at stake than a simple question of public policy. As the fears

39. [Philadelphia], *Report of the Committee,* 9–10.
40. Ibid., 9–12, 11.
41. Ibid., 13–14.

over paternal authority and responsibility, female sexuality and illegitimacy, intemperance and indolence, and charity and class conflict indicate, pauperism (like criminality) symbolized a rift in the social fabric itself. The growth of poverty and pauperism could mean only one of two things: either there was a fundamental flaw in the organization of society and economy, or society itself was menaced by an alien form within its boundaries. The Philadelphia gentlemen who elaborated the discourse on poverty after the War of 1812 refused the former position. Society and economy were not riven with internal contradictions; instead, they had not fully extended their sway over the population. The poor were to blame for their own ignorance; it was the duty of the state to reeducate them.

III

During the 1820s and 1830s, the Philadelphia Magdalen Society, seeking to overcome the resistance of prostitutes and the apathy of society, also transformed and extended its efforts. The Magdalen Society saw itself primarily in terms of Christian charity—fulfilling in a modern context Jesus' commandment to redeem prostitutes from sin. Leaders of the Magdalen Society stressed the importance of classification and subordination, sharing with poor-relief reformers an emphasis on the importance of charitable ignorance and sexual behavior and with proponents of the penitentiary a conviction of the centrality of separation and conscience. But more clearly than either, the travails of the Magdalen Society and its inmates demonstrated the class and gender contradictions of nineteenth-century social discipline. The leaders' efforts set them apart from the conventional desire of their class and sex to look away from the condition of the magdalens, and their understanding of prostitution—as a story of an individual woman's inexorable slide into sin—blinded them to the necessities of working-class womanhood. These contradictions helped shape the reform effort. In the end, the incomplete hold of the disciplinary project stimulated its expansion.

Philadelphians organized the Magdalen Society in 1800. Led by members of the city's religious, social, and economic elite, the Magdalen Society not only dispensed individual instruction but opened an asylum for prostitutes in 1808.[42] Men ran the society, although a female matron directed the day-to-day life of the asylum. Over time, the male leaders of the organization also enlisted the assistance of female visitors.

42. On the formation of the Magdalen Society and its ties to the city's financial and professional elite, see Marcia Roberta Carlisle, "Prostitutes and Their Reformers in Nineteenth Century Philadelphia" (Ph.D. diss., Rutgers University, 1982), 156–162. For an example of the Magdalen Society's early ideological message, see Magdalen Society of Philadelphia, *Advice to a Magdalen* (Philadelphia, 1800).

Most of the Magdalens were young women. Having either sought out the attention of the Magdalen Society or having been brought to the attention of the managers through a stay in the almshouse, they were secluded in the asylum under the supervision of the matron and her assistants. There they received religious instruction and training in domestic skills and suffered subjection to the discipline of the house. When they showed signs of repentance, or at least continued submission to the government of the matron, the Magdalen Society's managers attempted to return them to society. The asylum was a staging area for the reintegration of individual women into the family—either through marriage, indenture, or family reconciliation.[43] Like the reformed version of the poor-relief system, the Magdalen Society's aim and structure embodied a restored patriarchal authority.

The Magdalen Society and its asylum had limited reach. Unlike later antiprostitution societies, the managers of the Magdalen Society waited for young women to come to them or to be led to them by other institutions. Once a woman had made contact with a manager, her case was reviewed, and, if she appeared acceptable, she was admitted to the asylum. From 1808 to the mid-1830s, more than four hundred women entered the asylum, and the Magdalen Society claimed to have redeemed a sizeable number of their charges.[44]

Repentance among the asylum's inmates was sporadic. In fact, resistance and escape were constant occurrences in the asylum. Inmates violated the rules of the house, entered and left without the matron's permission, and, in many cases, "eloped" permanently. Despite the managers' vision of the asylum as a peaceable home for wayward and penitent women, in practice the house was riven with conflicts and struggles between the inmates and their governors.[45]

Consequently, throughout the 1820s and the 1830s, the managers produced a continuing narrative to explain the asylum experience and justify its labors. Their interpretation focused on the problems of indolence, habit, apathy,

43. On the age of the magdalens and their institutional experiences, see Carlisle, "Prostitutes and Their Reformers," 167–169. On the rules for the asylum, see ibid., 165–166. For early examples of the expectations of reform and the placing out of inmates, see MSCMS, Aug. 2, Nov. 1, 1808. For the labor within the asylum, see ibid., Feb. 7, 1809.

44. Magdalen Society of Philadelphia, *Report of the Managers of the Magdalen Asylum for 1835* (Philadelphia, 1836), 6–7. For other, more activist, prostitution societies, see Carlisle, "Prostitutes and Their Reformers," 125–136; Timothy J. Gilfoyle, *City of Eros: New York City, Prostitution, and the Commercialization of Sex, 1790–1920* (New York, 1992), 182–184; and, especially, Carroll Smith-Rosenberg, *Disorderly Conduct: Visions of Gender in Victorian America* (New York, 1985), 109–128.

45. Resistance began almost immediately in the asylum. For some indications of the continuing struggles over discipline or escapes (or "eloping" as the records had it), see MSCMS, Feb. 2, 1808, July 3, 1810, Sep. 4, 1811, July 7, 1812, Dec. 7, 1813, Feb. 1, 1814, Feb. 6, 1816, Feb. 2, 1819, Mar. 7, Apr. 3, May 2, 1826, Nov. 2, 1830.

contempt, and, most especially, on the dangers of duplicity. Priding themselves on their successes, they presented the Magdalen Society and its efforts
as heroic struggles against not only social indifference but the stained characters of their charges.

At the center of their analysis lay the tarnished nature of their inmates. In
the managers' perception of prostitution, seduction and duplicity took center
stage. Most obvious was the fall into prostitution, that initial seduction that
sent the magdalen sliding downward to her fate. But the magdalen herself, so
reformers feared, embodied duplicity, and her very presence threatened seduction. She was not only stained by others' lust, but she threatened to stain
the very effort of redemption.

The managers believed that prostitution left its victims bereft of good character and judgment. The limits to the asylum's success, therefore, were not
surprising. After all, the magdalens' "powers of mental perception appear to
be peculiarly weakened." They were "frequently observed to judge of acts and
their consequences by false standards," and even when they heard the call to
reform and honestly desired to repent, "yet unsubdued tempers, subtle per-
suasion of others, and the deceitfulness of the human heart" all posed "powerful obstacles to perseverance in the ways of rectitude."[46] In effect, the life of
prostitution had stripped the magdalens of their will to virtue. They were left
in constant danger of resisting the words of mercy and submitting to the seductions of vice.

To make matters worse, the enticements of vice were present within the asylum itself. The managers feared that duplicity stealthily infiltrated the asylum.
Young women, they claimed, entered the house without truly desiring redemption and reform, hoping to find temporary respite from their duties or
to seduce fellow inmates back to the trade. These women posed especial problems, for no matter how carefully the managers questioned them, there was
always the possibility that their mask of repentance would remain firm, that
their deception would work. It was "not in the power of man," the managers
noted, "to scrutinize the heart, and although abundant care is taken to ascertain that all applications are grounded in sincerity," it was not possible "to
search out every motive which influences a degraded female to enter such a
house."[47]

In part, the difficulties stemmed from the confusion of the inmates driven
to the house from temporary dangers or difficulties. If they did not truly desire penitence and continued in their indolent and vicious ways, they could
undermine the efforts of those truly struggling for penitence. Beyond this pos-

46. Magdalen Society, *Report for 1829* (Philadelphia, 1830), 5. See also *Report for 1826*
(Philadelphia, 1827), 9, *1828* (Philadelphia, 1829), 5.
47. Magdalen Society, *Report for 1826*, 9.

sibility lay a greater danger, that "a settled and deep design to entice away Magdalens in the house" led "some abandoned women to enter the asylum." These latter women threatened the very being of the asylum with their "deceitful allurements."[48] Given the weaknesses of the magdalens and their histories of vice, the possibility that these seducers would succeed seemed all too real.

To contain these dangers, the managers called for both more rigorous classification and expanded space. They argued that only greater separation of the magdalens (according to their relative progress toward penitence) as well as the isolation of all new magdalens could ensure the success of the asylum's efforts. Such separation would have two benefits. First, it would provide greater opportunities to observe, monitor, and evaluate new inmates. And, second, it would prevent those who retained their old values and practices from influencing those more subject to the rules and values of the asylum. In this way, the managers believed, the language of order, mercy, and repentance would no longer be contested by the language of pleasure, indolence, and sin.[49]

The managers of the Magdalen Society, then, recapitulated the logic of mimetic corruption and its institutional remedies. Confronted with a gap between their hopes and the realities of the asylum's success, they conceptualized the problem as a combination of dangerous communication and damaged subjectivity. The asylum's failures resulted when one of three elements was brought into play: a magdalen's inability to reform herself, an active and malicious duplicity, or the seductive presence of the unredeemed. The managers thus focused the problem of failure on the personality of their charges—explaining the limits of reformation in terms of the internal flaws of their subjects.

The Magdalen Society did not argue that prostitutes were inherently evil. Like many later and more feminist approaches to the question of prostitution, they argued that male lust lay at the origins of prostitutes' careers. Any "history of the inmates of a Magdalen Asylum would be a history of the treachery and shame of man." Indeed, this fact necessitated their efforts. Since men's desire lay at the root of prostitution, "we should do all in our power to repair the injuries which have been done by the base and reckless of our sex."[50] Their efforts, they believed, would bring a healing sympathy to the outcast.

48. Magdalen Society, *Report for 1826*, 9–10. See also, *Report for 1828*, 5; MSCMS, Feb. 8, 1826, Feb. 1, 1831.

49. Magdalen Society, *Report for 1826*, 10, *1827*, 8–9, *1828*, 5–6, *1829*, 6–7, *1830* (Philadelphia, 1831), 6–7.

50. Magdalen Society, *Report for 1834* (Philadelphia, 1835). For analyses of female, and more feminist, approaches to prostitution, see Smith-Rosenberg, *Disorderly Conduct*, 109–128; Judith R. Walkowitz, *Prostitution and Victorian Society: Women, Class, and the State* (Cambridge, 1980); Christine Stansell, *City of Women: Sex and Class in New York, 1789–1820* (New York, 1986), 69; and below for Philadelphia's Female Moral Reform Society.

But the Magdalen Society's managers coded this sympathy within the rhetoric of melodramatic seduction. Tracing the evolution of a prostitute from a position as an orphan "cast upon a friendless world," lacking in a "mother's voice" or a "father's blessing," left to fend for herself "without a guide, counsellor, protector, or friend," it was not surprising that she became a "dupe of some artful enemy" or, perhaps, was "beguiled into the path of licentious pleasure." Even those with parents could be "deceived, insulted, and abandoned."[51] Once entered on this path, the inner drive of her licentiousness and degradation led the prostitute into further sin. As a result, the managers focused their attention on the shape of individual character, not on prostitution as a social institution. The Magdalen Society understood its mission as individual rectification, not of men and their lusts, but of women engaged in sin. The fragility of childhood family structure may have made the magdalen susceptible to the advances of a deceiving rake, but the Magdalen Society did not aim to transform social organization.

The Magdalen Society's individualistic frame of reference also shaped their understanding of the asylum's relationship to prostitution in the city. Aware of their limited reach, the managers consistently bemoaned the small number of magdalens who came under their charge. As they saw it, failed communication and narrow vision underlay the small numbers. Prostitutes were simply unaware of the asylum and its benefits, and their ignorance kept them away. It struck the managers as "incredible, that of the number who have been betrayed or seduced into crime, and who are debarred from their homes as places of repentance," in 1834 "no more than twenty should seek the peaceful and secluded retreat" of the asylum. The only explanation, they believed, was that the city's prostitutes were misinformed about the purposes and practices of the asylum. Until this knowledge was widespread, "the institution may be regarded in the most repulsive light." "Its very privacy and quiet, which gives it the character of just such a home as the true penitent would choose, may cause it to be misrepresented as a place of gloomy imprisonment and restraint."[52]

If Philadelphia's prostitutes misunderstood the nature of the institution, the community displayed "a profound apathy" about prostitutes. In a city that teemed with charitable organizations, the managers charged that a "morbid sensibility" shaped popular feelings toward prostitutes. Contrary to Jesus' example, Philadelphians turned their backs on the "miserable beings" that the

---

51. Magdalen Society, *Report for 1830*, 3–4.

52. Magdalen Society, *Report for 1834*, 6–7. For similar attempts to analyze why prostitutes were not being drawn to the asylum, see *Report for 1833* (Philadelphia, 1834), 5–6, where lack of contact through the almshouse is blamed; MSCMS, Feb. 1, 1831, where the difficulty of reaching through the culture of prostitution is highlighted; and the *Report for 1835*, 5, where, once again, ignorance of the society's goals is blamed.

Magdalen Society attempted to salvage. Rather than seeking out the fallen in order to bring them back to the fold of decency, the "virtuous, amiable, high-minded, and even pious" of the city displayed little "pity" on "behalf of the hundreds who are rapidly rushing to ruin." At the same time, while citizens turned their backs on the suffering prostitute, they did nothing to punish those who caused the descent into vice, "the violators of the tenderest confidence, the destroyers of female purity, and the authors of untold miseries!"[53] The city at large reversed the proper order of condemnation. Leaving the prostitute in the vortex of vice, they welcomed her seducer into society. In doing so, they not only turned their backs on Christian charity but perpetuated the very vice they claimed to scorn.

From the vantage point of the managers, the prostitutes' ignorance and ignorance about the prostitutes were linked. And so long as they persisted, no real progress was possible. Consequently, in the 1830s, the managers welcomed the assistance of bourgeois women who proposed taking the Magdalen Society's message out to the fallen. In the middle of the decade, matrons began to visit both the asylum and the abodes of prostitutes. In the former, they sought to heighten the inmates' desire for reformation and discipline; in the latter, they hoped to encourage prostitutes to come to the asylum. In this way, the Magdalen Society aimed to expand its reach through home visits and to mobilize the efforts of women to transform both the city and the Magdalen Society's charges.[54]

Despite the increasing reliance on the aid of women, these efforts did not undermine the essentially patriarchal structure of the Magdalen Society or its asylum. The practices of the Magdalen Society stood in stark contrast to the short-lived efforts of the city's Female Moral Reform Society. Founded in 1837 by women concerned about the "increasing impurity of the day" and modeled on its predecessor in New York, the Female Moral Reform Society attempted to increase public attention and discussion of prostitution and seduction and to raise the public pressure on men who engaged in illicit sex. Unlike the Magdalen Society, the Female Moral Reform Society practiced public, self-activated, and evangelical intervention by pious women on the issue of illicit sexuality. They proposed distributing the radical *Moral Advocate* and actively exposing and ostracizing "licentious men."[55]

To their dismay, the Female Moral Reform Society received little or no

---

53. Magdalen Society, *Report for 1832* (Philadelphia, 1833), 7–8.

54. Magdalen Society, *Report for 1834*, 8; Minutes of the Managers of the Magdalen Society, Mar. 4, 1834, Magdalen Society Records, HSP.

55. Robert W. Landis, *An Address at the First Anniversary of the Female Moral Reform Society of Philadelphia, on the Evening of September 27th, 1838, to Which Is Appended the First Annual Report of the Society* (Philadelphia, 1838), 16–18, 18. This pamphlet contained not

support from existing moral reform agencies. Indeed, it reported, those who had "zealously engaged in the promotion of other moral and benevolent enterprises" had "evinced a coldness and indifference, and, in some instances, hostility" toward its efforts. The Magdalen Society does not appear to have supported its more active efforts. In the face of open hostility, the Female Reform Society, with its open challenge to the city's sex and gender systems, disappeared.[56]

In effect, the Female Moral Reform Society threatened to overturn the moral and sexual understanding of prostitution. Despite the Magdalen Society's acknowledgment of male responsibility for prostitution, its efforts remained centered on the moral character of the magdalens—it did not strive to reform men. The Female Moral Reform Society, on the other hand, focused its efforts as much on the seducers as on the seduced. Although each society continued to encode prostitution within a tale of individual moral failing, the Female Moral Reform Society endangered the liberties of male sexuality.

If its gender assumptions shaped the Magdalen Society, its class perspectives were equally binding. The Magdalen Society abstracted prostitution from its social environment and individualized both the causes and remedies for the prostitutes' condition. As the Magdalen Society saw it, prostitution was both sign and cause of a fundamentally moral and individual degeneration. Any woman engaging in illicit sex was "fallen," and the only possible response was to isolate her from her surroundings, reconstruct her character, and place her under the watchful control of a family. This perspective ignored the connections between prostitution and the necessities of working-class life and culture. On the one hand, most prostitution in the antebellum city was part of a wider continuum of male-female negotiation over sexual access and financial support. Despite the growing bourgeois idealization of love, sexual relations remained embedded in wider inequalities of economic power and physical force, and young women often engaged in prostitution as part of wider strategies of economic survival. On the other hand, prostitution was a form of wage labor and was tied both directly and indirectly to the larger wage economy. Women turned to prostitution to supplement inadequate wages or to escape from poverty or a difficult family situation.[57]

---

only an address on the subject but the first (and, as far as I have been able to determine, only) annual report of the Female Moral Reform Society along with its stated principles.

56. Ibid., 16. I am assuming the disappearance of the Female Moral Reform Society on the basis of the absence of any continuing records. In the 1840s, a new female-directed association for prostitutes, the Rosine Association, was created clearly as an attempt to overcome female dissatisfaction with the Magdalen Society. On the latter effort, see Carlisle, "Prostitutes and Their Reformers," 126–136.

57. Mathew Carey, *Miscellaneous Essays* ... (1830; reprint, New York, n.d.), 268; Carlisle, "Prostitutes and their Reformers," 11–14.

Young working-class women often moved back and forth between other forms of wage labor and prostitution. Driven by financial necessity, prostitutes were an accepted and understood part of working-class life. Rather than a rigid mark of social deviance and marginality, prostitution was a fluid social state for most of its practitioners.[58]

The managers of the Magdalen Society institutionalized the very social division they saw as inherent to prostitution. Even the cases when a magdalen returned to her family or left the asylum to marry contained no social message for the managers. They continued to assume that the prostitute was a creature apart, bereft, without resources, cast out by family and friends. Whereas the prostitutes appear to have used the asylum as a social way station, the managers understood it as a moral hospital. The walls of the asylum imposed the barriers between the magdalen and her community that the Magdalen Society claimed to overcome.

IV

If the history of the Magdalen Society demonstrated how disciplinary institutions helped sustain the barriers they sought to overcome, Philadelphia's House of Refuge revealed the growing dispersion and autonomy of the disciplinary realm itself. Incorporated in 1826 and opened in 1828, the House of Refuge incarcerated youthful delinquents, subjecting them to a regime of labor, vocational training, religious instruction, and discipline. The Refuge's managers constructed the institution as a supplement and alternative to the city's prison. But, in the end, their efforts helped transform the relationship of discipline not only to the prison but to the family. Seeking to supplement the prison, they reversed the relationship between discipline and penality. And, in doing so, they subordinated the claims of the family to the interests of institutional efficiency. As in the movements to institute public education or reform the poor-relief system, anxieties over the weakness of working-class parental authority served ultimately to expand the sway of disciplinary practice.

Beginning early in the 1820s, the Philadelphia Society for Alleviating the Miseries of Public Prisons began to investigate creating a separate institution for juveniles. Concerned with the dangers of depravity within the adult prison, they urged that youthful offenders be separated from their more corrupt elders and placed in a unique rehabilitative regime. Their aim, they assured the public, was to save youthful offenders from the corruptions of the prison and thereby help prevent the reproduction of criminality in the city. Encouraged by the success of similar institutions in New York and England, the Society

58. See Carlisle, "Prostitutes and Their Reformers," 33–40; Stansell, *City of Women*, 172–192.

enlisted the support of some of the city's leading figures (including United States senator John Sergeant) and pushed successfully for public support and state sanction.[59] The Refuge was a hybrid institution. Although it remained in private hands, it received state funds and was closely tied to magistrates in the city and throughout the state. Its hybridity gave it the practical flexibility, legal authority, and fiscal stability to extend the reach of the disciplinary apparatus further into the life of the city.

The Refuge's managers believed that a spiral of corruption haunted the penal system. Noting that "imitation is the natural propensity of youth," the managers bemoaned the condition of young offenders in the city's prison. Although recognizing that much had been accomplished in separating the less corrupt from the "votaries of crime," the segregation was incomplete and the dangers ever present: "Surrounded by those who have reached maturity of crime with maturity of years, the tendency to corruption is so obvious as scarcely to be resisted."[60] Unless some more permanent isolation of youthful offenders was achieved, punishment would serve merely to restrain, not to reform, and, in so doing, inadvertently contribute to perpetuating criminality.

But the origins of youthful criminality had deeper roots than the disorganized prison. Corruption began in the streets, and indiscipline resulted from the family. As John Sergeant stated the position, the children of the poor faced the greatest danger. "They are generally neglected and destitute," Sergeant maintained, "frequently without parents or friends to advise or direct them; and there are not wanting numerous instances in which abandoned parents, for their own gratification, direct their children into the paths of vice, by sending them into the streets to beg or to steal." Even when the intent of parents was not evil, as in "the case of the widowed mother," powerless to prevent her son's descent into the world of vice, the weaknesses of domestic authority among the poor necessitated the construction of new institutions of governance.[61] The working-class family, Refuge defenders argued, failed to produce the disciplined individual that liberal society needed to function. And, if laboring parents failed in this task, then the state or its delegated agents must act.

Proponents of the House of Refuge thereby joined the wider assault on working-class life that underlay the reformation of poor-relief and the re-

59. Minutes, Mar. 17, 1824, Apr. 12, 1824, Jan. 21, 1826, PSAMPP; [Philadelphia, House of Refuge], *An Address from the Managers of the House of Refuge to Their Fellow Citizens* (Philadelphia, 1826), 4–5, 12–16; John Sergeant, *An Address Delivered before the Citizens of Philadelphia, at the House of Refuge, on Saturday, the Twenty-ninth of November, 1828* (Philadelphia, 1828), 4–6. See Robert Forster to John Sergeant, Jan. 15, 1827, Vaux Papers, HSP, for a report on the London House of Refuge.

60. [Philadelphia, House of Refuge], *An Address from the Managers*, 5.

61. Sergeant, *An Address*, 18–19, quotation on 18.

invigoration of the Magdalen asylum. Their argument effectively naturalized poor youth, reducing them to "material" to be shaped. As they saw it, life among the laboring poor constituted a ferocious terrain. Whether through parental neglect or nefariousness, the blank slate of childhood innocence was turned too often into a "second nature" of vice and criminality. The House of Refuge, they contended, needed to remove the children of the poor from the control of their parents, isolate them from the culture of the streets, and then reshape their physical, mental, and moral character. They would be recreated as proper individuals—industrious, disciplined, deferential, and moral.

The managers encouraged city officials to sweep the streets of undomesticated children. "If the vigilance of the magistracy were so exerted, as to leave not one infant beggar in the streets, not one vagrant child . . . the darling hope might be realized of an almost total cessation of prison discipline." But, the managers cautioned, the hopes of the institution could be achieved only if poor children were seized early enough: "In proportion to the tenderness of years is the hope of reformation. . . . If the public, and especially the officers of justice, would enable us to withdraw the unhappy children of iniquity, in *actual childhood,* from the haunts and the practices, and the temptations of crime, we could almost insure their restoration to the world with virtuous habits formed, and hearts strengthened to resist the allurements of vice." Through misguided sympathy, however, magistrates and parents too often refrained from committing the very young to the institution. The result was that the "material" of youth had been turned into the "*second nature*" of the criminal; "the love of wickedness" turned into a "master passion in consequence of a long course of habitual indulgence."[62]

The physical organization of the House of Refuge represented the division between the Refuge and the streets. The grounds contained a main front building that held a library, offices, and living space for the managers, the officers, and the officers' families. Two wings of individual cells extended back from the front, one for male inmates and one for female. Each cell contained a small bed and shelf and was "exposed at all times to absolute superintendence and inspection." The dormitory wings also contained rooms for schools, and workshops were placed elsewhere within the compound. The institution held a kitchen, infirmary, and chapel—the latter large enough "to keep the different sexes from conversation and even from seeing each other." The complex as a whole, the managers assured the public, was spacious enough to allow for physical recreation within the outer walls.[63]

The entire regime of the House of Refuge endeavored to effect a transfor-

62. Philadelphia House of Refuge, *Second Annual Report* (Philadelphia, 1830), 6, *Fourth Annual Report* (Philadelphia, 1832), 5–6.

63. Philadelphia, House of Refuge, *First Annual Report* (Philadelphia, 1829), 4–5.

mation of character. Male inmates were awakened at quarter to five in the morning. At five, "after washing and combing," the boys were brought together for religious service. They then were sent to their respective classrooms. At seven in the morning, they breakfasted, and they labored from half past seven until noon, when they had lunch and then listened to "a lesson or lecture on some useful, moral, or scientific subject" until one in the afternoon. Four more hours of labor then followed—and if they finished their assigned tasks, "half an hour [was] allowed for recreation and play." The inmates then returned to school, where they remained until a quarter to eight in the evening, after which they engaged in evening prayer and then returned to their rooms. At this point, the managers reported, "the dormitories [were] all safely locked." The House of Refuge aimed to be, for its inmates at least, a world apart. Once they entered, contact with society would be controlled, visitors limited, and the spatial parameters of everyday life carefully set.[64]

The world of the Refuge was deeply gendered. Officials attempted to segregate boys from girls totally—providing them with separate wings and classrooms, designing the chapel for separate worship, and dividing the vocational training according to sex. A steward had general oversight of the institution and its inmates, but immediate oversight of the girls was in the hands of a matron and her assistant. Although the matron and her assistant were placed under the authority of the steward (they were only allowed to leave the premises with his permission), the steward's contact with the female inmates occurred through the mediation of the matron. Males were allowed into the female compartment only when accompanied by the matron or assistant matron, and only the matron or her assistant was allowed to "search or examine the female delinquents."[65]

The matron's duties were more explicitly religious than the steward's. She was to "unfold to those under her charge, the advantage of a moral and religious life, and to impress upon them a conviction of the evils and miseries that attend the wicked and profligate." A "ladies Committee," established in the initial organization of the Refuge, aided the matron. Drawn from among the female bourgeoisie (and in its initial year including Sarah Grimké), the

64. Ibid., 7–8. According to the report, "with some slight variations, the occupations and duties of the females are conducted in a like manner." Ibid., 8. For some sense of the attempt to control inmates' movement and location, see section XVI on "separation and classification," and section XVII on "general regulations" in *Rules and Regulations for the Government of the House of Refuge,* in Philadelphia, House of Refuge, *The Act Incorporating the House of Refuge and Laws Relative Thereto, Together with the Rules and Regulations for Its Government and List of Officers, Managers, Etc.* (Philadelphia, 1829), 13–24 (the relevant sections are on 23–24).

65. See sections VI and VII on the "Steward" and "Matron and Assistants" in *Rules and Regulations,* in Philadelphia, House of Refuge, *Act Incorporating the House of Refuge,* 18–20, quotation on 19.

ladies' committee not only inspected the female department but also was charged to "excite in the girls a sense of virtue and piety; to inculcate habits of industry, cleanliness, and strict attention to the direction of the Matron, and the rules of the House; and to reward those who have distinguished themselves for industry and good conduct." Like the Magdalen Society, its organizational structure embodied a patriarchal order—governed ultimately by men, with women and clergymen providing immediate moral and religious oversight. At the same time, and to a far greater degree than the social world outside its walls, it aimed at gender subordination and the separation of spheres.[66]

Nor did the gendered division of labor appear only on paper. The boys worked at a variety of tasks—making and cutting nails, boxes, cases, boots, and shoes, binding books, and picking wool, for example. The girls, on the other hand, were set to tailoring, sewing, knitting, and "housewifery." In fact, the girls were the main producers of clothing for the institution. This division continued after inmates left the institution. The House of Refuge prepared inmates for indenture, the managers seeking to bind out their subjects after a year in the Refuge. The boys were indentured to a variety of occupations (mostly farming but also various artisanal skills); the girls were dispatched as domestic servants.[67] If the Refuge aimed primarily to make the boys disciplined workers, the matron was tasked with preparing the girls to enter the domestic world as dutiful servants and wives.

In practice, the House of Refuge's charges, like the magdalens, were not al-

66. Ibid., 17, 20. I do not want to imply that no thought was given to the moral character of the boys or that the duties of the managers and the steward were not also geared to moral education. But I do want to draw attention to the ways in which the moral education of the girls was highlighted and that of the boys was largely subsumed under the larger disciplinary regime.

The concern for a proper domestic order, especially with regard to the females, emerges as well in the regulations governing the "Indenturing or Apprenticing Committee." Although there is a general prohibition of indenturing an inmate to "a tavern-keeper, or a retailer or distiller of spirituous liquors," there is also a specific command that "no girl shall be apprenticed to an unmarried man, nor placed in boarding houses, or in academies for boys." *Rules and Regulations,* in Philadelphia, House of Refuge, *Act Incorporating the House of Refuge,* 16. The concern to control female sexuality and to protect female charges from sexual abuse was at the heart of the social regulation of the institution.

67. Philadelphia, House of Refuge, *Fourth Annual Report,* 12. On indentures, see, for example, the numbers for May 1, 1829, to May 1, 1830, where it was reported that, of the boys, 16 were indentured to farmers, 1 to a miller, 1 to a shoemaker, 2 to cloth manufacturers, 1 to a tailor, 9 to screwmakers, 1 to a tobacconist, 1 to a merchant, 10 to whaling voyages (a sign that they were not disciplined), 1 to a carpenter, and 2 to papermakers; all 10 indentured girls were sent to housewifery (*Second Annual Report,* 28–29). A similar variation among the boys and the same uniformity among the girls can be found two years later. See, *Fourth Annual Report,* 12.

ways willing to submit to the Refuge's discipline. Reports revealed a series of runaways from the Refuge, individuals dismissed as "improper subjects," and apprentices "returned by their masters." The problems of resistance and recalcitrance, therefore, did not end with entry to the Refuge. Both boys and girls continued to insist on their own rights and to maintain their own behaviors.[68]

But once within the House of Refuge, youth were subject not only to the institution's rules but to its punishments. Disobedience (refusing or neglecting work, challenging the commands of Refuge officials, "profane or indecent language," breaking silence while in the dormitory or during meals, striking an officer or attempting to escape) was subject to a series of escalating punishments. First offenders or minor offenders could be deprived of play or exercise; more serious or continuing transgressions led to a loss of supper, reduction to only bread and water for meals, confinement in solitary cells, corporal punishment "if absolutely necessary," and, finally, "fetters and handcuffs, only in extreme cases."[69]

The infliction of punishment was intricately tied to the purposes and structure of the institution. Both the steward and the matron had authority to inflict immediate punishment. But responsibility lay with the steward. It was his duty to enforce all rules and regulations, record all offenses and punishments, and transmit this information to the managers' executive committee. The managers were insistent on ensuring that all infractions be punished— the principle of "certainty of punishment" had to be upheld so that there would be no "repetition of offence." Indeed, the steward was expected to maintain constant oversight and discipline within the Refuge—all life within its walls needed to be ordered and regular.[70]

68. Philadelphia, House of Refuge, *Fourth Annual Report*, 11–12. The Refuge's managers even recognized the possibility of legitimate resistance in noting that sometimes inappropriate masters were chosen by the indenture committee and that, as a consequence, "it was induced to believe that some of those who leave their place, have good reason for so doing" (12). This position, of course, implies the successful transformation of the inmates. But the larger issue still holds that the inmates were not passive receptacles of authority and that their role in shaping both the context of the Refuge and the practices of the Refuge should not be ignored. For a discussion of this problem, see Stansell, *City of Women*, 203–209, 214–216.

69. Section XIV, "Punishments," in *Rules and Regulations*, in Philadelphia, House of Refuge, *Act Incorporating the House of Refuge*, 22. When corporal punishment of females was called for, it was to be "done by or in the presence of the Matron." Ibid.

70. Ibid., 18–19, 19, 22. See the 10 duties ascribed to the steward, along with the relevant tasks of the matron, her assistants, and the assistant keepers, labor and instruction, and the arrangement of time, ibid., 18–21. As with the other bureaucratic arrangements, these rules were meant to regulate the exercise of authority. In the Refuge, at least, the aim was, not an unbridled control, but a carefully controlled one. In this, the *Rules and Regulations* resembled the original guidelines drawn up for the Walnut Street prison. For a further discussion of this attempt to regularize authority in the disciplinary realm, see below, Chapter 8.

The aim of punishment and regulation was subordination. The Refuge's managers, after all, were convinced that they had to remake the material of their charges, youthful delinquents on the road to the "second nature" of rebellion and criminality. The recurring theme of the Refuge's reports was the transformation from indiscipline and disobedience to regularity and compliance. "No. 35," for example, was from London and lost his father when "very young." His mother "was unable to manage him, and he spent most of his time in the streets, frequently absenting himself altogether." He ran away from two masters, and his mother "finding that the child was going to ruin," sent him to the Refuge when he was thirteen. After time in the Refuge, he and three others were indentured and, the Refuge managers reported proudly in 1830, were "making themselves very useful, and conduct themselves well." The importance of obedience emerges even more clearly in the tale of "No. 33," whose father had died when she was young and whose mother "took little care of her." Before her arrival at the Refuge, she had lived a "most irregular life" and was committed on the charge of vagrancy. But, after "she had been some time under the discipline of the institution, she became docile and obedient," and a place as a servant was found for her. Her new masters were quite pleased: "We believe her to be honest: she is industrious, obedient and kind." In addition, they reported that she had improved in school, attended public worship, and appeared "serious, and religiously inclined."[71] Discipline and dutifulness were the marks of successful transformation.

These practices of punishment highlighted an ideological problem for the institution. The Refuge was designed to remove youthful delinquents from the corrupting atmosphere of the prison—particularly the compartments that held those awaiting trial. The legislature empowered magistrates and the managers to commit youths accused of vagrancy when they judged them appropriate subjects for the Refuge's discipline.[72] But children then could be, and were, sent to the Refuge before their conviction for any offense. In other words, children could be subjected to an effectively penal regime without ever facing a jury.

In response, proponents of the House of Refuge articulated a vision of the Refuge as disciplinary but not penal. The Refuge, they argued, "is not a jail." As Sergeant argued, the jail was a "yawning monster." The Refuge, on the other hand, "inflicts no punishment: it affixes no badge of disgrace; it stamps

71. Philadelphia, House of Refuge, *Second Annual Report*, 25–28. Similar sentiments can be found in the letters from masters included in the *Fourth Annual Report*. Among the different descriptions of the subjects are: "willing to do all that I request of him," "smart, industrious, obedient, and honest," "attends to his work, and seems well satisfied with my treatment of him," "strictly honest, obedient, and industrious," and "sober, industrious, obedient, and honest." *Fourth Annual Report*, 14–15. The examples could be multiplied.

72. Philadelphia, House of Refuge, *Act Incorporating the House of Refuge*, 6–7, 9–10.

no degradation"; instead, it "imposes restraint, for restraint is necessary no less for the good of the subject, than for the security of society." In the Refuge, the city's grand jury argued in 1828, the "misguided and neglected, rather than the guilty child," would find a place, and there, "where virtue will be cherished, and vice repressed," they would overcome their early education in vice and thus be "enabled to bear his part of the public burthens." The managers themselves acknowledged that "the best intentioned individuals" had questioned whether the "restraints imposed in this establishment, were inconsistent with the liberty of the citizen," since many inmates did not have jury trials. In reality, the managers argued, the lack of a jury trial, rather than a sign of tyranny, was an indication of the mercy and justice that motivated the Refuge. The Refuge sought to eliminate not only the "sentence of infamy and pain" that accompanied trial and conviction "but to prevent trial and conviction itself." Although some came to the institution guilty of criminal offenses, a "much larger class happily finds a shelter here" who suffered from "criminal tendency and manifestations," inadequate "means of support," or a lack of "protection and guidance" from "their natural friends." These children were committed, not out of guilt, but because "adequate securities against guilt are wanting."[73]

Refuge officials maintained that their authority was no different from that of the Guardians of the Poor. The guardians, after all, compelled poor children to education and labor: "They confine them, and coerce them to a course of servitude and apprenticeship." This coercion was an act of mercy and indulgence that "flows from a spirit of kindness, which prevents them [the children] from injuring themselves." In sum, coercion could be a positive element for the young: "Miserable would be their condition, if this power were not vested somewhere."[74] Likewise with the Refuge. It was not a punishment to be sent to the Refuge; the Refuge meant the liberation from both punishment and vice.

The managers thereby inverted the relationship between discipline and the penal system and, at the same time, extended the reach of disciplinary practices. The Refuge, after all, had originally been designed to supplement penal authority. By strengthening the division between youthful delinquents and older offenders, its proponents hoped to eliminate the corrupting influence of imprisonment. But when supporters of the Refuge defended confinement without trial, they implied that the same practices could in one context be punishment and in another contain no penal aspect. Discipline, rather than simply being a technique of the penal system, had become a structure within which punishment operated.

73. Ibid., 10; Sergeant, *An Address*, 33, 30; "Presentment of the Grand Jury," ibid., 37; Philadelphia, House of Refuge, *Second Annual Report*, 8–9.

74. Philadelphia, House of Refuge, *Second Annual Report*, 10.

A similar dynamic was at work in the Refuge's relationship to the family. The Refuge aimed not only to correct the corruptive influences of the prison but also to supplement parental authority. The biographies of Refuge inmates who consistently resisted the authority of their parents and masters manifested the tattered state of familial discipline. But, just as in the case of the prison, what began as a supplement quickly assumed a dominant role. According to the Refuge's original rules for visitation, established in 1828, outsiders could visit the Refuge only on Wednesday afternoons and only with the permission of a manager. Family members' privileges were even more stringent. They could come only on the first Friday of each month and, again, only with the permission of the Visiting Committee. Four years later, however, even these limited rights had been substantially curtailed. Now "the parents, guardians, or near relations" could visit the inmates only once every three months, "under such regulations as the Executive Committee may make."[75] In effect, the Refuge intensified its control over the inmates, further lessening the connection between its subjects and their families.

Indeed, the managers suggested that one reason for confinement without trial lay in the added power it gave the institution to deal with families. Citing two cases of mothers who first sent their children to the Refuge and then requested their freedom, the managers reported that their authority enabled them to determine whether to accede to these maternal desires. Unlike the children's asylum, which could not resist parental demand, or the prison, which could not accede to it, the Refuge could exercise its own judgment about the appropriateness of the familial setting.[76] As the managers saw it, individual families had to prove their legitimacy once their children entered the orbit of the Refuge—it was not up to the Refuge to respond to the demands of the families.

V

In the areas of prostitution and delinquency, then, an intensification of discipline occurred during the 1820s and 1830s. Both the managers of the Magdalen Society and the managers of the House of Refuge focused their attention on

---

75. *Rules and Regulations,* in Philadelphia, House of Refuge, *Act Incorporating the House of Refuge,* 24. See the revised *Rules and Regulations of the House of Refuge,* in Philadelphia, House of Refuge, *Fourth Annual Report,* 28. For biographies of inmates, see, for example, Philadelphia, House of Refuge, *Second Annual Report,* 25–28. As the numbers of runaways from the Refuge, individuals dismissed as "improper subjects," and apprentices "returned by their masters" indicates, the problems of resistance and recalcitrance did not end with entry to the Refuge. Both boys and girls continued to insist on their own rights and to maintain their own behaviors. *Fourth Annual Report,* 11–12.

76. Philadelphia, House of Refuge, *Second Annual Report,* 7–8, 11–12.

removing individuals from their social surroundings and providing counter-weights to the structures of working-class life. In each area, as well, issues of proper familial organization and gender or sexual subordination loomed large. Both the Magdalen Society and the Refuge sought to contain and control the dangers of mimetic corruption. By constructing prostitution and delinquency as the result of individual flaws or familial weakness, they both justified the expansion of the disciplinary network and the individualization of the discourse and practice of social discipline.

These tendencies toward disciplinary intensification and individualization were not random practices. A series of statutes and legal decisions reshaped the legal organization of poor-relief, the prison, and the House of Refuge. In each area, the law aimed to strengthen and regularize the exercise of disciplinary authority. The end result was a disciplinary apparatus inscribed in the legal structure of the state.

In 1828, the legislature, responding to years of agitation on the issue of the city's poor, reorganized the structure and emphases of the poor law. They extended the terms of the Board of Guardians to three years (from one), severed the authority to raise the poor tax from the power to spend it, expanded the mechanism for collecting the tax, created the position of visitors of the poor, mandated the construction of a new and expanded complex for confining the poor, and reorganized the settlement laws.[77] In all, the new poor law expanded the capacity to oversee and govern the poor, placed confinement once again at the heart of poor relief, and drew the boundaries of public responsibility more tightly.

In part, these steps aimed to enforce economy. Separating the Board of Guardians (who had previously been empowered to set the poor rates) from the directors of the poor tax as well as establishing the visitors of the poor aimed at eliminating waste and guarding against deception. New regulations to ensure labor within the house of employment and the tightening of the settlement laws aimed at reducing the costs of the poor-relief system and limiting its numbers.[78] In these ways, the new system would lessen the responsibility of those with property for those without.

But the reforms operated at disciplinary and ideological levels as well. By compelling inmates to labor and constructing systems of accounting to credit their work and debit their costs, proponents hoped to drive the poor out of the house of employment into the wage economy and to impose self-discipline and self-regulation. Increasing the power of the Board of Guardians

77. "An Act for the Relief and Employment of the Poor of the City of Philadelphia, the District of Southwark, and the Townships of the Northern Liberties and Penn., Passed 6th March, 1828," in Hazard, ed., *Register of Pennsylvania*, I, 326–331.

78. On the creation of the different boards and their responsibilities, see ibid., 326–328. For the questions of labor and settlement, see ibid., 329–331.

to bind out the children of the poor aspired to control costs, but it also enabled greater intervention into, and control over, the lives of working-class families. The law, for example, empowered the guardians to prevent parents from leaving small children at the public charge and then claiming them when they were old enough to work.[79] Although justified in terms of institutional economy, this power had wider implications. Like the construction of the public schools, the law extended the reach of the paternal state, authorizing it to intervene in the social practices of the poor. And like public schools, it did so to construct a more regulated form of working-class subjectivity and individuality.

Indeed, the more general attack on outrelief and the tightening of discipline within the house of employment aimed to reconstruct a patriarchal family within the working class. The attack on outrelief was an attack on female-headed households. Women were the largest recipients of outrelief in the pre-reform system; men made up the majority of inmates in the house of employment.[80] Tightening the regulation within the institution not only aimed at retraining individuals and imposing new habits of self-discipline but at driving individuals from the relief system and back into the labor market. If reformers aimed to make punishment disciplinary, the reforms of the poor-relief system made discipline punitive. The revamped poor-relief system sought not only to compel males to enter the wage-economy but to tie women to wage earning men in reinvigorated relations of dependence. In these ways, both the market and the patriarchal family would be embedded within the culture of the city's laboring poor.

The state also moved to intensify the power of the penal system to operate on individuals. In 1829, the legislature drafted a new law to govern the operations of the Eastern State Penitentiary. The statute established a Board of Inspectors (appointed by the Supreme Court and serving two-year rather than one-year terms) charged with overseeing the penitentiary, providing the raw materials and other supplies needed in the prison, making reports to the legislature, investigating conditions within the prison, appointing a warden, physician, clerk, and religious instructor for the prison, and setting the salaries for all prison employees. The law required the warden to reside in the prison,

79. "*And whereas* it frequently happens that children, who have been receiving public support for indefinite periods, are claimed by their parents when they arrive at a proper age for being bound out as aforesaid, to prevent such binding.

"Therefore, *Be it enacted by the authority aforesaid,* That the said guardians are authorized to bind out, as aforesaid, all children that have or may receive public support, either in the alms house or children's asylum, although the parents may demand their discharge from said institutions, unless the expenses incurred in their support be refunded; *Provided always,* That care be taken to put all children as aforesaid to proper persons and in respectable families." Ibid., 330.

80. On the relative numbers of relief recipients both within and without the almshouse, see Clement, *Welfare and the Poor,* 70, 76.

see each inmate daily, maintain (with the approval of the inspectors) discipline in the prison, supervise prison record keeping, appoint and dismiss the overseers (or deputy keepers), and report all infractions of prison regulations. The law charged the overseers with continual oversight of the inmates, with each overseer required to visit those inmates under his care three times daily, report their conditions to the warden, and obey institutional rules and the legal orders of the warden. In addition, the legislature mandated the appointment of a prison physician and a religious instructor to "attend to the moral and religious instruction of the convicts." [81]

The law also regulated the treatment of inmates. Prisoners were to be "kept singly and separately at labour, in the cells or work yards of said prisons," be maintained with "wholesome food of a coarse quality, sufficient for the healthful support of life," and supplied "with clothing suited to their situation, at the descretion of the inspectors of said prisons." While imprisoned, "no access" to the inmates was allowed except for the inspectors and officers of the prison, the grand juries of the city and county, official visitors, and individuals admitted by the inspectors "for highly urgent reasons." [82]

The principles of segregation and individuation guided the treatment of the convicts. On arrival at the prison, inmates would be examined by the prison physician, stripped of their clothes, and dressed in prison uniforms. The warden, clerk, and overseers were then to examine the prisoner so that they could become familiar with the prisoner's physical and personal characteristics. All personal effects were to be removed, to be returned when the inmate was released. A standard prison uniform was established, and prisoners were forbidden tobacco and liquor except as the physician commanded. Finally, on release, the warden was to obtain the inmate's history: "what means of literary, moral or religious instruction he or she enjoyed; what early temptations to crime by wicked associations or otherwise he or she was exposed to; his or her general habits, predominant passions, and prevailing vices, and in what part of the country he or she purposes to fix his or her residence." All of these data were to be included in the prison's records. If the inspectors and warden were pleased with the convict's behavior, they could grant him or her a certificate of good behavior and four dollars, "whereby the temptation immediately to commit offences against society, before employment can be obtained, may be obviated." [83]

The legislature, then, structured the Eastern State Penitentiary to avoid the problems that had plagued the Walnut Street Jail. All contact between inmates was forbidden, and the powers and duties of the inspectors and staff were

81. Pennsylvania, Laws, Statutes, etc., *Acts of the General Assembly Relating to the Eastern State Penitentiary,* 11–13, 13, 14–15, 17.
82. Ibid., 7.
83. Ibid., 15–17.

both heightened and more rigorously defined. The law thereby endeavored to increase the capacity for individualization and the regularization of inmate behavior and institutional practice.

As the guidelines for inmate histories demonstrate, the law remained within the logic of mimetic corruption. The new penal apparatus treated the course of criminality as an individual failing rooted in temptation or insufficient education. From the solitary cells through the elaboration of inmate histories, reformed penitential practice sought to bring all the powers of authority to bear on the individual conscience. As the architectural form of the Eastern State Penitentiary hoped to fix the convict under the eye of authority, the new penal statute aimed to institute the bureaucratic mechanisms and institutional regularity to ensure that that authority never wavered. Mimetic corruption would not only be blocked, but its effects would be removed from the individual.

But the clearest indication of the transformed and increasingly autonomous realm of discipline occurred within the area of juvenile delinquency. In 1838, the state's Supreme Court ruled on the constitutionality of the House of Refuge's authority to confine children before a criminal conviction. The case involved the status of Mary Ann Crouse, committed by Morton McMichael, one of the city's justices of the peace, because of a complaint by the child's mother, Mary Crouse. The commitment alleged that "the said infant by reason of vicious conduct, has rendered her control beyond the power of the said complainant, and made it manifestly requisite that from regard to the moral and future welfare of the said infant she should be placed under the guardianship of the managers of the House of Refuge," to which complaint the magistrate agreed. The magistrate had validated the mother's position through testimony of other witnesses.[84] In response, the child's father brought a habeas corpus challenging the constitutionality of the commitment.

The court examined not only the appropriateness of the specific commitment but the constitutionality of the Refuge's authority. At issue was an 1835 statute that dramatically extended the reach of the Refuge. In that year, the legislature had determined that youths could be sent to the Refuge not only upon conviction or commitment for vagrancy but on the complaint of their parents if their "incorrigible or vicious conduct" had rendered them uncontrollable by parental authority. Indeed, children could be committed without parental consent when the child's conduct, combined with "the moral depravity or otherwise of the parent or next friend in whose custody such infant may be," indicated that "such parent or next friend is incapable or unwilling

---

84. "Ex Parte Crouse," in Thomas I. Wharton, *Reports of Cases Adjudged in the Supreme Court of Pennsylvania, in the Eastern District*, Vol. IV, *Containing the Cases Decided at December Term, 1838, and March Term, 1839*, ed. John Sword and I. Tyson Morris (Philadelphia, 1884), 9–10. See, as well, Stansell, *City of Women*, 214–216.

to exercise the proper care and discipline over such incorrigible or vicious infant."[85] The Refuge, thereby, was empowered not only to assist the legal system but to supplement and even override parental authority in the absence of crime.

The court legitimated the power of the Refuge. And it did so by explicitly accepting the notion that the parental power of the state overrode the power of parents. Once again asserting that the Refuge did not punish but educate, the court noted that "the public has a paramount interest in the virtue and knowledge of its members" and, although acknowledging that "parents are ordinarily intrusted with" education, suggested that this was because "it can seldom be put into better hands." But the court ruled, when parents "are incompetent or corrupt, what is there to prevent the public from withdrawing their faculties, held, as they obviously are, at its sufferance?"[86] In other words, the family, rather than being the base of the state, was a representative of it. Discipline, rather than being a supplement of parental authority, overrode it; the latter was suffered to control the familial domain—but only upon good behavior.

The 1820s and 1830s, then, marked the transformation of the disciplinary apparatus from a defensive enclave to an expansionist social strategy. Private reformers and public officials elaborated the disciplinary realm throughout the city. A heightened emphasis on individualization in punishment joined a growing interventionism in working-class life. But with the expansion of discipline came a heightening of its contradictions: new sites of resistance, revelations of its limits, challenges to its authority. Reformers thus revealed the excess proper to the disciplinary project.

Disciplinary institutions not only transformed the practice of discipline but altered their relationship to other sources of social power and authority. Most strikingly, the swarming of the disciplines subordinated the powers of the family while intensifying attention to individuals. This threefold process—of expansion, individualization, and familial reconstruction—lay at the heart of the reforms of the 1820s. Public officials and private reformers aimed to recast the family and the individual in the likeness of liberal society. Rapidly, however, this project of liberal transformation would confront its limit at the heart of the disciplinary realm—the Eastern State Penitentiary.

85. "Ex Parte Crouse," in Wharton, *Reports of Cases,* 10.
86. Ibid., 11.

CHAPTER EIGHT

The Penitential Imagination

T he reorganization of the disciplinary project culminated during the 1830s. Pennsylvania established separate confinement at the Eastern State Penitentiary and abolished public executions. Penitential reformers aimed not only to spiritualize the practice of punishment but to liberate it from the external intrusions that had marred the regime at Walnut Street Jail. At the same time, they strove to remove punishment further from the public at large. State officials and private reformers articulated ever greater claims for institutional autonomy and erected more powerful boundaries between the public and the disciplinary world.

This process, reformers hoped, would institute a new type of authority and give concrete form to the penitential imagination. Penitential proponents believed that Eastern State would enact a new ethics of governance and submission. Reformers hoped that Eastern State would transform not only the individuals subject to it but the very practice of authority; it would not only individualize punishment but spiritualize it. On the one hand, the prison's governors, aided by the power and restraint of penitential architecture, would govern mildly, attending to the souls and thoughts of the prisoners and representing society's quiet support. On the other, inmates, shorn of their contagious and vicious community, would look inward, internalize Christian morality, and meekly submit not only in appearance but in reality. The spirit of redemption would reign.

Yet, instead, the practices of the penitentiary sharpened the contradictions of discipline within liberal society. Rather than an emblem of disciplinary restraint and order, disarray and conflict haunted the new penitentiary. Rather than an exemplification of Enlightenment, the new penitentiary regime found itself charged with cruelty and degradation. And rather than a new form of power acting gently on the spirit, the new penitentiary intensified the materiality of imprisonment. From within the search for a spiritualized punishment, the body returned to the center of punishment; the reform of conscience re-

293

newed the corporality of power. In the end, as the body of the penitentiary acted on the bodies of prisoners, the dreams of redemption generated a dynamically expansive disciplinary realm.

I

The Eastern State Penitentiary opened in 1829. Five inspectors were appointed, including Judge Charles C. Coxe, Thomas Bradford, Jr., Benjamin Richards, and John Swift. Samuel R. Wood, a businessman and member of the Philadelphia Society for Alleviating the Miseries of Public Prisons, was appointed warden; and Franklin Bache, physician. Bradford, Richards, Swift, and Wood had been inspectors at Walnut Street. Richards and Swift also served terms as mayor of Philadelphia. The first inmate arrived on October 25, 1829. Charles Williams, an eighteen-year-old black man, had been convicted of burglary in Delaware County and sentenced to two years' imprisonment. He was examined by a doctor from the city and kept temporarily in the infirmary. On October 28, Williams requested to "be allowed" to work. But it was not until November 20 that he was put to shoemaking.[1] The Pennsylvania system of separate confinement had begun.

The inspectors were confident of the penitentiary's effects on individuals. In their *First and Second Annual Reports,* they reported that, on the arrival of a convict, "he is placed in a cell and left alone, without work and without any book. His mind can only operate on itself; generally, but few hours elapse before he petitions for something to do, and for a bible." If the inmate had a trade, such work was granted as a "favour"; if not, then one of the overseers, "all of whom are master workmen in the trades they respectively superintend and teach," would train him. Certain that "intemperance and thoughtless folly" were "the parents of crime" and that prisons were "peopled by those who have seldom seriously reflected," it was the "first object of the officers," the inspectors reported, "to turn the thoughts of the convict inwards upon himself, and to teach him how to think." To them, that was the genius of solitude. Shorn of his old companionship, the convict would eagerly seek out reading matter and conversation, and, in the penitentiary, he "can only read and hear, what is calculated to make him industrious and virtuous." Once the "prisoner has experienced the operation of the principles of this Institution on a broken spirit and contrite heart, he learns, and he feels, that moral and religious reflection, relieved by industrious occupation at his trade . . . divest his solitary cell of all its horrors, and his punishment of much of its severity."

1. Eastern State Penitentiary, "Warden's Daily Journal," Oct. 25, 28, Nov. 20, 1829, R.G. 15, PHMC; Board of Inspectors, *First and Second Annual Reports of the Inspectors of the Eastern State Penitentiary of Pennsylvania, Made to the Legislature at the Sessions of 1829–30, and 1830–31* (Philadelphia, 1831), 23.

Prison officials "cherished and fixed" this newfound pleasure in labor and reflection.[2]

The new system, the inspectors argued, embodied good policy and philanthropy. They proclaimed that Eastern State had inflicted "great terror . . . upon the minds of the convict community." The evidence that "the most knowing rogues" avoided committing crimes that might result in a penitentiary sentence, they insisted, were "powerful reasons for extending its operation, to those penitentiary offences not at present comprehended within the statute" of 1829. Indeed, the Board was convinced of "the humanity and excellence of this system of penitentiary punishments." "Its permanent establishment and extension" to all those crimes subject to imprisonment at hard labor, the inspectors concluded, would "be consistent with the purest principles of philanthropy, and calculated to advance the interests, and sustain the elevated character, of the Commonwealth of Pennsylvania."[3]

II

Advocates of the separate system of punishment believed that separate confinement signified an entirely new way of ruling, of exercising authority, and of achieving consent. For them, the new penitentiary avoided the cruelties of other penal systems, provided a purified and purifying space of redemption, and, in its distance from everyday life, ensured the terror of punishment while preventing the dangers of mimetic corruption. As the penitentiary acted on the spirits of inmates, its silent order would stand as a solemn caution to the society whose gaze stopped at its walls. For its proponents, the fact that the Eastern State Penitentiary did not act directly on the body was its preeminent superiority over other penal regimes.[4] The absence of the lash, they believed,

2. Board of Inspectors, *First and Second Annual Reports*, 9–10. As time went on, the inspectors acknowledged that few of their inmates were literate. See, for instance, Board of Inspectors, *Fourth Annual Report of the Inspectors of the Eastern State Penitentiary of Pennsylvania, Made to the Legislature at the Session of 1832–1833* (Philadelphia, 1833), 9, and Board of Inspectors, *Fifth Annual Report of the Inspectors of the Eastern Penitentiary of Pennsylvania, Accompanied with the Table of Prisoners in the Western Penitentiary, Read in Senate, February 12, 1834* (Harrisburg, 1834), 4.

The masculine gender pronoun is generally appropriate in the early years of the Eastern State Penitentiary. Between 1829 and 1835, only four women, all black, were sentenced to the penitentiary. Exactly why this is so is unclear as the proportion of women sent to the Walnut Street prison remained much higher. Some sense of the greater "sensibility" of women to confinement may have worked against sentencing them to Eastern State. That the penitentiary received those convicted of more serious crimes may have also worked against women being sent there.

3. Board of Inspectors, *First and Second Annual Reports*, 10–11, 12.

4. That is true not only of older corporal and capital punishments but also relative to other schemes for organizing penitentiaries—penitentiaries that depended on the whip to

marked an irrevocable divide between the separate system and all others. By addressing discourse to the soul, rather than force at the body, the penitentiary seemed to open up the possibility not merely of the transformation of behavior but of free submission to the law.

The critique of corporality linked penal reform to a wide variety of early-nineteenth-century social reforms. And the implications of the commitment to a notion of the penitentiary as disembodied authority can best be approached indirectly—through the connections between penitential ideology and antislavery sentiment. Some of the most ardent supporters of separate confinement and the spread of disciplinary institutions in the city (Roberts Vaux, John Sergeant, William White, Job Tyson) openly advocated antislavery or were members of Philadelphia's antislavery society. For both antislavery and penal reform, whipping symbolically condensed the evils of tyranny and barbarism. This condensation joined the critique of corporal punishment to an argument of moral incommensurability: the use of the lash in slavery (or in other penal regimes) became a symptom of an inveterate cruelty and lack of humanity. Penitential proponents, through their attack on flagellation, formulated appropriate patterns of governing and acceptable gender roles, and they proclaimed the distance between their vision and its alternatives in a powerfully embodied way. Whipping gave body to the injustice of social systems against which bourgeois sensibility defined itself.[5]

---

maintain discipline. See, for example, Charles Caldwell, *New Views of Penitentiary Discipline, and Moral Education and Reform* (Philadelphia, 1829), 1–10; Edward Livingston, *On the Advantages of the Pennsylvania System of Prison Discipline* (Philadelphia, 1828).

5. Myra C. Glenn has demonstrated that an aversion to corporal punishments (against prisoners, sailors, children, and wives, among others) motivated a wide range of reform movements in northern society in the early 19th century. To these movements, the deployment of the lash represented a barbaric remnant that a truly civilized nation should surpass. See Glenn, *Campaigns against Corporal Punishment: Prisoners, Sailors, Women, and Children in Antebellum America* (Albany, N.Y., 1984).

Almost all the members of the prison society through 1830 were members of the Pennsylvania Abolition Society. Peter Jonitas and Elizabeth Jonitas, "Members of the Prison Society: Biographical Vignettes, 1776–1830, of the Philadelphia Society for Assisting Distressed Prisoners and the Members of the PSAMPP, 1787–1830," II, 337, Department of Special Collections, Haverford College Library, Philadelphia, Pa., 1982. This biographical overlap is a microcosm of the larger tendency toward intersecting concerns among a wide variety of late-18th- and early-19th-century reform and humanitarian movements. For discussions of the interconnection between antislavery and other movements (including penal reform) that hoped to discipline while liberalizing society, see David Brion Davis, *The Problem of Slavery in the Age of Revolution, 1770–1823* (Ithaca, N.Y., 1975), 238–242; Thomas C. Holt, *The Problem of Freedom: Race, Labor, and Politics in Jamaica and Britain, 1832–1938* (Baltimore, 1992), 30–33; Ronald G. Walters, *The Antislavery Appeal: American Abolitionism after 1830* (Baltimore, 1976).

Like Benjamin Rush before them, penitential proponents and antislavery writers thought that whipping instigated a spiral of inhumane degradation. Just as the pillory, the whipping post, and the chain, according to Roberts Vaux, served only to "familiarize the mind with cruelty, and consequently to harden the hearts of those who suffered, and those who witnessed such punishments," so with the labor discipline of slavery. "Mankind have always been more forcibly operated upon by moral incentives, than by physical compulsion, and roused to greater exertions by the hope of a benefit, than by the fear of an evil. Among slaves the inflictions of the lash supply the place of moral incentives, and the fear of punishment is substituted for the hope of reward." To Vaux, the moral dangers of the whip seemed as great for those who employed it as for those subject to it. "In daily familiarity with cruel and degrading punishments," he asked of slave masters, "must not their feelings become callous and indifferent to human rights and sufferings? With evil examples constantly before them, with minds at leisure to multiply imaginary desires, with every facility to gratification and every temptation to crime, and unrestrained by discipline, necessity, or the moral feelings of the community, will they not become dissolute, licentious and criminal?" Job Tyson agreed. Any examination of the South "in its moral as its physical aspects" would be struck by the "sweeping desolation of its blight. The vice of indolence, and those other vices, which march in the train of inaction, are but too perceptible on every hand . . . instead of the hardy race which should fix upon solid ground the deep foundations of our republican edifice, we find them luxurious and effeminate, unequal to those vigorous exertions which a new system in a new country requires."[6]

Slavery's direct and violent seizure of the body symbolized its inherent inhumanity. Damningly, Vaux insisted, even slave mistresses fell under the sway of the power and degradation of the slave system: "Who will deny the tendency of slavery to corrupt the disposition and deprave the heart when it is testified by credible witnesses . . . that 'respectable ladies' frequently order, and superintend, the infliction of cruel punishments on their naked slaves,— nay, inflict them with their own hands! To be capable of such acts must they not have forfeited every claim to that humanity and delicacy of feeling which

---

For discussions of the ways a symptom gives body to inner antagonisms or conflicts, see Slavoj Zizek, *The Sublime Object of Ideology* (New York, 1989), 11–53; Zizek, *Tarrying with the Negative: Kant, Hegel, and the Critique of Ideology* (Durham, N.C., 1993), 58–69.

6. [George Washington Smith], *Description of the Eastern Penitentiary of Pennsylvania* (Philadelphia, 1829) 7; Roberts Vaux, "An Address on the Impolicy of Slavery, delivered Jan. 1, 1824 before an Association Formed for the Education of Men of Colour," 2, 8, American Philosophical Society, Philadelphia, Pa. See also, J. R. Tyson, *Discourse before the Young Men's Colonization Society* (Philadelphia, 1834), 8.

contribute so much to the interest and charm of the Sex!"[7] Here Vaux made clear the inversion that, he believed, slavery generated in human nature and social justice. Universalizing the assumptions of bourgeois womanhood, reporting that slavery undermined them, he cast slavery out as an inhumane system. Given the importance of a refined female sensibility to bourgeois culture, an importance that had been clear in the debates over poor reform, Vaux's outrage over southern women instigating whippings is not surprising. Nor is the fact that, once again, it is the issue of "cruel punishments on their naked slaves" that clinches the point. Women wielding the whip not only conjured up images of a world upside down but revealed a domestic system full of arbitrary and explosive violence.

Slavery proved the moral, economic, and political failure of the direct seizure of the body. To the slave, Vaux insisted, "whether the product of his labour is great or small, it is equally the same . . . he makes no acquisition, and sustains no loss, of property; he experiences no increase of comfort, and suffers no diminution of his scanty allowance: He therefore favours his natural indolence as much as he can." Citing efforts to "feudalize" plantations, the distinctions between the effects of task and gang systems, and the response of slaves to opportunities to produce for themselves and their families, Vaux believed that all evidence supported his claims for the superiority of desire over demand in encouraging labor and productivity. "The freeman tastes the reward which 'sweetens labour': He is compensated in proportion to his toil; makes a certain and secure acquisition of property, and obtains by his industry an increase of the comforts and enjoyments of life: it is therefore his interest to accomplish as much as possible." Within freedom, even "delusive" hopes stimulated greater exertion and provided comfort. The implicit genius of liberty was that it held open the possibility of enrichment and comfort. When such enrichment occurred, individuals achieved the security, stability, and discipline that accompanied property. But even when it did not occur, they remained tied to society and the law by virtue of their hopes.[8]

The critique of corporality, ultimately, was addressed simultaneously against older monarchical or aristocratic regimes and the contemporary slave

7. Vaux, "An Address on the Impolicy of Slavery," 9.

8. Ibid., 2, 2–3, 3–4. Vaux, for one, doubted the capacity of slaves to master freedom immediately. He believed gradual emancipation or colonization the most rational means of freeing slaves. Slaves needed to be educated into appropriate ways to desire and practice liberty. Gradually, then, former slaves could be drawn into the economy of desire that motivated free individuals. See ibid., 4–5; Vaux to Charles Miner, Jan. 26, 1830, Vaux Papers, HSP. I would like to thank Steven Hahn for suggesting the parallels between Vaux's gradualism and support for colonization and his penitential philosophy. On delusive hopes, see Vaux, "An Address on the Impolicy of Slavery," 3. On the ties between a "freeman" and the state that "protects his person, his property, and his rights," see 28–29.

regime. It was, in "despotic governments," Job Tyson declared, that "history informs us, excessive punishments almost always prevail." And, after all, whipping flourished in both the slave South and in Europe. In each case, the use of corporal punishments appeared to make visible the inherent injustice and antagonism of the social realm. It was precisely this inherent injustice that the spread of free labor was supposed to overcome. John Sergeant argued that slavery was at its heart a lawless act of power: "The reduction of a fellow creature to slavery, to a state where nothing is his own but his sorrows and his sufferings, is, if you please, an act of sovereign power, that is of sovereign force, which obeys no law but its own will, and knows no limits but the measure of its strength." [9]

Both the market and the spiritualization of punishment would demonstrate the extent to which northern society was realizing what Vaux and his allies believed was the inherent human disposition for liberty. Both penitential punishments and free labor aimed ultimately to create a productive and prudent work force. And they did so by denying that they acted on the body, insisting instead that they reformed and empowered the will. This denial of corporality was achieved through the abstraction of power. Market coercions and penitential architecture would replace the lash; the theater of conscience and the incentive of property would supplant the scaffold spectacle and the confrontation of master and slave.

Yet paradox haunted this critique of corporality. If for Vaux the propensity of slave mistresses to wield the whip demonstrated the evils of slavery and the distance between North and South, women exercising the whip also implicitly undermined the naturalness of the gender assumptions—that women were

9. Job Tyson, *Essay on the Penal Law of Pennsylvania* (Philadelphia, 1827), 9; John Sergeant, "Speech on the Missouri Question, Delivered in the House of Representatives of the United States, on the Eighth and Ninth of February, 1820," in *Speeches* (Philadelphia, 1832), 223. See also Vaux's comments: "To hold slaves is to impugn the sacred injunction, 'to do unto others as you would be done unto,' and to disregard the religious code in which it is contained. Those who 'love one another' cannot deprive each other of the dearest rights of man, but would let the captive and oppressed go free" (Vaux, "Address on the Impolicy of Slavery," 27). Adam Jay Hirsch has offered a somewhat different if, I believe, complementary reading of the connections between antislavery and penal reform. Examining the case of Massachusetts penal reformers, Hirsch suggests that individuals could simultaneously oppose slavery and call for penal confinement and forced labor because they believed that imprisonment was a transitory penalty that served the legitimate demands of justice, whereas slavery was a permanent condition of life. Although I agree with Hirsch's suggestions regarding the importance of these considerations, I would argue that much of the seeming paradox was overcome because of the ways that the penitentiary symbolized a new society, a society that stood in opposition to the slave society of the South. For Hirsch's careful arguments, see *The Rise of the Penitentiary: Prisons and Punishment in Early America* (New Haven, Conn., 1992), 71–111.

demure and filled with sensibility—that undergirded his critique. At the same time, if the propensity to flagellation marked slavery and other penal systems as cruel, it was the penal and anti-slavery reformers who repeatedly returned (if only imaginatively) to describe the whipping scene. It was their fascination that gave whipping its symbolic importance. The whipping scene became a fetish of reform. Reformers' gaze upon flagellation helped to propel the reform effort and constitute the distinctions between social systems.[10] Their desire to describe and imagine the whipping scene constituted flagellation as a symptom of systemic social difference. In their very emphasis on, and investment in, the importance of the lash, Vaux and his allies simultaneously affirmed and subverted the very distance they described.

Similar contradictions shadowed the spiritualization and the isolation of punishment. The growing emphasis on spirit and character, the demand to move away from the direct infliction of punishment upon the body, intensified concerns about the bodies of prisoners. In part, this regard for the body occurred because of anxiety about the effects of solitude on the physical well-being of inmates. Endless details about the body of the prison and its effects on the bodies of the prisoners filled the debates over new penal forms (their architecture, their regimes, their effects on physical and mental health). Still, the concern with the prisoners' bodies was tied to the spirituality of punishment. As the penal system became ever more concerned with character as opposed to behavior, deception and resistance haunted the penitential imagination. Prison officials worried lest they be misled, lest a prisoner, understanding all too well the codes of submission, fabricated the postures of the penitent and turned the desire for reformation against his keepers. The capacity to distinguish between false and true repentance marked, so prison reformers and officials claimed, the experienced prison official and distinguished him in turn from the gullible multitude.[11] Not only did the achievement of true re-

---

10. This fascination with flagellation operated within a larger set of images depicting the horrors of slavery, images that themselves tended to be gendered. Generally, the image of the debasement of the female slave was rape, whereas for the men it was whipping. Why Vaux inverts this pattern by stressing women's whipping others is not clear to me. But it does suggest the importance of gender considerations in the critique of corporality.

In his essay on fetishism, Freud suggested that a fetish was a mechanism to avoid an inner conflict and thereby keep desire active. As will become clear below, the fascination with whipping, I think, both helped motivate reform and deny the threats posed to the penitential imagination by the actual practices of prison authority. Sigmund Freud, "Fetishism," *Collected Papers*, ed. Ernest Jones et al., trans. Joan Riviere et al. (London, 1953), V, 198–204.

11. See the testimony of Thomas Bradford, Jr., in Thomas B. McElwee, *A Concise History of the Eastern Penitentiary of Pennsylvania, Together with a Detailed Statement of the Proceedings of the Committee, Appointed by the Legislature, December 6th, 1834, for the Purpose of Examining into the Economy and Management of That Institution, Embracing the Testimony Taken on That Occasion, and Legislative Proceedings Connected Therewith* (Philadel-

pentance come to be the ultimate justification for the penitential system, but the ability to recognize that repentance became the ultimate sign of prison officials' capacity to reform convicts.

This situation brought into play a complex hermeneutics of repentance. As the penitentiary aimed to reform inmates from the inside out, to penetrate more deeply into their character and their souls, any failing on the part of the inmate became an act of insubordination and resistance. Seeking knowledge of the noncorporeal soul, prison officials had only corporeal signs to decipher: what was said, what was labored, what was read. The aim of penitential discipline was a this-worldly rebirth; convicts needed to discard their old selves for a new one to be born. But this negation of the old, and the freedom that came with a new submission to the law, took place within the same body. Unlike Christian Redemption, where, at the Second Coming, the Word made flesh would turn the flesh into Word, penitential reformation was about the secular desires and discipline of the body first in prison and then in everyday life. Ostensibly about the spirit, the judgment of moral progress could not be about anything but the body, for it was only the body, its movements and expressions, that could be interpreted.

The penitentiary's annual reports textualized this attention to the penal body. These reports contained statements by the warden, the physician, and often documentary evidence about the inmates (including age, sex, offense, sentence, place of conviction) and focused on the condition of the prison population. Although the House of Refuge and the Magdalen Society had made similar public statements, these reports were a new effort for the penal apparatus (there were no consistent reports from the inspectors at Walnut Street). The reports themselves, in effect, signified the general transformation of the relationship of the public to punishment—from direct, corporal display to increasingly disembodied and indirect connection. Like the novels and pamphlets of the 1790s, these reports made possible the imaginative, intellectual connection between punishment and the community that Rush had dreamed of. As the state further concealed its punishments, the penal body came back before the public through the medium of print.

---

phia, 1835), II, 84, 86. For examples of debates over new penal forms, see Franklin Bache, *Observations and Reflections on the Penitentiary System: A Letter from Franklin Bache, M.D. to Roberts Vaux* (Philadelphia, 1829); Pennsylvania, Commissioners to Revise the Criminal Code, *Report of the Commissioners on the Penal Code, with the Accompanying Documents, Read in the Senate, January 4, 1828* (Harrisburg, 1828); Pennsylvania, Commissioners to Superintend the Erection of the Eastern Penitentiary, *Letter Report and Documents, on the Penal Code from the President and Commissioners Appointed to Superintend the Erection of the Eastern Penitentiary, Adopted and Modelled to the System of Solitary Confinement, Read in the Senate, January 8, 1828* (Harrisburg, 1828); [Smith], *Description of the Eastern Penitentiary of Pennsylvania.*

III

Just as the growing individualization of the disciplinary system had joined with its spatial expansion, so the separation of the cell intersected with the isolation of the penal structure itself. Throughout the 1830s, Pennsylvania moved to limit public access to penal matters and insulate the system of punishment from direct popular scrutiny. Shifting the appointment of the inspectors from the mayor and council to the Supreme Court had been merely the first step. The state also eliminated the capacity of grand juries to oversee prison conditions. Prison officials and their supporters believed that grand juries were unjustified intrusions into prison life—neither qualified to judge nor productive in their presence. Samuel Wood was especially hostile to such visits, noting in his journal after one grand jury had toured the penitentiary that he was "much struck with the folly and uselessness of such visits," and recording another occasion when he simply had not taken a grand jury to see any inmates but had "paid particular attention in escorting them around." [12]

Pennsylvania also moved to eliminate public executions. In 1833, a committee of the House of Representatives, responding to doubts about the efficacy of public capital penalties, called for their abolition. The committee drew on fifty years of arguments against public punishments and extended them to capital punishment. The committee reiterated the claims that had long been made against public punishments: they were remnants of barbaric times, spread violence and crime throughout society, offended Christian and enlightened sensibilities, transformed the condemned into heroic celebrities (in some cases, turning them into objects of pity and solicitude), did not deter crime, disrupted commerce and daily life, and the committee suggested that punishments, including capital punishments, performed out of the public view would produce more terror in the condemned and more effectively deter others. Pennsylvania needed to abolish public executions to complete its penal revolution. [13]

12. "Warden's Journal," June 28, 1832, Oct. 9, 1834, quoted in "Journal of the Committee," Jan. 10, 1835, in Anderson, *Report of the Joint Committee of the Legislature of Pennsylvania, Relative to the Eastern State Penitentiary, at Philadelphia, Read in the House of Representatives, Mar. 26, 1835* (Harrisburg, 1835), 58. For the statutory elimination of the grand jury's right to visit the penitentiary, see "An Act Relative to the Western and Eastern State Penitentiaries, and to the Philadelphia County Prisons," in *Laws of the General Assembly of the State of Pennsylvania, Passed at the Session 1832–1833 in the Fifty-Seventh Year of Independence* (Harrisburg, 1833), 56. For one grand jury's unhappy response, see Samuel Hazard, ed., *The Register of Pennsylvania, Devoted to the Preservation of Facts and Documents, and Every Other Kind of Useful Information respecting the State of Pennsylvania* (Philadelphia, 1828–1836), XV, 11.

13. "Report on the Expediency of Abolishing Public Executions," Dec. 12, 1833, in *Journal*

Soon thereafter Governor George Wolf signed into law an act abolishing the public theater of punishment in Pennsylvania. From that point on, "whenever hereafter any person shall be condemned to suffer death by hanging," the sentence would be carried out "within the walls or yard of the jail of the county in which he or she shall have been convicted." In this new practice, a select part of the community would represent the whole. The "sheriff or coroner" had to attend each execution, and he was instructed to "invite the presence of a physician, attorney general or deputy attorney of the county, and twelve reputable citizens" to act as public witnesses. Sheriff's deputies or members of the prison staff could be present and, if the prisoner requested, two ministers and the family of the condemned. It would "be only permitted to the persons above designated to witness the said execution"; the community at large had no place in the ritual. Consequently, the sheriff was to "make oath or affirmation" that the execution had occurred and to publish that statement in at least two of the county's newspapers.[14] As with punishment more generally, the public execution now would be public only through the mediation of textual representation.

No longer would the assembled community witness executions in public squares. Instead, the state would take life within county jails before an invited group of citizens. Interestingly, part of the rationale for excluding the public at large was the preservation of the public at large. The House committee recognized that thousands of people flocked to see executions, and they acknowledged that executions sometimes served to raise the criminal, and not the criminal law, in the eyes of the public. But it simultaneously held that these spectacles revolted a public who demanded their elimination. The "horrid spectacle" of executions, the committee noted, was "the only one left to shock the public eye," and, despite all the evidence of the popularity of the executions, "the innocent wish neither to hear the sighs nor to behold the tears of the guilty." Although it was "right that he should suffer," the committee argued, "let his punishment be as private as his crime." In this way, "the public, who have already suffered their share, will be spared the farther evils resulting

---

of the Forty-fourth House of Representatives of the Commonwealth of Pennsylvania (Harrisburg, 1834), II, 171–177. For an earlier report on the abolition of public executions, see Journal of the Thirty-fourth House of Representatives of the Commonwealth of Pennsylvania (Harrisburg, 1824), 706–709. Pennsylvania was one of several states to redefine the public status of capital punishment in the 1820s and 1830s. For a discussion of this movement throughout the Northeast and its wider implications for antebellum society, see Louis P. Masur, Rites of Execution: Capital Punishment and the Transformation of American Culture, 1776–1865 (New York, 1989), 93–116.

14. Laws of the General Assembly of the State of Pennsylvania, Passed at the Session 1833–1834 (Harrisburg, 1834), 234–235.

from a public execution."[15] From the committee's perspective, public executions were merely a further infliction upon the public itself.

The committee denied evidence drawn from the embodied public in order to construct an ideal one. It countered tokens of the public's interest with its sense that the spectacle was an imposition on the public, that it was an extension of the suffering caused by crime. This denial might have contained a hidden class dimension. Although the report of 1833 made distinctions only between the law-abiding and the lawbreaking elements of the community (around the issue of pickpockets), an earlier report of 1824 expressed its social assumptions more explicitly. As that committee saw it, "the serious and well disposed" might be "deeply and solemnly impressed with a sense of the awful demerit of crime" on witnessing a public execution. Unfortunately, the lawmakers insisted, execution crowds were "composed chiefly of those among whom moral feeling is extremely low" and who "retire from the execution evidently delighted, and as if privileged by what they have witnessed, permit themselves to be involved in scenes of disorder, debauchery, and intemperance, to the annoyance of the peaceable and well disposed." Rather than a unified whole, the public was divided between the "serious and well disposed" and those whose "moral feeling is extremely low." These class differences necessitated a rethinking of the nature of penal display. By the 1830s, legislators were convinced that they had to divide the public from what was carried out in its name. Only those with either a personal stake in the event, the professional skills to resist the seduction of the ritual, the social status to be entrusted with the community's honor, or the political position to symbolize the state could attend. In the committee's view, the public was best served when it was represented, not when it was present.[16]

The new penitential structure, then, presupposed an unstable separation and spiritualization of punishment. As the critics of flagellation repeatedly returned to a scene that revolted them, the attempt to spiritualize punishment magnified attention to the body; as the legislature abolished public penalties in the name of the public, it split the public in whose name it acted and reserved access to punishment to the "serious and well disposed." Each process maintained, while denying, the gaze on the penal body. Reformers hoped that the increasing abstraction of power offered the possibility to conceal the process of punishment while transcending the direct seizure of the body. But

15. "Report on the Expediency of Abolishing Public Executions," *Journal of the Forty-Fourth House of Representatives of the Commonwealth of Pennsylvania*, II, 176.

16. *Journal of the Thirty-Fourth House of Representatives of the Commonwealth of Pennsylvania*, 707. For two stimulating discussions of these developments that draw attention to the increasing delegation of visibility in punishment, see Masur, *Rites of Execution*, 95–113, and Randall McGowen, "Civilizing Punishment: The End of the Public Execution in England," *Journal of British Studies*, XXXIII (1994), 257–282.

this abstraction reverted incessantly to the materiality of prisoners' bodies. The penitential imagination was haunted by its own contradictions. Events rapidly would prove these contradictions more than imaginary.

IV

The new penitentiary rapidly plunged into crisis. In December 1834, a joint committee of the state legislature met in Philadelphia to investigate charges of moral and financial improprieties as well as acts of cruelty toward prisoners within the penitentiary. Pennsylvania attorney general George M. Dallas represented the state, and four attorneys, including Thomas Bradford, Jr., defended Samuel Wood and his assistants Richard Blundin and John Holloway. Sixty-five witnesses presented charges and countercharges about the penitentiary's affairs. Public attention and anxiety were focused on the institution— attention and anxiety that threatened to undermine the legitimacy of the penitential experiment.[17]

The attorney general indicted the authorities at Eastern State for violating both the letter of the penitentiary law and the spirit of proper penitentiary discipline. His allegations ranged from financial malfeasance through personal immorality to official cruelty and violence. First, Dallas charged Wood, Blundin, Blundin's wife, Holloway, and "others" with "practices and manners . . . licentious and immoral" among the officers and their families; second, he declared that the officers of the penitentiary had engaged in "embezzlement and misapplication of the public provisions and public property"; third, he alleged "cruel and unusual punishments inflicted by order of the warden upon refractory convicts"; and, lastly, Dallas accused the officers of practices "inconsistent with the object and principles of a penitentiary . . . subversive of its order, regularity, and security."[18]

Witnesses charged the inspectors, Wood, and his officers with appropriating materials and labor from the penitentiary for their own private use (either in the form of personal conveniences, or, in Wood's case, of supplies for his

17. "Eastern Penitentiary," *Pennsylvanian* (Philadelphia), Jan. 23, 1835. Thomas Bradford, Jr., did not give oral testimony but delivered a written statement to the committee after it had closed its hearings in Philadelphia. He thereby was both an attorney for the respondents and a witness in their defense (and without cross-examination). There were, then, 66 different testimonies. The actual testimony is known because Thomas B. McElwee, a member of the committee, chose to publish the testimony. I have drawn extensively from his *Concise History,* below. For McElwee's reasons for publishing the testimony, see I, 3. For another discussion of the investigation, see Negley K. Teeters and John D. Shearer, *The Prison at Philadelphia: Cherry Hill, the Separate System of Penal Discipline: 1829–1913* (New York, 1957), 93–107. On public attention, see G. M. Dallas to George Wolf, Dec. 21, 1834, Jan. 24, 1835, in George Wolf Papers, HSP.

18. Anderson, *Report of the Joint Committee,* 42.

private business). In part, the problem lay in the bewildering way that the inspectors had managed the financial records of the institution, mixing together different accounts and sources of state finance in a bewildering (and seemingly cavalier) way. But more was at issue than carelessness. The testimony suggested that Wood and his top assistants either participated in or connived at the actual theft of supplies and materials from the penitentiary. Witnesses accused Wood of diverting resources from the penitentiary to his own mill and farm, accused Richard Blundin's wife of systematically taking supplies meant for prisoners for her own family, and accused other staff members and some inspectors with receiving goods and services from the penitentiary on a smaller scale. They presented a picture of prison officials who, using Eastern State as a private reserve, subverted the distinction between public and private in order to enrich themselves and their personal concerns.[19]

Embezzlement, however, was merely part of a general disregard for penal discipline. The laxness of authority extended into the day-to-day life of the institution. The warden and staff members threw parties within the prison walls; Wood and the inspectors entertained guests, employed prisoners as cooks and waiters, allowed inmates to work outside their cells and in the company of paid laborers, and failed to separate inmates rigidly or conceal their identities fully.[20] Yet, even these charges were merely the tip of the iceberg.

V

The investigation also challenged the personal morality of the prison administration. As the association of flagellation with slavery made clear, critics of the whip identified corporal penalties with arbitrary and regressive systems of government that, Roberts Vaux declared, stimulated "licentious and dissolute" wishes. Their criticism of flogging began with, but exceeded, an aversion to the physical effects of corporal penalties. They advocated the penitentiary, in part, because its withdrawn and enclosed space would ensure a purified and moralized space of reflection. As the inspectors put it, the "convict removed from his former associates should breath none other than a moral atmosphere."[21] But, critics charged, the enclosed and withdrawn space of the peni-

19. On Wood's having private business in the Eastern State Penitentiary, see testimony of William Griffith, in McElwee, *A Concise History,* I, 174–176, testimony of Judge Charles Coxe, 194–195. On Mrs. Blundin and her family with prison goods, see Griffith, 174; testimony of William Parker, 206–210. On prisoners out of cells, see testimony of Silas Steel, 160–161; testimony of Philip Hahn, 168.

20. See testimony of James Torry, ibid., 145, testimony of Leonard Phleger, 151, testimony of William Griffith, 172–173.

21. Board of Inspectors, *Sixth Annual Report of the Inspectors of the Eastern State Penitentiary of Pennsylvania, Made to the Legislature at the Session of 1834–5* (Philadelphia, 1835), 5.

tentiary did not create a purified order. Instead, it was providing a mask to conceal rampant immorality within the prison's walls. Witnesses testified to intoxication, apparent sexual relations, and sexual diseases within the prison walls. The Eastern State Penitentiary, its critics implied, rather than transcending the immoral and vicious, sanctioned older forms of wickedness in a new setting.

Although claiming that immorality was widespread, extending in some cases even to inmates, witnesses against the penitentiary emphasized the alleged immorality of Richard Blundin's wife. William Parker, a former convict, declared that "though I have been in all parts of the world, with all sorts of women, I have never seen one as bad as she—whose general conduct was as bad." According to several male employees of the penitentiary, Mrs. Blundin constantly embezzled goods, was frequently drunk, often verbally abusive, had been infected with venereal disease, and engaged in intimate relationships with Wood and Holloway.[22]

Most explosive were the charges relating to Wood's relationship with Mrs. Blundin. As the witnesses described it, Wood allowed her the run of the institution. At best, they implied, he was willfully blind to her activities; at worst he actively took part in them. Philip Hahn testified that "Mrs. Blundin and Mr. Wood appeared to be very intimate and sociable." William Mayall reported that one Sunday Wood and Mrs. Blundin were "a great deal together—talking—and very familiar and friendly with each other. He was sitting down— and she was laughing and chatting and fondling round him." This relationship, they believed, led to more than just intimacy. Israel Averel reported that Mrs. Blundin had the use of the official carriage for her marketing, a privilege she employed to visit her friends and at least one "house of ill fame."[23] Others reported her removing bread and other foods from the penitentiary in Wood's presence.

In their minds, Mrs. Blundin was a mysterious power within the institution. Mayall declared that "Mrs. Blundin generally appeared to me to be master." This sense of her power was echoed by John Harvey, another former employee, who admitted having never reported Mrs. Blundin's use of public provisions to Wood. He told the committee: "I was under the impression that

22. Testimony of William Parker, in McElwee, A Concise History, I, 211, testimony of William Mayall, 226–227, testimony of William Torry, 144, 146, testimony of Philip Hahn, 166–167. Mrs. Blundin was never called to testify, nor was her first name ever used. Despite her centrality in the drama that unfolded, she was the only important player whose full name was never provided. She therefore occupied a peculiar place. She was at the heart of much of the testimony but never granted anything but a derivative identity. In this regard, she was the perfect template on which to project all of the different anxieties and obsessions expressed throughout the hearing.

23. Testimony of Philip Hahn, ibid., 167, testimony of William Mayall, 226, testimony of Israel G. Averel, 264.

if I said any thing about it, I would forfeit my situation there. I did not know of any person having forfeited his situation before that—but I had heard of Mrs. Blundin having so much influence over Mr. Wood that I thought it would be useless for me to make a complaint." Others testified that Mrs. Blundin abused both Wood and themselves and deployed prison services and facilities for her own pleasure and the pleasure of her family.[24] They claimed that Mrs. Blundin had gained control over Wood and then used her privileged position to dominate the life of the institution.

Critics of the penal regime, therefore, mobilized common misogynist imagery to attack Mrs. Blundin. As the testimony developed, they painted a picture of Mrs. Blundin as a diseased, vicious, and power-hungry woman, contemptuous of Wood, of propriety, and of the honor of the state. Systematically, they sought to separate her from her husband and to link her illicitly to Wood. At the same time, they aimed to undermine Wood's authority. These witnesses implied that Wood's own appetites had made him dependent on Mrs. Blundin, who, in turn, used the prerogatives of the penitentiary to engage in her own pleasures regardless of their moral or legal implications. Mrs. Blundin symbolized all that was arbitrary in the penitentiary. It was her violation of domestic propriety that marked the distance between the penitential imagination and the actual practices of the prison. And her perceived power, more than anything else, appeared to them to indicate a penitentiary out of order. What, after all, was a woman doing as "master"?

If Wood's accusers depicted a prison in disarray, Wood's defenders were hardly silent. Opposing the image of Wood as cavalier and immoral, they painted a picture of his character as beyond reproach. At the same time, they sought to turn the charges of immorality against Wood's accusers, implying that it was they, not the warden, who reeked of immorality. In the end, the warden's allies mobilized the language of character, seeking to convince the committee that Wood's class (in all senses of the word) was beyond question.

The witnesses allied with Wood embodied the very nature of the administration's defense. The major accusers, with the exception of Judge Coxe, were alienated former staff members drawn largely from artisanal ranks. The institution's witnesses, on the other hand, were chiefly men of authority and stature. Some of Wood's continuing employees did testify in his behalf, but members of the Board of Inspectors, administrators of other institutions, physicians, and penal reformers occupied center stage during the institution's defense.[25] These witnesses brought to bear their social standing and claims to

24. Testimony of William Mayall, ibid., 227, testimony of John Harvey, ibid., 272, testimony of William Griffith, 173–174, testimony of William Parker, 206–212.

25. Among those who testified on the warden's behalf against the charges were Thomas Bradford, Jr., William H. Hood, and Benjamin Richards, all inspectors; Francis Lieber,

deference; their very presence implied the class divide that marked the entire investigation.

In part, the warden's defenders sought to diminish the importance of the charges. They sought to justify social activity within the prison walls, the deployment of prisoners as laborers, and the practice of mixing inmates with paid workers. On the one hand, witnesses pointed to the official nature of the entertainments and the necessity for staff members residing within the walls to obtain relaxation. On the other, they reminded the committee that the construction of the penitentiary remained incomplete and that, under those circumstances, the state achieved financial benefits from employing prisoners to complete the prison. Moreover, the incompleteness of the buildings necessitated greater flexibility in penal discipline. As they saw it, rather than malfeasance in office, these activities were merely rational compromises to the real nature of the penitential setting.[26]

Defusing charges of immorality was more complicated. Here, the warden's defenders aimed to elevate the committee's perceptions of Wood. Witnesses testified to Wood's long-standing commitment to penal reform. Bradford as well as James J. Barclay and Francis Lieber (both members of the Philadelphia Society for Alleviating the Miseries of Public Prisons) informed the committee that Wood had studied the question of punishment carefully, traveled abroad to learn more about penal administration, and served as a Walnut Street inspector. Just as important, Bradford made it clear that Wood had not sought the office of warden but had it thrust on him by the reform community. In their telling, Wood was a dutiful public servant, studious in his approach to punishment, and lacking in either personal ambition or ulterior motives in directing Eastern State. The committee also heard testimonials to Wood's more general character. In all, the warden's allies sought to make the moral charges against him literally incredible—drawing on not only Wood's own image but their own standing in commending his character.[27]

James J. Barclay, and Reverend Charles R. Demmy, members of the Philadelphia Society for Alleviating the Miseries of Public Prisons; and physicians William E. Horner (professor of anatomy), William E. Gibson, and Charles Luken (physician at the Pennsylvania Hospital).

26. See, for instance, the testimony of William H. Hood, in McElwee, *A Concise History*, II, 66–67, testimony of Thomas Bradford, Jr., 83–84; and Anderson, *Report of the Joint Committee*, 17–18 (on the necessity of staff entertainments). If they viewed these activists as unavoidable given the state of the penitentiary, they still wanted them eliminated as quickly as possible. See, for instance, the testimony of Hood, in McElwee, *A Concise History*, II, 66–67.

27. See testimony of James J. Barclay in, McElwee, *A Concise History*, II, 14, testimony of Francis Lieber, 55, testimony of Thomas Bradford, Jr., 79–80, testimony of William Fry, 16–17, testimony of Charles R. Demmy, 19, testimony of Joseph Watson, 59.

They also sought to denigrate the character and motivation of Wood's accusers. In large part, that took the form of implying that Wood's accusers were engaged in an unholy conspiracy. As Wood's allies saw it, the entire set of charges had been hatched as a means of getting control of the penitentiary. William Hood testified that, although he had originally supported Coxe in his investigation, he believed that the former staff members "were a gossiping set, and had talked themselves into the existence of evils that were imaginary. There was a spice of ambition in some of them, who wanted to take the vacancies that might accrue in consequence." James Stewart reported that the staff had come to him and tried to get him to testify that he had witnessed improprieties and cruelty in the prison. He assured the committee that he had refused this entreaty.[28]

The attempt to undercut the character of Wood's accusers carried over into their testimony. Although only the answers, not the questions, of the committee testimony were printed, the statements of William Griffith, Silas Steel, Leonard Phleger, and others make clear that counsel for the defense pressed them continually on their communications with each other, hoping to demonstrate that their testimony was planned and could not be trusted as independent corroboration. Moreover, Bradford and others painted the accusers themselves as immoral.[29] Wood's allies contended that the former staff had been driven from the prison, not in retaliation for their charges, but as a necessary act to preserve the propriety of the penitential environment.

Wood's defenders, then, implied that the investigation turned on the personal credibility of a gentleman as opposed to his subordinates—and they left no doubt that it was the gentleman who should be believed. In the end, the committee's majority agreed. None of his accusers could prove sexual relations between the warden and Mrs. Blundin, and they could only report their belief that it was impossible that he did not know that she had pilfered public provisions. The ambiguity of the charges moved the proceeding into the realm of interpretation and reputation—and in that arena, the committee's majority believed, Wood held the upper hand. Noting the "evidence of the general good character" of Wood, they declared it a "well established principle" that, when a person's morality is questioned, if the "accused can make

28. Testimony of William H. Hood, in McElwee, *A Concise History,* II, 65–66, testimony of James Stewart, 33–34.

29. In fact, Bradford and Wood, before the legislative hearings, had come into conflict with Silas Steel, William Griffith, and William Mayall, whom they accused of spreading deist and Painite ideas among the inmates. Steel and Griffith denied the charges. See testimony of Thomas Bradford, Jr., in McElwee, *A Concise History,* II, 90–91, testimony of William Griffith, I, 181, testimony of Silas Steel, 161–162. On Mayall's religious beliefs, see his testimony, ibid., 233. Also see, "Warden's Daily Journal," Nov. 22, Dec. 22, 23, 1833, Eastern State Penitentiary, R.G. 15, PHMC. Wood recorded on Dec. 23, 1833, that Steel had left the institution.

out a general good character, it is strong and persuasive evidence, and in all good cases of doubt, or mere suspicion should lead to a full and honorable acquittal." Wood's "high moral character" had been attested to by "the evidence of persons of the first respectability." This presumption, they averred, was especially important vis-à-vis Mrs. Blundin. No effort was made to defend Mrs. Blundin's character. Both Wood's critics and defenders joined in the hostility toward her.[30] But Wood's defenders implied, and the majority concurred, that Wood's reputation was sufficient to acquit him of all charges of immorality.

V I

Whatever the truth of the charges about Wood's immorality, his accusers believed that the dangers his governance posed went far beyond the excesses of Mrs. Blundin. The witnesses arrayed against the warden charged him with arbitrary and cruel treatment of his inmates. By their telling, the hand of authority in the prison was anything but gentle and disembodied. Instead, it struck directly at the body of the prisoners.

The most serious charge related to Mathias Maccumsey, who, on the morning of June 27, 1833, died in Eastern State. Maccumsey, born in Lancaster County, Pennsylvania, forty-four years old, was, at the time of his death, serving the second year of a twelve-year sentence for murder. Because Maccumsey "on several occasions got the men next him talking, and being detected in the act," on the evening of the twenty-sixth, the warden ordered the "iron gag" placed on him during the morning of the twenty-seventh. The gag, an "iron instrument resembling the stiff bit of a blind bridle, having an iron palet in the centre, about an inch square, and chains at each end to pass round the neck and fasten behind," in this instance "was placed in the prisoners mouth, the iron palet over his tongue, the bit forced in as far as possible, the chains brought round the jaws to the back of the neck; the end of one chain was passed through the ring in the end of the other chain to 'the fourth link,' and fastened with a lock." Maccumsey's "hands were then forced into leather gloves in which were iron staples and crossed behind his back; leather straps

30. Anderson, *Report of the Joint Committee*, 8, 9. The Board of Inspectors themselves had conducted a prior investigation into the charges against Wood and had come to the same conclusions. The course of this investigation can be followed in the Board's Minutes. See the records for the meetings of Nov. 12, 1833, where the issue is taken up; Dec. 1, 1833, where Wood is granted permission to attend with counsel; Dec. 3, 1833, where Wood objects to restrictions placed on his actions if he attends; Dec. (?), 1833, when Coxe proposes reporting abuses to the legislature; Jan. 28, 1834, when Wood is granted permission to fire several of his staff; Feb. 1, 1834, when Coxe resigns in protest; and Feb. 3, 1834, when the Board received its first communication from Dallas of his concern over possible abuses within the penitentiary. Minutes of the Board of Inspectors of the Eastern State Penitentiary, R.G. 15, PHMC.

were passed through the staples, and from thence round the chains of the gag between the neck and the chains; the straps were drawn tight, the hands forced up toward the head." This was not the first time that Maccumsey had been subject to the gag. But in this instance it proved fatal. Shortly after it had been secured, he suffered fits and collapsed. All efforts to revive him proved futile, and, within the hour, he was dead. The prison physician, Franklin Bache, reported that Maccumsey had died of apoplexy.[31]

Maccumsey's death revealed a world of penal violence. The gag, it turned out, was only the most extreme of a series of measures prison officials employed to quiet noisy, or discipline refractory, inmates. These punishments ranged from depriving inmates of their time in exercise yards, increasingly severe reductions of food, confinement in a "dark cell" or dungeon, all the way to restraint in a straitjacket or the gag. All were designed to achieve what solitude could not: inmates' unquestioning obedience to the regulations of the institution. If Eastern State had been designed to make the whip superfluous, physical violence had reemerged at the very heart of its disciplinary practices.[32]

This point reappeared in the punishment of "ducking." Ducking, according to Thomas McElwee, a member of the legislative investigating committee, was "inflicted by suspending the offender from the yard wall by the wrists, and drenching him with water, poured on his head from buckets, in nature of a shower bath." It simultaneously cleansed and punished inmates. But in the case of Seneca Plimly, the practice might have caused madness. Plimly had been convicted in Bradford County of horse theft and sentenced to one year of incarceration. Wood and his staff considered him a "crazy man." But whatever the reality of his mental condition, Plimly was a problematic prisoner. Sometimes violent, often unclean, Plimly was regularly subjected to forced ducking, and, in the winter of 1831–1832, Plimly suffered a particularly severe shower bath. Isaac Cox reported that "it was a very cold day—as cold as I ever recollect it" when Plimly was ducked. Wood had ordered John Curran to duck Plimly, and, after some hesitation, "he went and brought the water, to the

31. See Eastern State Penitentiary, "Warden's Daily Journal," June 27, 28, 1833, R.G. 15, PHMC; McElwee, *A Concise History,* I, 18. Information on Maccumsey's biography and sentencing is drawn from the Board of Inspectors, *Fourth Annual Report of the Inspectors of the Eastern State Penitentiary,* 17; Board of Inspectors, *Fifth Annual Report of the Inspectors of the Eastern Penitentiary of Pennsylvania, Accompanied with the Table of Prisoners in the Western Penitentiary, Read in Senate, February 12, 1834* (Harrisburg, 1834), 9. For information on McCumsey's collapse, see "Warden's Daily Journal," June 27, 1833, R.G. 15, PHMC; testimony of Silas Steel, in McElwee, *A Concise History,* I, 158–159; testimony of Leonard Phleger, 149–150; testimony of William Griffith, 177–178; testimony of Charles S. Coxe, 186–187.

32. McElwee, *A Concise History,* I, 16–18. Maccumsey himself had been subject to physical violence—a beating—at the hands of Wood on a previous occasion. See testimony of William Griffith, 177.

amount of not less than 12 buckets—I stood by the ladder," Cox continued, and "ordered Curran to take the ice out so that it should not injure the man— there was ice in them—pretty thick on some of the buckets—icicles were hanging on his hair, all round his head, about one or two inches long. I helped untie him, after the buckets were poured. The ropes were so frozen, and the wet together, that we had a difficult job to get them off at all." Shortly there- after, Plimly was pardoned by reason of insanity, released, and transferred to the almshouse.[33]

As with the iron gag or deprivation of food, the shower bath was a physical supplement to the pressures of solitude. Here the rationale was more directly medicinal—the bath, after all, was designed to strengthen prison hygiene. But, rather than healing the prisoner, the shower bath subjected him to physical torment and possibly mental derangement. The bath once more indicated that solitude did not fully seize the soul of prisoners—and that the prison regime regularly deployed physical penalties beyond the mere fact of confinement.

The committee's investigation, therefore, demonstrated the presence of ex- tralegal penalties within the penitentiary. William Griffith himself admitted to striking another prisoner, and others testified to the use of violence in con- trolling inmates.[34] These forms of corporal struggle, restraint, and punish- ment were generated out of the very nature of separate confinement. Labor, after all, was designed as a relief from solitude. But what did one do with in- mates who refused to labor? The architecture was designed to prevent com- munication. But what additional solitude could be imposed for those who re- sisted the commands of silence? Solitude as a practice could not be intensified without limits. When it failed to seize the spirit, only the body was at the dis- posal of the authorities. Whether through the deprivation of food, increased physical restraint, or more direct if informal bodily violence, the separate sys- tem could not do without corporal discipline. Solitude released corporal coer- cion; the separate regime reinvented corporal punishment as its anchor.

In response, Wood's defenders turned to expertise and the particularity of the disciplinary domain. In this way, they made two separate arguments. First, the gag and the shower bath were incapable of causing the damage with which they were charged. And second, these instruments, although perhaps unwise,

33. Ibid., 17, testimony of William Griffith, 179, testimony of Isaac Cox, 259. A somewhat more sympathetic description is provided by William Adair, II, 31–32. Information on Plimly can be found in [Board of Inspectors], *Report of the Board of Inspectors of the Eastern Penitentiary of Pennsylvania, to the Legislature, Read in Senate, January 20, 1832* (Harrisburg, 1832), 6. He was prisoner number 75. On Plimly's pardon and departure from the peniten- tiary, see "Minutes of the Board of Inspectors of the Eastern State Penitentiary," Jan. 14, 1832, and "Warden's Daily Journal," Feb. 10, 1832, R.G. 15, PHMC.

34. Griffith's testimony on these issues is in McElwee, *A Concise History*, I, 183–184. See also testimony of Leonard Phleger and Philip Hahn, 152–153, 171.

were not cruel, because, within the disciplinary world, they were not unusual. Mobilizing both medical and professional authority, the warden's defenders aimed to show that laymen were not qualified to judge the necessities of penitential discipline. In their view, the disciplinary realm was a world apart—and could only be evaluated by immanent criteria.

Some of the city's physicians came before the committee to deny that the gag could have been fatal. The structure of the human head, they reported, precluded the gag from strangling Maccumsey. Thus, they concurred in Bache's assumption that he did not suffocate but rather died from apoplexy. George McClellan, testifying for the defense, argued that it was "impossible" for the gag to have caused apoplexy. "If the man had remained cool, and patiently submitted to the punishment, it could not have produced apoplexy." It was Maccumsey's resistance that had led to his death. William Horner, professor of anatomy at the University of Pennsylvania, could not "see any objection" to the gag. "The principal influence of an instrument of this kind would be morally; its moral effect would depend upon the temperament of the individual.—A quiet man would bear it easily another would be restless."[35]

The defense witnesses thereby turned responsibility for Maccumsey's death back on Maccumsey himself. Had Maccumsey accepted his punishment properly, they implied, he would still be alive. It was his violent attempt to escape from the gag, his refusal to submit patiently to his suffering, that had caused his death. Maccumsey, in effect, had overreacted, driving himself into a frenzy that ultimately killed him. The fault lay, not in the instrument of punishment that would affect its subject "morally," but in the disposition of the condemned. William Gibson suggested that the gag had "produced a moral and not a physical effect."[36] Had Maccumsey been a "quiet man," all would have been well.

A certain penitential logic inhered in these arguments. The gag, after all, condensed the entire symbolic structure of the separate system. Silent submission was the center of the penitentiary's discipline—the prime mechanism for promoting personal reformation. Breaking silence meant violating solitude, and without solitude the penitentiary could not function, nor could individuals be saved. As the legislative committee noted in its majority report, "Our system requires not only labor, but solitude, which combined are calculated to bring about reflection upon past misdeeds, and their evil consequences." It was necessary to ensure that these principles were not violated. "It will not do to allow the convict to interrupt that solitude by obstreperous noise, or to refuse to perform his work, or in any respect withhold the most implicit obe-

35. Testimony of George McClellan, ibid., II, 37–38. See also testimony of Benjamin H. Coates, 24, tstimony of William E. Horner, 42.

36. Testimony of William B. Gibson, ibid., 44.

dience to the order of the institution."[37] When Maccumsey attempted to speak to the inmate next to him, and "to get him talking," he challenged the very basis of the new prison. The gag was designed to ensure silence through restraint—in that it was a more personalized version of the penitentiary itself.

The arguments for Maccumsey's responsibility, however, also drew on a set of social assumptions. None of the physicians or officials who testified on the gag denied that it could cause suffering. "Such an instrument," William Gibson testified, "put into the mouth of a man of high temperament tightly would provoke coughing, reaching, and struggling." George McClellan allowed that the "instrument might excite coughing and difficult efforts at breathing," and "might irritate the parts." But these dangers were dependent on the character and qualities of the sufferer. The physicians thus sought to minimize the dangerousness of the gag by metaphorically reducing the humanity of its subjects. Gibson assured the committee that "if drawn with moderate tightness, I should say that it [the gag] would not produce more effect than a common mouthing bit upon a horse." McClellan shared his confidence, suggesting that the gag was "a safer instrument than if it were wood—as pieces cannot be masticated off—it is just like a machine for breaking young horses."[38] The doctors cast Maccumsey as somewhat less than fully human and the gag as equivalent to breaking a horse. The treatment of inmates, from this perspective, could not be judged by common notions of cruelty. Instead, it was necessary to recognize the animal propensities of the inmates. The doctors diminished the threat of the gag by reducing the stature of the convicts.

The committee's majority report made this vision of the inmates explicit. It reminded the public that, whatever the hopes of reformation, those subject to prison discipline "are men of idle habits, vicious propensities, and depraved passions." "Obedience" was the first necessity for reformation, and "with many convicts, if not all, [it] is a matter of much difficulty, requiring great firmness and discretion." Unfortunately, "gentle means" were not always sufficient to produce obedience, "and yet it must be produced, or nothing can be done." Consequently, "it becomes necessary to adopt some punishment beyond that which is inflicted under the sentence of the convict, and which is essential to secure his quiet subjection to that sentence."[39] The penitentiary was acting upon the "vicious" and the "depraved," and its control over them was always precarious. It was the fact of their corruption that made discipline necessary. The committee's majority thus concurred with witnesses

37. Anderson, *Report of the Joint Committee*, 12.

38. Testimony of William B. Gibson, in McElwee, *A Concise History*, II, 43, testimony of George McLellan, 37.

39. Anderson, *Report of the Joint Committee*, 12.

who believed that the inmates had to be broken, that their character placed them beyond the reach of normal practices of authority.

The warden's allies and the committee majority, therefore, formulated a rationale for an expanding and intensifying disciplinary realm. Whatever the humanitarian aims of its proponents, the penitentiary worked on recalcitrant matter. Inmates arrived at the institution debased and corrupt, and the gentle hand of solitude could only reform them after they had been subdued. The inmates' resistance, they suggested, was a sign of their continuing depravity, and an unmistakable subjection had to be imposed to combat it. As a result, a second discipline was required—a supplemental exercise of power where confinement failed. From this perspective, it was the character of the inmates that triggered the spiral of increasing discipline—and thus it was the prisoners who were responsible for their corporal restraint.

At the same time, the complexities of governing inmates meant that prison officers required much latitude. It was "from the necessity of the case," not "upon any well-defined legal rule" that supplemental punishments (including the gag) had been inflicted. Although the inspectors had power to make general rules of discipline, they had chosen not to do so, noting that the "difficulty of forming such rules must occur to every one." The case-by-case nature of discipline meant that "a large and liberal discretion" was usually "vested in the warden or superintendent." Indeed, they believed, such discretion was in the nature of things and "must be the case under any system of rules which could be devised." This discretion was not unlimited, however. The warden "naturally" would "regulate" himself by referring "to the practice of other institutions of a similar nature." Such comparison, of course, meant that he needed to be deeply involved with the wider disciplinary community. Thus it was fortunate that the state had access to Wood. The warden, the committee reported, was "well known" for possessing "great experience, a well established character for humanity, firmness and discretion." [40] His long study of penitential discipline and experience with prison government entitled him to much freedom in overseeing inmates.

The warden's witnesses presupposed, and the committee's majority accepted, the specificity of disciplinary knowledge. But this acknowledgment extended far beyond Wood's personal qualities and experience. Instead, defenders of Wood's administration expressed a vision of the disciplinary realm as a world apart—subject to its own special rules and justified in its own special practices. The committee made this explicit in its discussion of Maccumsey's case. Declaring that it "was in full proof" that the gag was employed in a wide range of disciplinary institutions (the navy, the Walnut Street prison, and, previously, on Maccumsey and others in the Eastern State Penitentiary),

40. Ibid., 12–13, 13.

they suggested that it was "not therefore an 'unusual punishment,' and it may be inferred from this that it had not been considered a cruel punishment." Pointing to Bache's acquiescence in the use of the gag, and reminding all that he was "distinguished for his humanity, intelligence, and service," the committee's majority argued that such medical approval, combined with a history of common usage, "goes far, if it does not entirely relieve the punishment in this case from all intentional cruelty on the part of those who had inflicted it."[41] The practices of disciplinary institutions had become self-referential.

Indeed, the notion that Eastern State could be defended through its similarities to other disciplinary spaces was a central theme in the majority's report. Beyond arguing that the gag or the shower bath could not have caused death or madness, witnesses for the warden pointed to their use in other institutions. Benjamin Coates testified that the shower bath had been used "extensively" at the Pennsylvania Hospital and as "a medical agent." As far as the committee could see, this was a decisive fact. Declaring that Plimly had been insane before his ducking, they recognized that this conviction raised a crucial question: "Was this punishment of this unfortunate prisoner cruel and unusual?" And to that question they had an unequivocal answer: It was not. Although "many buckets had been poured upon him on a very cold day," an action that was "indiscreet," the committee was confident that it was "deprived of all evidence of cruelty," which "always implies intention." That the shower bath was "frequently employed for insane patients, not only as curative, but disciplinary means, in the best institutions for this unfortunate class of men in the city and vicinity of Philadelphia" precluded any intention of cruelty. The shower bath "could not then, with any propriety be called unusual" and, as it was well known that its use was "familiar," went "far to demonstrate that its use was without cruelty."[42]

The warden's defenders argued that notions of cruelty were relative to the domain in which they operated. Since it was established that the gag and the shower bath, as well as other tools like the straitjacket, were used in an array of disciplinary institutions and approved by professionals in the field, charges of cruelty were misplaced. The disciplinary realm had to be judged by its own standards. These standards, witnesses and committee members suggested, were rooted in the nature of the disciplinary project and the human material that it confronted. They believed that a wide range of discretion had to be granted to those in charge of the penitentiary. And they argued that limits to that discretion were best established in comparison with other disciplinary sites—and not with common, everyday perceptions.

41. Ibid., 14.
42. Testimony of Benjamin Coates, in McElwee, *A Concise History,* II, 23, 24; Anderson, *Report of the Joint Committee,* 13.

The warden's allies, then, had adumbrated a discourse of character and knowledge. From their perspective, the combination of Wood's moral reputation, his long-standing involvement in penal reform, and the common practices of the disciplinary realm shielded him from blame. In making these claims, Wood's defenders conveyed a pair of assumptions about the nature of disciplinary authority and power. First, the class nature of the penal relation—represented by the characters of Wood and his subjects—necessitated leeway for supplemental punishments and discipline within the penitentiary. And, second, the limits to this supplemental power could be established only within the terms of the disciplinary community and its ideals. Discipline needed to be constantly expanding and intensifying, and its rules and regulations had to be self-referential.

The failures of solitude reveal the corporal underside of the theory of mimetic corruption. For fifty years, penal reformers had sought to escape from corporal penalties by arguing that the problem of criminality could be attacked through isolation and the control of communication. Embodied communication and display, they implied, blocked the operations of moral reflection. This emphasis on mimetic corruption had helped stimulate the ever-increasing separation and isolation of the penal system. As the ultimate enactment of segregative incarceration, the Eastern State Penitentiary sought to make the body all but superfluous to punishment; within its walls, authority would act directly on the spirit. Yet, ultimately, this attempted escape from the body led back to corporality. For if the theory of mimetic corruption had helped justify the separate system, it could not explain the continuation of resistance or insubordination within the penitentiary nor suggest a course of further reformative action. In the end, with no more separation to impose, prison officials had nowhere else to turn than to the body itself.

VII

Authority based on character and specialized knowledge, however, was a two-edged sword. Claiming that the disciplinary realm could be judged only by its own standard, and that its leaders' reputations lifted them above the criticisms of their subordinates, the warden's allies moved close to suggesting that the public had no ground from which to judge penal practices. As such, they were open to charges of class prejudice and antidemocratic sentiments. These charges were not long in coming. Thomas B. McElwee, an erstwhile Whig turned Democrat, a former Philadelphian representing rural Bedford County in the state House of Representatives, launched a vigorous dissent against the assumptions and conclusions of the committee's majority. McElwee was not alone in his assessment of the warden's guilt—Attorney General Dallas being equally convinced—but McElwee's was the most sustained and public objection to the dominant interpretation. In McElwee's view, the committee had ignored clear evidence of the warden's guilt and succumbed to the lure of class loyalty.[43]

McElwee was particularly scornful of the committee's deference to Wood's reputation. Convinced that the charges of immorality, embezzlement, and mismanagement had been established by the evidence, he believed that the majority had been swayed by the warden's social connections. Accusing them of "white-washing" Wood, he asserted that the warden's "*respectable connexions*" had shielded him from the implications of his "malversations in office, such as immoral conduct, public peculations, cruelty to those confided to his charge, murder, etc." McElwee sardonically compared the committee's deference to Wood's character with the opposite case: the poor accused who, "not surrounded by those trivial paraphernalia of the *best blood in the country*, respectable connexions, etc., . . . must be convicted to be sure, a sacrifice to expediency." "Wealth," McElwee continued, "too often screens the villain from the scrutiny of the law, and commands the courtesy of the world when the brand of infamy should decorate the forehead of the professor." The committee's actions amounted to "no humbug when they rush in a mass to the rescue of one of their number, let him be innocent or guilty, and *divest of caste,* or brand as perjured miscreants, those who have the courage to become their accusers."[44]

This deference, McElwee believed, had dangerous social implications. Noting "that there are a class of individuals, who place no confidence in the integrity of the witnesses for the Commonwealth," he argued that such class consciousness had no place in a public dispute. "If the higher classes are charged with criminal matter," he pointed out, "and the evidence of men in a more humble sphere is rejected as unworthy of belief," then there would be "no means of detecting the culprit, and crimes are committed with impunity—the tinselled ruffian revels in his guilt, secured from the grasp of justice, while the useful operative, the farmer, and the mechanic, are spurned as perjured miscreants possessing no rights." Under such a presumption, the

43. For Dallas's views of the investigation, see Dallas to George Wolf, Jan. 11, 24, 1835, George Wolf Papers, HSP. As far as I have determined, Roberts Vaux never expressed himself publicly or in writing on the results of the investigation. But a letter to Governor Wolf indicating concern over the administration and oversight of the penitentiary suggest that Vaux felt, at the least, that the institution's government needed serious reform. See Vaux to George Wolf, Nov. 27, 1835, in George Wolf Papers. For McElwee's conviction that Wood was guilty of the charges against him, see McElwee, *A Concise History,* I, 124, 129–132; McElwee, *Report of the Minority of the Joint Committee of the Legislature of Pennsylvania, Relative to the Eastern State Penitentiary, at Philadelphia, Read in the House of Representatives, March 26, 1835* (Harrisburg, 1835), 5–6.

44. McElwee, *A Concise History,* I, 130, 135–136. For McElwee's position on the veracity of the charges, see McElwee, *Report of the Minority,* 5–6.

poorer elements were left "having a mere right to live, to administer to the wants of their oppressors, who think the oppressed have no wants which should be gratified, no feelings, no sensibilities which should be respected."[45] The committee had merely put reputation above the facts. McElwee implied, however, that this presumption of character was itself at the heart of the dispute.

Equally skeptical of the claims to disciplinary discretion, McElwee argued that only a strict adherence to statutory sanctions be allowed. In his view, supplementing the punishment of imprisonment with added penalties was itself criminal. Those who increased sanctions were as guilty as those who evaded legal penalties: "There can be no justification for the increase of the miseries of the wretched—none for the infractions of the laws."[46] Shorn of the defense of character, the warden and his defenders were no different from common criminals—and perhaps more dangerous.

At the same time, McElwee believed that the penitentiary's administration violated the social bond and the rights of man. "The feelings of our nature," McElwee asserted, "revolt at the infliction of torture not authorized by a judicial tribunal." Such power was, in fact, a violation of the political compact: "Man is invested with power over his fellow men only to the extent of self-preservation and the good order of society; vengeance and mercy belong to the Deity." No matter what crimes an individual had committed, he was still "a MAN, and that title is enough to protect him from the illegal infliction of pain, and all punishment is an infliction of some sort, doing violence to the feelings of the culprit, and therefore producing pain."[47] Wood's defenders, he argued, promoted a law outside the law, a second law that threatened to create an engine of uncontrollable power within the state. For McElwee, however, there could be only one law—applicable to all, inmates and officials, without distinction.

To make matters worse, McElwee argued, the penitentiary had been shielded from genuine criticism. The committee's majority, who accepted the truth of the official representations, were aiding and abetting cruelty and injustice. McElwee's conflicts with his peers, evident during the hearings themselves, spilled over into the question of publishing the committee's records. McElwee sought to have the legislature officially publish the testimony, but he was rebuffed. As a result, he took matters into his own hands. "This work," he asserted in the early pages of his *A Concise History of the Eastern State Penitentiary*, "would not have been undertaken, had not the legislature refused to print the testimony, and thus excited serious apprehension in the minds of men friendly to the system." McElwee believed that the legislature was seeking

45. McElwee, *A Concise History*, II, 106–107.
46. McElwee, *Report of the Minority*, 8.
47. McElwee, *A Concise History*, I, 4.

to conceal the cover-up that the committee's findings constituted; it was engaged in a deliberate attempt to keep the public from understanding the issues and facts involved. He stood, he insisted, on other grounds: "Secrecy forms no part of the system; and every man has a right to know what transpires within the walls of an institution so important to the Commonwealth, and in which every citizen has a deep interest."[48]

McElwee, then, broke with both Eastern State and the joint committee on the issues of law and publicity. In doing so, he took up a position within the classical republican public sphere. From his perspective, the penitentiary was a public institution that needed constant, open, public scrutiny. Only such continuing vigilance could ensure that the penitentiary would institute the reason and values of its founders.[49] To his mind, the warden and his defenders, confusing the relationship between public and private, had reduced the penitentiary to an extension of Wood and his friends. Whether the question was one of public money, private parties, or institutional cruelties, McElwee believed that secrecy served only to defraud the public and debase the state.

He contended that the public had a natural, and justified, interest in the practices of the prison. Drawing on the widespread sentimental assumption that images of cruelty stimulated sympathy, McElwee firmly believed that the public would be outraged both by the cruelties of the penitentiary and by the legislature's refusal to condemn its perpetrators. In his book, McElwee included engravings of a prisoner undergoing the gag, the straitjacket, and the "tranquilizer chair" and suggested that merely seeing these "horrible sufferings" would stimulate "public indignation against the perpetrators of this inhuman infraction of the laws, prohibiting its repetition."[50] McElwee believed not only that he spoke for the rights of man but that "public indignation" would come to his aid.

*   *   *

In the end, McElwee's protest, overwhelmingly defeated both in committee and in the legislature, fell on deaf ears. No public outcry greeted the joint committee's *Report* or McElwee's *Concise History*. The history of the publicity of punishment presented the paradox of a self-dissolving public sphere. For nearly half a century, the state gradually had been removing the practice of punishment from the public realm. Finally, legislators, prodded by reform organizations within society, had removed and concealed the penal apparatus

48. Ibid., 3. For examples of continuing conflicts between McElwee and other committee members, see *Poulson's Daily Advertiser*, Apr. 11, 1835; *Saturday Evening Post* (Philadelphia), Apr. 18, 1835.

49. On this issue, see McElwee's plaintive call for Roberts Vaux to take up a public pen against the abuses of the system. McElwee, *A Concise History*, II, 134–136.

50. Ibid., I, 4.

from public view. McElwee sought to reclaim the tradition of the rights of man for inmates, but, in seeking to mobilize public outrage over the cruelties of the penitentiary, he sought support in a public sphere whose moment, at least with regard to penal issues, had passed.

McElwee's defeat disclosed the limits of sensibility as well. Whether presenting testimony of brutality, including engraved depictions of the prison's punishments, or describing "tortures" and invoking "horrible suffering," McElwee assumed and continued the language of humanity and sensibility that penal reformers had used from the late eighteenth century onward. In dwelling on the "illegal infliction of pain," McElwee aimed to redefine the penitentiary's practices as cruel, to transform them into symbols of barbarity, just as the critics of flagellation had done with the whip. But, whereas critics of the lash had successfully redefined whipping as cruel and had deployed images of flogging to symbolize larger social systems, McElwee was unable to reduce the gag and the shower to barbarism or grant them larger significance in the eyes of his contemporaries. Benjamin Rush had dreamed that enclosing punishment would increase the community's interest in the condition of inmates. But the process of separation, it seems, had placed prisoners outside the realm of public sensibility; subordinated to the claims of authority, the rights of man stopped at the prison's walls.[51]

But it also may be that the reemergence of corporality within the prison carried too much social meaning to be framed as McElwee wished. Penal reformers had made public displays of corporal violence the symptom of older structures of personalized, arbitrary, and cruel power.[52] To gaze on the whipping scene was to reaffirm distance and difference; insisting on its cruelty, they constructed their own position as humane. But if the penitentiary could produce practices that mirrored the cruelty of monarchical or slaveholding regimes, then the distance between North and South, liberty and slavery, enlightened and barbaric was less secure. Maintaining the disciplinary realm from the charges of cruelty, indeed maintaining the distance between disciplinary reason and everyday judgments, helped preserve those larger social distinctions. The penitentiary's punishments, its defenders insisted, neither derived from desire nor produced pleasure. They were imposed with the reluctance of necessity. And, in making this argument, the unsaid comparison

51. To make this point is not to imply that there was no interest in the inner workings of prisons. Not only were there journals, articles, books, and so forth, providing reformist descriptions and critiques of the prison in the 19th century, but also a popular literature of exposé. Moreover, there had been popular interest in the hearings themselves. But there does not seem to have been any popular desire to challenge the official interpretation of the practices at the Eastern State Penitentiary.

52. Robin Evans, *The Fabrication of Virtue: English Prison Architecture, 1750–1840* (New York, 1982), 418–419.

with flagellation and the sheer symbolic power of the whip—its painful presence and its allegedly dissolute and seductive pleasures—might have helped diminish the ideological force of the penitentiary's excesses. Reduced in symbolic power, linked to the insubordination of inmates, responsibility for the gag or shower could be placed on the prisoners' shoulders. If these punishments were the doing of inmates, signs, not of the penitential structure, but of convict recalcitrance, then the penitentiary, and indeed the social world it represented, could not be cruel—and the name of humanity and philanthropy was preserved.

Indeed, McElwee himself shared some of these assumptions. He believed that intensifying the implementation of discipline could save the disciplinary project. *A Concise History* sought to demonstrate that the administration of Eastern State did not taint its structure. "The fault," he argued, "lies not in the system but in the mal-administration of the system." From his perspective, it was Wood and his assistants who, "betraying their trust and violating the law," had "brought odium on the system."[53] In effect, he reduced the conflicts within the penitentiary to issues of administrative immorality. In this way, McElwee replicated the central move of the disciplinary project itself—turning systemic conflicts into personal failings. Despite his speaking with the voice of the law and the public against administrative arbitrariness, McElwee sought to complete, not overturn, the disciplinary regime.

On this point, McElwee joined with his opponents. Despite their differences, both sides believed that, shorn of extraneous presences, the penitentiary could fully implement its discipline.[54] This underlying unity appeared most clearly in the treatment of Mrs. Blundin and the understanding of supplemental punishment. Both issues revealed a commitment to a further purification of the penal realm. And each demonstrated the difficulty McElwee faced in challenging the logic and arguments of disciplinary authority.

Mrs. Blundin never testified at the hearing. Nor did anyone speak on her behalf. Alone of all the accused, her actions were universally reviled. The majority accused her of "very gross and improper deportment and practices, entirely unbecoming her sex and condition." They implied that she was guilty of

53. McElwee, *A Concise History,* II, 134.

54. McElwee's opponents did not, of course, share his perspective on the warden. From their perspective, the failings in prison administration could be traced to the incomplete nature of the penitentiary. Urging greater control over inmate movement, criticizing Wood's decisions to allow inmates out of their cells, and concerned over the confusing financial dealings of Eastern State, they urged an accelerated attempt to bring the penitential structure to completion. But, as with McElwee, they argued that these were problems of execution, not system; when the penitential system had been consolidated all irregularities and conflicts would disappear. See, Anderson, *Report of the Joint Committee,* 11, 15–16, 18–19.

the immoralities alleged by Dallas, explicitly condemned her for embezzling goods from the penitentiary, and expressed their regret that she "was ever permitted within the walls of the penitentiary," suggesting that "to this circumstance most of the mischiefs complained of may be traced." In the end, their relief that she had been expelled from the institution was almost palpable. McElwee's revulsion from Mrs. Blundin seemed to have no bounds. She was a "common harlot," a "woman so criminal, so abandoned, so infamous" that he could not conceal his "astonishment" that her "peculations, plunderings, and repeated larcenies" had "been so boldly enacted without check from the warden." McElwee believed that "censure" was the only appropriate response to Wood for allowing Mrs. Blundin to remain within the walls of Eastern State, declaring it "impossible" that Wood could not have realized her nature.[55]

For both sides, Mrs. Blundin's presence and behavior within the penitentiary threatened to dissolve the very boundaries of prison morality. As "matron," Mrs. Blundin, they believed, had violated codes of gender and class. From the perspective of McElwee and his fellow committeemen, she had refused her role as demure, domestic, bourgeois wife and sought to extend her power at Eastern State, engaged in illicit pleasure both within and without its walls, and inverted the proper relationship between the sexes. The two sides differed less on the extent of her evil than on the degree of damage done. The committee's majority believed that she had exercised less influence on Wood, Holloway, and the others than did McElwee and that her expulsion from the penitentiary settled the matter. McElwee, on the contrary, believed that her character had implicated the entire administration, all of whom were guilty of her actions.

Mrs. Blundin stood condemned of violating notions of domestic propriety and blurring public and private spheres. Her very presence within the institution, the committee believed, was a private intrusion within public space, and her appropriation of prison goods and services a private use of public resources. In this way, she threatened the penitential project. For the disciplinary expansion of the 1820s and 1830s had sought to impose ever more rigid boundaries on social space and was designed, in part, against the forms of working-class womanhood. When Mrs. Blundin displayed anger, threw parties, moved freely throughout the penitentiary and the city, assumed authority within the prison, or scavenged for public goods, she did more than overstep her official place. Mrs. Blundin marked the reemergence within the heart of the disciplinary project of the forms of subjectivity that the penitential imagination aimed to repress.

But if Mrs. Blundin could be expelled from the penitentiary, the same could

55. Ibid., 8–11; "Common harlot" is from McElwee, *A Concise History*, I, 133; the rest is from ibid., II, 99.

not be said for resistant prisoners. It was that fact that caused the committee to justify additional penalties aimed at the body. Individual resistance, they insisted, not official cruelty, caused additional punishments. However painful such penalties appeared, they were necessary tools of discipline. Francis Lieber made this point most explicitly. Arguing for deprivation of food as the ideal supplementary penalty to solitude, Lieber explained that it "depends entirely upon the convict to remove [the deprivation]—and if he will abstain until he dies, I should say, let him die—as obedience is the first means of discipline." Such punishments, Lieber believed, were the inmate's responsibility. It was up to the prisoner to accept the dictates of the structure—and thereby free himself or herself from restraint. McElwee disagreed with the defense of supplemental corporal punishments. He believed that the penitential spirit precluded them—only a deprivation of labor was acceptable. But he did not challenge the committee's presuppositions about the expansiveness of discipline or of inmate responsibility. The beauty of intensified solitude, he thought, was that it placed the responsibility for suffering on the prisoner—while sparing inmates additional physical pain.[56]

McElwee's position precluded any systematic questioning of the disciplinary project itself. His attempt to assault disciplinary discretion yet save the penitential project was ultimately impossible. For the penitential imagination did not simply fail to live up to the law—it exceeded it. As Foucault put it, "Disciplinary mechanisms secreted a 'penality of the norm,' which is irreducible in its principles and functioning to the traditional penality of the law."[57] McElwee's opponents recognized, as he did not, that disciplinary authority generated ever new strategies and techniques from within its own logic. Solitude needed supplement because conscience was not sufficient. The inspectors and their allies recognized that reformative incarceration was always subject to failure. What they had tried to do was to incorporate that failure within their expectations in advance. It was precisely this recognition that drove the disciplinary project onward. The very attempt to discipline inmates individually meant that authorities had to invent ever new methods of government—and that these methods could not be subject to any general law.

At the same time, confinement itself, in its very physicality, was already a corporal penalty. If solitude failed, the only recourse open to the state was to act further on the body. Far from being the most spiritual of penal arenas, the separate system had revealed the inextricable corporality of punishment.

56. Testimony of Francis Lieber, ibid., II, 56. For an earlier, more extensive defense of this form of punishment by Lieber, see Anderson, *Report of the Joint Committee*, 31. For McElwee's discussion of an experiment in denying inmates labor, see McElwee, *A Concise History*, I, 19–20.

57. Michel Foucault, *Discipline and Punish: The Birth of the Prison*, trans. Alan Sheridan (New York, 1977), 183.

McElwee failed to grasp that, like penal publicity, his call for a single law and an avoidance of the body was already anachronistic.

The penitentiary's defenders thus enacted on the ideological level what Sigmund Freud would later call "splitting of the ego." Freud suggested that some of his patients, when children, had been trapped between an instinctual desire and a threatened prohibition. The ego, he continued, "must now decide either to recognize the real danger," which would entail giving up the desire, "or to repudiate reality and persuade itself that there is no reason for fear, so that it may be able to retain the satisfaction." But, interestingly, neither course is taken exactly. Instead, Freud claimed the ego both "rejects reality and refuses to accept any prohibition" and "recognizes the danger of reality, takes over the fear of that danger as a symptom and tries subsequently to divest himself of the fear."[58] Freud believed that this psychic process derived from a transhistorical fear of castration. But the legislative response to prison conditions suggests that "splitting" can be a social and historical process, a way to preserve an identity by both accepting and denying social evidence. The penitentiary's defenders did not refuse to recognize the ways Eastern State exceeded the law. But they did deny that this excess entailed repudiating the penitential imagination. In both recognizing and denying the excesses of the penal apparatus, the inspectors and their allies turned a challenge to their identity into a source of institutional intensification and continued authority.

In the aftermath of the legislative investigation, then, penitential authority sought to stabilize itself through exclusion and denial. By excluding Mrs. Blundin and denying any structural roots for the penitentiary's excesses, legislators and prison officials sought to maintain the distinction between the "cruel and vindictive penalties which are in use in the European countries" and those "milder correctives" that Roberts Vaux had dreamed the penitentiary represented.[59] In doing so, they repeated yet inverted the fundamental gestures of penitential punishments. The critique of public punishments had aimed to prevent the penal from polluting the everyday; now the inspectors and their allies claimed that the everyday was polluting punishment. The critique of corporal and capital punishments had treated the dynamic and expansive degradation imposed by the scaffold and the whip as symptomatic of larger social structures; but now penitential proponents argued that the irreducible element of penal corporality had no larger meaning than the incorrigibility of individual inmates. Freed from external intrusions and larger symbolisms, the penitentiary, they hoped, would finally fulfill its obligations.

The disciplinary apparatus was consolidated in Philadelphia by the 1830s.

58. Sigmund Freud, "Splitting of the Ego in the Defensive Process," in *Collected Papers*, ed. Jones et al., trans. Reviere et al., V, 372–375.

59. [Smith], *Description of the Eastern Penitentiary*, 7.

Despite the criticisms levied against the Eastern State Penitentiary, its fundamental premises remained unscathed. Neither the prison's critics nor its defenders questioned the value of solitude. If the prison administration was controversial, the penitential idea itself remained beyond challenge. In defending Wood and the penitentiary from their critics, prison reformers, prison officials, and state legislators had articulated a doctrine of disciplinary discretion rooted in expertise and social authority. At the same time, notions of inmate responsibility and the permanence of prison were, if anything, more fully established. The spiritualization of punishment had led, ultimately, to the reemergence of the penal body.

In the end, both McElwee and his opponents avoided confronting the fundamental contradiction, for the liberal imagination, of penitential punishment. The separate system presumed that citizens could be produced by reducing individuals to silent labor. But the alleged essence of liberal citizenship, or liberal manhood at least, was exercising one's voice. Reformative imprisonment was paradoxical from its beginning in the post-Revolutionary era, and its contradictions were sharpest in the Eastern State Penitentiary. It was there that the paradox that underlay the disciplinary project—to produce citizens by denying them the capacity to exercise the practice of citizenship itself—assumed its clearest form. To confront that paradox directly would have meant acknowledging the structure of submission that underlay liberal society. And it was that structure that remained beyond challenge.

Indeed, the history of punishment embodied the evolving public order of late-eighteenth- and early-nineteenth-century Philadelphia. The Revolution triggered continuing struggles to define a new culture and society. These struggles made and remade class and gender relations while redefining the nature of the state and reshaping the public sphere. The history of punishment both reproduced and transformed these struggles. From the 1780s to the 1830s, from the experiment with public labor, through the deployment of reformative incarceration at Walnut Street, to the institutionalization of separate confinement at Eastern State, Philadelphians sought to create a rational and republican form of punishment and to stabilize the Revolutionary and post-Revolutionary public realms. In this project they failed. Each stage of punishment produced ever new contradictions while the effort to master these contradictions produced, in turn, new sites of struggle, disagreement, and disruption. The failure of the prison and the expansion of social contradictions went hand in hand; in their frenetic efforts to discipline the scene of punishment, elite Philadelphians produced ever more sites of conflict. The Revolutionary dream of a unified and unifying culture was exploded from within. The fractured and volatile urban realm of the late-eighteenth- and early-nineteenth-century city—fissured by class, ethnicity, gender, and race—

demanded and refused the stability sought by Revolutionaries and promised by the prison.

Ultimately, these paradoxes of punishment encapsulated the evolving contradictions of American liberalism. If the history of punishment in Philadelphia is singular, its meaning is not unique. It was not simply that the philosophies and institutions Philadelphians produced spread throughout the northern United States. From the Revolution onward, liberalism advanced under the sign of individual liberty and opportunity. Challenging first the British monarchy and then the slaveholding South, northern society proclaimed that limits to individual liberty existed only at its margins. But the history of punishment and social discipline teaches another story. There the very effort to produce liberal citizens engendered new forms of subordination, the emphasis on individuality denied social action its collective (especially class-based) contexts, and the efforts to spread liberal institutions generated ever new forms of struggle and disagreement.

Liberal society was predicated on a fundamental denial of its own contradictions and inequalities. The cult of the individual was enabled by the disavowal of the whole. Focusing its attention on the individual, liberalism substitutes the isolated self—a self constituted through the material practices of discipline—for the social body. Behind the blinding figure of the individually embodied self, the social body disappears. This disappearance, however, is always incomplete. For individuality is always produced through a social setting, and the social body, with its divisions, its conflicts, its hierarchies, haunts the individual it proclaims to free.

Thus, liberal discipline and the material individuality it imposed did not symbolize decline but impossibility. Discipline was a constantly failed attempt to suture the gap between Revolutionary ideals and the social realities of the new Republic; to sustain the fictions of a rational public sphere through the material retraining of its citizens. Rather than sites of decay and refuse, disciplinary institutions were shards of a dream broken at its very inception by its founders' vision.